CAPTIVATING TECHNOLOGY

Captivating Technology

RACE, CARCERAL

TECHNOSCIENCE, AND

LIBERATORY IMAGINATION

IN EVERYDAY LIFE

Ruha Benjamin, editor

.....

Duke University Press

Durham and London

2019

Library of Congress Cataloging-in-Publication Data

Names: Benjamin, Ruha, editor.

Title: Captivating technology : race, carceral technoscience, and liberatory imagination in everyday life / Ruha Benjamin, editor.

Description: Durham : Duke University Press, 2019. | Includes bibliographical references and index.

Identifiers: LCCN 2018042310 (print) | LCCN 2018056888 (ebook)

ISBN 9781478004493 (ebook)

ISBN 9781478003236 (hardcover : alk. paper)

ISBN 9781478003816 (pbk. : alk. paper)

Subjects: LCSH: Prisons—United States. | Electronic surveillance—Social aspects—United States. | Racial profiling in law enforcement—United States. | Discrimination in criminal justice administration—United States. | African Americans—Social conditions—21st century. | United States—Race relations—21st century. | Privacy, Right of—United States.

Classification: LCC HV9471 (ebook) | LCC HV9471 .C2825 2019 (print) | DDC 364.028/4—dc23

LC record available at https://lccn.loc.gov/2018042310

An earlier version of chapter 1, "Naturalizing Coersion," by Britt Rusert, was published as "'A Study of Nature': The Tuskegee Experiments and the New South Plantation," in *Journal of Medical Humanities* 30, no. 3 (summer 2009): 155–71. The author thanks Springer Nature for permission to publish an updated essay.

Chapter 13, "Scratch a Theory, You Find a Biography," the interview of Troy Duster by Alondra Nelson, originally appeared in the journal *Public Culture* 24, no. 2 (67): 283–302. Copyright 2012 by Duke University Press.

Duke University Press gratefully acknowledges Princeton University, which provided funds toward the publication of this book.

Cover art: Manzel Bowman, *Turbine*, 2016. Digital Collage.

for Khalil and Malachi

Contents

Foreword

.....

Troy Duster

Can a robot or an algorithm be racist? A simple question with a very simple answer. The reason why there is some confusion in the varied responses to this question is directly related to how much context and history is known about what goes into the computer programming. If the programmer knows little or nothing about the substance of the matter (e.g., from outside their own culture), the chances are very high that the seeming neutrality of "data in" will miss when there is racism embedded in the algorithm. Let's take two basic elements of a democratic society: voting rights and marriage eligibility. As a heuristic tool, it will be useful to contrast the voting access and marriage eligibility of a Japanese person of Burakumin descent (in Japan) with how American citizens of recent European or African descent in the United States are affected by voting rights and marriageability.

Here are the first lines from a *New York Times* report of September 1, 2017: "The calls started flooding in from hundreds of irate North Carolina voters just after 7 A.M. on Election Day last November. Dozens were told they were ineligible to vote and were turned away at the polls, even when they displayed current registration cards. Others were sent from one polling place to another, only to be rejected. Scores of voters were incorrectly told they had cast ballots days earlier. In one precinct, voting halted for two hours."[1]

On the surface, a strong social tradition or law determining the contours of eligibility can appear neutral, but a bit of knowledge about social history can easily reveal embedded racial or ethnic bias. As many Americans know, a fine example would be the "grandfather's clause" used in the post-Reconstruction South to prevent blacks (newly freed from slavery) from voting, as in, *one can vote only if one's grandfather voted.* This grandfather's clause had *disparate impact* on whites and blacks, and it is notable that in the last three decades, the right-tilting U.S. Supreme Court has substantially eroded "disparate impact" as grounds for challenging the constitutional standing of a law.

In the contemporary world of Japan, how might a parallel history provide access to (or denial of) voting rights—or marriage eligibility? Japanese parents spend several hundred million dollars every year paying detectives to ascertain information on whether their marriage-age children should either break off an engagement or marry. Why?

The Burakumin of Japan are a pariah caste at the base of Japanese culture and social stratification, and have occupied the bottom rung for over 1,200 years! The Japanese, like the Swedes and the Icelanders, are meticulously good, even rabid, record keepers. So they have birth records that go back several hundred years. The Burakumin were restricted to living in their own cordoned-off villages until the Meiji reforms of 1868–71, when the Tokugawa-era laws were overturned. Japanese birth records reveal not just when one was born, but with further research, one can use the *koseki* (birth certificates for every Japanese, with more info than a U.S. certificate), to find out where one's parents were born. So the Japanese hire researchers to surreptitiously (and illegally, since Meiji times) access the koseki and thus are able to trace back two, three, or even four generations of direct ancestry. This comes in handy, even in today's Japan, where parents of young couples who want to get married hire detectives (at a cost of over several hundred million dollars annually) to trace the koseki—to make certain that their offspring do not marry a Burakumin.

Now imagine that the Japanese could concoct an algorithm that could do such tracing and embed koseki information into voter eligibility. It would be the equivalent of our grandfather's clause but disguised as simply a neutral technology for tracing voter eligibility. Unless one knows about the history of the Burakumin, that machinery could be characterized as "neutral" by a computer programmer . . . and the embedded bias would be invisible without knowledge of Japanese history.

There is a parallel in the United States. Republican governors across a dozen states have pushed for voter registration that restricts access based upon "neutral" conditions such as state-issued identification cards with photos. All that would appear neutral to a computer programmer, oblivious to systemic and voter suppression strategies designed to intimidate or restrict black voters, overwhelmingly in the South, going back to the Jim Crow laws of the post-Reconstruction. A disproportionate number of blacks were affected by the grandfather's voting eligibility—just as a disproportionate number of blacks are affected by the "neutrality" of state-issued IDs, but oh so much more subtly. Disparate impact was blatant in the law that required evidence that one's grandfather had voted but has been "neutrally" disguised in photo ID laws. The answer to the question posed at the outset? Robots and algorithms can be as racist as the designers of the generated computer programs. *Captivating Technology* examines just such hidden interconnec-

Troy Duster

tions of seemingly neutral technologies, disentangling and identifying the social and historical, illuminating how and why it infuses the not-so-neutral "machinery."

Note

1. Nicole Perlroth, Michael Wines, and Matthew Rosenberg, "Russian Election Hacking Efforts, Wider Than Previously Known, Draw Little Scrutiny," *New York Times*, September 1, 2017, accessed January 25, 2018, https://www.nytimes.com/2017/09/01/us /politics/russia-election-hacking.html.

Acknowledgments

I am deeply grateful to the contributors to this volume for investing their energy and insights to bring this project to life. I had long admired each of them as thinkers, and now I stand in awe of their generosity and diligence as collaborators. I was told earlier in my career by more than one person that edited volumes were not a smart investment of time. I am so glad I did not listen! Habitual stubbornness for the win. Working on this book has been one of the most rewarding experiences and I have no doubt this is because I had the opportunity to work so closely with people who continually blow my mind *and* put it back together in new ways.

This book would not have been possible without the incredible support of Princeton University's Department of African American Studies. It is a rare thing, I suspect, to love, respect, *and* enjoy the company of one's colleagues. But that is the case here. Anna Arabindan-Kesson, Wendy Belcher, Wallace Best, Eddie Glaude, Reena Goldthree, Joshua Guild, Tera Hunter, Naomi Murakawa, Kinohi Nishikawa, Chika Okeke-Agulu, Imani Perry, Stacey Sinclair, Keeanga-Yamahtta Taylor, Judith Weisenfeld, and Autumn Womack teach me that is possible, even within old systems, to forge new ways of relating and being together. And it is an open secret that none of our work would be possible without the *incomparable* staff, past and present, Allison Bland, Elio Lleo, Jana Johnson, April Peters, and Dionne Worthy.

This department exemplifies the idea that technologies are not just "out there" in the world, but they include the everyday social tools that we all employ in our interactions with one another, containing or liberating, tearing each other down or building one another up. I am incredibly fortunate to work with people who choose the latter again and again. The freedom and encouragement I have experienced in this context teach me that it is possible to build new worlds in the midst of old ones.

The seeds of this project were first planted at the "Ferguson Is the Future" symposium at Princeton University in September 2015, which was funded by generous grants from the David A. Gardner '69 Magic Project in the Council of the Humanities and the Lewis Center for the Arts. The symposium was also cosponsored by the Princeton Department of English, Program in Gender and Sexuality Studies, and Department of African American Studies, Council on Science and Technology, Princeton Public Library, and

Octavia E. Butler Legacy Network. This gathering would not have happened without the collaboration of my extraordinary colleagues Moya Bailey and Ayana A. H. Jamieson, whose ongoing work on black feminist approaches to science, technology, and imagination continue to sharpen my own thinking and commitments. Also essential were Allison Bland and Elio Eleo's tech savvy, Iyabo Kwayana's film-making talent, and Ezelle Sanford III, Megan Eardley, and Destiny Crockett's planning prowess. Last but not least, Dionne Worthy: there are no words that can fully express her programming genius— but anyone who has experienced it *knows*.

There are also a number of venues where I, along with many of the contributing authors, had the chance to present this work and get feedback that helped us hone our ideas, including panels at the Eastern Sociological Society (2017), Society for the Social Studies of Science (2017), University of Pennsylvania Annenberg School for Communication, UC San Diego Science Studies Program, and Princeton StudioLab "Rethinking Mass Incarceration" Design Challenge series.

I was also very fortunate to receive sabbatical support from the Institute for Advanced Study in Princeton, and special thanks to Didier Fassin for creating such a wonderful space for scholars engaged in critical work at IAS. My deepest gratitude goes to my writing partners, Keisha-Khan Y. Perry and the late Lee Ann Fujii, who filled this year with so much joy and encouragement. They, along with Reuben and Janice Miller, helped me experience the sweetness of making new, lifelong friends in unlikely places, and reminded me that intellectual work thrives in the soil of friendship.

I also want to express my appreciation for those intellectual kin who have buoyed and grounded me over many years—Catherine Bliss, Dawn Dow, Alondra Nelson, Aaron Panofsky, Anne Pollock, and Tianna Paschel; as well as my graduate and postdoc advisors—Charis Thompson, Sheila Jasanoff, Stefan Timmermans, Loïc Wacquant, and Troy Duster whose early and ongoing support have been crucial to my development.

I also want to extend a very special thanks to students in my "Black to the Future" Seminar (fall 2017), Rachel Adler, Jean Bellamy, Taylor Branch, My Bui, Malachi Byrd, Maia Ezratty, Kenya Holland, Sara Howell, E Jeremijenko-Conley, Stefan Lee, Talya Nevins, Aparna Raghu, Leslie Robinson, Destiny Salter, Rosed Serrano, Max Stahl, Emmanuel Teferi, and Elena Tsemberis, who read an early draft of this book and provided invaluable feedback. The opportunity to work with so many incredible young scholars, including Kessie Alexandre, Kimberly Bain, Megan Blanchard, Chaya Chowder, Colleen Campbell, Janeria Easley, Nyle Fort, Emanuela Kucik, Tala Khanmalek,

Heath Pearson, Briana Payton, and Ezelle Sanford III, has energized and emboldened me over the last few years.

It goes without saying that Duke University Press was an incredible steward of this project! Without the expert guidance of Courtney Berger, Sandra Korn, the amazing editorial staff, and two anonymous reviewers who provided invaluable feedback, this book would not have been possible.

Last but not least, I thank my *day ones* (as my sons would put it), Malachi and Khalil for their surreality checks, Shawn for infusing the word *partner* with substance, and my mom, Behin, for always allowing me to walk free.

Introduction

DISCRIMINATORY DESIGN,
LIBERATING IMAGINATION

Ruha Benjamin

.....

All paradises, all utopias are designed by who is not there, by the people who are not allowed in.
—TONI MORRISON

What is so astonishing about the fact that our prisons resemble our factories, schools, military bases, and hospitals—all of which in turn resemble prisons?
—MICHEL FOUCAULT

Technology captivates.

Capturing bodies. Dashcams on the front of police vehicles recording traffic stops turned deadly, as with the arrest of Sandra Bland on a Texas highway. Robot cranes reaching thirty feet in the air, monitoring images and heat signatures throughout Camden, New Jersey, deepening police occupation of impoverished neighborhoods.[1] Crime prediction algorithms labeling black defendants "higher risk" than their white counterparts, reinforcing popular stereotypes of criminality and innocence behind a veneer of objectivity.[2] Electronic ankle monitors wrapping around the limbs of thousands of people as they await trial or serve parole . . . an "attractive alternative" to cages, more humane and cost-effective than jails, we are told. Tools, in this way, capture more than just people's bodies. They also capture the imagination, offering technological fixes for a wide range of social problems.

Electronic tracking and location systems are part of a growing suite of interventions dubbed "technocorrections."[3] Indeed, these interventions come bubble wrapped in rhetoric about *correcting*, not just individuals, but social disorders such as poverty and crime. In the first-ever report analyzing the impact of electronic monitoring of youth in California, we learn that e-monitoring entails a combination of onerous and arbitrary rules that end up forcing young people back into custody for "technical violations."[4] Attractive fixes, it turns out, produce new opportunities for youth to violate the law and, thereby, new grounds for penalizing them. But perhaps this is the point? Could it be that we don't need technocorrections to make us secure, that we need social insecurity to justify technocorrections?[5]

Captivating Technology examines how the management, control, and "correction" of poor and racialized people provide the raison d'être for investing in discriminatory designs.[6] The volume aims to contribute to a long-standing sociological concern with structures of inequality. These "default settings" encompass legal, economic, and now computer codes, and move past an individual's intention to discriminate, by focusing analysis on how technoscience reflects and reproduces social hierarchies, whether wittingly or not. From credit-scoring algorithms to workplace monitoring systems, novel techniques and devices are shown to routinely build upon and deepen inequality.[7] Racist and classist forms of social control, in this sense, are not limited to obvious forms of incarceration and punishment; rather, they entail what sociologist Carla Shedd calls a "carceral continuum" that scales over prison walls.[8]

Even what is now popularly known as the "prison industrial complex" is vaster than most of us realize. As the editors of *Captive Genders* Eric Stanley and Nat Smith catalog, it includes "[i]immigration enters, juvenile justice facilities, county jails, holding rooms, court rooms, sheriffs' offices, psychiatric institutes," along with an extensive set of social relations that include "prison labor, privatized prisons, prison guard unions, food suppliers, telephone companies, commissary suppliers, uniform producers, and beyond, the carceral landscape overwhelms."[9] Indeed, the enormity of the terrain is overwhelming, especially for those individuals, families, and communities that are caught in the crosshairs of this carceral regime.[10] But what the following pages reveal is that the sticky web of carcerality extends even further, into the everyday lives of those who are purportedly free, wrapping around hospitals, schools, banks, social service agencies, humanitarian organizations, shopping malls, and the digital service economy.[11] Technology is not just a bystander that happens to be at the scene of the crime; it actually aids and abets the process by which carcerality penetrates social life. It does so, in part, because technoscientific approaches seem to "fix" the problem of human bias when it comes to a wide range of activities. But as law profes-

Ruha Benjamin

sor Patricia J. Williams insists with respect to color-blind interventions more broadly, "the application of such quick fixes becomes not just a shortcut but a *short-circuiting* of the process."[12] And while there is some hope for broad-based solidarity precisely because of how far-reaching carceral logics are, racialized groups continue to pay a much higher price for this failure to deal squarely with the deep currents of social life.

THE NEW JIM CODE

So how should we understand the duplicity of technological fixes— purported solutions that nevertheless sediment existing hierarchies? First, it is important to reckon with the way that emerging technologies can reinforce interlocking forms of discrimination, especially when we presume they are insulated from human influence. This insidious combination of coded bias and imagined objectivity is what I call the *New Jim Code*—innovation that enables social containment while appearing fairer than discriminatory practices of a previous era. This riff on Michelle Alexander's *The New Jim Crow* considers how the reproduction of racist forms of social control in successive institutional forms (slavery, Jim Crow, ghettoization, mass incarceration), now entails a crucial sociotechnical component that hides not only the nature of domination, but allows it to penetrate every facet of social life.

As I have argued elsewhere, these "postracial upgrades appear necessary and even empowering, which is precisely what makes them so effective at exacerbating inequality. . . . In this way it is a kind of racial minimalism that allows for more and more racist violence to be less and less discernable."[13] Thus, truly transformative abolitionist projects must seek an end to carcerality in *all* its forms, from the state-sanctioned exercise of social control à la Big Brother, to everyday forms of surveillance that people engage in as workers, employers, consumers, and neighbors à la little brother.[14] Taken together, such an approach rests upon an expansive understanding of the "carceral" that attends to the institutional *and* imaginative underpinnings of oppressive systems.

Indeed, abolishing the carceral continuum requires investment in a *continuum* of alternatives to address the many social problems that the prison industry is tasked with managing but, thereby, perpetuates. In the words of Angela Y. Davis, the aim is not "prisonlike substitutes for the prison, such as house arrest safeguarded by electronic surveillance bracelets. Rather, positing decarceration as our overarching strategy, we would try to envision a continuum of alternatives to imprisonment—demilitarization of schools, revitalization of education at all levels, a health system that provides free physical and mental care to all, and a justice system based on reparation and reconciliation rather than retribution and vengeance."[15] A colossal undertaking indeed! This is why nothing short of the "creation of new institutions that lay claim to space now occupied by the prison" and all of its carceral antennae and appendages can form the basis of genuine social transformation. To that end, this discussion aims to buoy the vital scholarly and activist investment in abolition and transformative justice by offering the first sustained analysis of the carceral dimensions of emerging technologies across a wide range of social arenas.

The central questions animating the text are: Who and what are fixed in place to enable innovation in science and technology? What social groups are classified, corralled, coerced, and capitalized upon so others are free to tinker, experiment, design, and engineer the future? How are novel technologies deployed in carceral approaches to governing life well beyond the domain of policing? This book also asks: To what end do we imagine? How can innovation in terms of our political, cultural, and social norms work toward freedom? How might technoscience be appropriated and reimagined for more liberatory ends? Ultimately, this volume is about what people can do, *are doing* about it. From Frederick Douglass to Dorothy E. Roberts, African diasporic artists to black feminist abolitionists, the following pages also explore visions of fashioning the world in radically different ways.

DISCRIMINATORY DESIGN

In rethinking the relationship between technology and society, a more expansive conceptual tool kit is necessary, one that bridges science and technology studies (STS) and critical race studies, two fields not often put in direct conversation. This hybrid approach *illuminates* not only *how society is impacted by* technological development, as techno-determinists would argue, but how social norms, policies, and institutional frameworks shape a context that make some technologies appear inevitable and others impossible. This process of mutual constitution wherein technoscience and society shape one another is called *coproduction*.[16]

In her book *Dark Matters*, for example, sociologist Simone Browne examines how surveillance technologies coproduce notions of blackness, explaining that "surveillance is nothing new to black folks"; from slave ships and slave patrols to airport security checkpoints and stop-and-frisk policing practices, she points to the "facticity of surveillance in black life."[17] Challenging a technologically determinist approach, she argues that instead of "seeing surveillance as something inaugurated by new technologies . . . to see it as ongoing is to insist that we factor in how racism and anti-blackness *undergird* and *sustain* the intersecting surveillances of our present order."[18] Antiblack racism, in this context, is not only a by-product, but a *precondition* for the fabrication of such technologies—antiblack imagination put to work.

A coproductionist analysis calls for more than technological or scientific literacy, but a more far-reaching *sociotechnical imaginary* that examines not only how the technical *and* social components of design are intertwined, but also imagines how they might be configured differently.[19] To extricate carceral imaginaries and their attending logics and practices from our institutions, we will also have to free up our own thinking and question many of our starting assumptions, even the idea of "crime" itself.

Take, for instance, a parody project that begins by subverting the antiblack logics embedded in new high-tech approaches to crime prevention. Instead of using predictive policing techniques to forecast street crime, the White Collar Crime Early Warning System flips the script by creating a heat map that flags city blocks where financial crimes are likely to occur.[20] The system brings not only the hidden, but no less deadly, crimes of capitalism into view, but includes an app that alerts users when they enter high-risk areas to encourage "citizen policing and awareness."[21] Taking it one step further, the development team is working on a facial recognition program to flag individuals who are likely perpetrators, and the training set used to design the algorithm includes the profile photos of 7,000 corporate executives downloaded from the popular professional networking site LinkedIn. Not surprisingly, the "average" face of a criminal is white and male. To be sure, creative exercises like this are only comical if we ignore the fact that all of its features are drawn directly from actually existing proposals and practices "in the real world," including the use of facial images to predict criminality.[22]

By deliberately and inventively upsetting the status quo in this manner, analysts can better understand and expose the many forms of discrimination embedded in and enabled by technology. In fact, the late legal scholar Derrick A. Bell encouraged just this—a radical assessment of reality through creative methods and racial reversals, insisting that "[t]o see things as they really are, you must *imagine* them for what they might be."[23]

Discriminatory design, moreover, is a conceptual lens to investigate how social biases get coded, not only in laws and policies, but in many different objects and tools that we use in everyday life. Consider public benches designed with intermittent armrests that make it impossible to lie down. For the typical passerby, the inconvenience is negligible. But for a person who is homeless, it is another concrete reminder of one's denigrated status as "human refuse," kept out of sight, out of mind through techniques of "invisibilization."[24] Discriminatory design finds expression, too, in the spiked corners of luxury flats in London,[25] single-occupancy benches in Helsinki, and caged public seating in France.[26] In the last case, public criticism was swift and fierce, forcing city officials to remove the benches almost right away, demonstrating how everyday people can and should resist discriminatory designs as antithetical to the common good.

To illustrate how much of public life has been effectively privatized, German artist Fabian Brunsing created a metered bench that requires the user to pay in order for the spikes to retreat into the seat. Brunsing's artwork reminds us that, although discrimination may no longer be expressed in the form of "Whites Only" signs hanging in storefronts or painted on the back of benches as they once were, seemingly neutral "pay to use" policies enforce social boundaries and deepen inequities nonetheless. The metering of public life is evident in education, health care, policing, and more, where public goods that are nominally for everyone are structurally restrictive because historic and ongoing processes of discrimination ensure some people can easily feed the meter while others must contend with the spikes.

Keep in mind that well before eighteen-year-old Michael Brown was murdered by Officer Darren Wilson in the streets of Ferguson, Missouri, the municipality was exacting a pernicious form of economic terrorism by targeting the predominantly black citizenry for fees and fines in the millions of dollars. As one observer put it, "It's easy to see the drama of a fatal police shooting, but harder to understand the complexities of municipal finances that created many thousands of hostile encounters, one of which turned fatal."[27] Like an ordinary park bench enforcing the line between wanted and unwanted, public policies overseeing the most mundane aspects of social life act like so many skewers, violently prodding those who cannot pay up.

This metering of social life is a key feature of the carceral infrastructure that extends well beyond prison bars. It contributed to the tragic death of Sandra Bland, who was charged $5,000 in bail, and thereby skewered by a punitive apparatus, which those with means could have walked away from. According to a federal study, there are over half a million people sitting in city and county jails who have not been convicted of a crime.[28] In 2016 alone there were over eight hundred documented fatalities among those in lockup because they could not post bail[29] — a form of "premature death" that political geographer Ruth Wilson Gilmore defines as a key feature of racist state

Ruha Benjamin

violence.[30] And considering that a meter is a measurement tool, whether it is metered benches or metered public policies, the pervasive use of this technology to govern public life signifies a perverse calculus of human worth.

FERGUSON IS THE FUTURE

It started with a captivating image, then a question.

As the rebellion following the murder of eighteen-year-old Michael Brown in Ferguson, Missouri, was under way in the summer of 2015, I came across a photo online (figure 1.1) that arrested my attention. It showed a wall with the words *Ferguson Is the Future* spray-painted on the side.[31] A future, I wondered, of militarized police who terrorize residents using technologies of war *or* a future of courageous communities who demand dignity and justice using technologies of communication? The uncertainty, I think, is what we make of it.

Ultimately, these four words served as a catalyst for a symposium I co-organized with Moya Bailey and Ayana Jamieson, which we called "Ferguson Is the Future: Incubating Alternative Worlds through Arts, Activism, and Scholarship." This book, however, did not grow directly out of that gathering in the conventional way that talks turn into chapters; in fact, only four of the contributors (Benjamin, Gaskins, Nelson, and Roberts) participated in the symposium. Rather, the inspiration came from a less direct source—a question posed to the last panel by my colleague, legal and cultural studies scholar Imani Perry. In characteristic fashion, she pushed the conversation in a direction it had not yet gone:

> The question I have is about technology. . . . I was thinking about technologies like bullets and tanks and the weapons trade as a technology. One of the things that was so remarkable about Ferguson and why it captured the imagination is that people, with their flesh, confronted technologies of domination and stood in front of them. And so the question I have is about the ethical relationship to technology. It can be a tool for incredible imaginative exploration, but it is unquestionably the mechanism of our domination in the current era. And so how do we, particularly given how we are all implicated in technologies of domination . . . how do we all think about how to grapple with our relationship to these tools?[32]

Of all the incredible insights that grew out of "Ferguson Is the Future," this question lingered the longest for me because of the way it forces a clear-eyed view of the life-and-death stakes of technoscience. It does not permit a

FIGURE I.1. "Ferguson Is the Future." Photo by Paul Sableman.
Source: Flickr.com. Image reproduced through Creative Commons.

Twitter-friendly, formulaic response, but acts as an ongoing provocation that forces all those who seek to intervene in the deadly status quo to think anew about how to navigate material *and* ethical minefields. *Captivating Technology* offers one way forward—mapping technologies of domination that are often far more elusive than the bullets and teargas that meet protestors on the streets of U.S. cities, while pointing to alternative geographies where the very idea of "what tools are essential" for multispecies flourishing can engender ongoing experimentation and justice-oriented design.

RADIO IMAGINATION

This text engages with a number of foundational thinkers who have worked to develop an ethically grounded and sociologically informed orientation toward science and technology,[33] as well as more recent scholarship that explores how racial logics enter labs, clinics, public policies, pedagogies, and discourses about technoscience.[34] Whereas an overwhelming focus of previous work is on genetics and the life sciences more broadly, a number of scholars have broadened this emphasis to investigate the ways that racial and gender norms and hierarchies impact everything from basic health care to artificial

Ruha Benjamin

intelligence.[35] Some of the most exciting developments in this arena go on to articulate ideas for how to construct technoscience differently.[36]

Also crucial for this discussion is scholarship that examines how science and technology operate through, with, and against policing, prisons, and carceral systems.[37] A key feature of this work is the understanding that racialized groups are not only the objects of harm and neglect, but that the meaning and power of racial hierarchies are enacted through technoscientific processes. In a particularly disquieting example, Anne Pollock examines the case of the Scott sisters, whose dual life sentences were commuted by the governor of Mississippi on the condition that Gladys Scott donate a kidney to her ailing sister, Jamie.[38] Pollock shows how "[b]eing eligible to contribute a bodily resource can enact membership in a group, be it family or state. . . . In the United States, prison is not just a metaphor for power and control, but a potent way of organizing bodies in space, and constituting and depriving citizenship." The biomedical fix of organ transplantation is one of many techniques in which the rights, responsibilities, *and* coercive possibilities of political membership get enacted.

In attending to the underside of technoscience, the contributors to this volume remain attuned to the groans of bondage that echo whenever and wherever "liberty rings." Together, our aim is to cultivate what Octavia E. Butler called "the kind of imagination that hears . . . *radio imagination*."[39] Radio imagination, as offered here, serves as a methodological touchstone for ethical engagement with technoscience, where the zeal for making new things is tempered by an ability to listen to the sounds and stories of people and things already made. In the broadest sense, at stake is the category "human" itself[40]—who defines it, inherits it, wields it . . . who rents it, tills it, toils for it . . . who gets expelled from it, buried under it, or drowned as they risk everything to inhabit it?

REVIVING HUMANITY

The rhetoric of human betterment that surrounds technoscience is not only a shiny veneer that hides complexity and camouflages destructive processes. This feel-good grammar also makes it difficult to recognize, much less intervene in, the deadly status quo. Addressing such distortions, including the lack of attention to race in theorizing new technologies, black studies scholar Alexander Weheliye joins a wide range of thinkers who challenge the "liberal humanist figure of Man."[41] His intervention builds on black feminist theorizations of the human, particularly the work of Sylvia Wynter, who posits different "genres" of humanity that include "full humans, not-quite humans, and nonhumans,"[42] through which racial, gendered, and colonial hierarchies are encoded as natural distinctions. As literary scholar Zakiyyah Jackson aptly explains in her synthesis of an alternative genealogy of post-humanist thought, one that foregrounds Wynter, Frantz Fanon, and Aime Cesaire, "the figure 'man' . . . is a *technology* of slavery and colonialism that imposes its authority over 'the universal' through a racialized deployment of force."[43] And as several of the chapters in this volume make clear, fiction writing and other creative works offer some of the most compelling post-postracial visions for challenging entrenched social hierarchies in a way that do not flatten differences.

In their engagement with speculative fiction writer Octavia E. Butler, scholars Bailey and Jamieson explain how this "work concerns itself with the human problem, with the ways that humans' dual nature as both intelligent and hierarchical beings dooms them/us to destruction in an infinite number of ways."[44] A bleak vision, yes, but only if we decide not to activate a radio imagination that listens for and signals other ways of being human. In short, a black feminist approach to posthumanism and all of its technoscientific promises is not about including the oppressed in the fold of (Western liberal) humanism or about casting out humanism writ large, but about abolishing one particular genre that, by definition, dominates and devours all others. Ultimately, it is an approach to world-building in which myriad life forms can flourish.[45]

If, as argued, the rhetoric of human betterment distorts an understanding of the multifaceted interplay between technology and society, then a thoroughgoing commitment to justice has the potential to clarify and inspire possibilities for designing this relationship anew. Justice, in this sense, is not a static value but an ongoing methodology that can and should be incorporated into design processes. As JafariNaimi and colleagues powerfully contend, "we develop the value *justice* by testing and observing the work that the justice hypothesis does in various situations, and we recognize situations as just or unjust through reference to this learning."[46] As such, a justice-oriented approach to science and technology should not be limited to calls for "inclusion" as a vague multicultural platitude. Nor is it only about ensuring that a wide cross section of humanity can "access" technological goods and services. A fixation with barcodes, after all, has a way of barring more radical possibilities. As just one example of tech growth prompting socioeconomic decline, the rapid development of Silicon Valley has contributed to an alarming homeless rate in East Palo Alto, a predominantly black and Latino area

Ruha Benjamin

where more than one-third of schoolchildren now face housing instability.[47] How, then, might we craft a justice-oriented approach to technoscience?[48] It starts with questioning breathless claims of techno-utopianism, rethinking what counts as innovation, remaining alert to the ways that race and other hierarchies of difference get embedded in the creation of new designs, and ultimately refashioning the relationship between technology and society by prioritizing justice and equity.

REFASHIONING RACE AND TECHNOLOGY

As it turns out, the process of refashioning the relationship between race and technology may entail actual fashion. Hyphen-Labs, an international team of women of color working at the intersection of technology, art, science, and futurism,[49] is experimenting with a wide array of subversive designs, including earrings for recording police altercations, and visors and other clothing that prevent facial recognition, all part of their Not Safe as Fuck project. Interestingly, Hyphen-Labs created a neurocosmetology lab that creatively employs "hair braid electrodes to stimulate an increased flow of concentration,"[50] which finds its pedagogical counterpart in the work of researchers at Rensselaer Polytechnic Institute (RPI) led by one of the volume contributors, Ron Eglash, who are developing culturally situated design tools. One of the RPI projects, Cornrow Curves, focuses on "the underlying mathematical and computational thinking involved in cornrow braiding . . . [which] aligns with the mathematician's sense of fractal patterns as iterative scaling, and a computer scientist's sense of algorithm."[51] Cornrow Curves is part of a broader community informatics initiative, which is recasting what counts as technoscience and who we think of as innovators.[52] In the process, the creative, even *beautiful* dimensions of liberatory design abound!

Finally, you the reader are encouraged to explore the edges of your own imagination—the border patrols others have imposed, as well as the monitoring systems you may have installed yourself, including those gatekeepers squatting in the nooks and crannies of your thinking, forcing you down certain pathways and telling you to avoid others. How can we expect to change social structures when we continue to nurture the same habits of mind in our mental structures? Reflecting on mass incarceration and abolition, Angela Y. Davis advises, "*Dangerous limits have been placed on the very possibility of imagining alternatives. These ideological limits have to be contested. We have to begin to think in different ways. Our future is at stake.*"[53] Davis reminds us that the carceral imagination limits not only our beings and bodies, but also the many fixes proposed. *Captivating Technology* aspires to deepen our collective understanding of the significance of imagination, drawing on anthropologist Arjun Appadurai's formulation that imagination is

> no longer mere fantasy (opium for the masses whose real work is elsewhere), no longer simple escape (from a world defined principally by more concrete purposes and structures), no longer elite pastime (thus not relevant to the lives of ordinary people), and no longer mere contemplation (irrelevant for new forms of desire and subjectivity), the imagination has become an organized field of social practices, a form of work (both in the sense of labor and culturally organized practice) and a form of negotiation. . . . The imagination is now central to all forms of agency, is itself a social fact, and is the key component of the new global order.[54]

The task, then, is to challenge not only forms of discriminatory design in our inner and outer lives, but to work with others to imagine and create alternatives to the *techno quo* — business as usual when it comes to technoscience — as part of a larger struggle to materialize collective freedoms and flourishing. If, as emphasized in this book, the carceral imagination captures and contains, then a liberatory imagination opens up possibilities and pathways, creates new templates, and builds on a black radical tradition that has continually developed insights and strategies grounded in justice.

ONWARD!

The book is organized into three parts, beginning with traditional sites of carcerality "from plantation to prison," followed by more hidden arenas of carceral technoscience "from Facebook to fast fashion," and culminating in a sustained focus on justice-oriented approaches to science and technology "from abolitionists to Afrofuturists." This flow takes the reader from more familiar terrain, cast here in a new light, to less familiar territory, with a focus on continuities and discontinuities with the former. The final part blends the historical, speculative, and biographical to engender new connections that will hopefully inspire justice-oriented experiments in thinking and praxis that even we, the contributors, could not predict.

Part I, "Carceral Techniques from Plantation to Prison," examines the entanglement of succoring *and* suffering, in which forms of supervision and control typically associated with policing and punishment are incorporated in the health management of subordinate populations. Conversely,

Ruha Benjamin

techniques of prediction and prevention that animate novel approaches to "precision medicine" are shown to infuse the work of police and prisons. Each chapter grapples with the dialectic between helping and harming and illuminates the spatial logics of racial containment on plantations (Rusert), sanatoriums (Perreira), prisons (Hatch), urban neighborhoods (Miller), and fictional futurescapes (Scannell). Geographic space serves as a seemingly neutral proxy for the control of racialized populations; "places *not* people" are the focus (read: target), we are told. But whether it is the southern plantation, black ghetto, Brazilian favela, South African township, Palestinian territory, Indian slum, or now, algorithmically confirmed "hot spots" of crime and sickness, geographic and racial imaginaries remain deeply intertwined, the former naturalizing the latter, whereby "desirable" and "undesirable" serve as euphemistic codes for valuable and disposable people.

Part II, "Surveillance Systems from Facebook to Fast Fashion," investigates the relationship between surveillance and conceptions of the social good, where the latter encompasses the digital service economy (Poster), financial health (Nopper), child safety (Thakor), and a wide array of workplaces (Van Oort). Subjugation, after all, is hardly ever the explicit objective of science and technology; instead, noble aims such as "health" and "safety" serve as a kind of moral prophylactic for newfangled forms of social control. Each chapter traces how the twin processes of classification and containment extend well beyond the domain of policing, employing novel techniques offered as innovative solutions to entrenched social problems. Each demonstrates how such fixes encode inequity, and in many cases obscure racist logics and assumptions built into their design, ultimately making it more difficult to challenge and demand accountability.

Part III, "Retooling Liberation from Abolitionists to Afrofuturists," examines how those who are "fixed" by science and technology actively appropriate and reimagine technoscience for liberatory ends. While the first two parts of the book also explore different forms of resistance that take shape under oppressive conditions, this section focuses squarely on efforts to retool the relationship between science, technology, and social justice (Eglash, Gaskins, and Roth). This focus is guided by sociologist Alondra Nelson's query, "at what moments and through which tactics did black communities strive to tilt the balance of authority" toward collective freedom and flourishing?[55] Tactics, yes, and also a black radical imagination of the kind historian Robin D. G. Kelley envisions: "We must tap the well of our own collective imaginations, that we do what earlier generations have done: dream. . . . Without new visions we don't know what to build, only what to knock down. We not only end up confused, rudderless, and cynical but we forget that making a revolution is not a series of clever maneuvers and tactics but a process that can and must transform us."[56] Kelley's appeal, like that of Nelson, Davis, and many others gone before, reminds us that radical imagination is central to refusing discriminatory design and building a just and habitable world.

The last two chapters of this section are interviews conducted by Alondra Nelson and Ruha Benjamin, respectively, with two pioneers in the study of science, technology, and race—Berkeley Professor Emeritus Troy Duster and University of Pennsylvania Professor Dorothy Roberts. In classic sociological fashion, and consistent with Duster's reported fondness for saying "Scratch a theory, you find a biography,"[57] these conversations situate the individual scholar within family, community, and institutions, and trace the links between their early lives and their academic pursuits. From the headline "Black Radical Professor Attacks America" lodged against Duster to Roberts's experience as a young mother at a high-powered law firm in New York, the reader comes to appreciate how the personal is both sociological and political, and how such experiences shaped their intellectual interest in the "preframe" of science and technology.

In mapping how Duster's and Roberts's work disrupts dominant narratives of technoscience, the interviews themselves seek to unsettle a dominant social science tenet that divorces scholars' personal lives from their intellectual pursuits. Instead, a liberatory approach to social studies of science, technology, and race aims to ground knowledge in the social world. "Situating knowledge" is not only about revealing its historical and human contingency, but ultimately aims to make technoscientific accounts of the world *accountable* by excavating who, what, where, when, and why, rather than allowing this social infrastructure to remain invisible.[58] In this way, chapters 13 and 14 offer a model of scholarship that is at once foundational and *aspirational* for a new generation of thinkers who will see in the life stories of Duster and Roberts the symbiosis of everyday struggle and scholarly insight. Ultimately, my hope is for you, the reader, to imagine and craft the worlds you cannot live *without*, just as you dismantle the ones we cannot live *within*.

Notes

1. Pamela Engel, "The City of Camden, New Jersey Is under Intense, Military-Style Surveillance," *Business Insider*, December 30, 2013, accessed January 25, 2018, http:// www.businessinsider.com/camden-new-jersey-police-surveillance-2013–12.

2. Julia Angwin, Jeff Larson, Surya Mattu, and Lauren Kirchner, "Machine Bias," *ProPublica*, May 23, 2016, accessed January 25, 2018, https://www.propublica.org/article/machine-bias-risk-assessments-in-criminal-sentencing.

3. Anthony Hatch and Kym Bradley, "Prisons Matter: Psychotropics and the Trope of Silence in Technocorrections," in *Mattering: Feminism, Science, and Materialism*, ed. Victoria Pitts-Taylor, 224–40 (New York: NYU Press, 2016).

4. Leslie Gordon, "New Report Faults California's Electronic Monitoring of Youth," University of California–Berkeley School of Law, May 11, 2017, accessed January 25, 2018, https://www.law.berkeley.edu/article/new-report-faults-californias-electronic-monitoring-youth/; see also Victor M. Rios, *Punished: Policing the Lives of Black and Latino Boys* (New York: NYU Press, 2011), for a qualitative account of the modes of criminalization and resistance that shape the daily lives of Latino and African American boys in California; and Nikki Jones, *Between Good and Ghetto: African American Girls and Inner-City Violence* (New Brunswick, NJ: Rutgers University Press, 2009), for a qualitative account of African American girls and inner-city violence, which opens with an account of the elaborate school-based surveillance that students must undergo, including X-rays, patdowns, and ID checks that extends well past school hours into their everyday lives.

5. This is drawn from Roy's incisive query, "Do we need weapons to fight wars? Or do we need wars to create a market for weapons?" Arundhati Roy, *Capitalism: A Ghost Story* (Chicago: Haymarket, 2014), 43.

6. Wacquant elaborates on "the insatiable craving for bureaucratic innovations and technological gadgets: crime-watch groups and 'guarantors of place'; partnerships between police and other public services (schools, hospitals, social workers, the national tax office, etc.); video surveillance cameras and computerized mapping of offenses; compulsory drug testing, 'Tazers' and 'flash-ball' guns; fast-track judicial processing and the extension of the prerogatives of probation and parole officers; criminal profiling, satellite-aided electronic monitoring, and generalized finger-printing; enlargement and technological modernization of carceral facilities; multiplication of specialized detention centers (for foreigners waiting to be expelled, recidivist minors, women and the sick, convicts serving community sentences, etc.)." Loïc Wacquant, *Punishing the Poor: The Neoliberal Government of Social Insecurity* (Durham, NC: Duke University Press, 2009), 2.

7. As Virginia Eubanks writes, "technologies of poverty management are not neutral. They are shaped by our nation's fear of economic insecurity and hatred of the poor." Virginia Eubanks, *Automated Inequality: How High-Tech Tools Profile, Police, and Punish the Poor* (New York: St. Martin's, 2018), 9.

8. Carla Shedd, "Countering the Carceral Continuum: The Legacy of Mass Incarceration," *Criminology and Public Policy* 10, no. 3 (2011): 865–971; Carla Shedd, *Unequal City: Race, Schools, and Perceptions of Injustice* (New York: Russell Sage Foundation, 2015); see also Katherine Beckett and Naomi Murakawa, "Mapping the Shadow Carceral State: Toward an Institutionally Capacious Approach to Punishment," *Theoretical Criminology* 16, no. 2 (2012): 221–44.

9. Eric Stanley and Nat Smith, *Captive Genders: Trans Embodiment and the Prison Industrial Complex* (Oakland, CA: AK Press, 2015), 12.

10. For a discussion of the combination of "coercion and care" that characterizes what they call "carceral citizenship," see Reuben Jonathan Miller and Forrest Stuart, "Carceral Citizenship: Race, Rights and Responsibility in the Age of Mass Supervision," *Theoretical Criminology* 21, no. 4 (2017): 532–48; see also Bruce Western, *Punishment and Inequality in America* (New York: Russell Sage Foundation, 2006).

11. As political theorist Dilts cautions, "by focusing narrowly (on prisons, police, the death penalty, etc.) we also run the risk of abolishing institutions and practices but allowing their functions to thrive in a new and more deeply entrenched form." Andrew Dilts, "To Build a World That Is Otherwise: Andrew Dilts on Abolition," *Abolition Journal*, July 2, 2015, accessed January 25, 2018, https://abolitionjournal.org/andrew-dilts-abolition-statement/. For an examination of felon disenfranchisement as a "productive failure," see also Andrew Dilts, *Punishment and Inclusion: Race, Membership, and the Limits of American Liberalism* (New York: Fordham University Press, 2014); Andrew Dilts and Perry Zurn, eds., *Active Intolerance: Michel Foucault, the Prisons Information Group, and the Future of Abolition* (New York: Palgrave Macmillan, 2015). For a discussion of how surveillance technologies turn "public agencies like schools and social service offices into prisons," see Eubanks, *Automated Inequality*, 10; see also Cathy O'Neill, *Weapons of Mass Destruction: How Big Data Increases Inequality and Threatens Democracy* (New York: Broadway, 2017).

12. Patricia J. Williams, *Seeing a Color-Blind Future: The Paradox of Race* (New York: Noonday, 1998), 4, emphasis added.

13. For an elaboration of the New Jim Code, see Ruha Benjamin, *Race after Technology* (Cambridge: Polity, 2019). See Michelle Alexander, *The New Jim Crow: Mass Incarceration in the Age of Colorblindness* (New York: New Press, 2012).

14. Ruha Benjamin, "Innovating Inequity: If Race Is a Technology, Postracialism Is the Genius Bar," *Ethnic and Racial Studies* 39, no. 13 (2016): 1–8.

15. Miriam Schulman, "Little Brother Is Watching You," *Business and Society Review* 100–101, no. 1 (1998): 65–69.

16. Angela Y. Davis, *Are Prisons Obsolete?* (New York: Seven Stories, 2011), 107.

17. Coproduction, according to Jasanoff, "stresses the constant intertwining of the cognitive, the material, the social, and the normative," and "is not about ideas alone; it is equally about concrete, physical things." Sheila Jasanoff, *States of Knowledge: The Co-Production of Science and the Social Order* (New York: Routledge, 2004), 6. See also Jenny Reardon, *Race to the Finish: Identity and Governance in an Age of Genomics* (Princeton, NJ: Princeton University Press, 2002).

18. Simone Browne, *Dark Matters: On the Surveillance of Blackness* (Durham, NC: Duke University Press, 2015), 7.

19. Browne, *Dark Matters*, 8–9; emphasis added.

20. This focus builds upon Jasanoff and Kim's notion of "sociotechnical imaginaries," collective imaginations of the future that "encode not only visions of what is at-

Ruha Benjamin

tainable through science and technology, but also of how life ought, or ought not, to be lived; in this respect they express a society's shared understandings of good and evil" (4). As Jasanoff and Kim rightly note, competing imaginaries can coexist. In racialized societies, the hopes and capacities of some are routinely discredited in popular representations of progress or completely written out of futuristic visions, a kind of temporal penitentiary that locks the oppressed in a dystopic present. But, as the volume makes clear, counter-imaginaries persist and proliferate despite the odds. Sheila Jasanoff and Sang-Hyun Kim, *Dreamscapes of Modernity: Sociotechnical Imaginaries and the Fabrication of Power* (Chicago: University of Chicago Press, 2015).

21. Brian Clifton, Sam Lavigne, Francis Tseng, "The White Collar Crime Risk Zones," *The New Inquiry Magazine* 59, https://whitecollar.thenewinquiry.com.

22. See the white paper by Brian Clifton, Sam Levigne, and Francis Tseng, https://whitecollar.thenewinquiry.com/static/whitepaper.pdf

23. X. Wu and X. Zhang, "Automated Inference on Criminality Using Face Images," AI *Technology and Industry Review*, November 24, 2017, https://medium.com/syncedreview/automated-inference-on-criminality-using-face-images-aec51c312cd0.

24. Emphasis added; Derrick A. Bell, "Who's Afraid of Critical Race Theory?" *University of Illinois Law Review* 1995: 893.

25. See Wacquant: "Here penalization serves as a technique for the invisibilization of the social 'problems' that the state, as the bureaucratic lever of the collective will, no longer can or cares to treat at its roots, and the prison operates as a judicial garbage disposal into which the human refuse of the market society are thrown." Wacquant, *Punishing the Poor*, xxii.

26. Heather Saul, "Homeless Spikes outside London Flats Spark Outrage on Twitter," *The Independent*, June 7, 2014, accessed January 25, 2018, http://www.independent.co.uk/news/uk/home-news/homelessness-spikes-outside-london-flats-spark-outrage-on-twitter-9506390.html.

27. Henry Samuel, "French City Installs Anti-Homeless Cages around Benches," *The Telegraph*, December 26, 2014, accessed January 25, 2018, http://www.telegraph.co.uk/news/worldnews/europe/france/11314081/French-city-installs-anti-homeless-cages-around-benches.html.

28. Walter Johnson, "Ferguson's Fortune 500 Company," *The Atlantic*, April 26, 2015, accessed January 25, 2018, https://www.theatlantic.com/politics/archive/2015/04/fergusons-fortune-500-company/390492.

29. Todd D. Minton and Zhen Zheng, "Jail Inmates at Midyear 2014," U.S. Department of Justice, June 2015, accessed January 25, 2018, https://www.bjs.gov/content/pub/pdf/jim14.pdf.

30. Nick Wing, "Our Bail System Is Leaving Innocent People to Die in Jail Because They're Poor," Justice Policy Institute, July 14, 2016, accessed January 25, 2018, http://www.justicepolicy.org/news/10585; see also Dean A. Dabney, Joshua Page, and Volkan Topalli, "American Bail and the Tinting of Criminal Justice," *The Howard Journal of Crime and Justice* 56, no. 4 (2017): 397–418.

31. According to Gilmore, "Racism, specifically, is the state-sanctioned or extralegal production and exploitation of group-differentiated vulnerability to premature death." Ruth Wilson Gilmore, *Golden Gulag: Prisons, Surplus, Crises, and Opposition in Globalizing California* (Berkeley: University of California Press, 2007), 28.

32. "Black to the Future," video archive, accessed at https://blacktothefuture .princeton.edu/video/. Imani Perry's question at 1 hr 27 m 29 sec.

33. Troy Duster, 1970. *The Legislation of Morality: Law, Drugs, and Moral Judgement* (New York: Free Press, 1970); Troy Duster, *Backdoor to Eugenics*, 2nd ed. (New York: Routledge, 2003); Troy Duster, "Race and Reification in Science," *Science* 307, no. 5712 (2005): 1050–51; Troy Duster, "The Combustible Intersection: Genomics, Forensics, and Race," in *Race after the Internet*, edited by Lisa Nakamura and Peter Chow-White, 310–27 (New York: Routledge, 2012); Evelynn M. Hammonds, "New Technologies of Race," in *Processed Lives: Gender and Technology in Everyday Life*, edited by Melodie Calvery and Jennifer Terry, 74–85 (New York: Routledge, 1997); Dorothy Roberts, *Killing the Black Body: Race, Reproduction, and the Meaning of Liberty* (New York: Vintage, 1999); Dorothy Roberts, *Fatal Invention: How Science, Politics and Big Business Re-Create Race in the 21st Century* (New York: New Press, 2011).

34. Susan E. Bell and Anne E. Figert, *Reimagining (Bio)Medicalization, Pharmaceuticals, and Genetics: Old Critiques and New Engagements* (New York: Routledge, 2015); Catherine Bliss, *Race Decoded: The Genomic Fight for Social Justice* (Palo Alto, CA: Stanford University Press, 2012); Lundy Braun, *Breathing Race into the Machine: The Surprising Career of the Spirometer from Plantation to Genetics* (Minneapolis: University of Minnesota Press, 2014); Khiara M. Bridges, Terence Keel, and Osagie K. Obasogie, "Introduction: Critical Race Theory and the Health Sciences," *American Journal of Law and Medicine* 43 (2017): 179–82; Melissa Creary, "Biocultural Citizenship and Embodying Exceptionalism: Biopolitics for Sickle Cell Disease in Brazil," *Social Science and Medicine* 199 (2017): 123–31; Nadia A. El-Haj, "The Genetic Reinscription of Race," *Annual Review of Anthropology* 36 (2017): 283–300; Steven Epstein, *Inclusion: The Politics of Difference in Medical Research* (Chicago: University of Chicago Press, 2007); Joan H. Fujimura and Ramya Rajagopalan, "Different Differences: The Use of 'Genetic Ancestry' versus Race in Biomedical Human Genetic Research," *Social Studies of Science* 41, no. 1 (2010): 5–30; Duana Fullwiley, "The Biologistical Construction of Race: 'Admixture' Technology and the New Genetic Medicine," *Social Studies of Science* 38, no. 5 (2008): 695–735; Jonathan Kahn, *Race in a Bottle: The Story of BiDil and Racialized Medicine in a Post-Genomic Age* (New York: Columbia University Press, 2014); Michael J. Montoya, "Bioethnic Conscription: Genes, Race, and Mexicana/o Ethnicity in Diabetes Research," *Cultural Anthropology* 22, no. 1 (2007): 94–128; Ann Morning, *The Nature of Race: How Scientists Think and Teach and Human Difference* (Berkeley: University of California Press, 2011); Alondra Nelson, *Social Life of DNA: Race, Reparations, and Reconciliation after the Genome* (New York: Beacon Press, 2016); Aaron Panofsky, *Misbehaving Science: Controversy and the Development of Behavior Genetics* (Chicago: University of Chicago Press, 2014); Reardon, *Race to the Finish*; Sarah S. Richardson and Hallam Stevens, *Postgenomics: Perspectives on Biology*

Ruha Benjamin

after the Genome (Durham, NC: Duke University Press, 2015); Ernesto Schwartz-Marin and Peter Wade, "Explaining the Visible and the Invisible: Public Knowledge of Genetics, Ancestry, Physical Appearance, and Race in Colombia," *Social Studies of Science* 45, no. 6 (2015): 886–906; Kim TallBear, *Native American DNA: Tribal Belonging and the False Promise of Genetic Science* (Minneapolis: University of Minnesota Press, 2013); Charis Thompson, *Making Parents: The Ontological Choreography of Reproductive Technologies* (Cambridge, MA: MIT Press, 2007); Peter Wade, Carlos López Beltrán, Eduardo Restrepo, and Ricardo Ventura Santos, *Mestizo Genomics: Race Mixture, Nation, and Science in Latin America* (Durham, NC: Duke University Press, 2014); Johnny Eric Williams, *Decoding Racial Ideology in Genomics* (Lanham, MD: Lexington Books, 2016).

35. Geoffrey C. Bowker and Susan Leigh Star, *Sorting Things Out: Classification and Its Consequences* (Cambridge, MA: MIT Press, 2000); Wendy H. K. Chun, "Race and/as Technology or How to Do Things with Race," in *Race After the Internet*, edited by Lisa Nakamura and Peter Chow-White, 38–69 (New York: Routledge, 2011); Adele Clarke, Laura Mamo, Jennifer Ruth Fosket, Jennifer R. Fishman, and Janet K. Shim, *Biomedicalization: Technoscience, Health, and Illness in the U.S.* (Durham, NC: Duke University Press, 2010); Beth Coleman, "Race as Technology," *Camera Obscura* 24, no. 1 (2009): 177–207; Marie Hicks, *Programmed Inequality: How Britain Discarded Women Technologists and Lost Its Edge in Computing* (Cambridge, MA: MIT Press, 2017); David S. Jones and Ian Whitmarsh, eds., *What's the Use of Race? Modern Governance and the Biology of Difference* (Cambridge, MA: MIT Press, 2010); Lisa Nakamura, *Cybertypes: Race, Ethnicity, and Identity on the Internet* (New York: Routledge, 2002); Lisa Nakamura, *Digitizing Race* (Minneapolis: University of Minnesota Press, 2008); Safiya Umoja Noble, *Algorithms of Oppression: How Search Engines Reinforce Racism* (New York: NYU Press, 2018); Frank Pasquale, *The Black Box Society: The Secret Algorithms That Control Money and Information* (Cambridge, MA: Harvard University Press, 2014); Anne Pollock, *Medicating Race: Heart Disease and Durable Preoccupations with Difference* (Durham, NC: Duke University Press, 2012); Janet K. Shim, *Heart-Sick: The Politics of Risk, Inequality, and Heart Disease* (New York: NYU Press, 2014); Keith Wailoo, Alondra Nelson, and Catherine Lee, *Genetics and the Unsettled Past: The Collision of DNA, Race, and History* (New Brunswick, NJ: Rutgers University Press, 2012).

36. For example, Philip and colleagues describe *postcolonial computing* as "a bag of tools that affords us contingent tactics for continual, careful, collective, and always partial reinscriptions of a cultural-technical situation in which we all find ourselves." Kavita Philip, Lilly Irani, and Paul Dourish, "Postcolonial Computing: A Tactical Survey," *Science, Technology, and Human Values* 37, no. 1 (2012): 3. See also André Brock, "From the Blackhand Side: Twitter as a Cultural Conversation," *Journal of Broadcasting and Electronic Media* 56, no. 4 (2012): 529–49, and André Brock, Lynette Kvasny, and Kayla Hales, "Cultural Appropriations of Technical Capital: Black Women, Weblogs, and the Digital Divide," *Information, Communication, and Society* 13, no. 7 (2010): 1040–59, on "cultural appropriations of technical capital"; Ron Eglash, Jennifer L. Croissant, Giovanna Di Chiro, and Rayvon Fouché, *Appropriating Technology: Vernacular Science*

and Social Power (Minneapolis: University of Minnesota Press, 2004), on "appropriating technology"; Rayvon Fouché, "Say It Loud, I'm Black and I'm Proud: African Americans, American Artifactual Culture, and Black Vernacular Technological Creativity," *American Quarterly* 58, no. 3 (2013): 639–61, on "black vernacular technological creativity"; Alondra Nelson, Thuy Linh N. Tu, and Alicia Hedlam Hines, eds., *Technicolor: Race, Technology, and Everyday Life* (New York: NYU Press, 2001), and Laura Mamo and Jennifer Fishman, "Why Justice? Introduction to the Special Issue on Entanglements of Science, Ethics, and Justice," *Science, Technology, and Human Values* 38, no. 2 (2013): 159–75, on "justice and STS"; Banu Subramaniam, *Ghost Stories for Darwin: The Science of Variation and the Politics of Diversity* (Chicago: University of Illinois Press, 2014), on feminist approaches to the life sciences; Miriam E. Sweeney and André Brock, "Critical Informatics: New Methods and Practices," *Proceedings of the Association for Information Science and Technology* 51, no. 1 (2014): 1–8, on "critical informatics," among others. Ron Eglash, et al., *Appropriating Technology*.

37. danah boyd and Kate Crawford, "Critical Questions for Big Data: Provocations for a Cultural, Technological, and Scholarly Phenomenon," *Information, Communication and Society* 15, no. 5 (2012): 662–79; Sarah Brayne, "Surveillance and System Avoidance: Criminal Justice Contact and Institutional Attachment," *American Sociological Review* 79, no. 3: 367–91 (2014); Sarah Brayne, "Big Data Surveillance: The Case of Policing," *American Sociological Review* 82, no. 5 (2017): 997–1008; Andrew Guthrie Ferguson, *The Rise of Big Data Policing: Surveillance, Race, and the Future of Law Enforcement* (New York: NYU Press, 2017); Keith Guzik, "Discrimination by Design: Predictive Data Mining as Security Practice in the United States' 'War on Terrorism,'" *Surveillance and Society* 7, no. 1 (2009): 1–17; Bernard E. Harcourt, *Against Prediction: Profiling, Policing, and Punishing in an Actuarial Age* (Chicago: Chicago University Press, 2006); Richard Hindmarsh and Barbara Prainsack, eds., *Genetic Suspects: Global Governance of Forensic DNA Profiling and Databasing* (Cambridge: Cambridge University Press, 2010); Anthony Hatch and Kym Bradley, "Prisons Matter: Psychotropics and the Trope of Silence in Technocorrections," in *Mattering: Feminism, Science, and Materialism*, ed. Victoria Pitts-Taylor, 224–40 (New York: NYU Press, 2016); Elizabeth E. Joh, "The New Surveillance Discretion: Automated Suspicion, Big Data, and Policing," *Harvard Law and Policy Review* 10, no. 1 (2016): 15–42; Shiloh Krupar and Nadine Ehlers, "'When Treating Patients Like Criminals Makes Sense': Medical Hot Spotting, Race, and Debt," in *Subprime Health: The American Health-Care System and Race-Based Medicine*, ed. Nadine Ehlers and Leslie Hinkson, 31–54 (Minnesota: University of Minnesota Press, 2017); David Lyon, ed., *Surveillance as Social Sorting: Privacy, Risk, and Digital Discrimination* (New York: Routledge 2003); Peter K. Manning, *The Technology of Policing: Crime Mapping, Information Technology, and the Rationality of Crime Control* (New York: NYU Press, 2011); Gary T. Marx, *Windows into the Soul: Surveillance and Society in an Age of High Technology* (Chicago: University of Chicago Press, 2016); Amade M'Charek, "Beyond Fact or Fiction: On the Materiality of Race in Practice," *Cultural Anthropology* 28, no. 3 (2013): 420–42; Anne Pollock, "On the Suspended Sentences of the Scott Sisters: Mass Incarceration, Kidney

Ruha Benjamin

Donation, and the Biopolitics of Race in the United States," *Science, Technology, and Human Values* 40, no. 2 (2015): 250–71; Latanya Sweeney, "Discrimination in Online Ad Delivery," *Queue* 11, no. 3 (2013): 10–29; Tufeki Zeynup, *Twitter and Teargas: The Power and Fragility of Networked Protest* (New Haven, CT: Yale University Press, 2017).

38. Pollock, "On the Suspended Sentences of the Scott Sisters," 15–16.

39. Moya Bailey and Ayana A. H. Jamieson, "Palimpsests in the Life and Work of Octavia E. Butler," *Palimpsest: A Journal on Women, Gender, and the Black International* 6, no. 2 (2017): xi, emphasis added.

40. Many STS scholars have theorized the way that machines and other nonhumans exercise different forms of agency, narrating the blurred boundary between organisms and machines, showing how "myth and tool mutually constitute each other," and calling for a multispecies approach to justice. Chen's idea of animacy is to "theorize current anxieties around the production of humanness in contemporary times. . . . Animacy activates new theoretical formulations that trouble and undo stubborn binary systems of difference, including dynamism/stasis, life/death, subject/object, speech/non-speech, human/animal, natural body/cyborg." Mel Chen, *Animacies: Biopolitics, Racial Mattering, and Queer Affect* (Durham, NC: Duke University Press, 2012), 3. Relatedly, Haraway describes technologies as "frozen moments" that allow us to observe otherwise "fluid social interactions" at work. These "formalizations" are also instruments to enforce meaning, especially, I would add, racialized meanings that construct — not just reflect — the social world (302). Donna Haraway, *Simians, Cyborgs and Women: The Reinvention of Nature* (New York: Routledge, 1991), 302. See also Bruno Latour, "On Recalling ANT," *Sociological Review* 47, no. S1 (1999): 15–25; Eben Kirsky, ed., *The Multispecies Salon* (Durham, NC: Duke University Press, 2014); Donna Haraway, *Staying with the Trouble: Making Kin in the Chthulucene* (Durham, NC: Duke University Press, 2016).

41. Alexander Weheliye, *Habeas Viscus: Racializing Asssemblages, Biopolitics, and Black Feminist Theories of the Human* (Durham, NC: Duke University Press, 2014), 8.

42. Weheliye, *Habeas Viscus*, 3.

43. Zakiyyah Iman Jackson, "Animal: New Directions in the Theorization of Race and Posthumanism," *Feminist Studies* 39, no. 3 (2013): 640, emphasis added. See also Saidiya V. Hartman, *Scenes of Subjection: Terror, Slavery, and Self-Making in Nineteenth-Century America* (New York: Oxford University Press, 1997); Katherine McKittrick, ed., *Sylvia Wynter: On Being Human as Praxis* (Durham, NC: Duke University Press, 2014); Christina Sharpe, *In the Wake: On Blackness and Being* (Durham, NC: Duke University Press, 2016).

44. Bailey and Jamieson, "Palimpsests in the Life and Work of Octavia E. Butler," vi.

45. And for Wynter, the stakes are high: "all our present struggles with respect to race, class, gender, sexual orientation, ethnicity, struggles over the environment, global warming, severe climate change, the sharply unequal distribution of the earth resources . . . —these are all differing facets of the central ethnoclass Man vs Human struggle" (cf. Weheliye, *Habeas Viscus*, 29).

46. Nassim JafariNaimi, Lisa Nathan, and Ian Hargraves, "Values as Hypotheses: Design, Inquiry, and the Service of Values," *Design Issues* 31, no. 4 (2015): 38. See also

Nassim JafariNaimi, "Our Bodies in the Trolley's Path, or Why Self-driving Cars Must
Not Be Programmed to Kill," *Science, Technology, and Human Values,* accessed January 25, 2018, http://journals.sagepub.com/doi/pdf/10.1177/0162243917718942.

47. Alistair Gee, "More Than One-Third of Schoolchildren Are Homeless in Shadow
of Silicon Valley," *The Guardian,* December 28, 2016, accessed January 25, 2018, https://
www.theguardian.com/society/2016/dec/28/silicon-valley-homeless-east-palo-alto
-california-schools.

48. As Atanasoski and Vora posit, the aim is to track "how historical forms of domination and power, encompassing but not limited to social categories and hierarchies
of difference, get built into seemingly non-human objects and the infrastructures
that link them, thus sanitizing digital media [and a variety of other] technologies
as human-free." Neda Atanasoski and Kalindi Vora. "Surrogate Humanity: Posthuman
Networks and the (Racialized) Obsolescence of Labor," *Catalyst: Feminism, Theory,
Technoscience* 1, no. 1 (2015): 5.

49. See Hyphen-Labs, http://www.hyphen-labs.com/index.html.

50. Jessica Charlesworth, "Primer 2017: A Speculative Futures Conference." *Core77,*
March 21, 2017, accessed January 25, 2018, http://www.core77.com/posts/63489/Primer
-2017-A-Speculative-Futures-Conference.

51. Michael Lachney, "Culturally Responsive Computing as Brokerage: Toward
Asset Building with Education-Based Social Movements," *Learning, Media, and Technology* 42, no. 4 (2016): 7.

52. For Ron Eglash's "Community Informatics" projects, see http://homepages.rpi
.edu/~eglash/eglash.dir/ci.htm.

53. Angela Y. Davis, *The Meaning of Freedom: And Other Difficult Dialogues* (San Francisco: City Lights, 2012), 30.

54. Arjun Appadurai, *Modernity at Large: Cultural Dimensions of Globalization* (Minneapolis: University of Minnesota Press, 1996), 31.

55. Alondra Nelson, *Body and Soul: The Black Panther Party and the Fight against Medical Discrimination* (Minneapolis: University of Minneapolis Press, 2013), xii.

56. Robin D. G. Kelley, *Freedom Dreams: The Black Radical Imagination* (Boston: Beacon Press, 2003), xii; my emphasis.

57. American Sociologist Association. On Demand Content. http://www.asanet.org
/about-asa/asa-story/asa-history/past-asa-officers/past-asa-presidents/troy-duster.

58. See Donna Haraway, "Situated Knowledges: The Science Question in Feminism
and the Privilege of Partial Perspective," *Feminist Studies* 14, no. 3 (1988): 575–99.

Ruha Benjamin

(PART I)

CARCERAL TECHNIQUES FROM PLANTATION

TO PRISON

.....

1

Naturalizing Coercion

THE TUSKEGEE EXPERIMENTS
AND THE LABORATORY LIFE OF
THE PLANTATION

Britt Rusert

.....

I have often been asked to define the term "Black Belt." So far as I can learn, the term was first used to designate a part of the country which was distinguished by the colour of the soil. The part of the country possessing this thick, dark, and naturally rich soil was, of course, the part of the South where slaves were most profitable, and consequently they were taken there in the largest numbers. Later, and especially since the war, the term seems to be used wholly in a political sense — that is, to designate the counties where the black people outnumber the white.

—BOOKER T. WASHINGTON, *Up from Slavery*

[T]he procedures adopted for the captive flesh demarcate a total objectification, as the entire captive community becomes a living laboratory.

—HORTENSE SPILLERS, "Mama's Baby, Papa's Maybe:
An American Grammar Book"

A few years after the 1932 initiation of the Tuskegee Study, the U.S. Public Health Service's "observation" of "untreated syphilis in the male negro" in Alabama's Macon County, the first clinical article on the topic appeared in the *Journal of the American Medical Association*.[1] The paper was presented at the 1936 annual meeting of the organization and emphasized an "unusual opportunity" that arose after a survey of the "southern rural areas" revealed that a "considerable portion of the infected Negro population remained untreated during the entire course of syphilis."[2] The original survey, which provided treatment for rural populations with syphilis, was transformed by the Public Health Service (PHS) into a nontherapeutic study that tracked the natural course of the disease by following "the untreated syphilitic patient from the beginning of the disease to the death of the infected person."[3] As is now well known, the participants only remained untreated because the PHS withheld treatment over the course of the study and misled recruited clinical subjects into thinking they were being cared for by government doctors. Embedded within an emerging biopolitical regime in the early twentieth century while anticipating the uneven distribution of health under neoliberalism, the fiction of governmental "care" in the Tuskegee Study masked a structure of scientific exploitation that was racialized, gendered, classed, and deeply connected to the history and afterlife of slavery.[4] While the story of Tuskegee has been thoroughly detailed by scholars, it continues to provide powerful and prescient warnings about how "care" and "coercion" have been intertwined within and beyond the health "care" system under racial capitalism.[5]

Clinical articles published over the next four decades continued to invoke the uniqueness of this situation in the South and repeatedly referred to the investigation as a study of the "natural history of syphilis."[6] The test subjects were often figured in these accounts as mere incubators for the reproduction of the disease, their bodies effectively de-acculturated by the focus on natural history. As Allan Brandt has argued, the idea that "conditions in Tuskegee existed 'naturally'"—and were not influenced by institutionalized racism, widespread poverty, and socioeconomic inequality—enabled the PHS to present a deeply interventionist human experiment as a simple, observational "study in nature."[7] For example, researchers cited the geographic isolation of the research population to justify the test group's lack of access to "modern treatment."[8]

The PHS's dependence on a rhetoric of natural history in this geography of the U.S. South reveals an enduring scientific history on and of the plantation, which, in the age of slavery, served as an informal laboratory for all kinds of experimental investigations into the "natural history" of race. Despite the presence of an already established and pervasive discourse that the poor, rural plantation districts of Alabama existed outside of modern culture, an entrenched discourse about the South that certainly contributed to the study's conditions of possibility, researchers still worked hard to ensure their test subjects blended into the background of the laboratory's southern scene. The Tuskegee clinical articles, for example, represented the residents of Macon County as nonmodern folk who remained connected to a primitive agricultural landscape—the study was even scheduled around crop cycles to accommodate participants' work schedules. Most of the men selected for the syphilis experiments were sharecroppers who worked under white farmers in a system of debt peonage.

The PHS was clearly attuned to the role the plantation complex played in organizing the human and agricultural geography of Macon County. Researchers figured Macon County as an ideal laboratory, a perfectly enclosed system that was produced out of the peculiarities of an isolated and insular plantation system. In other words, an understanding of the plantation as a closed, even carceral, space that contained and enclosed a discrete population allowed PHS officials to figure Macon County as a scientific laboratory, cut off from the contingencies and unwanted variables of the outside world. Over and over again, researchers emphasized the "non-migratory nature" of their test population.[9] It is true that in 1932, Macon County was still very much tied to its plantation past, but that past was itself part of the movements, reorganizations, and upheavals of industrial capitalism. Ignoring the reality of the Great Migration, the literature *and* on-the-ground experiments of Tuskegee naturalized both the coerced containment and forced migration of African Americans within ongoing processes of dispossession and displacement.

In their attempts to figure Macon County as a sealed laboratory that effectively enclosed a stable experimental population, the Tuskegee researchers extended the laboratory life of the plantation into the twentieth century. This essay attends to a prehistory of the Tuskegee Study in order to better understand how experimental plantation geographies were reproduced and managed well after Emancipation and Reconstruction. I track how an emergent New South discourse at the turn of the twentieth century sought to maintain the integrity of the plantation as a closed system even as the natural resources of the South were being offered up to the national and global economy. After slavery, industrialists and farmers alike scrambled to recontain black laboring bodies—as well as nonlaboring, "surplus" bodies—within carceral geographies sited on old plantation grounds, new work camps, and a growing prison system.[10]

Turning to Booker T. Washington's Tuskegee Institute, which was founded in Macon County in 1881, this essay considers the relationships between the hygienic pedagogies of Washington's South and the kinds of spaces traversed—and bodies mined—for the benefit of the Tuskegee experiments. In many ways, what we discover in Washington's writings and speeches is an articulation of the relationship between blackness and what we would today call *biopower*, Michel Foucault's theory of the emergence of a new mode of governance in the nineteenth century in which the management of life, rather than death, became the object of power: "in this model of power, the expansion and efficiency of life, not its deduction, becomes the primary function of power, and deduction [death or debility] is merely an instrument in the service of expansion," and in the service of the "optimization" of life itself.[11] But rather than resisting regimes of biopower operating under the guise of health, care, and life, Washington actually advocated for the transformation of African Americans, especially former slaves of the South, into a coherent *population* for the purposes of biopolitical governance and intervention. In other words, it is as if Washington recognized this new, emerging form of power being organized in the nineteenth century, and sought to encourage and economize the folding of the anatamo-political black body, and a newly coherent black population, *into* biopolitical regimes of power. Indeed, throughout his writings and at the Tuskegee Institute, Washington was obsessed with making his students as well as a larger population of ex-slaves "useful" to the state, advertising the local population as another resource to be exploited in what the sociologist Robert Bullard has called the "sacrifice zone" of the South.[12] The focus on personal hygiene and cleanliness at the Tuskegee Institute opened the door for alliances with public health initiatives early in the twentieth century, making the school's student population as well as residents of surrounding counties subjects of intense hygienic surveillance. In short, the residents of Macon County had been transformed into a research population well before the 1932 initiation of the syphilis experiments.

Consistently and across several decades, Tuskegee researchers trafficked in discourses about the supposed "naturalness" of space and life in the Deep South to obscure technologies of experimentation that included the surveillance and coercive attempts to contain and control the research population for the purposes of the clinical study. Researchers and advocates benefited from the historical boundedness of blackness to the land in the plantation South to present the study as both noninvasive and controlled (it was neither). Moreover, researchers effectively ignored the historical reality of the Great Migration while dealing practically with the fact that the men in the study were continually moving, leaving, escaping all the time. Researchers drew on perceptions about the "primitiveness" and timelessness of black southern life to obscure the exploitations of the experiments at the same time as they understood the experiments to be central to a broader effort by the U.S. government to present itself as international leader in biomedicine in

Britt Rusert

the postwar period. In this way, the dialectic of innovation and inequity that characterizes contributions to this volume here takes on a distinctly racialized temporality: Tuskegee was used to establish the position of the United States at the forefront of scientific innovation in the period, over and above Germany, but the study "participants" were continually pushed back to a mythic premodern past in order to obscure the violences that enabled innovations in modern medical "care." The fiction of slavery as a nonmodern, feudal system of serfs wedded to the land also proved useful for mitigating worries about the contingencies and actual movement of the Tuskegee research population.

On the ground, and in the Tuskegee clinical literature, poor communities of the rural South were thus transformed into nonmodern enclaves that existed in a natural state, apart from the nation-state and beyond the jurisdiction of modern medicine. Such characterizations, of course, obscured the systematic withdrawal of resources from the post-Reconstruction South, removed blackness from modernity, and used—but not did not serve— southern black communities in the quest for establishing the centrality of the United States to a global scientific-technological modernity. In this way, Tuskegee's naturalization of socioeconomic inequalities, paired with the merging of black bodies with the southern environment, effectively resignified the commodifiable, exploitable enslaved body—or what Hortense Spillers refers to as captive "flesh," upon which anything can be done—for postslavery scientific modernity.[13] As under slavery, New South discourse and initiatives, from business journals to the showcasing of black talent at world's fairs and expos within and outside the United States, offered up black workers to the North and to emerging global labor markets as "natural resources," akin to and wedded to the rest of the exploitable South.[14] And as the history of the Tuskegee experiments demonstrates, if black southerners weren't able to work because they were ill or otherwise incapacitated, they would be put to "use" in other ways, in the name of science and life itself.

NATURAL RESOURCES OF THE NEW SOUTH

Although public health intervention in the southern states focused primarily on urban spaces, the rural plantation became a site of legitimate concern for the medical establishment by the mid-nineteenth century. James H. Cassedy marks the 1840s as the period in which "plantation hygiene" took shape in the context of the growth of medical topography, the rise of geological surveying, the establishment of the American Medical Association, the enthusiasm generated by sanitation reform in the North, and the increase in medical journalism in the South.[15] Observers of the period believed that disease emanated from recently cleared land: since the turning of soil was believed to unearth unhealthy elements, medical authorities encouraged planters to build their plantations quickly in order to counteract or minimize disease conditions. Experts directed planters to keep the entire architecture of the plantation, including the "culture of soil, building, drainage, ditching, and manure making,"[16] as organized as possible, since disordered plantation geographies were thought to engender disease. Plantation organization in the nineteenth century was, therefore, tightly conjoined with healthfulness: the ordered plantation, in these discourses, itself becomes the cure, the picture of health in the antebellum South. The plantation was figured as a kind of biopolitical institution of health management early on, as planters sought to keep an entire ecology of slaves, crops, animals, and environmental factors in a salubrious order.[17]

Just as the industrial factory was modeled on the colonial plantation, the plantation emerged at the frontier of biopolitical innovation, as an institution "where[in] certain subjects became objects of knowledge and at the same time objects of domination," but were transformed into such in the name of "health" and "life."[18] In the postbellum plantation South, African American labor could be separated from a concern with the body in a way that was impossible under the auspices of a plantation system that needed to keep an internal ecology of crops and enslaved laborers in balance to maximize profit. Of course, slavery was in no way a humane institution that properly cared for slave health, but it is crucial to draw attention to the important role of sickness management in the day-to-day operation of antebellum plantations.[19] Such regimes of plantation soundness established a kind of governance over African American subjects in the South that seemed to have become obsolete with emancipation. However, industrial schools and other training sites that were established for the education of ex-slaves effectively reanimated systems of health management in order to incorporate black subjects back into the coercive labor structures of the New South and into emerging regimes of biopolitical governance. Houston Baker has written on the ways in which particular institutions in the postwar South worked to confine African American subjects within "plantation arrangements" into the twentieth century.[20] Tuskegee serves as his prime example. Indeed, Tuskegee's success in propelling such plantation arrangements was due in large part to how health management at "Mr. Washington's plantation" stood central to the school's practices and pedagogies.[21] New South institutions picked up where the plantation left off:

continued interest in maintaining the health of an institutional environment enfolded the bodies of black subjects—not just their labor—back into intimate structures of the New South economy. As in so many plantation environments under enslavement, Tuskegee's management personnel were concerned with keeping the health of an entire institutional ecology in balance.

Washington foregrounds personal hygiene throughout his writings, most notably in his 1901 autobiography, *Up from Slavery*. Washington primed for his civilizing missions at Tuskegee in his domestic role as "house father" to Native American students at Hampton Normal and Agricultural Institute in Virginia. In 1881, Washington was invited upon General Armstrong's recommendation to head up an industrial school in Macon County, Alabama. The state legislature had recently approved an act that sought "to establish a Normal School for colored teachers at Tuskegee"[22] and granted the school $2,000 annually, a meager sum compared to the allowances given to other educational institutions in the state. Washington eagerly took up the mission to bring the Hampton model of education into the Deep South, to provide students with a "practical education" that favored practice in agricultural and work-related tasks over a classical curriculum that would apparently go unused in the rural South. In the process of "working with the hands," students would grow to love the menial tasks that differed little from the toil of the (old South) plantation.[23]

Washington finds something almost pathetic in the ex-slave's aspiration to both class and geographic mobility through book learning. In his touring of the rural districts surrounding Tuskegee, he reports happening upon a sad scene (he says it was "one of the saddest things I saw during the month of travel") in which "a young man, who had attended some high school, [was] sitting down in a one-room cabin, with grease on his clothing, filth all around him, and weeds in the yard and garden, engaged in studying a French grammar."[24] This rural scene of instruction visualizes the superiority of practical pedagogies of hygiene over the supposed civilizing influences of an education in "French grammar." The young man's classical education does little, if anything, to instruct him in the proper ways of civilization. At Tuskegee, the cleaning up of rural "filth"—both the grimy rural subject and the weedy, overgrown space he or she occupied—became the primary aim of a decent education. Washington saw honor and dignity in schooling that picked up on the kinds of mechanical arts traditions of the plantation under slavery. In many ways, he viewed industrial training as a simple extension of skills learned on the antebellum plantation: he did, after all, refer to the peculiar institution as the "school of slavery." Throughout Washington's autobiography and in other works, nothing, at times, seems more disgusting to him than black class aspiration, an aspiration for class mobility that gets coded as both foppish and morally degrading. Of course, Washington would eventually gain fame, mobility, and wealth through accommodationist rhetoric, becoming the urbane "New Negro" he claimed to despise. While he gained increased mobility in northern, white, philanthropic circles, he encouraged black southerners to "cast down your bucket where you are."[25] Washington favored an industrial education because he did not want his students to consider moving up in the world by moving out of the South. Rather, he, along with other New South proponents, worried about black laborers completely abandoning the agricultural spaces of the South. Washington's pedagogies at Tuskegee, while couched in the language of northern, industrial modernity, encouraged students to remain in the plantation districts managing the New South plantation.

Extending his civilizing, near missionary work with the Native American students at Hampton, Washington engaged in strict pedagogies of hygiene on the New South plantation at Tuskegee in order to indoctrinate a lazy, wasteful southern population into the clean, thrifty moral order of the U.S. North. In fact, Washington held out hope that African Americans trained in northern hygiene brought south would turn a fallow South into a newly (re) productive landscape. Soon after his famous "cast down your bucket" line in the Atlanta Exposition Address, Washington assures white Southern listeners that if they reach out to aid the plight of their Negro brethren, they will find "that they will buy your surplus land, *make blossom the waste places in your fields*, and run your factories."[26] A few lines later he insists that if the southern black population is not aided, they "shall prove a veritable body of death, stagnating, depressing, retarding every effort to advance the body politic."[27] In the postbellum period, anxieties over the productivity of the landscape in the South continued to be intimately linked with the health (or death) of its black laboring population. At Tuskegee, Washington carefully ensured the propagation of a healthy, clean black citizenry willing to make "blossom the waste places in your fields."

Many scholars have documented the nearly obsessive regimes of hygiene and orderliness that stifled students, staff, and faculty in their daily activities at Tuskegee.[28] Washington writes in *Up from Slavery*, "Over and over again the students were reminded in those first years—and are reminded now—that people would excuse us for our poverty, for our lack of comforts and conveniences, but that they would not excuse us for dirt."[29] There was, however, a clear problem with the attempt to sweep the dirt of the Tuskegee

Britt Rusert

plantation from out of public view. In *Working with the Hands*, Washington describes racial uplift in distinctively agricultural terms: "Our pathway must be up through the soil."[30] There is a paradox here: Washington insists upon a kind of impossible cleanliness of the bodies and spaces of Tuskegee at the very same time as he encourages racial uplift through hard, dirty toil in the southern soil. Just pages after Washington insists in *Up from Slavery* that "absolute cleanliness of the body has been insisted upon from the first," readers are offered a scene in which students work to erect the campus's first building, "digging out the dirt in order to allow of the laying of the foundations."[31] Ultimately, Washington must come to terms with the dirt of the still agriculturally dependent South to make black labor in the New South's soil a noble endeavor.

DIRT AND DISORDER: THE PUBLIC HEALTH CONNECTION

At Tuskegee, ideas about moral uncleanliness circulated through the actual dirt of the plantation. Washington negotiated northern, and perhaps even bacteriological, models of sanitation with the agricultural roots of the rural South, a necessarily "soiled" society. In her 1966 study of the role of purity in primitive and modern cultures, Mary Douglas understands dirt as both matter out of place and the mark of a system.[32] Modern taboos surrounding pollution are often tied to particular aesthetic and hygienic concerns, but dirt is also constituted by modern systems of classification. In the preface to the 2002 edition of *Purity and Danger*, she writes, "there is no such thing as dirt; no single item is dirty apart from a particular system of classification in which it does not fit."[33] Since dirt is disorder, "eliminating it is not a negative movement, but a positive effort to organise the environment."[34] Upon arriving at Tuskegee, Washington was heartened to find that the bodies and souls of African Americans in Alabama had not been weakened and degraded as in the cities. At the same time, he is struck by the disorganization of the plantation districts. Washington's obsession with dirt elimination is an effort to organize an environment.

In this light, the alliance between Washington's Tuskegee and the U.S. Public Health Service was an ideal partnership. In the mid-nineteenth century, public health in the United States emerged primarily in industrial centers of the North, focusing on the containment of disease and promotion of sanitation measures in increasingly crowded, immigrant-populated cities. The "unhygienic practices" of dispossessed populations were specifically blamed for contributing to disease miasmas in the North. The association between disorder, disease, and the underclass prompted public health authorities and sanitation officers (the medical police) to criminalize immigrant communities as diseased populations that needed to be separated from the rest of the population through quarantine, zoning regulations, and other methods of urban organization and containment. Into the late nineteenth and early twentieth centuries, public health efforts began to take more interest in the South as fears over yellow fever outbreaks proliferated alongside worries over a decaying plantation system's deleterious effects on the southern body politic.[35]

Like Washington's efforts at Tuskegee, the southern public health movement was highly invested in organizing dangerous geographies in the South, particularly those socioeconomic units like the plantation that had been dismantled by the Civil War. Tuskegee's formalized relationship with official public health initiatives included Washington's establishment in 1915 of a "National Negro Health Week," a 1909 conference held at the school entitled "General Health Conditions of Negroes in the Southern States," and the regular publication of health and sanitation pamphlets for the education of the public. Tuskegee's public health pedagogies thus extended far beyond the school's well-guarded boundaries. As part of their participation in the Women's Club of Tuskegee, for example, students made home visits in order to teach local residents about the principles of hygiene.[36]

Roderick Ferguson marks the post-emancipation moment in which imperial and military tactics used in territories outside of the United States were simultaneously turned against marginalized populations on the domestic front, as one in which "sexuality becomes a mode of racialized domestic governmentality."[37] Aligned with the intensification of a form of power and governance that claims to operate on behalf of the well-being and health of the population (biopower), pedagogies of health and hygiene thus became a prime concern of black industrial schools in the pursuit of producing sexually and gender-normalized African American citizen-subjects. Although he clearly would not have called it "biopower," Washington seems to have understood how power was increasingly targeting the population rather than the family, as well as how racialized governmentality depended upon the production of sexual and gendered norms. In an age when sexual practices became the objects of power and discipline through the production and proliferation of discrete sexual identities (Foucault famously said that the "homosexual" did not exist before 1870), syphilis itself was treated as a sexual "perversion," one that justified forms of racialized governmentality and discipline in the plantation districts of Tuskegee. Indeed, the figuration of syphilis itself as a

Britt Rusert

kind of sexual "perversion" helped to more tightly corral infected black men into the "population" and into forms of biomedical intervention for the purposes of the Tuskegee experiments.

THE TUSKEGEE EXPERIMENT(S)

During the antebellum period, the entire plantation was represented as a domestic household in which slaves were enfolded, if only rhetorically, into the plantation "family." Under Reconstruction and during the intensification of biopower later in the nineteenth century, black laborers still inhabiting plantation geographies were effectively transformed into a population, a transformation that Washington both recognized and sought to streamline. Ultimately, it was this contained, "nonmigratory population" that provided the perfect laboratory conditions for the Tuskegee clinical study.[38]

The Tuskegee Study emerged out of an earlier therapeutic program that had been jointly funded by the Public Health Service and the philanthropic Julius Rosenwald Fund. Rosenwald, who was the president of Sears, Roebuck, had a long history of investment in the health of the South and was also a trustee of the Tuskegee Institute and a good friend to Washington.[39] With the beginning of the Great Depression, the Rosenwald Fund withdrew its funding, and the PHS worried that their hard work would go to waste. On the suggestion of Dr. Taliaferro Clark of the PHS, the study was transformed from a therapeutic study, in which participants received treatment after a six-month observation period, into a "study in nature," in which doctors observed the course of the disease as it wreaked havoc on its victims, an experimental group composed of around four hundred men.[40] The Tuskegee Institute was also an active participant with varying levels of involvement during different stages of the experiments. Conductors of the study went so far to protect the integrity of their research as to prevent participants from receiving penicillin when it became available in the late 1940s as the standard treatment for the disease. The grotesque violation of these men's bodies extended even after death: family members were required to turn over the bodies of the deceased for autopsies to secure funeral benefits.[41]

The study continued for forty years until a young PHS officer broke the story to a reporter from the Associated Press in 1972. However, the Tuskegee experiments had never been a secret: in addition to the regular clinical reports published in medical journals, the study was well known among public health officials, other governmental authorities, and medical personnel. Since the years in which the Tuskegee syphilis experiments were first made public, it still remains a shocking case study in the history of medical ethics violations in the United States. Today, Tuskegee is held up as being *representative* of a long and brutal history of antiblack racism and exploitation in medicine at the same time as it is *exceptionalized* and thus made unassimilable into a history of medicine already filled with countless cases of mistreatment, negligence, and abuse.

An earlier history of hygienic intervention in the South illuminates at least one crucial condition of possibility for the study: the priming of Macon County as an experimental site. Tuskegee, along with its surrounding counties, had long been established as a site of both experimental knowledge production and intensive hygienic intervention. In his years of fund-raising for the school, Washington relied upon the rhetoric of an educational experiment that would ultimately prove to northern observers the worth and capability of ex-slaves working their way up and out of the bondage of ignorance. Washington regularly invited wealthy northern visitors to campus to be firsthand witnesses to the kind of educational experiments performed at the school. Rosenwald was himself a contributor to the spectacular "Tuskegee Experiment" at the Institute; in 1915, he even "brought a private railroad car full of wealthy and prominent Chicagoans to see Tuskegee for themselves, and used the railroad journey to imbue his guests with his own enthusiasm."[42] Through the presentation of Tuskegee as an exceptional spectacle for northern philanthropic consumption, the campus and its surrounding areas emerged as a "unique" empirical site for the (social) scientific observation of blackness.

The empirical surveying of the region continued with the 1934 publication of Charles Johnson's *Shadow of the Plantation*, a sociological study of rural life in the South. Johnson studied over six hundred families in Macon County to determine the impact of a disintegrated plantation system on the disenfranchised populations still inhabiting the Black Belt region of Alabama. *Shadow of the Plantation* is compelling for several reasons, particularly since the volume was published just two years after the Tuskegee Syphilis Study's inception and was funded by both the Rosenwald Fund and the U.S. Public Health Service. In his acknowledgments, Johnson notes, "The study itself was made possible by the Julius Rosenwald Fund, through Dr. Michael Davis, who has been interested and in turn has interested the United States Public Health Service in certain of the health problems of this and several other similar counties of the South."[43] In a chapter entitled "Survival," Johnson makes a passing reference to the beginning years of the Tuskegee Study, calling it "a special demonstration instituted as an experiment by the Rosenwald Fund."[44] Johnson's influential arguments about the lasting legacy of the plantation complex were even used as evidence to support particular aspects of the Tuskegee experiments in a 1954 article in *Public Health Reports*.[45]

In his introduction to *Shadow of the Plantation*, Robert E. Park repeatedly invokes the multiple valences of the "experiment" at the Tuskegee Institute. In the years before he arrived at the University of Chicago, Park lived and worked at Tuskegee as Washington's personal secretary. He was likely considered a particularly knowledgeable authority on Johnson's geography of inquiry. Park calls Tuskegee a "rural laboratory" where Washington "carried on his experiments in rural education — experiments which graduates of his school and others, with the assistance of the Rosenwald Fund, have extended to most other parts of the South."[46] He also refers to the ways in which the division of the South into various administrative units — the old plantation districts — made the work of compiling and analyzing statistical data an easier task for the social scientist: "available statistics . . . have been collected and classified on the basis of existing administrative units rather than of the region or of any other sort of natural area."[47] Indeed, Park's presentation of Tuskegee and its surrounding county as a "rural laboratory" configures the area as an ideal experimental site — a geography primed for the accumulation of empirical data extracted from the bodies that occupied such laboratory spaces.

In a 1995 article published in the *Journal of the National Medical Association*, Benjamin Roy makes the bold argument that contemporary scholarship on Tuskegee has neglected a crucial point: Tuskegee was *not* a clinical study.[48] He argues that the experiment was "instead the economic exploitation of humans as a *natural resource* of a disease that could not be cultivated in culture or animals in order to establish and sustain U.S. superiority in patented commercial biotechnology."[49] Roy argues that the Tuskegee Study was actually applied science, used first to standardize existing syphilis tests and later to provide sera that had been extracted from the research subjects to develop serological tests. Ultimately, the continual extraction of "renewable culture sources" from Tuskegee's test subjects allowed "U.S. investigators and biotechnology to wrest control from German researchers to dominate and maintain leadership in syphilis serology."[50]

Roy's provocative essay suggests that Tuskegee test subjects quite literally served as natural resources mined in the government's quest for biomedical dominance on the global stage, connecting an apparently insular and exceptional experiment in the Deep South with the transnational commercial networks of U.S. science. The combination of "experiment" and "hygiene" in this rural plantation geography ultimately produced something that has been called by some commentators a form of genocide. Houston Baker refers to the syphilis experiments as "nothing other than a direct, disciplinary power-and-knowledge corollary of disciplinary enclosures, exercises, and tactics of the Tuskegee plantation."[51] Indeed, there are significant links between the hygienic pedagogies of the Tuskegee Institute, New South ideology, and the Tuskegee experiments, which took Macon County's experimental population as fodder for the production of modern scientific knowledge. Susan Reverby's discovery of a set of "sister experiments" in Guatemala immediately following World War II, in which PHS researchers infected prisoners, soldiers, and sex workers with syphilis and gonorrhea, further illuminates the transnational reach of the dialectic of innovation and exploitation in mid-century syphilis research in the United States and how the syphilis experiments in the "insular" Deep South connected to a broader agenda of the U.S. government to forge scientific innovation out of the world that the war (and slavery) made.[52]

Here, we might add Colin Dayan's arguments about how, in the modern United States, care has been used by the state to justify coercion and legitimate state violence.[53] "Care" and the interventions made under its name are the perfect cover for intensive surveillance, oversight, and exploitation, especially in a biopolitical regime in which life must be supported—and indeed produced—at all costs, even when it tends toward the death of individual subjects. Dayan writes about how the Department of Defense presented "coercion as care" in its 2009 review of practices at Guantánamo; in the case of forced feeding of prisoners on hunger strike at Guantánamo, care was actually torture.[54] In the Tuskegee experiments, care became lethal: a social experiment in social abandonment was framed through a suite of benefits offered to study "participants," including the covering of funeral costs. The Tuskegee experiments brutally and powerfully illustrate, on the ground, how the dialectic of social control and social abandonment always works in tandem: it was the intensive oversight of this particular population in the Black Belt that justified and obscured their actual abandonment by the state.

FROM TUSKEGEE TO TODAY

The deep connection between the Tuskegee experiments and what Jarvis McInnis refers to as the "afterlife of the plantation" sheds light on the specific historical circumstances that allowed an exploitative, nontherapeutic experiment to operate under cover in the U.S. South for over forty years, during

Britt Rusert

the advent of a new age of scientific-technological modernity in the early and mid-twentieth century.[55] But this concrete, on-the-ground history also points toward a more general conclusion: experiments with human populations have long depended on the processes of underdevelopment that are central to capitalist modernity. As Walter Rodney masterfully laid out in *How Europe Underdeveloped Africa*—published, coincidentally, in 1972, the year a whistleblower exposed the Tuskegee experiments to the general public—the uneven development of different regions under capital is highly racialized. Beginning with the inauguration of the slave trade, and continuing through the colonial and postcolonial occupation of Africa, the development of the so-called West has depended on the systematic withdrawal of both people and natural resources from Africa.[56] The *development* of Europe (and increasingly, Asia) thus depends on the *underdevelopment* of Africa. With Rodney's thesis about Africa in mind, we might think about how particular geographies *within* the United States have historically been—and continue to be—used to enrich and develop the nation at the expense of their own development.

Scientific and medical innovation has routinely taken advantage of and benefited from the racialization and uneven development of space: case in point, clinical studies are routinely sited in places from which capital has already taken flight. As capital moves on to new frontiers, experimental science swoops in, from the old "plantation districts" in Alabama to hospital rooms in Baltimore, Maryland.[57] The use of research populations outside the United States makes it even easier to evade ethical expectations and regulations to return resources to individuals who participate in research studies.[58] In the Caribbean, for example, there is no need to serve the communities that participate in clinical studies, since there aren't any people there anyway. The lack of media coverage and popular silence around the environmental/economic crises in Puerto Rico over the past few years further emphasize that from the perspective of the United States, the colonial logic of *terra nullis* still applies to the Global South, as already depopulated geographies to be used at whim for U.S. tourism, militarization, waste disposal, and extraction (of resources, debt, and knowledge).[59]

I thus want to suggest that the concept of *uneven development* be more squarely situated within studies of contemporary bioscience and medicine.[60] Bioscientific innovation continues to be supported by the underdevelopment of—and systematic withdrawal of resources from—vulnerable populations. This centering of racialized regimes of underdevelopment—and underdevelopment's production of uneven geographies—in the study of bioscience and medicine not only promises to bring new perspective to past histories of human experimentation, but may help to anticipate where such experiments are headed next. Looking forward, we should, for example, be attuned to how experimental studies sneak in under the cover of the "innovations" and "opportunities" produced by disaster capital, and should be especially attentive to how science may increasingly piggyback on the hurricane seasons and other environmental-socioeconomic disasters intensifying across the Global South.[61] And while the plantation, as a physical space, no longer organizes populations as it once did, at least not in the United States, the racialization of space, and the underdevelopment of spaces coded as "black," continues to authorize and naturalize the enclosure of experimental populations.

New patterns of human migration and displacement due to climate change and other socioeconomic disasters and global instabilities raise further questions about whether or not the plantation can still be used to produce fictions of stable, enclosed populations (carceral imaginaries) for science, medicine, and commerce. For example, climate change presents new opportunities for disaster capitalism, but it also presents clear challenges for the development of biomedicine in the future, especially since clinical trials require some semblance of static, nonmoving research populations. In this future of migration and dispossession (which is already our present), and which is in many ways, in Mbembe's words, the "becoming black" of the world itself, racialized carceral geographies like the hospital, the refugee camp, and the prison will likely only intensify in importance as sites of human experimentation.[62] These are spaces that by their very nature can be depended upon to capture and contain human populations in a world of precarity, movement, and migration.[63] The containment of populations within institutions may appear to challenge Foucault's understanding of the transformation from disciplinary societies to control societies under biopower, where the centrality of institutions to correct human behavior (discipline and punish) gives way to a much more diffusive and expansive form of power (biopower) in which individuals work on/discipline themselves (care of the self). But Foucault is clear that disciplinary structures do not disappear under the conditions of biopower; they are simply embedded in new structures of power and perform different types of work. It may be the case that present conditions simply require an intensification and reorganization of disciplinary structures that are still in existence today, especially the prison, the hospital, and the refugee camp.

Today, the experimental logic of the plantation has largely transferred from the plantation to the prison and adjacent spaces of detainment. And yet the "shadow of the plantation" still looms. The long history of planta-

Britt Rusert

tion science, from Marion Sym's founding of modern gynecology, through abusive experiments conducted on enslaved women, to the Tuskegee syphilis experiments, prefigures forms of experimental science and medicine that continue to require practices—or fictions—of stability and enclosure in the twenty-first century.[64] The plantation may no longer exist as it did in its antebellum form, but the carceral arrangement it birthed—and which ironically articulates the noncoercive containment of racialized subjects, people rooted in place "naturally," disconnected from the forced migrations that brought them to that particular place—continues to animate the contemporary biopolitical landscape.[65]

CODA

From Charles Chesnutt's *The Conjure Tales* (1899) to Jean Toomer's *Cane* (1923), African American literature exposed the logic and history of the Tuskegee Syphilis Study decades before they were uncovered and made public in 1972. The uncanny anticipation of the syphilis experiments in both Chesnutt's and Toomer's representation of an extractive, experimental New South economy still moored to the violences and geographies of enslavement—of the laboratory life of the plantation given new life in the post-Reconstruction, industrializing South—might be read as a kind of prophecy about an event that had not yet come to pass. Alternatively, these works may be simply *diagnostic*, reflecting the fact that the experimental logic of the plantation—and its specific tethering of blackness to plantation geographies—was already established and ingrained before the start of the Tuskegee trials. As this essay has detailed, the Tuskegee researchers took advantage of a space and a population already primed for an exploitative clinical study.

But these texts do not just register the conditions that abetted the syphilis experiments and enabled them to operate under cover for so long; they also turn to the resources of fiction to create alternative geographies, or more specifically to create what Katherine McKittrick calls "black geographies."[66] More than simply illuminating how domination takes shape through the displacement of difference in and across space, McKittrick's black geographies seek to capture practices and narratives that challenge regimes of "spatial domination.[67] Since people of African descent have been historically deemed "ungeographic," McKittrick insists on the importance of shifting attention from charts and maps to stories, poetry, songs, drama, and other imaginative and theoretical works that help to articulate "cartographies of struggle" among diasporic populations, especially among black women, whose bodies have been tied to the land (and sea) and excluded from geography in a very specific way.[68]

Charles Chesnutt's *The Conjure Tales* is a particularly powerful example of a black narrative that challenges dominant conceptions of geography, while representing tactics for undermining racial-spatial domination in postslavery plantation spaces. In an essay that calls for sociological imagination and speculative methods—including fiction-making—to be taken seriously in both the study and actualization of social transformation, Ruha Benjamin notes that racism is both "innovative" and "future-oriented." In a world where antiracism seems to be always "playing catch-up" with racial and racist innovation, Benjamin suggests that speculative fiction plays a central role in keeping ahead of the innovative technologies of racialization.[69] While *The Conjure Tales* is framed as a set of plantation tales that look backward at a violent past of coercion and enslavement, they might be also interpreted as future-looking, speculative fictions concerned with showing how post-Reconstruction southern "laboratories" are constructed through the uneven geographies established by slavery. Much has been written about how Chesnutt upends and ironizes white nostalgia for the "good old days of slavery" that ran through popular plantation fictions in the post–Civil War period, but these tales are perhaps more notable, I would argue, as "near future" fictions that illuminate not exactly the boundedness of blackness to the past, but rather how particular structures and narratives about the plantation past become usable—or resourceable—for the racial innovations of the scientific-technological-entrepreneurial, post-Reconstruction present.[70]

Across *The Conjure Tales*, Julius's stories encode cautionary tales about how the exploitations of plantation coercion were being repackaged in and for a New South economy. In "The Goophered Grapevine," Julius warns Yankee transplants to the South, a married white couple named John and Annie, that they should not purchase the vineyard on the property because it had been cursed in the old days of slavery. He goes on to tell a fantastical tale about how Master Dugal asked a free conjure woman, Aunt Peggy, to curse—or "goopher"—the vineyard so that enslaved men and women on the property would no longer "steal" from the scuppernong grape harvest. When no one tells Henry, a new slave on the property, about the conjured vines, he eats some scuppernongs and finds himself transformed into a kind of human grapevine. Subject to the changes in seasons and the growth cycle of the grapevines themselves, Master Dugal finds a way to maximize his profit from Henry's person and labor: every spring, "w'en de sap rise en Henry's hair commence' ter sprout, Mars Dugal sol' 'im," and when he "withered" in

Britt Rusert

the winter, he would buy him back, at a low price. Bought and sold, sent away from and then retrieved back to the planation, over and over again, Mars Dugal made a "thousan' dollars a year off'n" Henry until the grapevine itself "withered en turned yaller en died." Inexorably tied to the plantation landscape and its forms of production, once the grapevines died, "Henry died too."[71] Filtered through the antebellum frame, Chesnutt's narrative of a man bought and sold every season chillingly registers the common practice of "leasing out" slaves in the antebellum period, but it also uncannily reflects the forms of convict leasing, debt peonage, sharecropping, and other forms of coercive control that used black subjects as "natural resources" in New South experimental landscapes—landscapes of both precarious abandonment and coercive containment.

While "The Goophered Grapevine" glimpses the continuation, and in some cases intensification, of regimes of racialized and geographic exploitation after the Civil War, another story, "Po' Sandy," perhaps more fully captures the extension of the "laboratory life" of the plantation into the postbellum period, in which black bodies and racialized lands were viewed as interlocking, extractive resources. In the story, an enslaved man named Sandy is turned into a tree by his conjuring wife, Tenie, so that he can't be sold away from her. He remains rooted to the plantation landscape, close to his wife, who turns him back into a man every evening, until one day, while in tree form, he is chopped down by two men. Tenie must then listen to Sandy's moans and groans as he is pushed through a sawmill and used as lumber in the construction of a schoolhouse, of all things, on the plantation grounds. "Po' Sandy" is a brutal allegory for how the legal assignment of enslaved people to the category of chattel property, alongside everything else within the master's purview, justified and abetted regimes of violent exploitation and harm. But the allegory of Sandy's violent exploitation and death while in the form of a tree may actually resonate *more* with New Southern timber and turpentine industries than with antebellum plantation production and regimes of ownership. In this way, "Po' Sandy" powerfully expresses how black bodies continued to be acted upon as commodifiable, bare "flesh" in postslavery plantation geographies. While racialized violence and exploitation were shrouded behind the ideologies of the plantation pastoral in the antebellum period, Chesnutt's *Conjure Tales* suggest that the naturalization of coercion became more blatant and more visible in the postwar period, as African Americans were violently and more openly chained to the southern landscape while being transformed into a discrete *population* for the purposes of biopolitical management and intervention.

Ultimately, the "plantation fiction" frame of *The Conjure Tales* is part and parcel of the "trick" in these trickster tales: not only do Julius's stories subvert the quaint "nostalgia" for the good old days of slavery that characterizes white plantation fictions of the late nineteenth century, but Chesnutt uses narratives about life, land, and labor in the antebellum South to *denaturalize* the forms of exploitation taking shape in the 1880s and 1890s, amid the transformation of the plantation South into a new form of a "living laboratory" in New South discourse and practice. In the end, as we learn from Julius in "The Goophered Grapevine," the cursed grapevines from the age of slavery cannot be disentangled from the new (South) vines. Furthermore, if, as Benjamin writes, racism is in the "business of manufacturing natures," Chesnutt, like Jean Toomer in *Cane*, turns to an industrial, manufacturing South to denaturalize those natures while further illuminating how the plantation itself serves as a powerful technology of naturalization.[72]

It is worth noting that most of the subjects transformed into commodifiable, exploitable "flesh" in *The Conjure Tales* are masculine bodies. Black women—as conjurors—possess forms of omnipotence and power, while their particular plights and forms of subjection are largely rendered invisible. Here we should recall that McKittrick's emphasis in *Demonic Grounds* is not just on "black geographies," but "black feminist geographies," a framework that moves toward the specific articulations of black femininity with and to colonial space, but also serves as a reminder that space is not just racialized, but also gendered in historically contingent ways. In the case of Tuskegee, a "black feminist geography" would pose the question of how both race and gender were naturalized in New South plantation laboratories. With this intersectional frame in mind, we might then return to the fact that the Tuskegee research population was composed solely of black men. While adjacent New South discourses and practices—with Washington at the helm—attempted to incorporate individual black subjects into a productive and normalized population, black masculine syphilitic subjects were both nonproductive and even feminized, aligned with the land itself, lying fallow and nonproductive. As part of the biopolitical management of blackness in the South, Tuskegee researchers took a population of purportedly nonproductive bodies and made them productive for a New Southern project that was directly linked to a *national* project of scientific modernization as well as transnational experiments intended to establish the United States' superiority in both war-making and science-making. In an age of biopolitical innovation that continued to rely on tools and methods of slave management inherited from the antebellum period, clinical studies became an ideal site

Britt Rusert

through which to put nonnormative, "unproductive" subjects "back to work," supporting biopower's need to manage and optimize "life," even if that meant the sacrifice of individual lives. And it is here that the insistent and persistent refusal of work across *The Conjure Tales* might be read as a resistant, even revolutionary, position, oriented against the profit-driven machinations of biopower itself.

Notes

1. R. A. Vonderlehr, et al., "Untreated Syphilis in the Male Negro: A Comparative Study of Treated and Untreated Cases," *Journal of the American Medical Association*, 107 (September 12, 1936): 856–60.

2. Vonderlehr, et al., "Untreated Syphilis in the Male Negro," 856.

3. Vonderlehr, et al., "Untreated Syphilis in the Male Negro," 856.

4. Two exemplary recent studies highlight the historical and geographic specificities of biopower as well as its transformations from the nineteenth to the twenty-first century: Kyla Schuller, *The Biopolitics of Feeling: Race, Sex, and Science in the Nineteenth Century* (Durham, NC: Duke University Press, 2018); Jasbir Puar, *The Right to Maim: Debility, Capacity, Disability* (Durham, NC: Duke University Press, 2017).

5. Colin Dayan, *The Law Is a White Dog: How Legal Rituals Make and Unmake Persons*, repr. ed. (Princeton, NJ: Princeton University Press, 2013); Colin Dayan, *The Story of Cruel and Unusual* (Cambridge, MA: MIT Press, 2007); Evelyn Nakano Glen, *Forced to Care: Coercion and Caregiving in America* (Cambridge, MA: Harvard University Press, 2012); João Biehl, *Vita: Life in a Zone of Social Abandonment* (Berkeley: University of California Press, 2005).

6. See, for example, A. V. Deibert and M. C. Bruyere, "Untreated Syphilis in the Male Negro: Evidence of Cardiovascular Abnormalities and Other Forms of Morbidity," *Journal of Venereal Disease Information* 27 (1946): 301–14.

7. See Allan Brandt, "Racism and Research: The Case of the Tuskegee Syphilis Experiment," in *Tuskegee's Truths: Rethinking the Tuskegee Syphilis Study*, ed. Susan M. Reverby (Chapel Hill: University of North Carolina Press, 2000), 18. Brandt outlines the distinctions between an experiment and a "study in nature," as put forward by the French physiologist Claude Bernard in 1865. While a study in nature requires only observation, an experiment involves intervention into the study's conditions. Brandt concludes that Tuskegee was clearly an experiment.

8. Vonderlehr, "Untreated Syphilis in the Male Negro," 856.

9. P. J. Pesare, T. J. Bauer, and G. A. Gleeson, "Untreated Syphilis in the Male Negro," *American Journal of Syphilis, Gonorrhea, and Venereal Diseases* 34, no. 3 (1950): 202. In a 1954 article, the authors note, "geographic isolation was a factor in favoring the unchanging nature of the group." See S. Olansky, L. Simpson, and S. Schuman, "Environmental Factors in the Tuskegee Study of Untreated Syphilis," *Public Health Reports* 69, no. 7 (1954): 693. As the study continued, researchers became increasingly worried

about the increased mobility of the experimental group. See, for example, Stanley H. Schuman, et al., "Untreated Syphilis in the Male Negro: Background and Current Status of Patients in the Tuskegee Study," *Journal of Chronic Diseases* 2 (1955): 543–58.

10. On the convict leasing system, see Sarah Haley, *No Mercy Here: Gender, Punishment, and the Making of Jim Crow Modernity* (Chapel Hill: University of Chapel Hill, 2016); Douglas A. Blackmon, *Slavery by Another Name: The Re-Enslavement of Black Americans from the Civil War to World War II*, repr. (New York: Anchor Books, 2009).

11. Vernon W. Cisney and Nicolae Morar, "Introduction: Why Biopower? Why Now?," in *Biopower: Foucault and Beyond*, ed. Vernon W. Cisney and Nicolae Morar (Chicago: University of Chicago Press, 2016), 4.

12. Robert D. Bullard, *Dumping in Dixie: Race, Class, and Environmental Quality* (Boulder, CO: Westview, 1990).

13. Hortense Spillers, "Mama's Baby, Papa's Maybe: An American Grammar Book," *Diacritics* 17, no. 2 (1987): 67.

14. Mabel O. Wilson, *Negro Building: Black Americans in the World of Fairs and Museums* (Berkeley: University of California Press, 2012), 99.

15. James H. Cassedy, "Medical Men and the Ecology of the Old South," in *Science and Medicine in the Old South*, ed. Ronald L. Numbers and Todd L. Savitt (Baton Rouge: Louisiana State University Press, 1989), 172.

16. Cassedy, "Medical Men and the Ecology of the Old South," 171.

17. Britt Rusert, "Shackled in the Garden: Ecology and Race in American Plantation Cultures," PhD dissertation, Duke University, 2009.

18. Michel Foucault, "Subjectivity and Truth," in *The Politics of Truth*, 2nd ed. (Los Angeles: Semiotext(e), 2007), 153; on the plantation as a frontier biopolitical institution, see Alex Weheliye, *Habeas Viscus: Racializing Asssemblages, Biopolitics, and Black Feminist Theories of the Human* (Durham, NC: Duke University Press, 2014).

19. Fett argues that plantation owners attended to slave ailments in terms of soundness. See Sharla Fett, *Working Cures: Healing, Health, and Power on Southern Slave Plantations* (Chapel Hill: University of North Carolina Press, 2007).

20. Houston A. Baker Jr., *Turning South Again: Re-Thinking Modernism/Re-Reading Booker T.* (Durham, NC: Duke University Press, 2001), 81.

21. Local residents in Macon County would colloquially refer to the institute as "Mr. Washington's Plantation." Baker notes this in *Turning South Again*, as does Louis R. Harlan in *Booker T. Washington: The Making of a Black Leader* (New York: Oxford University Press, 1972).

22. Quoted in Harlan, *Booker T. Washington*, 114.

23. "Working with the hands" is a reference to Washington's 1904 sequel to *Up from Slavery*. See Booker T. Washington, *Working with the Hands* (New York: Arno Press, 1969).

24. Washington, *Up from Slavery* (New York: Modern Library, 1999), 81.

25. The Exposition address is reprinted in chapter 14, Washington, *Up from Slavery*, 142–54.

26. Washington, *Up from Slavery*, 144; italics are mine.

27. Washington, *Up from Slavery*, 145.

28. See, for example, Harlan's *Booker T. Washington*. Donald Spivey documents the hostility of students, and sometimes even faculty and staff, to Washington's impossible expectations. Incredibly, Spivey reports that during the last ten years of Washington's leadership at Tuskegee, faculty even feared that students were armed and ready to attack. In 1903, students waged a strike based on their objections to the rigid order at the school. See Donald Spivey, *Schooling for the New Slavery: Black Industrial Education, 1868–1915* (Trenton, NJ: Africa World Press, 2007).

29. Washington, *Up from Slavery*, 115.

30. Washington, *Working with the Hands*, 29.

31. Washington, *Up from Slavery*, 115, 118.

32. Mary Douglas, *Purity and Danger: An Analysis of the Concept of Pollution and Danger*, repr. (New York: Routledge, 2002).

33. Douglas, *Purity and Danger*, xvii.

34. Douglas, *Purity and Danger*, 2.

35. See Cassedy, "Medical Men and the Ecology of the Old South," 172. See also Margaret Humphreys, *Yellow Fever in the South* (New Brunswick, NJ: Rutgers University Press, 1992).

36. John A. Kenney, "Health Problems of the Negroes," *Annals of the American Academy of Political and Social Science* 37, no. 2 (1911): 110–20.

37. Roderick Ferguson, "Of Our Normative Strivings: African American Studies and the Histories of Sexuality," *Social Text* 23, no. 3–4 (2005): 90.

38. For a more comprehensive overview of the Tuskegee syphilis experiments, see Susan M. Reverby, ed., *Tuskegee's Truths: Rethinking the Tuskegee Syphilis Study* (Chapel Hill: University of North Carolina Press, 2000). The older, and still very helpful, study is James H. Jones, *Bad Blood: The Tuskegee Syphilis Experiment*, rev. ed. (New York: Free Press, 1993), originally published in 1981.

39. On the involvement of the Rosenwald Fund in the therapeutic stages of the 1929 syphilis survey, see Peter Ascoli, *Julius Rosenwald: The Man Who Built Sears, Roebuck and Advanced the Cause of Black Education in the American South* (Bloomington: Indiana University Press, 2006), 314. It should be noted that by 1929 the fund was being run by Edwin Embree, who was especially enthusiastic about directing money to health initiatives in the South and to research in the social sciences. Rosenwald, who died in 1932, had taken a back seat in the organization's operations by this time. However, the fund's early involvement in the syphilis survey still reflects and extends upon Rosenwald's longtime philanthropic interest in African American education and health in the South.

40. The control group consisted of around two hundred men. The exact number in the experimental and control groups is unclear since researchers, in violation of standard research protocol, placed some subjects from the control group into the experimental group after they had become infected or were discovered to have already

had syphilis. See "Selections from the Final Report of the Ad Hoc Tuskegee Syphilis Study Panel," in Reverby, *Tuskegee's Truths*, 165.

41. The promise that family members would not be financially burdened by their deaths was likely a major participation incentive for many of the test subjects. The burial costs were subsidized through the Milbank Fund, another major northern philanthropy.

42. Harlan, *Booker T. Washington*, 141; Ascoli, *Julius Rosenwald*, 143.

43. Charles S. Johnson, *Shadow of the Plantation* (Chicago: University of Chicago Press, 1934), vii.

44. Johnson, *Shadow of the Plantation*, 187.

45. Olansky, et al., "Environmental Factors in the Tuskegee Study of Untreated Syphilis," 693.

46. Johnson, *Shadow of the Plantation*, xv.

47. Johnson, *Shadow of the Plantation*, xv.

48. Benjamin Roy, "The Tuskegee Syphilis Experiment: Biotechnology and the Administrative State," reprinted in Reverby, *Tuskegee's Truths*, 299–317.

49. Roy, "The Tuskegee Syphilis Experiment," 299.

50. Roy, "The Tuskegee Syphilis Experiment," 313.

51. Baker, *Turning South Again*, 96.

52. Susan M. Reverby, "'Normal Exposure' and Inoculation Syphilis: A PHS 'Tuskegee' Doctor in Guatemala, 1946–48," *Journal of Policy History* 23, no. 1 (2011): 6–28.

53. Dayan, *The Law Is a White Dog*.

54. Dayan, *The Law Is a White Dog*, 28.

55. Jarvis McInnis, "'Behold the Land': W. E. B. Du Bois, Cotton Futures, and the Afterlife of the Plantation in the US South," *The Global South* 10, no. 2 (fall 2016): 70–98.

56. Walter Rodney, *How Europe Underdeveloped Africa* (Cape Town: Pambazuka Press, 2012).

57. Bettina Judd, *Patient* (Pittsburgh: Black Lawrence Press, 2014); Rebecca Skloot, *The Immortal Life of Henrietta Lacks* (New York: Broadway, 2011).

58. Adriana Petryna, *When Experiments Travel: Clinical Trials and the Global Search for Human Subjects* (Princeton, NJ: Princeton University Press, 2009).

59. See Beatriz Llenín-Figueroa, "'I Believe in the Future of "Small Countries"': Édouard Glissant's Archipelagic Scale in Dialog with Other Caribbean Writers," *Discourse* 36, no. 1 (2014): 87–111.

60. Neil Smith, *Uneven Development: Nature, Capital, and the Production of Space*, 3rd ed. (Athens: University of Georgia Press, 2008).

61. Naomi Klein, *The Shock Doctrine: The Rise of Disaster Capitalism* (New York: Picador, 2007).

62. Achille Mbeme, *Critique of Black Reason*, translated by Laurent Dubois (Durham, NC: Duke University Press, 2017).

63. Michel Foucault, *"Society Must Be Defended": Lectures at the Collège de France, 1975-1976* (New York: Picador, 2003), 242. See also Gilles Deleuze, "Postscript on the Societies of Control," *October* 59 (winter 1992): 3–7.

Britt Rusert

64. "Remembering Anarcha, Lucy, and Betsey: The Mothers of Modern Gynecology," *Hidden Brain* (NPR), February 16, 2016.

65. On the use of debilitation and incapacitation as settler colonial tools of social control and exploitation of racialized populations, see Puar, *The Right to Maim*.

66. Katherine McKittrick, *Demonic Grounds: Black Women and the Cartographies of Struggle* (Minneapolis: University of Minnesota, 2006); see also Katherine McKittrick and Clyde Woods, eds., *Black Geographies and the Politics of Place* (Cambridge, MA: South End Press, 2007).

67. McKittrick, *Demonic Grounds*, xix.

68. McKittrick, *Demonic Grounds*, xxiii.

69. Ruha Benjamin, "Racial Fictions, Biological Facts: Expanding the Sociological Imagination through Speculative Methods," *Catalyst: Feminism, Theory, Technoscience* 2, no. 2 (2016): 22.

70. Deleuze's "near future," cited in Paul Rabinow and Nikolas Rose, "Biopower Today," in Cisney and Morar, *Biopower: Foucault and Beyond*, 323.

71. Charles Chesnutt, *The Conjure Tales* (New York: W. W. Norton, 2011), 13.

72. Benjamin, "Racial Fictions, Biological Facts," 22; see also Ruha Benjamin, "Innovating Inequity: If Race Is a Technology, Postracialism Is the Genius Bar," *Racial and Ethnic Studies* 39, no. 13 (2016): 1–8.

2

Consumed by Disease

MEDICAL ARCHIVES,
LATINO FICTIONS, AND CARCERAL
HEALTH IMAGINARIES

Christopher Perreira

.....

A better term [for the Olive View Sanatorium] might have been a priso[n].
—IRWIN ZIMENT, Chief of Medicine at Olive View, UCLA Medical Center

The sanatorium is jail. I'm not being treated here. I'm being punished! I'm a
political prisoner because I suffer from a political disease!
—ALEJANDRO MORALES, *The Captain of All These Men of Death*

The October 28, 1995, issue of the *Los Angeles Times* covered the seventy-fifth
anniversary celebration of the Olive View Sanatorium. At the reopening celebration, the *Times* reporter observed: "There were speeches and cake Friday
to honor the hospital that has been transformed into a modern facility from
a collection of wood-frame buildings where the sick and dying tuberculosis
patients were forced by law to stay."[1] With interviews of the former medical staff and surviving patients who attended the event, the article frames the
inauguration of the new medical facilities, which were built to replace the old
residential wards and buildings erected in the 1920s, as a celebration. The story
quickly turns, however, to the participants' memories of a distinctly violent,
carceral experience. The chief of medicine at Olive View, Dr. Irwin Ziment,
for instance, notes that while the sanatorium was always known as a center
of medical innovation, perhaps "a better term [for the sanatorium] might
have been a priso[n]." Former patients depicted their post-diagnosis TB experiences as systematic subjection to "horrifying and probably ineffective

treatments." Others remembered a prison-like experience in which doctors and Los Angeles County public health officials could have people arrested with "a stroke of the pen." While acknowledging these unsettling policies and practices, Director J. P. Myles Black maintained that many officials understood these police actions as necessary to protect the public: "They had to be controlled. Not because they had a disease, but because they were spreading it." Director Black identifies the threat as being found largely with "salad makers, waiters, [and] dishwashers."

During the first half of the twentieth century, Southern California had established firm foundations on which to think about race through the lenses of citizenship, disease, and containment, finding currency in the institution of public health. In 1944, for example, the medical journal *California and Western Medicine* (CWM) published the short public health essay "Migratory Agricultural Workers of California: Their Health Care," which, along with other medical journals, attempted to draw attention to so-called threats emanating from Mexican and Mexican American communities working in and around Los Angeles.[2] At a moment of heightened suburbanization across the United States, where suburbs grew exponentially faster than city centers, the article voices the urgent concern for the medical community to respond to the ways California's agricultural industry impacted its city dwellers, emphasizing the Los Angeles area as an important site of concern.[3] It does this by bringing together exaggerated discourses that circulated around poor, racialized laborers, substandard living conditions at migrant labor camps, contagious diseases, and the nation's duty to protect "the State." The article cautions readers: "Physicians need not stretch their imagination to visualize how such itinerant [Mexican] workers, who are often poorly nourished and diseased, when grouped together under conditions not by any means sanitary, may become a menace not only to themselves, but so to the citizens of nearby communities, and so to the people of the State at large."[4] The article frames this as protecting the public, yet the scenario depicted depends on physicians holding back the impulse to imagine a threat ("need not stretch their imagination") so they may see ("visualize") the actual threat that exists before them. The statement at once cautions those positioned to "protect" the state from this imminently *real* danger, while at the same time it imagines, indeed conjures up, an enemy of the state—one that traveled from south of the U.S.-Mexico borderlands, is positioned to infect "citizens of nearby communities," and therefore urgently needs containing.

Public health agents perceived such scenarios not only as threats to residents of Los Angeles, but also to people living in other large cities across the state. There was, the CWM article suggests, an urgent need to deal with the "thousands of needy agricultural workers, both those who are residents of California and the larger number who voluntarily, or through Federal aid as in the case of the Mexicans, are brought into the State."[5] While physicians and scientists debated how migrant labor shifted policy focus around race and disease, contributors to medical journals of the time often entangled and conflated discourses of public health and public security as social goods and necessary evils. In the 1940s, CWM was one of several influential medical and scientific journals presenting authoritative notions that the "thousands of needy [Mexican] agricultural workers" — Mexican workers in California before and after the establishment of the Bracero Program (1942–65) — could be dealt with as a single homogenous group, "poorly nourished and diseased," and "a menace not only to themselves" but potentially to the whole of the United States. The article was taking part in an ongoing debate in medicine and public health over this "menace," often referred to as "the Mexican problem."[6] Such print culture helped to produce and grant legitimacy to ideas about how the built environment emerged in response to perceived threats as spaces of protection and as technologies of containment.

This chapter examines discourses of racialized disease produced in a California public health context by placing it in dialogue with the memories of patients depicted in Chicano fiction. Alejandro Morales's 2008 novel *The Captain of All These Men of Death* centers collective memories of the Los Angeles Olive View Sanatorium in the 1940s and 1950s as a contested space of uneasy belonging. Building on scholarship in critical medical studies and cultural studies, I look to Morales's novel because it presents a platform for interpreting patient experiences documenting the logics of medicine from a cultural point of view. By doing so, the novel unsettles narratives produced within official accounts of U.S. medical science. *The Captain* recasts those racial, political, and social categories that undergird the policies of public health and security, to instead foreground the lived experiences of communities impacted most by those medical institutions. The novel, in other words, makes those narratives central to the production of their own histories, while at the same time it interprets acts of medical violence as constitutive to narratives of scientific progress and benevolence. The book explores the temporalities of medical technologies, the lives that live within them, and the ways racialized patients were both moved through and contained in what I am calling carceral health imaginaries. Arguing for a more robust understanding of what constitutes the medical archive, the essay suggests that the past remains deeply contested at the intersections of culture, and

Christopher Perreira

exists where cultural production *remembers* against the firm, often immovable scientific record. One goal of this essay, then, is to put some pressure on the structures of hierarchized knowledge, to interrogate its stabilizing effect on the archive, and to reconsider things not often understood as part of the official record.

MEDICAL HISTORIES AND OLIVE VIEW CARCERAL HEALTH IMAGINARIES

The compounded impact of racialized disease, as a discourse that marks a threat to white Californians, animates public health to shift more directly to bolster white settler protections. Those official shifts were understood largely as acts to secure the public through law, carried out by respected and powerful figures in medicine.[7] Natalia Molina traces connections between medical diagnosis and policing, detaining, and deporting migrant labor in California and the ways in which policing technologies were refined to "mark undesirable immigrant groups as outsiders."[8] Alexandra Minna Stern highlights those regularized exclusionary practices targeting racialized communities, suggesting that they were not at all fringe acts carried out by "hacks and mad scientists."[9] Indeed, Ruha Benjamin shows that those acts were consistently orchestrated by "prominent doctors, philanthropists, journalists, academicians, and administrators who wished to amplify the reach of an extensive eugenics agenda that dated back to the turn of the century."[10] What produced notions that medicine could self-govern and transgress laws with impunity came from, in part, the ability to carry on robust dialogues while operating in relative isolation and away from the scrutiny of a broader public.[11] Unearthing and rereading municipal archives, specifically those that framed public health as an issue of state or national security, brings such exclusionary mechanisms into sharper view.

In the early twentieth century, Los Angeles intensified efforts to target and criminalize entire groups of Mexican and Mexican American workers and communities around the understanding that communicable diseases needed to be contained. Sociological research played significant roles in developing these ideas, as historian David Gutiérrez has noted. In 1928, the Los Angeles County Health Department developed a housing stock numerical rating system for the county, finding Mexicans' residential patterns to be "the worst in the area."[12] Rates of infection by communicable disease—tuberculosis in particular—were intimately tied to living conditions and the city's efforts to exclude. Similarly, Vicki Ruíz asserts that labor and living

Consumed by Disease

(53

conditions for racialized communities in Los Angeles have often been tied to narratives surrounding contagious disease. Ruíz points to sanitation policies to clarify this point, noting that the works of "social scientists, Protestant missionaries, and social workers uniformly deplore the overcrowded, unsanitary conditions in which Mexicans were compelled to live."[13] Natalia Molina argues that the conflation of racial identity and contagious disease, specifically in relation to Chinese, Japanese, and Mexican communities in the late nineteenth and early twentieth centuries, began in the 1870s, prompting a steady pattern among city health officials that connected "any blemish on the pristine image of Los Angeles—including all forms of disease and any manner of disorder—to the city's marginalized communities."[14] Scientific authority was more firmly anchored in the institutionalization of public health as a securitizing imperative, tasked with protecting the city from communicable disease. Molina shows how this task was woven into the shored-up xenophobic duty of removing "rotten spots" (i.e., ethnic communities) from a raced and gendered public.

The archival trace of racialized exclusion in Los Angeles government records rested firmly on the backs of Mexican communities, and the county Department of Health aggressively sought out reasons to narrate high rates of tuberculosis in those communities specifically as a racialized discourse. To that end, statistical documentation overwhelmed the discussion, selectively framing Mexican Americans as the city's public health threat, burden, and obstacle to investment in public resources. Emily Abel observes that public health records indicate that government funding for tuberculosis care nearly vanished during the Depression, and the resource-burden narrative that framed health care for Mexicans in Olive View, as well as in city and county clinics, prompted nativist politicians and policymakers to argue against allocating funds for poor residents.[15] Through public health campaigns, this notion played a crucial role in creating the figure of representative disease-carrying Mexicans in the form of brown bodies. Molina points to one such example, where public health and the protection of the public were usefully confused—what she describes as the moment when public health as a science is blurred as a public service, demonstrating how scientific discourse could and does "bleed into policy considerations."[16] Overseeing the operations of Olive View, the Department of Charities conducted a study that resulted in a report featuring a Mexican immigrant couple with tuberculosis. The report alleged that the couple infected eighty-three people, all reported to be members of the couple's own family network. Such de-

Christopher Perreira

pictions positioned Mexicans as a burden to the public health system and a racialized contagious threat to a so-called general public. These imaginaries extended nativist, eugenicist conceptions of race in the mainstream, leading to more aggressive uses of public health as a tool of quarantine, deportation, and incarceration.[17]

Prior to the 1924 Immigration Act, which placed restrictions on "undesirable groups" migrating to the United States, there were significantly fewer concerns about stopping movement into the United States from Mexico. The decades following this legislation mark an important shift in the perception of Mexican laborers from "a racially inferior but generally malleable workforce" to the intensified and enduring representations of Mexicans as "criminal, a social burden, diseased, and inassimilable."[18] Furthermore, Mexican laborers were regularly identified as foreign, despite their status as residents, laborers, or citizens. In some cases, families were quarantined and subjected to experimental treatments, including those influenced by collapsed lung theory, which induced the collapse of the lung by surgically removing rib bones.[19] While tuberculosis was often framed in public health educational programs as an indiscriminate killer — infecting equally across social, racial, and cultural categories — the conflation of tuberculosis with race, class, gender, and nationality significantly shaped policy and practice. Public health in the early twentieth century advances yet another carceral technology in Los Angeles, where race and citizenship provided useful and effective frameworks for policing and containing racialized populations. Indeed, this carceral imaginary narrates the necessity of containing, quarantining, removing, and *cutting out* what is perceived as the rot of public space.

Reframing the official scientific record, these histories help to confront not only a dominant perception of the role of medicine — that it is, at its core, a benevolent and humanitarian endeavor — but also to critically examine the outcomes of archival knowledge, the definitions of progress in use, and the visions of futurity contained within. Reconsidering archival knowledge in this way — what it is, who it belongs to, and where it is sanctioned — sheds light on frameworks anchored in racial, ableist, gendered, and settler colonial logics maintaining it. In this context, the next section looks to Alejandro Morales's novel *The Captain of All These Men of Death* as a cultural text that reconfigures narratives of progress and individual freedom to consider what resistance in the archive can reveal, and to do so without seeking to resolve archival contradictions.[20] The "terrain of the national culture," Lisa Lowe argues, functions as a site of immersion into "the repertoire of American memories, events, and narratives," simultaneously locating the terrain where hierar-chical dynamics of social, legal, and political representation in the United States are worked out, and the space for collective memory to negotiate otherwise.[21] While the discourse of law is perhaps the one that most literally governs citizenship through "collectively forged images, histories, and nar-ratives that place, displace, and replace individuals in relation to the national polity," cultural production has the potential to rewrite those scripts and to shape how people forget and remember. To center more expansive forms of resistance around refusal and remembering across antiracist, feminist, and migrant experiences presents questions differently, allowing an inquiry through unlikely frameworks such as temporalities, memories, and cultural representation.

CRITICAL MEMORY AND *THE CAPTAIN OF ALL THESE MEN OF DEATH*

Frankly, knowing the histories of these buildings sheds a completely differ-ent perspective on what having tuberculosis was and meant, on what medi-cine was and has accomplished, on how medicine became abusive and how the patients, especially those of us who were poor, Mexican, and black kept our mouths shut and didn't say a word about what the doctors and nurses did to us. Unfortunately, all this was so easily forgotten.

—ALEJANDRO MORALES, *The Captain of All These Men of Death*[22]

If you are going to try to break, contest or interrupt some of these tenden-tial historical connections, you have to know when you are moving against the grain of historical formations. If you want to move [or] re-articulate [them] in another way, you are going to come across all the grooves that have articulated [them] already.

—STUART HALL, "An Interview with Stuart Hall"[23]

The Captain of All These Men of Death begins in the 1990s with the protagonist, Robert Contreras, casually addressing readers with reflections about his life: "You see, nothing really exciting happened in my life. I led a normal life. The strangest thing that happened was when my nephew came to visit with his son, who asked me for an interview."[24] The interview, conducted by the au-thor and his son, Gregory Morales, sought to record his experiences at Olive View Sanitorium (now the UCLA–Olive View Medical Center) from the mid-

Christopher Perreira

1940s to the mid-1950s, in part as research for Gregory's medical thesis and cultural history of tuberculosis. In part, the novel was inspired by the actual UCLA med-school thesis written by Gregory Morales.[25] Both engage the history of Olive View Sanitorium, the people who lived and worked there, and the cultural and medical histories that shaped and emerged from the hospital. Robert Contreras, who, as noted in the novel's preface, was modeled after the author's uncle, pieces together buried memories, temporal landscapes, historical pasts and presents—all of which collide as uncollected experiences to make up the novel's fragmented archive of a forgotten moment in Los Angeles history. When thinking back, Robert recalls the "wonderful images of the past, [like] photos in my mind," evoking depictions of Olive View that resemble photos and illustrated postcards sold to resident patients and their families in the first half of the twentieth century. Those images present the grounds as utopian landscapes, a *no-place* in the foothills of the Sierra Madre Mountains, set outside the Los Angeles city-space and away from the businesses and the general hospital in downtown. The serene pastoral landscapes, like much of Southern California's histories, are designed to remind residents of a romantic eighteenth-century Spanish missionary past, while at the same time very carefully erasing the indigenous presence and dispossession that the San Fernando Mission manufactured.[26]

From this emerges several tensions between Robert's recovered experiences as a racialized, wartime tuberculosis patient (a "TBer") and the titanic weight of medical knowledge and authority. The novel shifts to a first-person account, beginning with Robert's nearly forgotten attempts to enlist in the U.S. Army in 1944. Before he can enlist, the army physician diagnoses Robert with tuberculosis, which launches him into years of medical surveillance under the Los Angeles Public Health Department. He is moved from one hospital to another, until finally landing at the Olive View Sanatorium in Sylmar, which was known in the mid-twentieth century as the Los Angeles medical center serving poor, itinerant patients, and known nationally as the premier hospital researching the treatment and containment of tuberculosis on the U.S. West Coast. While living as an Olive View patient for nearly a decade, Robert experiences the mundane routines of patient life, but he also witnesses forced incarceration of suspected TBers, experimental, often fatal medical procedures carried out on poor people of color, and various forms of patient activism and resistance. Through the lens of memory, then, *The Captain* blurs the lines of archival recovery and official documentation of medical violence. Unsettling medical history as the major achievements of scientists and physicians, the novel instead situates settler colonial histories of the region as the conditions for California medicine, centering individual and collective experiences of racialized patients to tell the story of Olive View.

Scholars have discussed Morales's use of historical framing to ground the fictional content as something more than storytelling, and Morales himself has done much in his own writing to undermine the notion that "history" and "fiction" are easily separated.[27] He describes the problem of his work as "an attempt to conjure a fantasy of accuracy inhabited by those persons living or dead who intentionally, by their own free will, with pleasure or torment, read and identify themselves in the story."[28] While at Olive View, for example, Robert joins the volunteer staff of patient-journalists and contributes to the hospital newspaper *Olive View Point* as both writer and journalist. Based on the historical publication produced at Olive View Sanatorium, this fictional version of the newspaper traces the history of tuberculosis and its treatment over centuries, showing how the disease impacted governments and marginalized communities of both the past and present. Robert notes that his first writing assignment was to research the Mission San Fernando Valley, significant as a site of settler colonial histories impacting both the discourse of disease and the carceral legacies of the Spanish empire.[29] Covered in a story from the *Olive View Point*, the attention to this longer arc of history foregrounds the novel's attention to the ways Los Angeles infrastructure has been built on Tongva territory through settler colonial logics.[30]

The novel poses several sets of problems for readers to work out: Is medical violence a fact of the past and, if so, whose past? Is it contained by history, or do those histories haunt the present and continue to structure the future? Perhaps more importantly, what might it mean for a novel so invested in the official histories of the region to take seriously the constitutive relationships between memory and those carceral structures shaping medicine? Characters in this novel, for instance, struggle to come to terms with their own fidelities to medical authority, and at the same time to confront the reality that racialized bodies have long histories of being used as raw materials for scientific experimentation and advancement. The novel questions the definitions of progress underpinning the narration of science and medicine as a humanistic project by reframing it as a racial project. The way this is configured in theoretical terms troubles formulations of personhood that are structured by the logics of modernity and coloniality.[31] Robert suggests, in other words, that the power of historical scripts animating medical science as a benevolent force helps to explain, in part, why marginalized patients, "especially those of us who were poor, Mexican, and black," often "kept their mouths shut," and why such a form of medical violence is "so easily forgot-ten" in mainstream histories of medicine.[32]

Describing "another side of the tuberculosis crusade," Robert suggests that "the willingness of tuberculants to be test patients, sanatorium guinea pigs, or experimental rats" has everything to do with how they are racialized, and specifically how that process situates entire groups as powerless within the larger structures of medicine.[33] Robert continues:

> A dangerous selfishness compelled them to try any experimental drug presented to them. "If it works, I'll be the first to be cured!" I over-heard their justifications, their rationalization as they swallowed, injected, inhaled, or worse, went up to La Loma for experimental sur-gery. Aware of the possibility of disastrous setbacks such as devastat-ing physical abnormalities or fatal unexpected reactions, they became desperate and eagerly accepted whatever the doctors suggested. They were no longer willing or capable of struggling with the drudgery of their illness, and being bedridden had become overwhelmingly in-tolerable. . . . I could see it in their faces, in their calm demeanor: they were happy about their decision to be cured or die as quickly as possible.[34]

As time goes on, the possibility of consenting to such experimental medi-cines becomes more fraught as patients existing on the margins are either disappeared or killed, nearly always with impunity.[35] Robert notices that patients, overnight, "would be gone with no explanation," and that "[b]eing queer was a risky, dangerous business." The social realities demonstrate yet another layer of medical violence, where one could be "isolated, ignored, denied treatment, be found dead suddenly and mysteriously, or [be] mur-dered."[36] The novel details the ways in which patients of color have navigated vidence in medical spaces. Robert continues to critically observe the lives of Mexican, black, women, and queer patients, as well as patients with "a repu-tation of being a subversive, a political or social troublemaker on the out-side."[37] Such patients would go up to "La Loma"—the surgical unit and large laboratory that blocked the view of the experimental ward, a place that "re-minded everyone of Frankenstein and his castle where the good doctor had created a monster"—never to be seen again. "What I didn't know," Robert confesses as he remembers this time of his life, "was that they weren't always taken up there only for surgery, but also for tests, chemical experiments."

The novel itself, then, emerges as a catalogue of medical misery and car-ceral memory, listing not only Robert's observations but those of many patients over several years. Narrating his first encounter with La Loma, Robert recalls meeting with Consuelo Anzur, a patient who "had signed a waiver to participate in testing a new drug." Another patient and friend of Consuelo explains, "She didn't know what she was doing. They scared her and got her to do it. She barely understands English. She has no relatives, no friends, nobody to check on her. The experimental drug made her worse." Finally, urging Robert to leverage the newspaper as a political tool, she says: "Put this in the *Point*, Bob. Tell the patients how they use us as guinea pigs or experimental monkeys!"[38] Further experiments are carried out on prisoners and people who are homeless, many "who came from the county hospital and jail, both men and women" and "didn't know exactly what kind of treatment they were receiving."[39] As his own health improves, Robert indeed sees something predatory happening to those around him, and he becomes more attuned to the radical critique emerging from those politically marginalized in the hospital and beyond.

If memory in *The Captain* operates as I have suggested, that is, as a narrative device, the novel also shows how cultural texts in the twenty-first century can restage official histories as contested, as always-already negotiating refusal and resistance as counter-hegemonic responses. This refusal is perhaps most evident in the character Sandro Díez, an incarcerated patient at Olive View who seeks to disrupt the fantasy of the sanatorium as a benevolent institution. Rather, Díez sees a carceral operation with economic and political agendas. A former Pacific Pipe Clay and Cement Company employee with "a reputation of being a subversive, political or social troublemaker," he insists to Contreras that he be allowed to narrate his own position as an exploited, racialized radical laborer, and to be represented as such in the *Point*.[40] Díez is admitted to Olive View after the company doctor claims he has been infected with tuberculosis. He tells Robert that he rejected the diagnosis and, after momentarily resisting Díez's version of what happened with the doctors, finally agrees to write an account of Díez's arrest and incarceration for the *Point*. In it, he recounts the arrest and detainment of his family, who are also labeled as contagious TB carriers, explaining that the real motivation behind their arrest had to do with Díez's subversive politics as a union organizer. The Pacific Pipe Clay and Cement Company's exploitative and abusive working conditions drive Díez to seek, unsuccessfully, help from the other workers and their union: "They listened to me but were too afraid for their jobs to act. It took something ugly to make them finally respond."[41] He initiates a protest after seeing another beating, a sexual assault, and other routine acts of violence. His actions, Díez insists, prompt the com-

Christopher Perreira

pany to use quarantine laws as a tool to incarcerate, but what astonishes him most is the fact that such violence is sanctioned and unexceptional. Public displays of violence at the clay yard are represented as ongoing, mundane spectacles—the foreman smashing "his fist into the woman's face," yet Díez recognizes that it would take "something ugly to make them finally respond." The connection between the hospital and the prison is made explicit in this scene, and Díez claims that, for him, "the sanatorium is jail. I'm not being treated here. I'm being punished! I'm a political prisoner because I suffer from a political disease!"[42]

Díez's fictionalized narrative is likely based on an actual event. In an interview recorded in 1996, Morales refers to a conversation he had about someone's family incarceration at a hospital: "A man came to me about [my earlier novels]. He mentioned . . . how sometimes in the 1950s Chicanos were disappearing, and I asked, 'What do you mean disappearing? Were they being deported?' and he said, 'No, no, no. They took my dad and my brothers and me away, and they said that we had tuberculosis. They took us here, to the county hospital in Orange Country, and they held us for about a year. But we were never sick.'" Morales pressed the man for details, who continued: "They thought we were some kind of political radicals and that we were organizing certain unions and doing this and that. So that was a way of taking us out of circulation."[43] As a cultural text, *The Captain* documents an archival experience through the memories of those who were "gathered for experimental surgery," who "signed waivers without even knowing how to read," and, perhaps most difficult to navigate, those stories nowhere to be found in the archive or official records.

What does a meditation on memory such as this tell us about what is missing and what is absent? Here, in that tension between fiction and history, is where we might locate an important engagement with the historical framing of medical technologies. These fictional characters recognize this distinction between official history and a more collective memory, as a narrative tug that frames their story as one with political stakes and historical importance. The everyday lives of the people in the sanatorium, as Contreras in his later years comes to understand, ought to be documented: "Almost fifty years later [after Olive View] I would read the fascinating and little-known history of this beautiful place in a thesis my great-nephew . . . wrote while he was a medical student at the University of California, Los Angeles. In Olive View's history, Gregory deciphered the sanatorium's mystical, romantic, and frightful dimensions and how they intersected with its staff's, doctors', and patients' lives. . . . Gregory considered my life, like Olive View's history, important and valuable enough to be recorded and saved in his study." If "knowing the history of these buildings sheds a completely different perspective on what having tuberculosis was and meant," what medicine represents on a cultural front and as a politics of representation is the critical capacity to examine not only "how medicine became abusive" but to interrogate the narratives of medical progress and the possessiveness of knowledge, how it is always already racialized and gendered, and what is at stake in remembering what is easily forgotten.

Notes

1. Jill Leovy, "Breathing New Life: Olive View: Opened as a TB Sanitarium in 1920, the Hospital, Now a Modern Facility, Turned 75 This Week," *Los Angeles Times*, October 28, 1995, http://articles.latimes.com/1995-10-28/local/me-62120_1_olive-view.

2. *California and Western Medicine* is only one of many journals discussing public health and racialized communities during this time. Other articles published by members of the medical community in California include Karl L. Schaupp, "Medical Care of Migratory Agricultural Workers: A Story of Accomplishment—Presidential Address," *California and Western Medicine* 60, no. 65 (May 1944); "Health Education Media among California's Mexican-Americans," "Tuberculosis among Chinese," "Negroes in California," "Mexicans and Tuberculosis," and "Tuberculosis Programs among the Mexicans," *California and Western Medicine* 61, no. 2 (August 1944).

3. Eric Avila, *Popular Culture in the Age of White Flight: Fear and Fantasy in Suburban Los Angeles* (Berkeley: University of California Press, 2004), 4; Kelly Lytle Hernández, *City of Inmates: Conquest, Rebellion, and the Rise of Human Caging in Los Angeles, 1771–1965* (Chapel Hill: University of North Carolina Press, 2017), 167.

4. "Migratory Agricultural Workers of California: Their Health Care," *California and Western Medicine* 60, no. 2 (1944): 49.

5. "Migratory Agricultural Workers of California," 49.

6. Gilbert G. Gonzalez, *Chicano Education in the Era of Segregation* (Dallas: University of North Texas Press, 2013), 5–6. Gonzalez defines the "Mexican Problem" as "a culture," one that relies on a belief that "predisposed Mexican to laziness and poverty, to a 'Manana syndrome,' a proclivity to violence and heavy drinking, low intellectual abilities and more." See also Emily K. Abel, *Tuberculosis and the Politics of Exclusion: A History of Public Health and Migration to Los Angeles* (New Brunswick, NJ: Rutgers University Press, 2007); Lee Bebout, *Whiteness on the Border: Mapping the U.S. Racial Imagination in Brown and White* (New York: NYU Press, 2016); Mike Davis, *City of Quartz: Excavating the Future in Los Angeles* (London: Verso, 2006); Kelly Lytle Hernández, *Migra! A History of the U.S. Border Patrol* (Berkeley: University of California Press, 2010); Natalia Molina, *Fit to Be Citizens? Public Health and Race in Los Angeles, 1879–1939* (Berkeley: University of California Press, 2006); Natalia Molina, *How Race Is Made in America: Immigration,*

Christopher Perreira

Citizenship, and the Historical Power of Racial Scripts (Berkeley: University of California Press, 2014).

7. See also Tomás Almaguer, *Racial Fault Lines: The Historical Origins of White Supremacy in California* (Berkeley: University of California Press, 1994); Luis Alvarez, *The Power of the Zoot: Youth Culture and Resistance During World War II* (Berkeley: University of California Press, 2008); Ruha Benjamin, *People's Science: Bodies and Rights on the Stem Cell Frontier* (Stanford, CA: Stanford University Press, 2013); Nayan Shah, *Contagious Divides: Epidemics and Race in San Francisco's Chinatown* (Berkeley: University of California Press, 2001); Alexandra Stern, *Eugenic Nation: Faults and Frontiers of Better Breeding in Modern America* (Berkeley: University of California Press, 2005); Harriet A. Washington, *Medical Apartheid: The Dark History of Medical Experimentation on Black Americans From Colonial Times to the Present* (New York: Doubleday, 2006).

8. Molina, *How Race Is Made in America*, 100.

9. Stern, *Eugenic Nation*, 102.

10. Benjamin, *People's Science*, 3.

11. See Laurie B. Green, John Raymond McKiernan-González, and Martin Anthony Summers, "Introduction: Making Race, Making Health," in *Precarious Prescriptions: Contested Histories of Race and Health in North America*, edited by Laurie B. Green, John Raymond McKiernan-González, and Martin Anthony Summers (Minneapolis: University of Minnesota Press, 2014), vii–xxviii.

12. David Gutiérrez, *Walls and Mirrors: Mexican Americans, Mexican Immigrants, and the Politics of Ethnicity* (Berkeley: University of California Press, 1995), 91.

13. Vicki Ruíz, *Cannery Women, Cannery Lives: Mexican Women, Unionization, and the California Food Processing Industry, 1930–1950* (Albuquerque: University of New Mexico Press, 1987), 7. The conflation of race and disease shaped the ways the state sought to manage the development of the city not only around a color line, but out of the nativism that persisted through narratives of foreignness and noncitizenship. On the framing of community health, diet, and contagious disease in Mexican labor camps and houses, Gutiérrez's notes that of the Mexican families documented (1,668 individuals), over half reported having little or no meat in their regular diet, just under half reported rarely having fresh vegetables, and under half said their children had milk daily. Gutiérrez concludes that "even before the depths of the Great Depression, Mexican Americans and Mexican immigrants in Los Angeles County suffered infant mortality rates that ranged from twice as high as to five times higher than those of the general population."

14. Molina, *Fit to Be Citizens?*, 1.

15. Abel, *Tuberculosis and the Politics of Exclusion*, 86–87. There were, however, ongoing campaigns to raise funds, and charity organizations such as the Jewish Consumptive Relief Association ultimately played crucial roles in acquiring funds and shaping the narratives of need, philanthropy, and benevolence.

16. Molina, *Fit to Be Citizens?*, 143.

17. For the intersecting ways these discourses surface around race and representation, see Lytle Hernández, *Migra!*, and Curtis Marez, *Drug Wars: The Political Economy of Narcotics* (Minneapolis: University of Minnesota Press, 2004).

18. Molina, *How Race Is Made in America*, 35.

19. Thomas Dormandy, *The White Death: A History of Tuberculosis* (New York: NYU Press, 2000).

20. Lisa Lowe, *The Intimacies of Four Continents* (Durham, NC: Duke University Press, 2015), 3–4. Lowe argues for understanding "archives of liberalism" as a model for analyzing economies of "affirmation and forgetting" that structures and formalizes in official archives "liberalism, and liberal ways of understanding." The notion of freedom for "man," as defined by European and North American philosophical frameworks, at the same time relegates others to "geographical and temporal spaces that are constituted as backward, uncivilized, and unfree." The model is particularly important for reading narratives of freedom made possible by forgetting, denying, or erasing colonial slavery, dispossession, and displaced peoples across continents. It problematizes the notion that social inequality is resolvable through rights discourse defined by groups categorized as fully "human," while at the same time locating other subjects, practices, and geographies "at a distance from 'the human.'"

21. Lisa Lowe, *Immigrant Acts: An Asian American Cultural Politics* (Durham, NC: Duke University Press, 1996), 2.

22. Alejandro Morales, *The Captain of All These Men of Death* (Tempe, AZ: Bilingual Press/Editorial Bilingüe), 3.

23. Lawrence Grossberg, "On Postmodernism and Articulation: An Interview with Stuart Hall," in *Stuart Hall: Critical Dialogues in Cultural Studies*, ed. Kuan-Hsing Chen and David Morley (London: Routledge, 1996), 142–43.

24. Gregory Morales, "The Captain of All These Men of Death: Tuberculosis at the Olive View Sanitarium," MA thesis (University of California, Los Angeles, 1996), 1.

25. G. Morales, "The Captain of All These Men of Death."

26. On critical histories of California's twentieth-century Spanish colonial fantasies, see Carey McWilliams, *California: The Great Exception*, rev. ed. (Berkeley: University of California Press, 1999); Carey McWilliams, *North from Mexico; The Spanish-Speaking People of the United States* (Philadelphia: J. B. Lippincott, 1949); and more recently Mike Davis, Kelly Mayhew, and Jim Miller, *Under the Perfect Sun: The San Diego Tourists Never See* (New York: New Press, 2005).

27. See John Gamber, *Positive Pollutions and Cultural Toxins: Waste and Contamination in Contemporary U.S. Ethnic Literatures* (Lincoln: University of Nebraska Press, 2012), 57–90; Marc García-Martínez, *The Flesh-and-Blood Aesthetics of Alejandro Morales: Disease, Sex, and Figuration* (San Diego: San Diego State University Press, 2014); José Garza, "Social Turbulence as Reflected in Alejandro Morales' Novelistic Techniques," PhD diss. (Indiana University), 2006; José Antonio Palacios Gurpegui, *Alejandro Morales: Fiction Past, Present, Future Perfect* (Tempe, AZ: Bilingual Review/Press, 1996); Shimberlee Jirón-King, "Illness, Observation, and Contradiction: Intertext and

Christopher Perreira

Intrahistory in Alejandro Morales's *The Captain of All These Men of Death*," *Bilingual Review/La Revista Bilingüe* 29, no. 1 (2008): 3–13; James Kyung-Jin Lee, *Urban Triage: Race and the Fictions of Multiculturalism* (Minneapolis: University of Minnesota Press, 2004), 36–63.

28. Morales, *The Captain of All These Men of Death*, xii. Morales's other novels provide important cues for identifying Morales's theorizations of history through cultural production. His most critically acclaimed novel, *The Brick People* (1988), for example, fictionalizes generations of Mexican brickmakers and laborers at the Los Angeles Simons Brick Company. The story depicts northern Mexico and California labor and cultural history through the eyes of these workers, yet the engagement with a deep historical archive as well as his own family's narratives are hauntingly present.

29. Morales, *The Captain of All These Men of Death*, 150.

30. Lytle Hernández, *City of Inmates*, 25–27. Kelly Lytle Hernández has described the Spanish colonial period as "the first experiment in human caging" in Tongva territory. In the 1770s, Spanish settlers used caging to discipline Native rebellion and to control, coerce, and ultimately convert unmarried Tongva women and girls by locking them in dormitories at night. Priests used caging as a method of conversion by forcing thousands of baptisms. As Los Angeles developed, the legal designation of Native peoples as "minors" effectively subjugated the population as wards of the church and state.

31. See Lowe, *The Intimacies of Four Continents*; Walter Mignolo, *Local Histories/Global Designs: Coloniality, Subaltern Knowledges, and Border Thinking* (Princeton, NJ; Princeton University Press, 2012); Alexander G. Weheliye, *Habeas Viscus: Racializing Assemblages, Biopolitics, and Black Feminist Theories of the Human* (Durham, NC: Duke University Press, 2014); Sylvia Wynter, "Unsettling the Coloniality of Being/Power/Truth/Freedom: Towards the Human, after Man, Its Overrepresentation—An Argument," CR: *The New Centennial Review* 3, no. 3 (2003): 257–337.

32. Morales, *The Captain of All These Men of Death*, 3.

33. Morales, *The Captain of All These Men of Death*, 96.

34. Morales, *The Captain of All These Men of Death*, 96–97.

35. For detailed and systemic techniques developed to enable scientists to perform experiments on prisoners, see Allen M. Hornblum, *Acres of Skin: Human Experiments at Holmesburg Prison: A Story of Abuse and Exploitation in the Name of Medical Science* (New York: Routledge, 1998); Washington, *Medical Apartheid*, 244–70.

36. Morales, *The Captain of All These Men of Death*, 97. For an analysis of the eugenics movement in the United States and its enduring impact on gender, race, and sexuality, see Nancy Ordover, *American Eugenics: Race, Queer Anatomy, and the Science of Nationalism* (Minneapolis: University of Minnesota Press, 2003).

37. Morales, *The Captain of All These Men of Death*, 97. This section of the novel depicts multiple examples of social, state, and medical violence to tease out the disciplinary nature of the sanatorium, focusing on the racial violence of the Zoot Suit riots, the mundane and dangerous realities for queer patients, and more.

38. Along with animals (monkeys and guinea pigs), medical facilities developing treatments were testing them in dangerously high doses. Mukundan and colleagues note that Dapsone was used at Carville Leprosarium in the 1940s, and that Dapsone, at a dose of 100 mg, eventually became the standard treatment for leprosy, but only after six years of experimenting with it at high levels. Morales represents the distribution of Dapsone at Olive View at doses of 1,000 and 2,000 mg. See Harshini Mukundan, et al., *Tuberculosis, Leprosy and Other Mycobacterial Diseases of Man and Animals: The Many Hosts of Mycobacteria* (Boston: CABI, 2015), 481.

39. Morales, *The Captain of All These Men of Death*, 222–23.

40. Morales, *The Captain of All These Men of Death*, 97.

41. Morales, *The Captain of All These Men of Death*, 193.

42. Morales, *The Captain of All These Men of Death*, 176.

43. Gurpegui, *Alejandro Morales*, 8.

Christopher Perreira

3

Billions Served

PRISON FOOD REGIMES, NUTRITIONAL PUNISHMENT, AND GASTRONOMICAL RESISTANCE

Anthony Ryan Hatch

.....

After attending the 2015 American Correctional Association's trade show for the prison industrial complex, *New York Times* writer David Segal asks "Is there anything that cannot be turned into a weapon?"[1] From textiles to industrial lighting systems, design efforts to de-weaponize all sorts of prison structures and commodities have become a big selling point, creating massive new markets. Designing carceral environments that minimize the risk of interpersonal violence and maximize security is a recurring technological challenge. As one of the few commodities that prisoners cannot easily use *directly* as a weapon against guards or other prisoners, food is a powerful technology for direct and indirect political struggles in prison environments.

With over two million people held in U.S. prisons, detention facilities, and jails, the state serves billions of meals to people warehoused in the prison industrial complex. While meeting their constitutional responsibilities to provide daily calorie counts and minimum nutrient intake, prisons use food to control prisoners in obvious and not so obvious ways. By nutritional punishment, I am referring to a set of practices through which prison officials use the quantity or nutritional quality of consumed food as a form of punishment. Food is material biotechnology that continually transforms people's bodies and cultures, and structures social relationships.[2] The production and consumption of food is a cornerstone of prison life—and serves as the medium for forms of carceral domination.

Yet, through the practice of refusing to eat food, prisoners can use their bodies as counter-weapons to neutralize the power prisons wield over their lives. By gastronomical resistance, I am referring to a set of practices through which prisoners use the gastrointestinal systems of the body as a site for pushback against not only forms of nutritional punishment but against unjust and punitive conditions of confinement. Further still, prisons use the practice of force-feeding food as a counter-counter-weapon to neutralize prisoners' use of their own bodies in acts of resistance. Taken together, nutritional punishment and gastronomical resistance both unfold within food regimes specifically designed for prison environments. With a few recent and notable exceptions, these food politics within the U.S. prison industrial complex have not been sufficiently interrogated.[3] I ask: Through what techno-political relationships do prison food systems operate? How does the *fixing/refusal* of prison food simultaneously *innovate* techniques of carcerality and modes of resistance to the prison? I examine these questions across forms of nutritional punishment and gastronomical resistance within prison food regimes, drawing attention to both the political economy and technological infrastructures that manufacture prison food.

PRISON FOOD REGIMES

As U.S.-style mass imprisonment continues largely unfazed and under-challenged, the old cultural idea of prisons providing a crust of bread and water to emaciated inmates must give way to the contemporary reality of a massive system of industrial agriculture. Food regime analysis frames the complex and unequal power relationships that structure food systems in the U.S. carceral state. A food regime is a historically contingent constellation of political and economic structures (mainly in the form of rules, contracts, and trade relationships) and technoscientific practices (principally in terms of agricultural industrialization and the scientization of both farming and eating) that pattern the production and consumption of food globally. Building on the theorizations by Harriett Friedman and Philip McMichael, food regime analysis historicizes the food system by tracing patterns of crisis, transformation, and transition in the formation of the global political economy.[4] It is important to recognize that these patterns of change are not always linear and therefore do not always represent progress for people. This approach also features an analytic focus on agricultural technologies, such as biocides and genetically modified organisms, as tactics of domination and resistance within the global political economy of food.

Anthony Ryan Hatch

According to McMichael's periodization, there have been roughly three major global food regimes over the past four hundred years.[5] The first regime emerged in the early 1800s and lasted through the post–World War I years; it was defined principally by primary capital accumulation through settler colonialism and forced labor under chattel slavery and export to markets dominated by Europeans and their descendants in the United States, Australia, and Canada. As this periodization suggests, food regimes are best conceived through the lens of intersectionality, which recognizes how capitalist and colonial systems, marinated in a toxic brew of racism and heteropatriarchy, have produced gross social and economic inequalities between and within societies. Stated differently, food regimes are racial and gendered social formations based on the exploitation of labor of the black and brown global peasantry. The second regime took hold in the post–World War II period, lasting through the late 1970s; it involved the export of surplus food from the United States to postcolonial states, the widespread adoption of Green Revolution technologies as strategies for national development (i.e., mechanization, biocides, extensive monocropping), and land reforms that suppressed peasant uprisings in the global postcolony. The Green Revolution in particular represented a violent extension of technological domination into colonial states through a wholesale reconfiguration of local ecologies, economies, foodways, and bodies.[6] The first and second regimes were largely driven by European and U.S. national interests, whereas the third regime is based on corporate expansion and market dominance. The third regime is defined by the further application of food biotechnologies, global distribution and transportation systems, the supermarket revolution, animal protein–based food chains, and a grossly bifurcated food system that provides abundant animal proteins, fresh fruits, and vegetables to world's wealthy populations while perpetual food crises and high prices recur in the lives of billions of global working and poor populations.

In the carceral context, food operates simultaneously as a symbol of power and a material biotechnology of power that continually transforms people's bodies and cultures and structures social relationships. Food regime analysis relies on a substantive focus on the role of technology in generating and maintaining particular food systems. These conjoined processes of cultural signification and material transformation unfold through the dialectic relationship between food production and consumption. At the same time, these rituals and practices of food production and consumption are culturally mediated through race, ethnicity, sexuality, and gender.[7] Foods signal relationships of social power between groups in prisons: between the jailers and the jailed, between those who work in the prison kitchen preparing food and guarding the stockroom and those who file into the mess hall to eat what they are served, among prisoners like themselves. In this way, food operates as a currency within the prison economy, symbolizing who has the capacity to control others' lives and hoard the necessities of life.[8]

Prison systems obtain food through some combination of producing it themselves and/or purchasing from multinational food service corporations. Multinationals like Aramark and Trinity Services Group, along with the food service professionals who work in prison food services, are part of a global institutional structure that forms prison food regimes. Together, Aramark and Trinity provide food for 950 prisons and jails nationwide.[9] Aramark provides services to a wide range of social institutions; Trinity focuses its work exclusively on the prison business. Trinity has been in the prison food business since 1990, Aramark since 1978. These corporations rely on the brute purchasing power of scale, experience with food management software, and teams of bureaucrats to put together complex bids for state prison contracts.

Prison food regimes are one node in a much larger global structure. Their historicity is very important, and the role that food technologies play in their unfolding is critical. As prison populations increased in the late 1970s and early 1980s, food regimes shifted in response. Because they were feeding many more people now, prisons had to cultivate ways to keep costs down while not aggravating already contentious dynamics within facilities. In other words, prisons had to feed more people decent food than ever before. Until this new crisis of scale, prisons could get by with a combination of their own agricultural production plus contracts with local producers and distributors. Then, within the span of a few years in the early 1990s, they were faced with a new problem of scale. Simultaneously, multinational food service corporations were gifted a new opportunity. Take, for example, Aramark. By its own count, it has been in the corrections market for thirty-nine years. That means that they got into the corrections market in 1978. Nixon inaugurated the federal War on Drugs in 1971. By the time Aramark got into the game, prison populations had started to climb nationwide. They were well positioned to take advantage of a new, captive, and rapidly expanding market for heavily subsidized agricultural commodities.

According to its website, the Association of Correctional Food Service Affiliates (ACFSA) was formed in 1969 to "enhance, represent, and promote the correctional segment of the foodservice industry."[10] Defining itself as a mechanism for professional development and occupational advancement for workers, ACFSA also doubles as an organizational structure that helps

Anthony Ryan Hatch

link private corporations, prison administrators and decision makers, and food service workers. ACFSA members are the food service professionals who work in prisons, hence the claimed mission of the organization is to "develop and promote education programs and networking activities to improve professionalism and provide an opportunity for broadening knowledge." Each year, ACFSA hosts an "international conference and vendor showcase"—the theme for 2017 is "Doing More with Less."[11] The conference features sessions on nutrition, facility planning and design, networking, and accessing vendors. The ACFSA periodical, *Insider*, is filled with advertisements for food storage, preparation, distribution, and waste removal technologies: refrigerators, garbage disposals, temperature sensors, portion control devises, worker clothing.

In 2014, Aramark signed a $145 million contract with the Michigan Department of Corrections, after the Republican-led legislature decided it was a solid conservative idea to privatize their prison food regime. They serve meals to 45,000 prisoners daily at four dollars a day per prisoner (which is quite expensive, as you will see). Their contract stated that they have to provide each prisoner with 2,600 calories per day. The Michigan Aramark contract was terminated in July 2015 due to a series of revelations about food safety and Aramark employees' sexual exploitation of prisoners, and was replaced by a contract with Trinity Services Group for $12 million more per year, yet many of the same problems remained. This is just one case of corporate malfeasance; there are others. In response to the crisis in Michigan, Aramark was also subjected to an investigation by the Ohio inspector general in 2016, this time for overcharging the state due to erroneous counting procedures linked to its food management software (more on this shortly).

Technology is implicated in the shift of prison food regimes from local suppliers to multinational food conglomerates. A new Aramark–Pennsylvania deal provides an illustrative example of this shift from local to multinational corporate control of prison food regimes. Aramark has been aggressively pursuing prison food business across the nation, presumably because of its profitability. In February 2017, Pennsylvania awarded Aramark Correctional Industries a three-year, $154 million contract to provide food purchasing, logistics, and inventory systems services to the state's twenty-six facilities.[12] Under the contract, the state Department of Corrections (DOC) will continue to prepare, inspect, and control prisoners' food. The state hopes to save a little more than $16 million over three years by "taking advantage of Aramark's software system to deliver more efficient services."[13] The deal was negotiated under the auspices of Pennsylvania's "GO-TIME" initiative (which stands for the Governor's Office of Transformation, Innovation, Management, and Efficiency), which is supposed to "leverage resources, streamline processes, and create efficiencies" in state bureaucratic operations.[14]

Soon after the first Aramark prisons came online, the *Pittsburgh Post-Gazette* reported that local food and dairy producers in Pennsylvania were upset because they now found themselves locked out of the lucrative and reliable prison business. Prior to the new Aramark contract, local farms could enter into short-term contracts with one or more of the twenty-six facilities. John Friedmann, president of Karetas Foods, told the *Post-Gazette*, "A lot of companies in Pennsylvania relied on that. . . . More than 100 million in contracts, and everyone was just left out in the cold, period. The profits went to Aramark and their contractor."[15]

A different but related problem has been unfolding in Ohio, where state public unions compete against private multinationals for prison food service contracts. According to reporting from the *Ohio Dispatch* and the *Detroit Metro Times*, Aramark and the Ohio Civil Service Employees Association, the union for state workers, have been fighting for the lucrative state prison food contract. For years, food for Ohio's fifty thousand prisoners was produced by state workers, but Aramark won its first contract to take over this function in 2013. After a litany of problems including maggots, rodent feces, substandard food, and unsanitary conditions, Ohio terminated the Aramark contract in favor of a contract with Trinity.[16] For their sins, Aramark was fined $272,300 and received 240 citations for shorting inmates on food. The Aramark contract was renewed again in 2015 for two years and was set to expire on June 30, 2017. The union submitted a proposal for the new contract, claiming to offer prisoners food "with a cost of $1.226 per meal, compared to Aramark's current price of $1.313 per meal."[17] Even though the union claimed that they could save the state $4.4 million annually, the state is still (as of this writing) weighing its options. A similar situation unfolded in Shelby County, Tennessee, with thirty-one nonunionized food service workers whose jobs would be eliminated under a $3.65 million Aramark contract.[18] These political contestations are fundamentally about the health of state economies and the ways in which prisons serve to prop up local economies that would otherwise be in crisis.[19] Part of the public negotiation over these contracts is about how many local jobs are gained/lost, whether the profits from prison sales stay in the home state, and how all of this impacts state prison expenditures.

For prison officials, food service management software justifies itself based on claims of cost savings and bureaucratic innovation. On its correctional

Anthony Ryan Hatch

food service website, Trinity Services Group boasts that it uses a program called NetMenu®, now owned by the CBORD Group.[20] CBORD provides food service systems (i.e., card readers, interfaces) for colleges and universities, hospitals, senior living facilities, and businesses. NetMenu is a "configurable menu program which provides a unified interface to online information systems."[21] NetMenu now enables Trinity "to instantly update standards and share common recipes, menus, and settings across all of our operations, as well as access nutritional information, manage inventory and purchasing, and generate production reports."[22] Sometimes, the claims of technical efficiencies that result from these systems are overblown. The efficacy of food management software systems, like all technologies, is limited by the training of users and their proper application. For example, in 2016 Aramark was the "only qualified bidder" for an estimated five-year $118 million food services contract with the state of Tennessee.[23] The only other bid, from Trinity Services Group, was somehow not in compliance with bidding rules. In contrast to the claims made in the Pennsylvania case, Aramark's bid earned low scores in the "technical qualifications, experience, and approach" category.

Prison farms (i.e., plantations) still exist as a major part of prison food regimes, too. According to the most recent data from the 2002 National Criminal Justice Reference Service, twenty-eight states and the Federal Bureau of Prisons had prisoners working in agriculture.[24] Cheap prison labor combined with substantial arable land and economies of scale position prison farms as cost-saving public–private enterprises for the State. *All fifty states* run "correctional industries" that use prison labor to produce commodities exclusively for sale to other state agencies within the same state. For instance, in 2012 the Mississippi State Penitentiary at Parchman used "600,000 man-hours, planting over 5,700 acres in vegetables, rice, corn, wheat, and soybeans and producing over two tons of vegetables worth more than $1.3 million and almost half a million eggs."[25] Oklahoma's farm system, Agri-Services, "produces or processes 723,000 pounds of beef, 115,000 pounds of pork, 1,445,000 pounds of processed meat, and 580,000 gallons of milk" in a "typical year." In Georgia, the per-inmate food cost is 30 percent lower than the national average because of its ten-thousand-acre plantation system including a modern food processing and distribution network.[26] As agricultural practices in the nation as a whole were transformed through mechanization and the postwar use of biocides and monoculture, so too were these shifts effective in transforming prison agricultural practices. Yet, prison farms are also being repackaged discursively as ways to reduce aggression, reduce recidivism, reduce costs, and improve prisoner nutrition. Next, prison farms will be repackaged as part of the "farm-to-table" movement organized around locally sourced and sustainably produced agriculture.

The prison commissary is another place where prisoners can access food. It is also a place where prisons and private food service corporations can siphon money off prisoners and their families. A quick internet search reveals the price sheets for several prison commissaries. A limited menu of snack foods is available at inflated prices, many provided by multinational food conglomerates like the Hershey Corporation and Lay's. According to one study of prison uprisings, between 1900 and 1995, only forty out of 1,334 uprisings were about food, but among these events, the most common prisoner grievance was access to the commissary.[27] As jurisdictions look to spend less on food services and cut back on the number of meals, portion size, and food quality, prisoners are forced to rely more heavily on the commissary as a source of food. Consequently, prison commissary firms generate $1.6 billion per year in revenue.[28] Keefe Group, one of the largest prison commissary firms, has been working in prisons since 1975. In 2016, Stephen Raher of Prison Policy Initiative reported that H.I.G. Capital, the firm that owns Trinity Services Group, was trying to buy Keefe. This strong evidence of the consolidation and monopolization of prison food should raise serious questions for U.S. regulators. Unfortunately, prison food systems fall outside the normative regulatory structure.

As these stories suggest, transformations in prison food regimes are linked to a unique regulatory structure. Unlike in the so-called free society, the Food and Drug Administration and the U.S. Department of Agriculture do not function in prisons. They do not conduct inspections, they do not monitor equipment, they do not check the nutritional quality of food or verify the biological safety of food preparation practices. They do not perform a regulatory function. Instead, prison food systems are self-regulated by individual jurisdictions and facility bosses. As a safety matter, the food itself and its storage, preparation, and waste removal are all handled in-house or by private contractors. The heterogeneity that defines this patchwork of rules and regulations makes macro/national analysis difficult.

As a legal matter, food is the subject of vast U.S. case law, mainly pertaining to the First and Eighth Amendments to the U.S. Constitution. Prison food law deals with the constitutional frameworks and regulatory systems that situate prison food regimes between U.S. prison law and U.S. food regimes. Prisoners have rights to the free practice of religion, which grants them access to religiously prescribed diets. The struggle between prisoners' religious

Anthony Ryan Hatch

practices and prison demands for uniformity and control takes place in state and federal courts. The basic idea is that religious diets must adhere to strict guidelines (e.g., halal, kosher, vegetarian) and thereby may be better-quality food. Prisons are not obligated to serve religious meals under lockdown or disciplinary conditions, although these dynamics are often the subject of litigation. Prisoners also have protected access to medically necessary diets—say, for diabetes. These diets may involve specialty foods or modified eating schedules. Again, in practice, the courts have given prisons wide latitude in terms of the consistency with which they must provide these special diets. In general, medical diets are covered under the Eighth Amendment, which protects prisoners against the deliberate indifference of prison officials with regard to their health. There is some question as to whether a prisoner's hunger strike, which I discuss later, is protected as free speech under the First Amendment.[29]

The only institutions that monitor prison food are U.S. courts, the independent media, and prisoner advocacy organizations, like the ACLU Prison Project. Unfortunately, each of these institutions is limited with respect to its access to, interest in, and power over prison food. For example, there has been great independent reporting on prison food systems since the Great Recession of 2008–9 as jurisdictions were looking for ways to trim their prison budgets by eliminating meals, providing less food, or not serving fruits and vegetables. While these reports bring to light practices that otherwise would remain hidden from public view, they have not had a discernible effect at the contractual or regulatory levels—prisons are free to continue business as usual. It can take years for prisoners' formal complaints to wind their way through the courts, and although they might result in policy changes, they are often local, temporary, and future-oriented, with little in the way of compensation for harms done. This is why resistance to prison food regimes emanates from the very bodies of prisoners—only through their own bodies can prisoners seek to force prison officials to change.

NUTRITIONAL PUNISHMENT

The nutritional quality of prison food directly impacts the physical and mental health of prisoners and increases the burdens on prison health care systems. Prisoners experience high rates of physical and mental health problems, many of which result from or are exacerbated by prison food. Analyses of the nutritional quality of prison food demonstrate that food to be high in calories, sugar, sodium, and fat. Prison food is produced from the cheapest ingredients on the market. Prisons apply a very narrow and unscientific conception of what constitutes a nutritious diet — it is minimally a diet that will not invite lawsuits. Prison diets are quantified according to the number of calories they contain in relationship to their cost. Food is provided that transfers enough calories to the prisoners so as not to let them wither away (except in cases where that is exactly the plan). They ask: How can we provide each prisoner enough calories at the lowest price so as not to bump up against constitutional limits? Recent reports suggest prisons are turning to nutritional supplements to augment food-based diets. In fact, there is a body of research that investigates the relationship between supplement consumption, criminal behavior, and mental health in prison populations.[30]

Raw starvation is not a major problem in U.S. prisons, but well-designed hunger is. Excellent reporting by the Marshall Project documents the extent of the problems of hunger and nutrition in the context of a neoliberal fixation on controlling food costs. The high costs of feeding so many prisoners in the context of national economic insecurity and stretched state budgets has led many departments of correction to consider ways to cut down on the cost of food. This economic analysis is often conceptualized in terms of the cost of feeding a single inmate for one day. In places like Gordon County, Georgia, the Marshall Project reports cases of jail inmates "licking syrup packets and drinking excessive amounts of water" to stave off hunger. Other jail officials in other jurisdictions boast of providing the "cheapest meals in the U.S." (in Arizona), or "I think [the prisoners] eat better than some of the people on the streets" (in Montana).[31]

Stories of stale, dangerous, parasite-infested food from these "professional partners" in prison abound, stories that have impacted their ability to maintain their contracts with systems. If you think Chipotle has a food PR problem, prison food nightmares shock the gastrointestinal sensibilities of taste, texture, and pleasure — like food porn, but in reverse. The food services giant Aramark, which provides food for six hundred prison systems, has been especially good at this.[32] Aramark is responsible for "maggot-related incidents," serving prisoners food pulled out of the trash, rat-eaten cakes, mold infestations, and rotten chicken on taco night.[33]

Is there a legally mandated number of meals that a prisoner must receive each day? No. Is there a legally mandated number of calories that prisoner must receive each day? No. Are there any legally enforceable mechanisms that regulate the quantity or nutritional quality of prison food? No. There are any number of recommendations from professional organizations as to these standards, but no prison is obligated to follow them as a matter of

Anthony Ryan Hatch

law.[34] What, then, is the legal standard for *not* violating the Eighth Amendment regarding food? The determination that a prison food practice violates the Eighth Amendment must meet two tests. First, the practice must be objectively cruel and unusual, which means that it must violate contemporary standards of decency. Second, prisoners must prove that prison officials were deliberately indifferent to the specific problems in the case — only conditions that are known to responsible prison officials can be unlawful under the Eighth Amendment. How does this translate into real-world practice? It feels like a world steeped in capriciousness and hypocrisy. In reality, current U.S. prison food law means that prison officials can use food to whatever ends they choose in individual cases, they can oversee serious lapses in sanitation or nutritional quality, and they can police and inspect themselves. Prisons cannot easily deprive *groups* of prisoners of basic human needs like food, shelter, warmth, medical care, and exercise, but they are largely free to deprive *individual* prisoners of these basic needs. It is important to remember that the state reserves for itself the right to kill its own citizens, either with or without due process. Not feeding prisoners healthy, life-sustaining meals seems trivial next to the sovereign's absolute right over death.

In *Hutto v. Finley*, a group of Arkansas prisoners sued the state under the Eighth Amendment over being fed "grue," a hard-baked mélange of meat, potatoes, syrup, vegetables, eggs, margarine, and seasonings.[35] An unending diet of grue in overcrowded and filthy cells, the court found, violated the Eighth Amendment and constituted the use of food as a form of cruel and unusual punishment. One of the more visible and recent contestations over the constitutionality of prison food emerged in late 2015 as the Cuomo administration in New York decided to stop serving something called nutraloaf to prisoners in solitary confinement. Nutraloaf (or prison loaf or disciplinary loaf) is as functional as it sounds — it is an oven-baked loaf of nutrients extracted from surplus foods, often served with a side of "fuck you." As reported in the *New York Times*, nutraloaf was reserved for prisoners in solitary who needed *further* punishment for "throwing food" or "bodily waste" or "refusing to obey orders from correctional officers during mealtimes." Nutraloaf for breakfast, lunch, and dinner. They even made kosher versions of nutraloaf for Jewish inmates.

GASTRONOMICAL RESISTANCE

Practices of prisoners intentionally and systematically refusing to eat the food prisons serve them (or any food) are linked to biopolitical struggles against unjust treatment. Forms of prisoner noncompliance are better understood as multiple forms of gastronomical resistance—consumptive practices that aim to disrupt/interrupt the use of state food as a form of nutritional punishment. Prisoners not allowing themselves to be fed transgress the sovereign's right to make die or let live. Jailed suffragettes in Britain in the early 1900s were the first to use the hunger strike as a form of gastronomical resistance against the state's refusal to recognize their protests against disenfranchisement as political rather than criminal acts.[36] Since then, the hunger strike has become a powerful form of resistance against state violence.[37] As Banu Bargu reminds us, when people have no weapons, they use the body as a weapon in a perverse form of necropolitics.[38] The hunger strike has been used as a collective form of resistance to great effect in places like California, where a series of coordinated strikes, one of *twelve thousand prisoners* in 2011 and another of *thirty thousand prisoners* in 2013, have raised the profile of prisoners' claims of unjust and inhumane treatment, including indefinite detention in solitary confinement, opaque gang classification criteria, group punishment, sleep deprivation, and inadequate food.

Alabama has also been a site of gastronomical resistance via hunger strike. The Free Alabama Movement, led by Kinetic Justice-Amun (formerly Robert Earl Council) participated in a general labor strike explicitly against Aramark in 2017.[39] In Alabama, prisoners waged at least twenty-seven hunger strikes between 2013 and 2017 to protest various forms of unjust treatment.[40] Kinetic Justice-Amun also personally participated in a hunger strike in October 2016.[41] Prisoners in the Alabama system report that one of the tactics prison officials are now using to break these hunger strikes is turning off the water to the prisoner's cell.

Yet the state enforces biological limits on the hunger strike as a form of gastronomical resistance—here, the state wields a perverse form of biopower to make prisoners live. Suffragettes, so-called enemy combatants in the war on terror, and civil detainees held for immigration violations have all been subjected to the practice of force-feeding, a practice that U.S. courts have permitted in order to "save the lives" of hunger-striking detainees and prisoners. Contemporary force-feeding practices involve the administration of liquid nutritional supplements, like Ensure or Boost, through nasalgastric tubes. This practice requires that a subject be strapped in five-point restraints so that she cannot remove the olive oil–lubricated tubing that snakes through the nasal passage, down the esophagus and into the stomach. Keep in mind that this practice is not supposed to constitute torture. As a pair, force-feeding and hunger strikes constitute the most rare and extreme forms of gastronomical resistance and nutritional punishment, practices

Anthony Ryan Hatch

that position prisoners' bodies at the knife edge of death. Yet more mundane practices also demonstrate how social groups in prison weaponize food in different ways.

Hacking prison food is a tactic for transforming commissary food into something that generates desire and pleasure. This hacking signals novel forms of gastronomical resistance that prisoners develop to minimize the everyday nutritional punishment they face. Simultaneously, hacking food has sprouted a new genre of prison food cookbooks, the circulation of which in so-called free society contributes to the normalization of prison culture. Think of *Prison Ramen* by Clifton Collins Jr., Gustavo "Goose" Alvarez, and Samuel L. Jackson, and *Commissary Kitchen* by Albert "Prodigy" Johnson (yes, the brilliant rap artist) and Kathy Iandoli. In this world, our incarcerated neighbors are like participants in a perverse form of "maker culture," in which their ability to produce palatable food out of refuse should amaze and astound. "It actually tastes good!" One 2015 story in the *Detroit Metro Times*, written by a formerly incarcerated citizen in the Oakland County Jail who goes by the pseudonym "Stephen Katz," describes a twist on the jail burrito, complete with Flamin' Hot Cheetos–flavored rice, tortillas, pickles, jalapeños, and squeeze cheese.[42] This brings to mind a dark, carceral version of the Food Network program *Chopped*, in which contestants compete for a $10,000 cash prize and bragging rights if they can wow three esteemed (and well-paid) chefs with their creativity in assembling a three-course meal out of fun baskets filled with surprise ingredients. The carceral iteration is sometimes called a "cook-up." "The resourcefulness in food preparation in jail was impressive," Katz boasts. "Everything was reused or repurposed or altered in some way to prepare the meal or improve the flavor." While prisoners are able to create fleeting moments of pleasure and community around the commissary hack, this culinary ingenuity is expensive for prisoners and their families. Prisons and prison services corporations are positioned to weaponize private food in economic terms. Prison commissaries inflate food prices to extract surplus profits directly from prisoners and their families.

CONCLUSION

In the late afternoon of September 21, 2011, Brother Troy Davis refused his last meal.[43] After twenty years of waiting for the people of the state of Georgia to kill him by lethal injection in the Jackson Diagnostic and Classification Prison, for the alleged shooting death of off-duty police offer Mark MacPhail, Mr. Davis refused to accept the food offered to him by the state as a breathtaking sign of faith—faith that his life would be spared. "It will not be my last meal," people present heard him say. While he ultimately refused to eat it, Mr. Davis requested the same meal given to the other 2,100 prisoners that day: a grilled cheeseburger, oven-baked potatoes, baked beans, coleslaw, cookies, and a grape drink.[44] The suicide watch guard tasked with ensuring that condemned prisoners do not kill themselves before the state can do so was supposed to write down how much or how little food Brother Davis ate before his execution. He didn't do his job. Troy Davis's symbolic act of gastronomical resistance, his act of refusal, served to push back against the state's devilish manipulation of the bodily and earthly pleasures in the "last meal." As Troy Davis understood with profound clarity, food is a living technology and symbol of the carceral imagination run amok.

Left with few options, prisoners weaponize and sacrifice their bodies to resist the violence that prisons food regimes create. Carceral seppuku—a knife through the stomach as a ritual act of honor and selflessness. For those of us who stand in solidary with our incarcerated kinfolk, we cannot stand by and only bear witness. The prison abolition movement and the food justice movement need to establish common cause against their common enemies, who have formed a dangerous duo—a violent carceral state and a voracious corporate food system. We cannot achieve food justice outside prisons while new forms of nutritional punishment bubble along inside prison walls. Bourgeois conceptions of gastronomical resistance cannot be limited to shopping at Whole Foods and supporting community farmers' markets. Simultaneously, we cannot achieve prison abolition while ignoring the entrenchment of corporate food regimes through the carceral system. The linkage between these two systems of power has to be severed at the spine.

Notes

1. David Segal, "Prison Vendors Continue to See Signs of a Captive Market," *New York Times*, August 29, 2015, accessed July 10, 2017, https://www.nytimes.com/2015/08/30/business/prison-vendors-see-continued-signs-of-a-captive-market.html?mcubz=3.

2. Anthony Ryan Hatch, *Blood Sugar: Racial Pharmacology and Food Justice in Black America* (Minneapolis: University of Minnesota Press, 2016); Gill Valentine, "In-Corporations: Food, Bodies and Organizations," *Body and Society* 8, no. 2 (2002): 1–20.

3. Erika Camplin, *Prison Food in America* (Lanham, MD: Rowman and Littlefield, 2017); Amy B. Smoyer and Giza Lopes, "Hungry on the Inside: Prison Food as Concrete and Symbolic Punishment in a Women's Prison," *Punishment and Society* 19, no. 2 (2017): 240–55; Caitlin Watkins, "Industrialized Bodies: Women, Food, and Environ-

Anthony Ryan Hatch

mental Justice in the Criminal Justice System," in *Addressing Environmental and Food Justice toward Dismantling the School-to-Prison Pipeline Poisoning and Imprisoning Youth*, ed. Anthony Nocella, K. Animashaun Ducre, and Johhn Lupinacci, 137–60 (New York: Palgrave Macmillan. 2017).

4. Harriet Friedmann, "The Political Economy of Food: A Global Crisis," *New Left Review* 197 (1993): 29–57; Phillip D. McMichael, "A Food Regime Genealogy," *Journal of Peasant Studies* 36 (2009): 139–69.

5. Phillip D. McMichael, "A Food Regime Genealogy," *Journal of Peasant Studies* 36 (2009): 139–69.

6. Deane Curtin, "Making Peace with the Earth: Indigenous Agriculture and the Green Revolution," *Environmental Ethics* 17, no. 1 (1995): 59–73.

7. Amy B. Smoyer and Giza Lopes, "Hungry on the Inside: Prison Food as Concrete and Symbolic Punishment in a Women's Prison."*Punishment and Society* 19, no. 2 (2017): 240–55.

8. Deborah Lupton, "Food, Memory and Meaning: The Symbolic and Social Nature of Food Events," *The Sociological Review* 42, no. 4 (1994): 664–85; Gill Valentine and Beth Longstaff, "Doing Porridge: Food and Social Relations in a Male Prison," *Journal of Material Culture* 3, no. 2 (1998): 131–52.

9. Tom Perkins, "Something Still Stinks in Michigan and Ohio's Prison Kitchens," *Detroit Metro Times*, February 17, 2016, accessed July 6, 2017, https://www.metrotimes.com/detroit/something-still-stinks-in-michigan-and-ohios-prison-kitchens/Content?oid=2396672.

10. Association of Correctional Food Service Affiliates, "About ACFSA," accessed July 8, 2017, http://www.acfsa.org/about.php.

11. Association of Correctional Food Service Affiliates, "Invitation to Attend 2017 Conference," accessed July 8, 2017, http://www.acfsa.org/documents/2017Conf/2017InvitationToAttend.pdf.

12. State of Pennsylvania, "Governor's Office GO-TIME Announcement," accessed July 10, 2017, https://www.governor.pa.gov/go-time-department-of-corrections-food-procurement-services-and-management-software-system-contract-to-save-an-estimated-16-6-million-over-three-years/.

13. Jerry Gaul, "Aramark Wins Food Services Contract for Prisons; Pa. Says Deal Saves Taxpayers Millions," *Philly Voice*, February 15, 2017, accessed July 9, 2017, http://www.phillyvoice.com/aramark-awarded-food-services-contract-prisons-pa-says-deal-saves-taxpayers-16-million/.

14. State of Pennsylvania, "Governor's Office GO-TIME Announcement."

15. Daniel Moore, "Food, Dairy Companies Supplying State Prisons Unhappy with Contract Changes," *Pittsburgh Post Gazette*, May 30, 2017, accessed July 9, 2017, http://www.post-gazette.com/news/state/2017/05/30/aramark-pittsburgh-Food-dairy-companies-supplying-state-prisons-unhappy-with-contract-changes/stories/201704230011.

16. State of Michigan. "Department of Corrections Testimony," accessed July 9, 2017, http://house.michigan.gov/hfa/PDF/Corrections/DOC_Subcmte_Testimony(Det roitMetroTimesArticle_3-3-16).pdf.

17. Alan Johnson, "Union Says Its Prison Food Contract Would Save Ohio Taxpayers 44 Million," *The Columbus Dispatch*, February 1, 2017, accessed July 9, 2017, http://www .dispatch.com/news/20170201/union-says-its-prison-food-contract-would-save-ohio -taxpayers-44-million.

18. Linda Moore, "Shelby County Employees Plead While Commissioners Ponder Food Service Contract," *Commercial Appeal*, March 16, 2015, accessed July 10, 2017, http://archive.commercialappeal.com/news/government/county/shelby-county -employees-plead-while-commissioners-ponder-food-service-contract-ep-993775200 -324443731.html.

19. Ruth Gilmore, *Golden Gulag Prisons, Surplus, Crisis, and Opposition in Globalizing California* (Berkeley: University of California Press, 2006).

20. Created at Yale in 1992 as the Yale School of Medicine and its medical library's first workstation interface, NetMenu was written in the C programming language and was unique in the early nineties for being usable on both Macintosh and DOS platforms. It offered its users local networked access to the Yale Hospital information system, Micromedex (a drug/toxicology database), the Medical School Library, Clinical Advice Services, and electronic mail. I cannot determine exactly when or under what conditions Yale sold NetMenu to CBORD, but CBORD filed a trademark application for the program on October 16, 2003.

21. Mark A. Shifman, Jeffrey I. Clyman, John A. Paton, Seth M. Powsner, Nancy K. Roderer, and Perry L. Miller, "NetMenu: Experience in the Implementation of an Institutional Menu of Information Sources," *Proceedings of the Annual Symposium on Computer Application in Medical Care* (1993): 554–58.

22. Trinity Services Group, "Correctional Food Service," accessed July 9, 2017, https://www.trinityservicesgroup.com/food-service-2/.

23. Dave Boucher, "Aramark Lone Bidder for Tennessee Food Service Con- tract," *Tennessean*, August 12, 2016, accessed July 8, 2017, http://www.tennessean .com/story/news/2016/08/12/aramark-lone-bidder-tennessee-prison-food-contract /88446156/.

24. Criminal Justice Institute, Inc., *Corrections Yearbook: Adult Corrections 2002*, ed. Camille Graham Camp (Middletown: Criminal Justice Institute, 2003).

25. Robert Winters, "Evaluating the Effectiveness of Prison Farm Programs," Cor- rections.com, September 23, 2013, accessed July 18, 2017, http://www.corrections.com /news/article/33907-evaluating-the-effectiveness-of-prison-farm-programs.

26. "Georgia's Prison Farms," *Corrections Forum* 8, no. 4 (July/August 1999), https:// www.questia.com/magazine/1P3-44023228/georgia-s-prison-farms.

27. Reid H. Montgomery Jr., Gordon A. Crews, and William Crawley, *A History of Correctional Violence: An Examination of Reported Causes of Riots and Disturbances* (Washington, DC: American Correctional Association, 1998).

Anthony Ryan Hatch

28. Stephen Raher, "Paging Anti-Trust Lawyers: Prison Giants Prepare to Merge," *Prison Policy Initiative*, July 5, 2016, accessed July 14, 2017, http://www.prisonpolicy.org/blog/2016/07/05/commissary-merger/.

29. Naoki Kanaboshi, "Prison Inmates' Right to Hunger Strike," *Criminal Justice Review* 39, no. 2 (2014): 121–39.

30. See Ap Zaalberg, Henk Nijman, Erik Bulten, Luwe Stroosma, and Cees van der Staak, "Effects of Nutritional Supplements on Aggression, Rule-Breaking, and Psychopathology among Young Adult Prisoners," *Aggressive Behavior* 36, no. 2 (2010): 117–26; Stephen Schoenthaler, Stephen Amos, Walter Doraz, Mary-Ann Kelly, George Muedeking, and James Wakefield Jr., "The Effect of Randomized Vitamin-Mineral Supplementation on Violent and Non-Violent Antisocial Behavior among Incarcerated Juveniles," *Journal of Nutritional and Environmental Medicine* 7 (1997): 343–52; Gesch C. Bernard, Sean M. Hammond, Sarah E. Hampson, Anita Eves, and Martin J. Crowder, "Influence of Supplementary Vitamins, Minerals and Essential Fatty Acids on the Antisocial Behaviour of Young Adult Prisoners: A Randomised, Placebo-Controlled Trial," *British Journal of Psychiatry* 181 (2002): 22–28.

31. Alysia Santo and Lisa Iaboni. "What's in a Prison Meal?," The Marshall Project, July 7, 2015, accessed November 10, 2016, https://www.themarshallproject.org/2015/07/07/what-s-in-a-prison-meal?ref=collections#.oG4UiMzq9.

32. Christopher Zoukis and Rod L. Bower, "Aramark's Correctional Food Services: Meals, Maggots, and Misconduct," *Prison Legal News*, December 2, 2015, accessed March 10, 2017, https://www.prisonlegalnews.org/news/2015/dec/2/aramarks-correctional-food-services-meals-maggots-and-misconduct/.

33. State of Michigan, "Department of Corrections Testimony," accessed July 9, 2017, http://house.michigan.gov/hfa/PDF/Corrections/DOC_Subcmte_Testimony(DetroitMetroTimesArticle_3-3-16).pdf.

34. The American Correctional Association has produced nutritional recommendations for prisons since 1975, but the current recommendations are not made publicly available.

35. *Hutto v. Finney* 437 U.S. 678, 1978.

36. June Purvis, "Suffragette Hunger Strikes, 100 Years On," *The Guardian*, July 6, 2009, accessed March 10, 2017, https://www.theguardian.com/commentisfree/libertycentral/2009/jul/06/suffragette-hunger-strike-protest.

37. Stephen J. Scanlan, Laurie Cooper Stoll, and Kimberly Lumm, "Starving for Change: The Hunger Strike and Nonviolent Action, 1906–2004," in *Research in Social Movements, Conflicts and Change* Volume 28, edited by Patrick G. Coy, 275–323 (Bingley, UK: Emerald Group Publishing, 2008).

38. Banu Bargu, *Starve and Immolate: The Politics of Human Weapons* (New York: Columbia University Press, 2015).

39. Kamala Kelkar, "Prison Strike Organizers to Protest Food Giant Aramark," The PBS Newshour, January 8, 2017, accessed July 7, 2017, http://www.pbs.org/newshour/updates/prison-strike-protest-aramark/.

40. Connor Sheets, "I'm Not a Dog: Hunger Strikes inside Alabama Prisons, from Protests to Force Feeding," www.al.com, April 30, 2017, accessed on July 10, 2017, http://www.al.com/news/index.ssf/2017/04/im_not_a_dog_hunger_strikes_in.html.

41. Connor Sheets, "Incarcerated Alabama Prison Strike Leader Goes on Hunger Strike as Advocate Decries 'Human Torture.'" www.al.com, October 28, 2016, accessed July 10, 2017.

42. Stephen Katz, "What It's Like to Actually Eat the Food in Oakland County Jail," *Detroit Metro Times*, July 8, 2015, accessed November 10, 2016, https://www.metrotimes.com/detroit/what-its-like-to-actually-eat-the-food-in-oakland-county-jail/Content?oid=2354552.

43. Benjamin Jealous, "Troy Davis Will Refuse His Last Meal," posted September 20, 2011, accessed August 5, 2016, http://www.naacp.org/blog/entry/troy-davis-will-refuse-his-last-meal.

44. Rhonda Cook, "Davis' Last Day: A Goodbye to Family," *Atlanta Journal-Constitution*, September 21, 2011, accessed on August 5, 2016, http://www.ajc.com/news/news/local/davis-last-day-a-goodbye-to-family/nQL2s/.

4

Shadows of War, Traces of Policing

THE WEAPONIZATION OF

SPACE AND THE SENSIBLE

IN PREEMPTION

Andrea Miller

.....

On a muggy July night in Atlanta, a local organizer and I drove fifteen minutes northeast of the city to Stone Mountain Park, home to the infamous 1.57-acre Confederate carving of Jefferson Davis, Thomas "Stonewall" Jackson, and Robert E. Lee. As we found our way into the park's grassy amphitheater, we joined visitors gathered with lawn chairs and blankets and picnic baskets to watch the nightly lasershow. Noted for its racist Confederate imagery and kitschy musical montages, this summer's theme was "Lasershow Drone Wars: The Mountain Awakens." Despite living in the Southeast for more than ten years, I had never seen the Confederate monument in person before. Illuminated by lights from the ground below and a full moon, the carving looked both imposing and much smaller than I had imagined. The night was, in fact, structured around contradictions between what I experienced when I got to the park and what I had imagined and expected of Stone Mountain. A sacred site for the Muscogee peoples where histories of racial violence are inscribed onto the mountain itself, Stone Mountain is both the site of the Ku Klux Klan's 1915 rebirth and a present-day rallying point for white supremacist organizations. Not least of all of the night's contradictions was that while it was called "Lasershow Drone Wars: The Mountain Awakens," the lasershow featured not a single drone. In fact, the only reference to drones at all appeared implicitly during the title sequence of a brief segment that featured a confusing and poorly narrativized version of *Star Wars* projecting spacecraft at war across the mountain's Confederate carving. Grainy images of laser-shooting spaceships were bookended by visual appeals to post-9/11 nationalism, Dixie nostalgia, tributes to the victims of the recent Bastille Day attack in Nice, France, and the 1986 Space Shuttle *Challenger* disaster. My friend and I left confused: why reference drones at all?

Through its absence in the lasershow, the specter of the drone emerged that night through entanglements between the antebellum South and the U.S. Civil War, anxieties about Cold War–era technological failure and present-day terrorist threat, and what is often presented as the inaugural moment of the United States's ongoing war on terror, September 11, 2001. Taking up the material absence of the drone in the park's lasershow as a point of departure, I consider wide-scale unmanned aerial systems (UAS) development in Metro Atlanta as the backdrop to the use of predictive policing technologies in the city's historically black neighborhoods. Coupling these two forms of preemptive policing, where preemption signals actions in the present that work to contain and suppress perceived threats in an imagined future, I ask how we can interrogate preemption as not simply the modus operandi of imperialist expansion elsewhere but also as the racializing infrastructure for settler expansion within the geopolitical borders of the United States. For example, as Atlanta increasingly relies on technologies such as PredPol predictive policing software and expands its surveillance network of cameras and license plate readers throughout Atlanta's six policing zones, it is necessary to trace the connections and departures between these technologies and those that provide the digital infrastructure for drone policing in Iraq, Afghanistan, North-West Pakistan, Yemen, Somalia, and Syria.[1] This chapter, then, echoes the recent work of Tyler Wall, who locates drone policing alongside domestic police power and anti-Black violence in the United States.[2] Building on scholarship such as Wall's that calls into question the historical and contemporary distinctions between war power abroad and civil policing practices within the United States, I ask how we can begin to think about these practices of preemption along a spectrum of force distribution for the nation-state and those actors and institutions deputized in its service.[3] I ask how preemption articulated through predictive policing in Atlanta works to produce material and imagined zones of environmental carcerality for racialized and poor persons: fixing, tracking, and containing circuits of mobility and dwelling.

Drawing from fieldwork conducted in 2016–17, I begin to examine the spatiality of preemption in Atlanta and how this relates to preemptive policing in drone war abroad. In addition to the city's adoption of algorithmically driven policing technologies that imagine and reimagine the city's six polic-

Andrea Miller

ing zones, I consider an expansive definition of preemptive policing that can account for both everyday enactments of threat management and speculative finance that both produce and foreclose capacities for living and being. While I cannot fully address the financial valences of preemption in this chapter, they function as the shadow practices to the digital and not-only digital practices of preemption that emerge through predictive policing in Atlanta, where the built environment of the city itself is and has historically been weaponized to produce and delimit the possibility for life capacities to emerge and sustain themselves.[4] Situating these spatial practices of preemptive policing with and alongside each other, it becomes possible to understand policing as integral to the colonial project of nation-*building*, an ongoing and incomplete process of enclosure and expansion whose continuation is perpetually articulated through a language of counterinsurgency and threat prevention.

In order to trace the connections and divergences across registers of policing, from drone war to predictive policing in Atlanta, I begin by articulating a framework of police power as it emerges through histories of colonial war-making and nation-building. I argue that discourses of preemption work not only through imperialist constructions of racialized threat and otherness but also through racialized discourses and anti-Blackness for U.S. settler colonial power. Situating preemption in drone warfare as the backdrop to localized modes of preemption in Atlanta, I ask how these practices are historically and contemporarily refracted through predictive policing technologies and imaginaries of the built environment. Understanding the preemptive infrastructures of algorithmic, technohuman practices of policing and surveillance as never only digital and never only enacted within the auspices of the police proper, I interrogate the adoption of PredPol predictive policing software and the expansion of Atlanta's Operation Shield Video Integration Center (VIC) by the Atlanta Police Department. Finally, I return to Stone Mountain's lasershow by exploring the cultural production of the lasershow as a sense-making event of wartime. How can the drone's absence in the lasershow point us toward an alternate reading of policing in the present? Further, what forms of political possibility and scholarly praxis might open up if we think with rather than against the insensible?

POLICING AND PREEMPTION: A COLONIAL PROJECT

In this section, I situate drone policing and civil policing as preemptive practices within the colonial project of nation-building, a project for the United States that emerges through both settler-colonial and expansionist registers.

In this way, I take seriously Mark Neocleous's assertion that "we need an argument that works on and with the nexus of war power and police power," where the generation of the police to pacify civil disorder cannot be disentangled from its honing and application in militarized, colonial governance practices.[5] Tracing a genealogy of policing through circuits of counterinsurgency technologies both within and outside of the geopolitical borders of the United States, I ask about the partial connections across these terrains of policing.[6] Additionally, I argue that current articulations of preemption most often located as emerging from Cold War–era policies of prevention and deterrence must instead be traced through the *longue durée* of U.S. colonialism as the active form of policing the United States's multiple and shifting borders—territorial, racial, and perceptual. In this way, racialized and racializing technologies such as digital and biometric surveillance systems and predictive policing software do not signal an altogether new form of preemption. Rather, they supplement and rearticulate other historical and nondigital or not-only digital forms.[7]

Early iterations of the police in the United States include the slave patrols and night watches of the U.S. South and Northeast dating back to the early eighteenth century; the Texas Rangers established in 1835 in the Southwest; and anti-labor police formations in the late 1800s and early 1900s modeled after colonial occupation forces elsewhere. For example, the Pennsylvania State Police (PSP), the first of its kind when formed in 1905, was explicitly modeled on Britain's Royal Irish Constabulary (1836–1922) and Spain's Guardia Civil in the Philippines (1868–98). Known as the Black Hussars for their black uniforms, military-style cavalry units and training, and the terror they generated across the Pennsylvania countryside, the PSP were flanked by carefully culled military veterans.[8] A hybrid of military and civil policing practices in both formation and practice, the PSP became a model of state police formations first exported to the state of New York in 1917 and then, gradually, to other states around the United States. Here, and as policing practices by the state were supplemented by private security firms like the infamous Pinkerton and Baldwin-Felts agencies, we see circuits of technology, training, practices, and personnel that move into and out of the geopolitical borders of the United States. These historical circuits are currently mirrored through practices such as the U.S. 1033 Program, designed to redirect military surplus into the hands of domestic police forces and academic institutions, and through training exchange programs such as Atlanta's GILEE (Georgia International Law Enforcement Exchange), which sends Atlanta law enforcement

Andrea Miller

to Israel to train in counterterrorism practices in exchange for training Israeli law enforcement in drug war policing tactics.[9]

Further, it is necessary to trace the historical relationship between geographies of policing practices and the ways those practices explicitly seek to quell the perceived threat of ethnic and racial minorities. As the first PSP superintendent, John C. Groome, is quoted in Katherine Mayo's 1917 ode to the virtues of the Pennsylvania State Police, "One State Policeman should be able to handle one hundred foreigners."[10] Here, we see not only the historical enmeshment of military and civil policing practices but also how these practices are animated by discourses of racialized threat. The relationship between policing practices and racialized threat is also clearly elaborated in Major General Sir Charles Gwynn's writings on imperial policing. Serving in the British Army from 1890 to 1931 in India, North-West Pakistan, Iraq, Afghanistan, and Palestine, Gwynn wrote of military policing and small wars alongside British military contemporaries such as Colonel C. E. Calwell and George Nathaniel Curzon.[11] Gwynn defines civil and military policing through practices of "concentration and offensive action," where both emerge as extensions of imperial small wars. In what could be called an economy of force distribution, civil and military police are always already entangled in the pursuit to achieve a "unity of control" for the colonial state.[12] Gwynn's description of the relationship between civil and military policing is worth lingering on, where the two are imbricated through policing as practice and along a continuum of violence.

This concentration of force for Gwynn is not exercised against individual targets but is spatially distributed to envelop and overtake emerging concentrations of insurgency through collective and individual punishment, where what Gwynn refers to as the "hostile . . . citizens of Empire" are overcome by passion and emerge as a threat to order.[13] For Gwynn, distribution of force and violence must necessarily match and exceed concentrations of impassioned racialized insurgents that "become a danger to life and valuable property."[14] The passions that Gwynn describes in 1934 and that vitalized the early formations of policing units in the United States can be situated alongside discourses of affective, racialized threat animating contemporary state violence,[15] from the overwhelming lethal force and carceral displacement and warehousing of Black, brown, and Native persons in the United States to the use of drones against Muslim and Arab persons abroad.

Gwynn's theorization of policing also demonstrates in no uncertain terms that police power does not reside solely in the sphere of population control within the geopolitical borders of the state. Rather, policing as a set of practices animates state power to produce and maintain both territorial and infrastructural capacities across multiple registers. In this way, rather than thinking of policing as defined and limited by the borders that separate the state from its others, policing can be understood as that which instead iteratively and anxiously produces and works to maintain those borders.[16] Policing performs the territorial work of enclosure, producing multiscalar thresholds of interiority and exteriority that must be perpetually imagined and reimagined—from the level of the hyperlocal to the geospatial boundaries of the nation-state to those emergent territorial concerns that exceed the state's explicit borders.[17] It is thus vital to situate policing as practice alongside scholarship that calls into question the distinctions between war power and police power, as well as attendant relationships between war and peace, invisible and hypervisible forms of violence, and spatiotemporal constructions of distance and proximity.

In this regard, U.S. policing practices have historically emerged through entanglements of, and at times collisions between, settler-colonialism, expansionism, and capital. These adaptive practices involve managing national anxieties of disorder and dismemberment of the body politic from fictional withins *and* withouts. This shifting perceptual border is policed through the model of prevention, concentrating deployments of force in sites and against those persons and places identified as imbued with criminogenic potential, most often along lines of race and class. In this way, perhaps paradoxically, practices of preemptive policing and their technological infrastructures enforce fantasies of a coherent territorial whole through material practices of exclusion, containment, calculation, and killing across a spectrum of targets spanning the levels of individual, place, and population.[18]

If the police are the territorializing apparatus of state power that manages the state's infrastructural and productive capacity, the attendant work of policing is to manage, enact, and contain the emergence of life capacities. I draw from the work of Marisol de la Cadena, Simone Browne, Ruth Wilson Gilmore, and Sylvia Wynter to understand that policing not only works to manage culturally, economically, and historically produced lines of race, class, and ways of being in the world. Policing also works to engineer and produce the very conditions for their emergence and the terms of both recognition and nonrecognition.[19] Gilmore's definition of racism is instructive here, which she defines as the "state-sanctioned or extra-legal production and exploitation of group-differentiated vulnerability to premature death."

Andrea Miller

Gilmore identifies the nexus between property and population management as a capacity, and one that is necessarily racializing and racialized, where "the state's power to organize these various factors of production, or enable them to be disorganized or abandoned outright, is not a thing but rather a capacity."[20] Following Gilmore, we can understand police power as a broader entanglement of bureaucratic, territorializing, and force-distributing actors managing the interplay between the infrastructural capacity of the state and the life capacities of those enmeshed either directly or indirectly in its current or prospective territories. In this way, persons, places, and the built and ambient environment are constructed as integral to the development of infrastructural capacities through dynamic practices of inclusion and exclusion. These inclusions and exclusions, which are neither static nor fixed but rather mobile and adaptive practices, can include extractive inclusion (vis-à-vis labor, information, or resource expropriation), displacement or dispossession, modes of neglect and disinvestment, or exposure to violence and premature or slow death.

Further, the management of life potentials and capacities through policing practices points us toward policing as the register of preemptive practices for and by the state and its deputies. Here, preemptive practices emerge differentially though relatedly through the technologically and algorithmically driven language of innovation and precision. These practices aim to manage the future in the present, where preemption supplements and at times supplants the language of pacification, prevention, and peacekeeping in civil and military policing.[21] Within preemptive discourse, technological innovation provides a contemporary analog to other historical discourses of prevention and pacification. Practices such as the data mining and social media monitoring that animate Atlanta's Operation Shield Video Integration Center, the "disposition matrix" database used to identify terrorist suspects and targets, and algorithmic risk assessment used to determine creditworthiness are but a few examples. Through preemption's technological veneer, pacification and prevention take on what are presented as novel spatiotemporal characteristics whereby the state acts in the present based on its perceived ability to apprehend virtual, future risks.

Preemptive logic follows a line of reasoning whereby future catastrophe, imagined as imminent threat, is avoided through exercises of state violence in the present. Modeled and sterilized through its reliance on statistical analysis and myths of scientific precision, the large numbers of preemption's dead and injured, such as many of the nearly ten thousand people believed to have been killed in U.S. drones strikes in Afghanistan, Iraq, Pakistan, Somalia, Syria, and Yemen, are circumscribed to the margin of error called "collateral damage."[22] As I demonstrate elsewhere, preemption emerges through a dynamic relationship between discourses of scientific precision and a colonial imagination that must perpetually police the threshold whereby racialized future threat may cohere.[23] Tweaking slightly Brian Massumi's assertion that preemption demonstrates an "umbilical link into the prototerritory of emergence," preemption might instead be thought of as the enactment of emergent infrastructures aimed to maximize and expand colonial capacity.[24] As Louise Amoore adeptly points out, preemption does not simply seek to forestall potential futures. Rather, preemption seeks to territorialize those futures by delimiting the possibilities for their emergence.[25] While preemption involves the production and management of future threat, that threat must also be understood as a site of colonial opportunity and innovation—perhaps most perversely though accurately described by the military term *target of opportunity*.[26]

As it is enacted in the present, preemption's material practices include legal sanction and detention, the exercise of force to enact bodily harm and even death, and acts of dispossession and displacement (whether through foreclosure and eviction, land theft, or the forced relocations of war). As practices that circle various spatial, temporal, and discursive registers, it is necessary to interrogate forms of preemption that may not at once appear to be related, even as they rely on similar technological and discursive infrastructures. For example, the ability to use license plate readers (LPRs) to construct a pattern of mobility for vehicles and drivers on Atlanta roadways cannot be disentangled from pattern-of-life analyses used to identify and track potential drone strike targets. Grégoire Chamayou refers to these practices as the abstraction of individuals into "indivisible chronospatial units." Through the geospatial tracking of individuals' patterns of movement, "regular routes progressively thicken on the screen, like paths frequently taken by a flock dig their furrows in the grass of a field." Within this highly paranoid chrono-geography that characterizes preemptive technologies from the U.S. military to the Atlanta Police Department (APD), aberrations in movements and patterns can only be rearticulated as evidence of threat.[27] In both APD's use of LPRs and pattern-of-life analysis in drone warfare, then, the signatures of persons as chronospatial units identify those persons as different iterations of the target of opportunity.

Andrea Miller

Understanding that policing practices historically and contemporarily emerge through local and transnational circuits of infrastructure, training, protocols, and personnel, it becomes possible to ask about the connections between unmanned aerial systems development in the Atlanta Metro region and localized forms of surveillance and policing that rely on similarly preemptive logics and technologies. Further, the absence of the drone in the Stone Mountain lasershow must be interrogated through and alongside an absence of the U.S. South in discussions of contemporary U.S. militarization more broadly, particularly when it comes to the highly coveted technologies operationalized in U.S. drone policing in the war on terror. Having spent much of my life living and thinking in the U.S. South, this absence has appeared as a thick and sinewy one of unspoken notions of regional and national belonging and nonbelonging, deeply sensed even in those moments when it is most stridently dismissed. This absence doggedly persists despite the fact that Atlanta is a major site in the development of military systems technology in a state currently ranked seventh in defense spending, where leading defense and aerospace companies in the state include Lockheed Martin, General Dynamics, and Northrop Grumman. The Georgia Tech Applied Research Corporation (GTARC)—the business face of the Georgia Tech Research Institute (GTRI) of the Georgia Institute of Technology—ranks second only to Lockheed Martin in the state for defense contracts. Most recently valued at receiving $288.4 million in contracts, GTARC outranks both General Dynamics ($151.4 million) and Northrop Grumman ($103.9 million) as a defense contractor in the state.[28]

Among the most recent projects boasted by GTARC and GTRI has been the development of fully autonomous collaborative military swarm systems. In what GTRI described as "what may have been the first aerial encounter of its kind," GTRI swarms participated in an aerial dogfight with a Naval Postgraduate School swarm at Camp Roberts in California in February 2017.[29] Even as it is important not to understate the extent to which drones often provide tactical support for other forms of aerial technologies and ground troops rather than functioning completely autonomously as popular mainstream accounts often present them,[30] it is significant here that economies of knowledge production within Atlanta are directly engaged in engineering innovative technologies that animate a drone imaginary of future war.[31]

Within the imagined future of drone war, fully autonomous weaponry fulfills an imperial fantasy of perfectly asymmetrical warfare, whereby the perceived risk of racialized threat and otherness is managed and contained through fully technologized means.[32]

This fantasy is perhaps most fully elucidated by Georgia Tech roboticist Ronald Arkin, who has endeavored to create fully autonomous weapons capable of making ethical targeting decisions based on international laws of war.[33] In Arkin's case, desires animated by notions of technological precision and legal justice converge in an imperial fantasy of the future where reliable algorithms replace the wavering capacities of human decision making and error.[34] This fantasy of the future also underwrites contemporary preemptive governance in the war on terror. Within this articulation of preemption, algorithmically driven futures provide a speculative basis of innovation and scientific testing through which myriad forms of technologized killing and harm can be justified in the present. By this logic, the development of unmanned systems in Atlanta used to distribute lethal force across racialized populations in Afghanistan, Iraq, Pakistan, Somalia, Syria, and Yemen does not simply operationalize harm through a logic of collateral damage in present warfare but also through a logic of collateral damage that is necessary to feed a speculative military economy.[35]

In addition to the work being undertaken by GTRI and other Georgia Tech faculty like Arkin, algorithmically driven technologies in the Atlanta Metro region are not solely located within the sphere of military and defense spending. Atlanta-area police have historically used the city as a laboratory for the development and testing of new policing technologies, including PredPol predictive policing software, surveillance drones, and social media monitoring.[36] PredPol predictive policing software, adopted by APD in 2013, is marketed as predicting the "what, where, and when — not who" of crime.[37] One of several predictive policing technologies used by law enforcement across the United States, PredPol is an algorithmically driven technology that uses past crime data to predict locations of future crime. Generating five-hundred-by-five-hundred-foot "hotspot" boxes identifying where crimes are most likely to occur, PredPol offers a mode of policing that presents itself as a mathematically precise, unbiased, and efficient way to allocate resource dispositions. Significantly, the deployment of PredPol software offers two corollaries with those technologies used in drone policing abroad: First, PredPol utilizes predictive analytics to purportedly generate locations of imminent future threat. As with preemptive strikes in drone war, these predictive capacities are fueled through discourses of risk management that seek to contain racialized threat. Second, the implementation of PredPol follows a discursive logic of the war on terror whereby the language of technological precision and innovation is used to mask the force of state violence and its historical trajectories.

Take, for example, this description of PredPol software's efficacy by former APD police chief George Turner during the system's ninety-day implementation period:

> Using real-time data piped in from Atlanta's records management system, PredPol's methodology uses high-powered mathematics to calculate probabilities of where and when crime will occur today. . . . What matters most is that the mathematics allow police to not only characterize past crime, but also use past crime to forecast with great accuracy the locations where crime will occur in the immediate future. . . . The mathematics also allow Atlanta police to forecast crime at a very fine scale while constantly adapting to crime patterns as they change from day to day. PredPol predictions identify 500 × 500 foot boxes that are at the greatest risk of crime in the coming shift.[38]

Here, Turner gestures to the software's precision and how a reliance on mathematics and big data is believed to offer an innovative and scientifically driven approach to the spatial policing of risk. Turner also points toward the role of scale in data-driven policing practices, where large volumes of data can be spatially translated into a "very fine scale" at a local level. PredPol policing software is used in concert with other digital policing technologies, such as those operationalized at APD's Operation Shield Video Integration Center (VIC), where more than 7,500 video cameras and license plate readers work to provide real-time video feeds of Atlanta's six policing zones. Through the integration of these technologies, the built environment of Atlanta is fragmented into spaces of differentially distributed risk.

While the scale and application of force between drone policing and predictive policing cannot be conflated, they both emerge through circuits of civil and military policing enmeshed through shared technologies, protocols, personnel, and goals. First, the integration of digital technologies to predict locations of imminent threat without explicit concerns with the identity of suspects mirrors the logic of drone policing and "signature strikes" in the war on terror. While the dominant discourse espoused by military and government officials cites the precision of drone policing as one of its greatest assets—drastically reducing civilian casualties—the material practices of drone war reveal a population-centric mode of waging war that inflicts forms of environmental terror in addition to more punctuated exercises of lethal force.[39] Importantly, these modes of distributing harm emerge through environmental logics whereby space and place are themselves rendered criminogenic — so saturated with racialized threat that persons within those spaces cannot be otherwise than suspect.[40] The attribution of threat sufficient to warrant targeting based on bodily movement, the heat signatures of metal objects, and signals intelligence (SIGINT) and social media intelligence (SOCMINT) that comb through social media, cellular data, and digital correspondences is amplified for those bodies located within criminogenic spaces and regions.[41]

It is this same criminogenic environmental logic that emerges through predictive policing practices in Atlanta, which combine the use of software like PredPol with technologies such as social media monitoring, real-time camera feeds, and license plate readers. Here, military intelligence-gathering practices that are imagined as being used only in distant locations abroad provide the technological infrastructure for racialized policing practices throughout Atlanta. In the same article mentioned above, former chief Turner describes that Atlanta's Zone 4 was one of two police zones where PredPol was originally tested in the city. Zone 4 encompasses an area of twenty-one square miles of southwest Atlanta, an area of historically Black neighborhoods that were some of the hardest hit during the foreclosure crisis from 2008 to 2011.[42] Further, Zone 4 is popularly presented as a persistent problem area for the APD and local residents.[43] It is not without note, then, that Zone 4 was one of the first chosen as a test site for APD's use of PredPol software. First, the rollout of PredPol in this area of the city demonstrates the consonance between technologized policing of risk in both military and civil policing. Further, it also usefully demonstrates how these technologized practices supplement historical geographies of racialized threat rather than imagine them anew.

Zone 4 includes an area of the city where the built environment has historically been endowed with threat potential and weaponized to police the mobility and presence of Black Atlantans. As Kevin Kruse describes in his history of white flight from the city, the Peyton Forest neighborhood, located in what is currently police Zone 4, became a battleground of racial politics in the city in 1962 when city construction workers erected barricades across Peyton and Harlan Roads, known as the Peyton Wall. According to Kruse, "As all Atlantans understood, the roadblocks stood at the precise fault line between black and white sections of the city."[44] Paraphrasing Barbara Ryckley, an officer of the Southwest Citizens community organization, Kruse describes that white residents of Peyton Forest imagined themselves as besieged by the threat of Blackness: "not just Peyton Forest but all of white Atlanta was 'endangered' by black expansion."[45] Kruse goes on to describe how the purchase of three homes on nearby Lynhurst Drive by Black residents was viewed as a "flank attack" on white neighborhoods. Before the Atlanta courts ruled against the barricades, they were torn down twice, set afire once, and then rebuilt by the city under the watch of Klansmen patrolling the streets.[46]

This episode in the spatial history of Zone 4 usefully points toward forms of policing that both delimit circuits of racialized mobility and property acquisition and perceive racialized threat as an environmental phenomenon against which war must be waged. While it exceeds the aims of this chapter, the relationship between this weaponization of the built environment in Atlanta warrants further inquiry to draw out connections between current speculative urban development practices and the use of predictive policing to manage urban space. How do the forms of place-making and territory operationalized through predictive policing practices create and foreclose capacities for living, here the possibilities for Black life and property? Moreover, how do discourses of racialized threat as requisite of policing work to both consolidate and conceal white property-holding as the basis of the colonial and imperial state? Here, localized discourses of threat are both assuaged by and operationalized through bureaucratic practices that manage the holdings of the state in its nation-building project.

This episode also draws our attention toward the circuits of policing whereby preemptive measures are operationalized not only by the state but also by deputized groups such as the KKK and the broader citizenry, particularly through militarized language and logics to contain what is perceived to be creeping racialized threat. Racialized threat in both the Peyton Wall incident and in contemporary practices aimed at policing Zone 4 is not unlike the insurgent passions described by Gwynn in British imperial policing or those forms of threat ascribed to Muslim and Arab bodies imbued with terrorist potential and targeted by drone policing. As I argue elsewhere, these logics of imminent threat disarticulate risk from the individual subject and, instead, render threat atmospheric and diffuse, capable of saturating environments.[47] Further, the historical spatial policing of Atlanta's Zone 4 demonstrates that contemporary preemption cannot be situated as an explicitly and only digital phenomenon. Rather, digital technologies used to police and produce space emerge through historical confluences of place, racialized threat, and the weaponization of the built environment. In this way, rather than affirming discourses of the militarization of police that have predominated media discussions post-Ferguson in the United States, it is useful instead to ask about the historical consonances between military and civil policing and preemption and how these practices produce particular environments as criminogenic sites to be contained.

CONCLUSION

I conclude this chapter by returning to the Stone Mountain lasershow to consider the drone's absence despite its appearance in the event's name, "Lasershow Drone Wars: The Mountain Awakens." How should we consider the explicit absence of the drone amid a region in which unmanned systems development is a major area of defense spending and where drone war technologies are rearticulated to aid in policing racialized threat locally? I want to suggest that the lasershow emerges as a sense-*making* event of "wartime," an event that obscures even as it produces understandings of state and capitalist technics of preemption and colonial power. The event of the lasershow displaces practices of violence, dispossession, policing, and surveillance backward into a memorialized past or into a future saturated with racialized threat.[48] As a sense-making event, the lasershow utilizes digital technology to remotely display imagery across and to interact with the mountain, even at times appearing to rearrange its rock carving like a jigsaw puzzle—a dynamic montage of a national, and even Euro-American, history of war, violence, and trauma narratives distributed across and in spite of time and space (see figure 4.1). The shadow of the drone that is cast but never materializes in the lasershow is instructive as an analytical framework through which to think about colonial projects of remote sensing. As one of the material practices of preemptive policing in both its military and civil iterations, remote sensing—sensing at a distance—has elsewhere been described as the form of sensing that characterizes modernity itself.[49]

In her work on remote sense-making and the emergence of panoramic paintings, Caren Kaplan notes that the term *sense-making* cannot be disentangled from its purchase as a contemporary military term, "incorporating the commander's understanding of a situation, with the primacy of geographical information as a given, as a technique of decision-making."[50] However, as Kaplan notes of eighteenth-century panoramas, sense-making takes on additional valences of the sensory that exceed visual and military registers. Panoramic paintings not only worked to make sense of war through

Andrea Miller

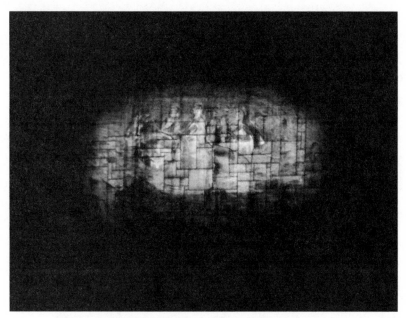

FIGURE 4.1. Stone Mountain lasershow, July 2016.
Photograph by Andrea Miller.

visual mastery and line of sight but, also, instructed spectators *how* to sense war. "Immersion in the panoramic scene induced dizziness, confusion, and fright as well as joy and wonder, generating new sights and sensibilities while foreclosing others. . . . the new format produced far more ways of seeing and sensing than the reinscription of a masterful gaze from above."[51] In this context, the contemporary panorama of the lasershow engages in a similar practice of remote sense-making for the spectator. Fireworks, beams of colors and light, and flames shooting up from the base of the mountain extend beyond the borders of the mountain's visible surface to envelop the viewing space and immerse spectators in "Mountain Vision," as it is called at the park. Following Kaplan's theorization of sense-making and wartime, the lasershow's gesture to the drone, through its absence, might indicate a particular sensorial aporia related to drone policing and its material and practical infrastructures. The lasershow seems to instruct its viewer to simultaneously understand the drone as an insensible object in the present while imagining the work of the drone as a floating signifier that can encapsulate a variety of past and future practices of war-making. Here, through fantastical projections of wartimes past and future—from the Civil War to Vietnam and the U.S. war on

FIGURE 4.2. Stone Mountain lasershow, July 2016.
Photograph by Andrea Miller.

terror to the space war of science fiction—diffuse histories and geographies
of war are folded into the sign of the drone (see figure 4.2). Additionally, these
histories and futures are collapsed into a present that simultaneously highlights and occludes contemporary practices of drone policing and preemption as well as territorial registers of colonial dispossession and violence. The
mountain's historical legacies as a site of capitalist extraction, which neces-
sitated the dispossession of the Muscogee people who held Stone Mountain
sacred, are anxiously erased through a perpetual process of *terra nullius*
during the lasershow. Night after night each summer, the mountain is iteratively dispossessed of its own histories and transformed into a tableau for
colonial mythologies of discovery, property, and nation-building. The lasershow, then, works to render multiple and entangled histories and speculative
economies of military and civil policing insensible for the spectator. While
suturing together events and affects of wartime that span the American Civil
War to an embattled present saturated by terrorist threat, this "imaginative
geography" of the lasershow instructs its spectators how to perceive, or not
perceive as it were, the connections between drone policing in the U.S. war
on terror and spatial policing practices that are imagining and reimagining

Andrea Miller

streets and neighborhoods throughout the Metro Atlanta region.[52] Perhaps also, though, this imaginative geography can offer an alternative entry point into thinking with, through, and against histories of policing, where that which must be anxiously repeated also points to instabilities and fissures in the colonial project of nation-building.

What other temporal and spatial possibilities and ways of being might the lasershow's imaginative geographies work to conceal, submerge, or render insensible? To close, I want to begin to ask: How might we read the lasershow otherwise? How might thinking with the insensible point us toward forms of politics that exceed, even as they hold space for, a politics of recognition? Drawing from Rancière's "partition of the perceptible," Marisol de la Cadena describes that *"r*ecognition is an offer for inclusion that—not surprisingly—can transpire only in the terms of state cognition."[53] In de la Cadena's ethnographic work on Runakuna practices, recognition, an instruction on the sensible, is never a complete or totalizing process. Rather, recognition and the production of the sensible are processes of translation that are necessarily attended by excess. These ways of doing, being, and knowing that exceed representational capture nevertheless transform those political beings with which they interact.[54] So if, as Rancière tells us, policing is the work of delimiting the sensible, we must ask how we might begin to think with the insensible, even if partially. To think with the insensible is not to discount explicit and more easily recognizable forms of insurgency, such as an April 2016 counterprotest at a KKK and white supremacist rally at Stone Mountain, where hundreds of demonstrators clashed with police and shut down access to the park by paying the fifteen-dollar parking fee in pennies. Rather, it is to inquire into a more expansive politics, one that can also account for what Simone Browne describes as "dark sousveillance," a Black epistemology of countersurveillance that works on and through the unseen, the invisible, and at the limits of the sensible.[55] Maybe it is in thinking *with* rather than against the insensible that we can begin to inquire not simply into other futures but also into other, perhaps less recognizable or altogether unrecognizable, presents, politics, and historical archives.[56]

Notes

1. Nefertiti Jaquez, "Atlanta Police's High-Tech Cameras Helping Catch Criminals," WSBTV, February 24, 2017, http://www.wsbtv.com/news/local/atlanta/atlanta-polices-high-tech-cameras-helping-catch-criminals/494039551.

2. Tyler Wall, "Ordinary Emergency: Drones, Police, and Geographies of Legal Terror," *Antipode* 48, no. 4 (September 2016): 1124.

3. Wall, "Ordinary Emergency"; Mark Neocleous, *War Power, Police Power* (Edinburgh: Edinburgh University Press, 2014); Mark Neocleous, "Air Power as Police Power," *Environment and Planning D: Society and Space* 31, no. 4 (2013): 578–93; Mark Neocleous, George Rigakos, and Tyler Wall, "On Pacification: Introduction to the Special Issue," *Socialist Studies/Études socialistes* 9, no. 2 (winter 2013): 1–6; Madiha Tahir, "The Containment Zone," in *Life in the Age of Drone Warfare*, ed. Lisa Parks and Caren Kaplan, 220–40 (Durham, NC: Duke University Press, 2017); Madiha Tahir, "The Ground Was Always in Play," *Public Culture* 29, no. 1 (2017): 5–16; Priya Satia, "The Defense of Inhumanity: Air Control and the British Idea of Arabia," *American Historical Review* 111, no. 1 (2006): 16–51.

4. For a discussion of the relationship between racialization and finance, see Zenia Kish and Justin Leroy, "Bonded Life: Technologies of Racial Finance from Slave Insurance to Philanthrocapital," *Cultural Studies* 29, no. 5–6 (2015): 630–51.

5. Neocleous, "Air Power as Police Power," 587. See also Neocleous, *War Power, Police Power*.

6. Marilyn Strathern, *Partial Connections* (Walnut Creek, CA: AltaMira, 2005); Marisol de la Cadena, *Earth Beings: Ecologies of Practice Across Andean Worlds* (Durham, NC: Duke University Press, 2015), 31–34.

7. Thinking through the digital, nondigital, and not-only digital forms preemptive policing and surveillance may take, I am indebted to the work of Simone Browne in *Dark Matter: On the Surveillance of Blackness*. In particular, I draw from Browne's discussion of "racializing surveillance" and "critical biometric consciousness." Following Browne and her discussion of those forms of branding and illumination Black bodies have been historically subject to, it is necessary to consider forms of biometric surveillance and policing that are all too often eclipsed through conversations of contemporary surveillance that can only account for their digital iterations. Simone Browne, *Dark Matters: On the Surveillance of Blackness* (Durham, NC: Duke University Press, 2015), 16, 118. Additionally, in describing the not-only digital, I take up the phrase "not only" in the spirit of Marisol de la Cadena, where "not only" describes those practices of being, doing, and knowing that exceed categorization in translational processes between worlds. Marisol de la Cadena, *Earth Beings*, 15, 275–76; see also Marisol de la Cadena, "Runa: Human but *Not Only*," HAU: *Journal of Ethnographic Theory* 4, no. 2 (2014): 253–59. For an extended discussion of the not only digital, see Andrea Miller, "Protocological Violence and the Colonial Database," *Antipode*, May 19, 2017, https://radicalantipode.files.wordpress.com/2017/05/6-andrea-miller.pdf.

8. Katherine Mayo, *Justice to All: The Story of the Pennsylvania State Police* (New York: G. P. Putnam's Sons, 1917), 14–23.

9. See Glenn Greenwald, "The Militarization of the U.S. Police: Finally Dragged into the Light by the Horrors of Ferguson," *The Intercept*, August 14, 2014, https://theintercept.com/2014/08/14/militarization-u-s-police-dragged-light-horrors-ferguson/; Jordain Carney, "Paul: Police Should Give Back Military Gear," *The Hill*, May 27, 2015, http://thehill.com/blogs/floor-action/senate/243203-rand-paul-police

Andrea Miller

-should-be-forced-to-give-back-military-gear; Dan Bauman, "Campus Police Acquire Military Weapons," *New York Times*, September 21, 2014, https://www.nytimes.com /2014/09/22/world/americas/campus-police-acquire-military-weapons.html; Rania Khalek, "Atlanta Mayor Rejects Demand to End Israel Police Training," *Electronic Intifada*, July 21, 2016, https://electronicintifada.net/blogs/rania-khalek/atlanta-mayor -rejects-demand-end-israel-police-training.

10. Mayo, *Justice for All*, 24–25.

11. For contemporary and historical analyses of small wars and their pursuant military practices, see the *Small Wars Journal*, run by the Small Wars Foundation.

12. Charles W. Gwynn, *Imperial Policing* (London: Macmillan, 1934), 16, 20–21. For an extended conversation about Gwynn in North-West Pakistan, see Tahir, "The Containment Zone," 220–40.

13. Gwynn, *Imperial Policing*, 14, 23.

14. Gwynn, *Imperial Policing*, 27.

15. See Andrea Miller, "(Im)Material Terror: Incitement to Violence Discourse as Racializing Technology in the War on Terror," in *Life in the Age of Drone Warfare*, ed. Lisa Parks and Caren Kaplan, 112–33 (Durham, NC: Duke University Press, 2017).

16. Ngai discusses how the U.S. Border Patrol in particular worked to produce notions of the Mexico-U.S. border following the Immigration Act of 1924. See Mai M. Ngai, "The Strange Case of the Illegal Alien: Immigration Restriction and Deportation Policy in the United States, 1921–1965," *Law and History Review* 21, no. 1 (spring 2003): 71–72, 81–89. See also Amy Kaplan, *The Anarchy of Empire in the Making of U.S. Culture* (Cambridge, MA: Harvard University Press, 2002).

17. For a discussion of the development of early policing during the period of Enclosure in England, see Neocleous, Rigakos, and Wall, "On Pacification," 2. See also Neocleous, *War Power, Police Power.*

18. On the spatiality of policing practices, see Steve Herbert, *Policing Space: Territoriality and the Los Angeles Police Department* (Minneapolis: University of Minnesota Press, 1997). See also Michel Foucault, *Security, Territory, Population: Lectures at the Collège de France, 1977–1978*, edited by Michel Senellart (New York: Picador, 2007).

19. Ruth Wilson Gilmore, *Golden Gulag: Prisons, Surplus, Crisis, and Opposition in Globalizing California* (Berkeley: University of California Press, 2007); De la Cadena, *Earth Beings*; De la Cadena, "Runa"; Sylvia Wynter, "Unsettling the Coloniality of Being/Power/ Truth/Freedom: Towards the Human, After Man, Its Overrepresentation—An Argument," CR: *The New Centennial Review* 3, no. 3 (2003): 257–337; Browne, *Dark Matters.* Here, I also draw from Rancière's definition of policing as those practices that "define the configuration of the perceptible." Jacques Rancière, *Disagreement: Politics and Philosophy*, translated by Julie Rose (Minneapolis: University of Minnesota Press, 2004), 29.

20. Gilmore, *Golden Gulag*, 28.

21. See Tyler Wall, "Unmanning the Police Manhunt: Vertical Security As Pacification," *Socialist Studies/Études socialistes* 9, no. 2 (2013): 32–56; Louise Amoore, *The Politics of Possibility: Risk and Security Beyond Probability* (Durham, NC: Duke University Press,

2013); Neocleous, *War Power, Police Power*, 1–36; Neocleous, Rigakos, and Wall, "On Pacification."

22. See "Drone Wars: The Full Data," Bureau of Investigative Journalism, 2017, https://www.thebureauinvestigates.com/stories/2017-01-01/drone-wars-the-full-data. Significantly, these figures do not account for U.S. strikes in Syria, nor do they account for those killed in air strikes for which drones provide tactical air support.

23. Miller, "(Im)Material Terror." See also Louise Amoore, "Security and the Incalculable," *Security Dialogue* 45, no. 5 (2014): 423–39; Amoore, *The Politics of Possibility*; Brian Massumi, *Ontopower: War, Powers, and the State of Perception* (Durham, NC: Duke University Press, 2015).

24. Massumi, *Ontopower*, 57.

25. Amoore, *The Politics of Possibility*, 153.

26. Chairman of the Joint Chiefs of Staff, *DoD Dictionary of Military and Associated Terms*, Department of Defense, July 2017, http://www.dtic.mil/doctrine/dod_dictionary /. See also Louise Amoore, "Algorithmic War: Everyday Geographies of the War on Terror," *Antipode* 41, no. 1 (January 2009): 58–59, 61; Samuel Weber, *Targets of Opportunity: On the Militarization of Thinking* (New York: Fordham University Press, 2005).

27. Grégoire Chamayou, "Patterns of Life: A Very Short History of Schematic Bodies by Grégoire Chamayou," *The Funambulist: Bodies, Designs and Politics*, December 14, 2014, http://thefunambulist.net/2014/12/04/the-funambulist-papers-57-schematic -bodies-notes-on-a-patterns-genealogy-by-gregoire-chamayou/; Cyrus Farivar, "We Know Where You've Been: Ars Acquires 4.6M License Plate Scans from the Cops," *Ars Technica*, March 24, 2015, https://arstechnica.com/tech-policy/2015/03/we-know-where -youve-been-ars-acquires-4-6m-license-plate-scans-from-the-cops/. For a discussion of how these forms of geospatial tracking impact borders and how they intersect with commercial uses of RFIDs, see (respectively), Amoore, *The Politics of Possibility*, 79–104; Amoore, "Algorithmic War," 58–59.

28. Office of Economic Adjustment, "Defense Spending by State Fiscal Year 2015," U.S. Department of Defense, 19.

29. John Toon, "Case Study: Swarms of Autonomous Aerial Vehicles Test New Dogfighting Skills," Georgia Tech Research Institute, April 21, 2017, http://www.news .gatech.edu/2017/04/21/swarms-autonomous-aerial-vehicles-test-new-dogfighting -skills.

30. Derek Gregory, "Drone Geographies," *Radical Philosophy* 183 (January/February 2014): 9–10. In articulating the zeitgeist of contemporary drone technologies, Caren Kaplan refers to this as the "drone-o-rama." See Caren Kaplan, "Drone-o-Rama," in *Life in the Age of Drone Warfare*, ed. Lisa Parks and Caren Kaplan, 161–77 (Durham, NC: Duke University Press, 2017).

31. The drone imaginary of future warfare and policing echoes what Shaw and Akhter refer to as the "dronification of state violence," where drone technologies in warfare are increasingly being redirected to produce urban spaces in the Global North. While Shaw identifies this as an inevitable future, in this chapter, dronification in a

Andrea Miller

total sense functions as an imperial desire in an imaginary future of autonomous warfare. See Ian Shaw, "The Urbanization of Drone Warfare: Policing Surplus Populations in the Dronepolis," *Geographica Helvetica* 71 (2016): 19–28. See also Ian Shaw and Majed Akhter, "The Dronification of State Violence," *Critical Asian Studies* 46, no. 2 (2014): 211–34; Ian Shaw, *Predator Empire* (Minneapolis: University of Minnesota Press, 2016).

32. Inderpal Grewal, "Drone Imaginaries: The Technopolitics of Visuality in Postcolony and Empire," in *Life in the Age of Drone Warfare*, ed. Lisa Parks and Caren Kaplan, 343–65 (Durham, NC: Duke University Press, 2017).

33. Ronald Arkin, *Governing Lethal Behavior in Autonomous Robots* (Boca Raton, FL: Chapman and Hall, 2009). For an extended discussion of Arkin, see Grégoire Chamayou, *A Theory of the Drone*, trans. Janet Lloyd (New York: New Press, 2015), 207–9.

34. See Jeremy Packer and Joshua Reeves, "Taking People Out: Drones, Media/ Weapons, and the Coming Humanectomy," in *Life in the Age of Drone Warfare*, ed. Lisa Parks and Caren Kaplan, 261–81 (Durham, NC: Duke University Press, 2017); Jeremy Packer and Joshua Reeves, "Romancing the Drone: Military Desire and Anthropophobia from SAGE to Swarm," *Canadian Journal of Communication* 38 (2013): 309–31.

35. For an extended discussion of collateral damage, the uses of medical metaphors such as surgical strikes in the U.S. war on terror, and practices of military speculation, see Jennifer Terry, *Attachments to War: Biomedical Logics and Violence in Twenty-First-Century America* (Durham, NC: Duke University Press, 2017), 35, 50–51. See also Melinda Cooper, *Life as Surplus: Biotechnology and Capitalism in the Neoliberal Era* (Seattle: University of Washington Press, 2008), 74–100.

36. See Electronic Frontier Foundation, "Georgia Tech Police Department Drone Records," https://www.eff.org/document/georgia-tech-police-dept; Jaquez, "Atlanta Police's High-Tech Cameras Helping Catch Criminals"; Nathalie Pozo, "Veterans Help Put More Atlanta Police Officers on the Street," Fox5Atlanta, June 30, 2017, http://www.fox5atlanta.com/news/265040835-story.

37. "About PredPol," PredPol, 2015, http://www.predpol.com/about/.

38. George Turner, Jeff Brantingham, and George Mohler, "Technology Talk: Predictive Policing in Action in Atlanta, Georgia," *Police Chief Magazine*, 2014, http://www.policechiefmagazine.org/predictive-policing-in-action-in-atlanta-georgia/.

39. See Tahir, "The Containment Zone"; Nasser Hussain, "The Sound of Terror: A Phenomenology of a Drone Strike," *Boston Review*, October 16, 2013, https://bostonreview.net/world/hussain-drone-phenomenology.

40. Lisa Marie Cacho, *Social Death: Racialized Rightlessness and the Criminalization of the Unprotected* (New York: NYU Press, 2012), 72–76. See also Keith Feldman, "Empire's Verticality: The Af/Pak Frontier, Visual Culture, and Racialization from Above," *Comparative American Studies* 9, no. 4 (2011): 325–41; Mimi Thi Nguyen, "The Hoodie as Sign, Screen, Expectation, and Force," *Signs: Journal of Women in Culture and Society* 40, no. 4 (summer 2015): 791–816. For a historical overview of how forms of air policing have relied on identifying criminogenic potential through place, see Priya Satia, "The

Defense of Inhumanity: Air Control and the British Idea of Arabia," *American Historical Review* 111, no. 1 (2006): 16–51; Neocleous, "Air Power as Police Power."

41. Jutta Weber, "Keep Adding: On Kill Lists, Drone Warfare and the Politics of Databases," *Environment and Planning D: Society and Space* 34, no. 1 (2016): 111–12.

42. Dan Immergluck and Jonathan Law, "Speculating in Crisis: The Intrametropolitan Geography of Investing in Foreclosed Homes in Atlanta," *Urban Geography* 35, no. 1 (2014): 1–5.

43. For current APD internal data, see "Crime Data Downloads," Atlanta Police Department, last modified 2017, http://www.atlantapd.org/i-want-to/crime-data -downloads. See also Brittany Miller, "Atlanta Neighbors Fed Up with Crime in Zone 4," CBS46.com, October 25, 2016, http://www.cbs46.com/story/33043327/neighbors-fed-up -with-crime-in-zone-4#ixzz4m4rKJIbL.

44. Kevin M. Kruse, *White Flight: Atlanta and the Making of Modern Conservatism* (Princeton, NJ: Princeton University Press, 2007), 3.

45. Kruse, *White Flight*, 4.

46. Kruse, *White Flight*, 4–5.

47. Miller, "(Im)Material Terror."

48. Mary Favret, *War at a Distance: Romanticism and the Making of Modern Wartime* (Princeton, NJ: Princeton University Press, 2010), 18.

49. See Caren Kaplan, *Aerial Aftermaths: Wartime from Above* (Durham, NC: Duke University Press, 2017), 21–22, 35–37, 55–57, 94–97; Derek McCormack, "Remotely Sensing Affective Afterlives: The Spectral Geographies of Material Remains," *Annals of the Association of American Geographers* 100, no. 3 (July 2010): 640–54. See also the discussion of wartime in Favret, *War at a Distance*.

50. Kaplan, *Aerial Aftermaths*, 36–37.

51. Kaplan, *Aerial Aftermaths*, 105.

52. Derek Gregory, *The Colonial Present: Afghanistan, Palestine, Iraq* (Malden, MA: Blackwell, 2004), 18–19.

53. De la Cadena, *Earth Beings*, 277, emphasis in original. See also Rancière, *Disagreement*.

54. De la Cadena, *Earth Beings*, 14–15.

55. Browne, *Dark Matters*, 21–24, 68, 162–64.

56. See also de la Cadena on the "eventfulness of the ahistorical." De la Cadena, *Earth Beings*, 135–36, 145–48.

5

This Is Not *Minority Report*

PREDICTIVE POLICING

AND POPULATION RACISM

R. Joshua Scannell

.....

"I'm tired. I'm tired of the future." —Agatha, from *Minority Report* (2002)

In November 2015, writer and antiracist activist Shaun King penned a widely circulated op-ed in the *New York Daily News* titled "Predictive Policing Is 'Technological Racism.'" In it, King raises a version of what data scientists call the "garbage in, garbage out" problem. In so many words: Any automated system will only ever be as good as the data it is based on. The racist history of American policing means that any predictive system's data are garbage. Therefore, predictive policing programs will be racist garbage.[1] This is true, but the framing raises an inevitable counterpoint. If it were possible to account for that history and code it out—in effect, to unskew the data— wouldn't predictive policing be an improvement over the status quo? Isn't relying on the insights afforded by an impartial equation interpreting hard math be preferable to the possible prejudices of a "bad apple" beat cop?

This is the problematic that, in the last decade, has dominated debates around predictive policing technologies. Skeptics point to the fact that a predictive policing system based on past police practice will reproduce the racial, sexual, and classed structures that organize state violence.[2] This is as obvious to developers as it is to their critics, and they have increasingly cast their surveillance net across an ever-widening spectrum of daily practices and affects in order to code their way out of "bias."[3]

But the terms of this debate are wrong. They revolve around an essentially liberal, reformist concept of policing that obscures the broader and more fundamental violence enacted by digitizing the decision-making capacities of the carceral state.[4] This depends on assumptions that I hope to dispel in this chapter: First, that people do something that is called "crime" outside of a relation with something called "the police." Crime does not exist prior to policing. Policing produces crime.[5] Second, that policing can, has, or will exist separate from the active production of racial difference. Policing does not have a "racist history." Policing *makes* race and is inextricable from it.[6] Algorithms cannot "code out" race from American policing because race is an originary policing technology, just as policing is a bedrock racializing technology.[7] Third, that policing has limits—that there is some sort of onto-logical red line beyond which policing cannot traverse. That has never been true, but criminal justice agencies' adoption of digital computers and data mining technologies has triggered a sort of generalized carceral unheim-lich.[8] Who knows what the computer knows about us?[9]

And it is that sensation—that affective prime—that predictive policing troubles the most.[10] It is what inevitably points discussion of the technology back to its magnetic north: *Minority Report*.

There are two *Minority Reports* worth mentioning. The original is a typi-cally paranoid Philip K. Dick story from 1956. Steven Spielberg adapted it for Twentieth Century Fox in 2002, and cast Tom Cruise as the leading man. They're normally framed as futural, dystopian warnings against concen-trating technological power in the hands of the state. But presenting them in this way misses a more fundamental point. The future is already here, and it always has been.[11] Both *Minority Reports* are stories about American racial capitalism's intrinsic entanglement with eugenics, carcerality, and enslavement.[12]

In Dick's version, the national state abducts children born with hydro-cephaly and transforms them into living computers. They're interred for life in the basements of government bureaus and financial houses, where machines extract short-term prophecies. Police have eliminated crime by preemptively placing people that the "precogs" envision breaking the law in detention camps indefinitely and without trial.

Spielberg resets the story in near-future Washington, DC, in the wake of an epidemic of a drug he calls "neuroin" (a thinly veiled stand-in for heroin and crack). In the story, the impure form of the drug to which the poor have ac-cess causes neonatal brain damage in children. It turns out that some of these children can "see" future murders in their dreams. The police take advantage of this by enslaving the children, permanently sedating them, and arresting the people they dream about. Rather than the mass camps of 1956, the con-

R. Joshua Scannell

demned of 2002 are rendered forever unconscious and interred in individuated cubby cells where they remain on life support until they die.

Both stories' plots follow Anderton, the head of the Precrime department,
as he tries to clear his name after precogs name him as a future murderer. He
sort of succeeds, although in neither case is the Precrime system "wrong." At
any rate, more important for our purposes than the travails of a self-pitying
white hetero police officer are the ways in which the stories depend on reproducing American matrices of domination.[13] The "precog mutants" in Dick's
story are "babbling idiots" and "monkeys." Their prisons are "monkey wings."
They're presumed not to feel pain, or have emotions, or mind their enslavement. They're tools, and nothing more. They waste away quickly and die
young. The society built on their labor cannot survive without them. They
quickly disappear, unmissed, from Anderton's narrative. This American hon-
esty is altogether too real for Spielberg, who recasts socially dead precogs
as "oracles" in one unit in one controversial police department. The action
centers on a national referendum on whether to expand the program.

We can trace a particular liberal-reparative trajectory of thought across
these two narratives. Dick's future is a relentless nightmare in which wealth
accumulation, mass incarceration, and state power mutually articulate one
another. The cyborg labor of the enslaved, justified by eugenicist ableism, is
taken for granted and goes unquestioned. Not so for Spielberg, for whom
Precrime is an unfortunate excessive moment, out of character with the
nature of American power. The unfortunate ill use of human beings in the
service of security is merely a temporary and isolated failure to live up to enduring American egalitarian-democratic norms. Spielberg's movie, in other
words, is a fable. It is a warning, rather than a critique. He gives the impression that the carceral state and American racial capitalism are not intrinsic
to one another, or that the technoscientific ratchet of police power is up for
popular debate. Dick, more accurately reflecting American history, doesn't
bother.

It is little surprise, then, that Spielberg's spurious liberal humanism animates the debates around predictive policing. In posing technoscientific
police overreach as a problem that can be addressed, it doubly articulates as
a parable whose lessons can be learned. That this deliberately and program-
matically elides the racial, sexual, and ableist logics that are the condition
of possibility for the neoliberal warfare state's political economic structure
is, of course, the point.[14] Prediction is, in fact, supposedly meant to alleviate
those very logics of inequity, all while denying their centrality to American
social organization.[15] And so the job of social improvement redounds once

again to the police, who, in our democratic state, can supposedly "learn the lessons" of *Minority Report*.

In 2013, the RAND corporation released a report called *Predictive Policing: The Roles of Crime Forecasting in Law Enforcement Operations*. In a subchapter titled "The Nature of Predictive Policing: This Is Not *Minority Report*," the authors note that "'predictions' are generated through statistical calculations that produce estimates, at best; like all techniques that extrapolate the future based on the past, they assume that the past is prologue."[16]

That all past is prologue is what speculative fiction assumes. Dick, writing in the 1950s, imagines detention camps full of people rendered criminal by a paranoid state. Spielberg, fifty years later, barely bothers with implication when he names the drug that ravages America's poor "neuroin." But if in both cases the science fictional points to a reality of mass incarceration and organized dispossession, it also enacts a "forgery of memory and meaning" that rewrites the history of American democracy as somehow apart from the history of racial oppression and exploitation that is both the real and the imagined world's condition of possibility.[17] In the original, race is notably absent. Considering how closely the tactics of the police state seem to be patterned on the internments of Japanese Americans during World War II, and how clearly the justifications for enslaving the precogs are based on eugenic ideologies of racial difference, it is telling that Dick never mentions race. But if Dick fails to acknowledge the racial structure of his dystopia, Spielberg's film actively disavows it.

Choosing, in 2002, to cast the instigators, tools, and victims (not mutually exclusive) of speculative state violence as entirely white is a predictable erasure that underscores what Frank Wilderson calls "socially engaged feature film's . . . bad faith of civic invitation."[18] *Minority Report* restages the racialized violence of the heroin and crack crises and crackdowns as speculative fiction: What if, in a dystopian future, the government invoked a drug epidemic to justify expansive and preemptive violence against the vulnerable? That Hollywood's capacity to think abstractly about questions like carceral violence depends on the sanctity of white bodies is not news. But it is telling that imagining an overreaching predictive future necessarily erases the certainty of past violence.

It is this particular type of amnesia that RAND researchers demonstrate when they defend predictive police technologies on the grounds that "the results are probabilistic, not certain."[19] Quantifying American policing's racist history does, in fact, certify the results of prediction. The penal consequences of transforming ruling ideologies of racial difference into quantitative tech-

        R. Joshua Scannell

niques for improving efficiencies and "objectivity" are not speculative—they are historical fact.[20] It is not a surprise that contemporary studies confirm that predictive policing ratchets up state violence.[21]

RAND's argument that "the results [of predictive policing] are probabilistic, not certain" is cunning. It reassures that probability doesn't threaten liberty, individualized suspicion, or protection against unreasonable search and seizure. That such formalities have not, do not, and cannot secure the well-being of those who are exploited and oppressed by American racial, sexual, and class structures is an obvious and predictable problem with RAND's case.[22]

Nevertheless, I take the RAND Corporation at their word on two counts: that all past is prologue, and that it is therefore the ontological ground that organizes livable lives.[23] Advances in the logistical capacity to deploy and circulate police forces will "probably" reproduce and expand carceral violence. Christina Sharpe has recently theorized that the racist contours of American history are such that we live "in the wake" of "the still unfolding aftermaths of Atlantic chattel slavery."[24] In that wake, the semiotics of the slave ship continue: from the forced movements of the enslaved to the forced movements of the migrant and the refugee, to the regulation of black people in North American streets and neighborhoods, to those ongoing crossings of and drownings in the Mediterranean Sea, to the brutal colonial reimaginings of the slave ship and the ark to the reappearances of the slave ship in everyday life in the form of the prison, the camp, and the school.[25]

Commercially available software does not and cannot "know" who will commit what crimes, or when. It will never "know" such things because crime is a social relation produced by the state and the police. It does not exist outside of state interdiction. More profoundly, the organizing logic of American criminal justice is not premised on individuated guilt and punishment, but on "the state-sanctioned or extralegal production and exploitation of group-differentiated vulnerability to premature death."[26] That is to say, it is premised on racism. In the inverted world of predictive policing, group-differentiated vulnerability is translated into probable criminal "risk." Predictive policing software uses almost every conceivable measure of vulnerability and victimization under American racial capitalism. It translates lived realities of oppression into a speculated likelihood of something called "crime." In doing so, it rationalizes the lie that black, brown, queer, and poor people and the places where they live are intrinsically threatening to the broader public.[27] This digital reformulation of the "dangerous poor" is deracinated and re-presented as hot spots and "mission areas": a "prescriptive" geography digitally manufactured to legitimate proactive police incursion.[28] And it is on the basis of this manufactured geography of "high risk," with that designation's concomitant relaxed "standards for what constitutes reasonable suspicion" that predictive policing programs proceed.[29] Labeling areas as "at-risk" appears to pose fewer problems to police departments because, in that case, individuals are not being directly targeted. The U.S. Supreme Court has ruled that standards for what constitutes reasonable suspicion are relaxed in "high-crime areas."[30]

Leading predictive policing programs like PredPol and HunchLab mine social data, employ prevailing criminological theories to model it, and project these models into the future as geospatially rendered probabilities of violence and disruption. Police commanders then direct units to respond to the map. Predictive policing systems are labor management tools. They leverage the digital information infrastructures of computational capitalism to occult the American carceral state's constitutive "population racism."[31] Systems like HunchLab do not rely only on crime data to make their predictions. Instead, they blend mundane police surveillance like request for service (911) calls with punitive renderings of the built environment (tracking for items like number of take-out restaurants, schools, or bars within a geographic range) and cosmic processes (weather, time of year) to "forecast" where and when crimes are most likely to occur, and direct police power accordingly.

But, while this sort of "holistic" surveillance may correct for "bias" in police reports, it does so by mobilizing an American political economic infrastructure that defines group-differentiated exploitation and death as normal and depends on its racialized maintenance to function.[32] When companies like Azavea build "race-blind" algorithms to model future crime, they are not working against the deadly organization of American populations.[33] They are (at best) simply denying the entanglements between race, carcerality, and capital.

The effect, as Safiya Noble argues in her critique of Google Search, is to reinstantiate "race" as an unspoken and unspeakable remainder, rather than an axial structure of American political economy. Or, as Noble puts it: "This rhetoric of post-racialism and colorblindness places the onus of discrimination or racism on the individual, or in the case of Google, on the algorithm. Rather than situating problems affecting racialized groups in social structures, those who call attention to the problems are made the problems themselves." What follows, then, is not intended to evaluate the effectiveness of a particular algorithm. Instead, I interrogate how predictive policing produces and regulates populations for control, containment, and extraction. In

R. Joshua Scannell

the first section, "The Fix Is In," I discuss a leading contemporary predictive policing product in order to examine the logics underlying the development and deployment of predictive policing systems. Most arguments in favor of predictive policing rest on a purported ethic of care and remediation. But the recourse to digital transparency is in fact a product of surveillant regimes of violence.[34] Predictive policing systems refigure contact between the police and the policed as a site of punitive data accumulation. This, in turn, feeds a self-sustaining logic of intelligence gathering, so that reformation becomes indistinguishable from technologies of sovereign control.[35]

In the second section, "Fixed in Place," I reread *Minority Report*(s) through an engagement with Sharpe to show how the fantasies and fears that animate much of the discussion around predictive policing reproduce virulent racial logics. I want to take Sharpe's concept of the weather as a ground to think through the deferrals and refusals of racialized life in the algorithmic architecture of predictive policing. This means pushing past the insufficient critique that such systems *run the risk* of reproducing racial inequalities. Rather, producing racialized oppression *is all that they can do*. Predictive policing depends on a "common sense" that criminalizing the characteristics of a settled community is ameliorative, rather than constitutive, of population racism.[36] But systems like HunchLab go even further and enlist the planet itself as an agent of racialized state power, by rendering "criminogenic" the temperature, rain, and wind—the weather.

I conclude the essay by returning to the *Minority Report*s and offer the not-so-radical idea that we are better off without them. Dystopian fiction has its uses and its pleasures, but combating American penal democracy demands an expansive imaginary of radically other worlds. That speculative fiction exists. The excellent *Octavia's Brood* is an example of the work that can and must be done to make the change that's needed—to not merely make the world a better place, but instead to create a wholly different one.

THE FIX IS IN

Predictive policing gained popularity during the budget crises created by the Great Recession of 2007–9. In November 2009, then LAPD chief of detectives (and current chief of the LAPD) Charlie Beck and data scientist Colleen McCue laid out in *The Police Chief* the first full-throated rationale for the "Public Safety Community's" adoption of "advanced analytics" innovated by Walmart and Amazon. Beck and McCue argue that widely adopting predictive data mining techniques would reveal nonintuitive relationships that would enable officers to "enter the decision cycle of our adversaries" in order to develop "preventing, thwarting, and information-based response." Beck and McCue imagine that such a process would increase departmental efficiency and allow officers to "do more with less," making up for recessionary shortfalls in personnel.[37] This, in turn, would allow the police to focus on "measuring what matters" in "underserved" communities and would allow the police to do the "real work" of "fixing" public safety.[38]

Beck and McCue's article ran just before the National Institute of Justice held the first of two national symposia on predictive policing technology. Laurie O. Robinson, the assistant attorney general for the Office of Justice Programs, argued that the aim of the symposium was twofold. The first was to define predictive policing, and the second was to "communicate what we're doing in terms that the community can accept" in order to "convince the public that we're acting in good faith."[39] The second goal overshadowed the first. Over the course of the symposium, participants worried about how to convince a skeptical public that the goal of the police is to be "less intrusive, not more," and to excise "that old Tom Cruise movie *Minority Report*" from their imaginations.[40] Or, as Chief Jim Bueerman of the Redlands, California, Police Department put it, "predictive policing holds the promise of enhancing police legitimacy in the community."[41]

The repeated invocation of negative perceptions and compromised legitimacy in the "community" belies the work that term does as racial euphemism. Polls of public attitudes toward the police consistently show sharp divergence between racial groups, with white Americans ranking the police as one of the most trusted institutions in the country, and black Americans significantly more skeptical. There are specific "communities" in which the police face a legitimacy crisis, and they are not usually white.[42]

The utility of this "community" euphemism is multiple. Disavowing race facilitates the increased policing of black and brown places that are defined as inherently and overwhelmingly deviant and criminal rather than not white.[43] They are, therefore, based on "the facts," the targets of police attention. In the first NIJ symposium, Dr. Theron Bowman, the chief of police in Arlington, Texas, showed exactly how this process works.

Describing his department's working model of predictive policing, he explained that Arlington PD uses "code violations" as a marker of "social disorganization" to identify "fragile neighborhood[s]."[44] Police then use this identification to allocate resources and thereby "prevent" crime. In 2016, according to the Arlington Police Department's own analysis on racial profiling, "African" and "Hispanic" motorists combined made up 56 percent of

R. Joshua Scannell

all traffic stops.[45] African motorists accounted for 34 percent, and Hispanics 22 percent. Those groups cumulatively make up 33 percent of the households in the city "with vehicle access" (Africans accounting for just 14 percent of those households). According to Census View, as of the 2010 census, Arlington is 18.8 percent black, 27.4 percent Latinx, and 59 percent white. Arlington police officers reported that, of their 112,004 vehicle stops in 2016, they knew the driver's "race or ethnicity" prior to stopping in 26.04 percent of cases. This discrepancy has one of three explanations: (1) the police are lying, (2) black and Latinx people are terrible drivers, or (3) the police are particularly active in black and Latinx neighborhoods (presumably because they are "fragile").

Finally, the "community" euphemism facilitates the transformation of race into metrics that open up policing to liberal logics of care, accountability, and objectivity. If, the thinking goes, police work can be based on the numbers, then policing can be made truly objective.

Azavea, the software company that makes the HunchLab predictive policing system, is an excellent example of how liberal egalitarian ethics expand the datafied imaginaries of a morphing carceral state.[46] Azavea is a Certified B Corporation, meaning "a for-profit company with a social mission." Their mission is "to apply geospatial data and software to create more sustainable, vital and livable communities while advancing the state-of-the-art through research."[47] HunchLab 2.0 is their effort to repair policing. Azavea describes the product as "a web-based proactive patrol management system. Advanced statistical models forecast when and where crimes are likely to emerge" and specialize in *"figuring out the best way to respond."*[48] To that end, they "pride [themselves] on transparency, a commitment to reducing harm associated with over-policing, and a focus on helping officers find the best tactical solutions to improve their communities."[49]

In pursuit of this mission, HunchLab offers several services to police departments. First, a mapping tool called "Predictive Missions" that trawls available databases to automatically generate "Missions." Unsatisfied with crime forecasting models that focus on crime reports, HunchLab dramatically expands the scope of its analysis: "For example, we can incorporate concepts such as: temporal patterns (day of week, seasonality); weather; risk terrain modeling (locations of bars, bus stops, etc.); socioeconomic indicators; historic crime levels; and near repeat patterns. The system automatically learns what is important for each crime type and provides recommendations of where to focus the resources that you have available. If you don't have particular datasets (such as bars or bus stops), the system simply adapts to use the data available in a given jurisdiction."[50] The Missions are geographically and temporally specific crimes that the program deems most likely to occur, most likely to be preventable by police patrol, and calibrated for optimal "dosage" (the company's term for optimal number of missions in a particular neighborhood). It arrives at these recommendations in a few ways. It "uses ensemble machine learning approaches" that incorporate and analyze data associated with a variety of crime forecasting models. Then it displays a chart showing how effective a particular theory is at explaining the likelihood of a crime. It compiles this with "patrol efficacy" (a measure of patrolling's impact on the incidence of the crime in question) and "severity weight." The "severity weight" is evaluated in dollars of "sum of predicted cost of preventable crime" crossed with the value of allocating patrol resources to prevent that crime. In the case of rape in Lincoln, Nebraska, the dollar value of the crime is evaluated at $217,866. But the likelihood of preventability, apparently zero, makes it "not really that important in terms of allocating patrol resources."[51] Commanders customize each crime's "weight," but the system measures this against the likelihood that patrolling will be an effective deterrent. It prescribes Missions based on the resulting dollar value cost-benefit analysis. HunchLab then paints these Missions on a map that streams to officers through GPS-enabled tablets and smartphones equipped with the Sidekick app.

When HunchLab recognizes the officers to be in a designated Mission zone, it triggers the product's second feature. This tool, called "Advisor" suggests two tactics and asks that officers select one. The system then starts an approximately fifteen-minute timer based on the "Koper curve," a criminological theory that short and intense patrols are as effective a deterrent as sustained surveillance.[52]

During those fifteen minutes the officers are expected to prosecute their chosen tactic. At the end of the window, they stop, respond to an "exit question," and proceed to the next Mission. Exit questions include[53]

- Did you have a positive interaction with the community?
- Did you feel that the mission location was appropriate?
- Did you feel that the risk fingerprint was correct?
- Should we send you here less often?
- Should we send you here more often?
- Should we set the mission timer higher here?
- Should we set the mission timer lower here?
- Was it difficult to patrol this location?

R. Joshua Scannell

The exit questions are designed to collect data, which are then run through decision trees that automatically revise suggested tactics and mission prescriptions. The company also hopes that leading questions like "Did you have a positive interaction with the community?" will affect future officer behavior by reminding them that they *ought* to be having positive interactions.

Finally, HunchLab offers a service called "Dashboard" (funded by a grant from Homeland Security) that "automatically keeps track of key performance indicators." Azavea suggests that Dashboard be made available to officers as well as management, suggesting that departments "keep KPIS on display in station houses through low-cost wall displays" so that "officers know how their metrics compare to the rest of the department."[54] It is hard to think of a clearer realization of Gilles Deleuze's model for "societies of control" than this.

My description of HunchLab raises a few points about how predictive policing works at peak benevolence.

First, HunchLab is designed as a riposte to the methodology of the largest predictive policing firm, PredPol. PredPol bases its predictions on three variables: crime history, location, and time. It employs an algorithm originally developed to predict earthquake aftershocks, to analyze that data and build its forecasts.[55] It has come under fire for being reductive, and overly dependent on biased police data.[56] HunchLab, by contrast, strives to be as holistic as possible. It maximizes the reach of its datasets and runs a number of forecasting models simultaneously. It does so by transforming the policed "community" into a field of criminogenic data. Take-out restaurants, schools, bus stops, bars, zoning regulations, temperature, weather, holidays, and more are all assigned criminogenic weights, and analyzed based on density; a preponderance of inexpensive food options becomes a nexus of criminal activity. Gastronomy and budget transform into criminality and risk, thereby mathematizing and forecasting the "community" euphemism.[57]

Second, the neoliberal tactics of gamification[58] and surveillance that plague the tech industry eclipse HunchLab's field of vision. Prediction, presented as a method of harm reduction, makes no effort to change the structural inequalities and violence of the American carceral state. Instead, Azavea relies on postindustrial labor management strategies and a framework that calculates social harm in dollar amounts to bend police agencies toward "reform." That these techniques all systematize American racial capitalism is elided through the imaginary of neoliberal efficiency. This is the sociopathic logic of Silicon Valley: that the conflicts and inequalities of the social world are ultimately an engineering problem born of human inefficiency. "Fixing" those problems is merely a question of applying algorithms to mitigate the drag on the ideal functioning of the system. Doing so will, in turn, "make the world a better place."

Finally, to quote Foucault, "visibility is a trap." HunchLab does not target individuals but "a certain concerted distribution of bodies, surfaces, lights, gazes; in an arrangement whose internal mechanisms produce the relation in which individuals are caught up."[59] But whereas Foucault argued that the panopticon individuates the effects of power, so that particular "inmates" learn to comport with the desired norms of the penal house, HunchLab produces a panopticon without inmates; surveillance without subjects; criminality without criminals. Humans as such are incidental to the model and its effects.[60] This reflects the company's Californian ideology discussed above.[61] But it also suggests a mode of power that weaponizes transparency. The constant agglomeration and analysis of data culled from the lived existence of persons and places under American racial capitalism renders contact between the police and the policed an open moment of data accumulation. In this encounter of the neoliberal, the digital, and the corporeal, the physical, metaphysical, and social violence ensconced in the mechanics of carcerality transform into anodyne "exit questions." The company then translates officers' responses into data and analyzes them with automated decision trees that granulate and distribute the lived oppressions of captivating technology into a "reparative" metric of reform. Inequitable policing is not a consequence of insufficiently detailed knowledge of the working life of the police, and efforts to present it as such hide the fundamental, structural role that policing plays in reproducing inequality.

FIXED IN PLACE

There is a moment at the beginning of Spielberg's *Minority Report* in which Colin Farrell's agent Witwer asks the Precrime unit "why [the precogs] can't see rapes? Or assaults, or suicides?" To which an agent Fletcher replies, "Because of the nature of murder. There is nothing more destructive to the metaphysical fabric that binds us than the untimely murder of one person by another." Pausing, first, to reflect on the murderous work that the word *untimely* does here, the bare minimum response to this proto-All-Lives-Matter armchair philosophizing is incredulity. One wonders how many killing officers exonerated by American courts and judges would, in this alternate universe, find themselves incarcerated in the Precrime unit's meat lockers. If, as

R. Joshua Scannell

RAND reassures us, "all past is prologue," then the answer hovers near zero. Presumably, those murders were all timely.

But focusing exclusively on murders inevitably occludes the myriad ways in which social death operates in the everyday. In addition to spectacular cases of state violence, any analysis of the mechanics of the racial state must attend to "more mundane displays of power and the border where it is difficult to discern domination from recreation."[62] This, of course, includes those instances in which racism explicitly becomes recreational qua entertainment, as in *Minority Report*. But, more broadly, it means the ways in which inequity affectively charges the *jouissance* of everyday domination. To reformulate Saidiya Hartman's argument that "innocent amusements" and pleasurable sentiments undergirded racial slavery, and Cedric Robinson's point that such pleasures have remained infrastructural to American popular media technologies, we can say that *to entertain the idea* that "crime control" can be outside, or other to racial capitalism is *to be entertained* by the notion that crime is extricable from the diamond compression of genocide, enslavement, institutional rape, organized accumulation by dispossession, organized food insecurity, Bourbon trap economics, mass incarceration, block busting, rate busting, skull busting, school busting (the list goes on), into neutral and objective technologies of population management.[63] This, contra Spielberg, is the *actual* "metaphysical fabric" that binds American together.

Christina Sharpe names this set of forces the Wake. American criminal justice doesn't detect rips in humans' collective lifeworld. It systematically excises black and brown lives from the repertoire of "human" beings for which the carceral state bears a pastoral responsibility of care.[64] Noting that "the list of nonindictments in the wake of state murders of black people continues to grow: Michael Brown, John Crawford, Aiyana Stanley Jones, Sandra Bland, Jonathan Ferrell, Miriam Carey, Tamir Rice, Rekia Boyd," Sharpe argues that "Black being appears in the space of the asterisked human as the insurance for, as that which underwrites, white circulation as the human. Always, black beings seemed lodged between cargo and being. *Wake: in the line of recoil of (a gun). Wake: The track left on the water's surface by a ship. Wake: the watching of relatives and friends beside the body of the dead person.*"[65]

Centering Sharpe's analysis shows how the American carceral state reorganizes pastoral pretensions like Spielberg's under the rubrics of data-driven strategic and tactical deployments. Spielberg's invocation of murder as the only crime that the Precrime unit can detect is an enormous change from Dick's original world. Dick's "Minority Report" is a more prescient vision of our actually existing datalogical dystopia.[66] The "Monkey Wings" in Dick's story are in most government bureaus, financial houses, and industrial sites, and the police borrowed the idea to use this captive labor from Wall Street. Real-world police borrowed the idea from Wall Street, but also from Amazon and Walmart.[67]

In Dick's vision, precogs can see a variety of crimes, and officers arbitrarily decide which arrests to make. In a telling moment, Dick's Anderton pulls a stack of cards with names and crimes written on them and tosses them sight unseen to a subordinate, telling him to "see which ones we want. Use your own judgment." Murder might be the particular crime of which Anderton is accused, but Dick's point is not to meditate on the boundaries between security and justice. Instead, his is a Cold War warning about the impact of black-boxed, unaccountably broad-based police power vested in vast and unknowable data generation.

Dick's story is also unfortunately prescient in that it tethers fear of creeping extrajuridical police power to a science fictional critique of the potential uses and misuses of digital technologies. In so doing, he and his later interlocutors (Spielberg, but also the journalists, academics, and researchers that see "The Minority Report" coming to life in contemporary policing techniques) miss the punch line that the punitive, unaccountable, terrifying organization of the relationship between police and policed is neither new nor "technological." It is, instead, an undergirding logic of the American racial state.[68] There is obviously something deeply unsettling about one's being transmuted to "risk." But it is also telling that critics and proponents alike constantly point to science fiction to articulate this fear. For people of color, for women, for queer people, the state presumption of abjection has never been science fictional. Neither Jim Crow nor Zero Tolerance required the deployment of massive computational power. Bodies themselves did that work. It is the structure of American racial antagonisms rather than the advent of new technology that underwrites the biopolitics of actually existing America.[69] As Simone Browne points out in *Dark Matters*, biometrics is from the beginning a racial technology. It is impossible to distinguish between efforts to inscribe "race" and racial difference on human bodies and efforts to quantify, compare, evaluate, and surveil the human.

At any rate, Spielberg characteristically transforms Dick's diagnostic of where-America-is-going into a morality play about the dilemma of how even good (white) men can, when invested with too much power, fray the inherent decency of American civil society. The ghost that haunts the film is the then-novel PATRIOT Act, whose effects were in 2002 only beginning to be

R. Joshua Scannell

felt, and whose novel technics of control are nodded to in the film world's saturation with biometric technology.[70] And, in a recuperative act of American liberal nationalism, Spielberg reimagines the actually existing surveilled, accused, hunted, detained target of the war on terror as an upstanding, heteronormative, white police officer.[71] It is only by doing so that he can pose the question: How far is too far?

The public has widely drawn the lesson that what is at stake in debates over predictive policing is how to properly balance the legal rights of individuals with "security." When journalists, pundits, and critics discuss predictive policing technologies, they autonomically invoke *Minority Report* (the movie) and wonder whether it could possibly be legal for the police to arrest you before you've committed any crime. The technical answer is no. It is legally impermissible (even if practically normal) to target and arrest individuals for crimes they have not committed. But it is telling that, when faced with widespread public nausea at the *idea* of predictive, preemptive, proactive, prescriptive policing, defenders point to Amendments One, Four, and Five of the Bill of Rights and assure the public that their programs comport with those strictures. Even if law enforcement *wanted* to take full advantage of the prognostic powers of digital technologies, the amendments formally forbid them from doing so. Though such a legalistic defense against the absolute power of the carceral state is certainly not *nothing*, it comes close to it in a country that historically prosecutes its terrors in prideful accordance with, and in credulous defense of, the letter of its law.[72]

I am arguing that predictive policing and its carceral cousins in the ever-expanding field of "data driven public safety solutions" does the groundwork of methodically and methodologically organizing racial state violence. It does so, in part, by lending a putatively objective and unprejudiced veneer to the ongoing "deputization of white civil society" that stands "at the heart of the American policing modality." Far from the remedial gesture of course correcting failed strategies of mass incarceration, like those suggested by the President's Task Force on 21st Century Policing, data-driven policing constitutes an enormous expansion of both the carceral field of vision and the neoliberal calculative logics under which racism is imagined and enacted.[73] The incorporation of ever-increasing, ever-more-granular data points and models aimed at building a perfectly "accurate" policing regime does not reduce harms associated with "over-policing." Instead, it cements a perverse digital mysticism as practical, mathematical common sense. This contemporary consensus looks to transform the affective, the climactic, and the geographic into raw material for a seemingly limitless expansion of the carceral state's datalogical paranoia.[74] At the root of this mission creep is not the transparently fascist call to Make America Great Again. Instead, it is a liberal injunction to reduce harm rendered in the narrowest practical sense. That is, (to borrow Axon, formerly Taser's slogan), to "Protect Life." In demanding that (all?) life matters, reformers endlessly reenact the fantasy that metrics will absolve the state of its "prejudices" and fulfill the supposedly bedrock promises of a just and egalitarian nation, all the while enjoying the fruits of the Wake.

We come full circle. The Axon Corporation takes up Spielberg's formulation that there is "nothing more destructive to the metaphysical fabric that binds us all than the untimely murder of one person by another," truncates it, extends its reach, and expands its domain to "Protect Life." To that end we are offered the dystopian prospect of "a team committed to pushing the boundaries of technology to help you [read: 'law enforcement, militaries, and citizens alike'] *feel more confident* in the field, at the station, and in court. From Smart Weapons, like our TASER devices, to police body cameras and digital evidence management systems, *every product works together as a single network. Seamlessly integrated. Completely connected.* And designed to help police, sheriffs, and law enforcement agencies everywhere *make the world a safer place*"[75] (emphasis added). This is a political formulation, although it is one that companies selling criminal justice software reflexively disavow. To acknowledge *politics* rather than constitutional comportment requires acknowledgment that the *point* of digitizing the carceral is to manufacture an end run around the narrow legalistic protections nominally afforded to Americans. It is precisely the speculative use of risks, rates, and probabilities that works around these constraints while invoking a quasi-progressive adherence to "smarter," more transparent policing. And, as we have seen, advocates like Azavea imagine predictive policing as reducing harm and protecting civil liberties. But the approach renders lifeways, foodways, and lifeworlds criminal, or probably so. Also, it suspects rain, heat, daylight, wind—weather. In the name of protecting life, crime control condemns the cosmological or planetary inevitabilities of living on a rock with atmosphere.[76]

Taking the absurd logic of criminogenic weather to its conclusion, criminality increasingly becomes a direct consequence of anthropogenic climate change and ecological crisis. Far beyond the slow violence that Rob Nixon has identified as a slow-burning biopolitical attack on the poor, the irreversible transformation of the earth's temperature becomes a vital virtual variable in local police departments' deployment decisions and strategic initiatives.

R. Joshua Scannell

Here is the ontological wager: probabilistic, uncertain results require the adjudication of the real. All is uncertain and ontologically unstable. But decisions must be made in the present to foreclose undesirable futures.[77] This is why predictive policing *really* isn't like "Minority Report." In that story, the mutant precogs can "see" the future. It is "real" and ontologically stable. Things already "exist" for them. But predictive policing does not produce a real. It produces "instabilities" that justify state violence. It produces risk. This risk, unfolding as an archive from the future, is policed.

Predictive policing consolidates and operationalizes risk, possibility, and insecurity. It drags the future and its volatility into the present and destabilizes the real. This engenders a state of constant crisis that demands the constant expansion and application of apparatuses of security. No one knows what the future consequences of *not* acting on a *possible* problem will be, so the security state must fan out to control all imaginable contingencies. From the perp not arrested to the stock not shorted, the future materializes as demand for action in the present, and as a constant failure of not having acted otherwise. Prediction rearticulates the power to make live or let die as a reasonable, calculated, technocratic "best guess." Algorithmic necropolitics is transmuted into a digital calculus of best practices in which killing or arresting someone is okay so long as they pose a future "risk to society." To prevent the worst possible outcome, or to amplify the best one, apparatuses of security must always be brought to bear.[78] In practical terms, this is realized as an intensification of policing surveillance logics and practices, and circulations of risk historically generated by the carceral archipelagos of racial capitalism.[79]

To close, I want to issue a minority report on "Minority Report" as a parable for the moment. Dystopian policing is neither speculative nor futural. It is actually existing, now, in the present. To imagine that the threat is in the future works to normalize and expand the carceral imagination. The idea *must* be to imagine the world as a space for freedom. Doing so depends on reckoning with the intense depth of the contemporary world's constitutive unfreedom. As Octavia Butler demonstrated throughout the course of her career, and as writers working in her tradition today—her "brood," to borrow the term from Walidah Imarisha and adrienne maree brown—continue to demonstrate, one does not need to misremember or misrecognize the historical horrors of the country in order to dream and demand liberation now and in the future.[80] On the contrary, if we intend to imagine a freer future, then we must reckon honestly with the terms of our world as it is.

If the parameters of the world we live in are so limited and so blinkered that we are incapable of imagining the carceral present unfolding into anything other than deeper, future-shocked dystopia, then the terms of engagement must change. We ought not to be concerned about making the world "a better place," but demand a radically different one. Insofar as the world drags the planet into paranoid collusion to reproduce racialized logics of command and control, then the world must go.

Notes

1. Shaun King, "Predictive Policing Is 'Technological Racism,'" *New York Daily News*, November 5, 2015, accessed December 28, 2017, http://www.nydailynews.com/new -york/king-predictive-policing-technological-racism-article-1.2425028.

2. Andrew Selbst, "Disparate Impact in Big Data Policing," *Georgia Law Review* 52, no. 109 (2017).

3. Andrew Ferguson, *The Rise of Big Data Policing: Surveillance, Race, and the Future of Law Enforcement* (New York: NYU Press, 2017).

4. Katherine Beckett and Naomi Murakawa, "Mapping the Shadow Carceral State: Toward an Institutionally Capacious Approach to Punishment," *Theoretical Criminology* 16, no. 2 (2012): 221–44.

5. Stewart Hall, Chas Chritcher, Tony Jefferson, John Clarke, and Brian Roberts, *Policing the Crisis: Mugging, the State and Law and Order*, 2nd ed. (New York: Palgrave Macmillan 2013); Ana Muñiz, *Police, Power, and the Production of Racial Boundaries* (New Brunswick, NJ: Rutgers University Press, 2015).

6. Joy James, "Introduction," *Warfare in the American Homeland: Policing and Prison in a Penal Democracy* (Durham, NC: Duke University Press, 2007); Kelly Lytle Hernandez, *Migra! A History of the U.S. Border Patrol* (Berkeley: University of California Press, 2010); Paul Amar, "Introduction: New Racial Missions of Policing: Comparative Studies of State Authority, Urban Governance, and Security Technology in the Twenty-first Century," *Ethnic and Racial Studies* 33, no. 4 (2010): 575–92.

7. Simone Browne, *Dark Matters: On the Surveillance of Blackness* (Durham, NC: Duke University Press, 2015); Eduardo Moncada, "Counting Bodies: Crime Mapping, Policing and Race in Colombia," *Ethnic and Racial Studies* 33, no. 4 (2010): 696–716.

8. Bernard Harcourt, *The Illusion of Free Markets: Punishment and the Myth of Natural Order* (Cambridge, MA: Harvard University Press, 2011); Bernard Harcourt, *Exposed: Desire and Disobedience in the Digital Age* (Cambridge, MA: Harvard University Press, 2015).

9. John Cheney-Lippold, *We Are Data: Algorithms and the Making of Our Digital Selves* (New York: NYU Press, 2017); Benjamin H. Bratton, *The Stack: On Software and Sovereignty* (Cambridge, MA: MIT Press, 2016); danah boyd and Kate Crawford, "Criti-

R. Joshua Scannell

cal Questions for Big Data: Provocations for a Cultural, Technological, and Scholarly Phenomenon," *Information, Communication and Society* 15, no. 5 (2012): 662–79.

10. Brian Massumi, *Parables for the Virtual: Movement, Affect, Sensation* (Durham, NC: Duke University Press, 2002); Eugene Thacker, *The Global Genome: Biotechnology, Politics, and Culture* (Cambridge, MA: MIT Press, 2005).

11. Rayvon Fouché, "From Black Inventors to One Laptop per Child: Exporting a Racial Politics of Technology," in *Race after the Internet*, ed. Lisa Nakamura and Peter A. Chow-White (New York: Routledge, 2012).

12. Catherine Bliss, *Race Decoded: The Genomic Fight for Social Justice* (Palo Alto, CA: Stanford University Press, 2012); Troy Duster, "The Combustible Intersection: Genomics, Forensics, and Race," in *Race after the Internet*, ed. Nakamura, and Chow-White; Alondra Nelson, *The Social Life of DNA: Race, Reparations, and Reconciliation after the Genome* (Boston: Beacon Press, 2016).

13. Patricia Hill Collins, *Black Feminist Thought: Knowledge, Consciousness, and the Politics of Empowerment* (New York: Routledge, 2000).

14. Ruth Wilson Gilmore, "Globalisation and US Prison Growth: From Military Keynesianism to Post-Keynesian Militarism," *Race and Class*, 40, no. 2/3 (1999): 171–88; Katherine McKittrick, "Plantation Futures," *Small Axe* 17, no. 3 (42) (2013): 1–15; Walter Johnson, *River of Dark Dreams: Slavery and Empire in the Cotton Kingdom* (Cambridge, MA: Harvard University Press, 2013); James, *Warfare in the American Homeland*.

15. Marion Fourcade and Kieran Healy, "Classification Situations: Life Changes in the Neoliberal Era," *Accounting, Organizations and Society* 38 (2013): 559–72; Duster, "The Combustible Intersection"; Oscar Gandy and Lemy Baruh, "Racial Profiling: They Said It Was Against the Law!," *University of Ottawa Law and Technology Journal* 3, no. 1. (2006): 297–327.

16. Walter L. Perry, Brian McInnis, Cart C. Price, Susan C. Smith, and John S. Hollywood, *Predictive Policing: The Role of Crime Forecasting in Law Enforcement Operations* (Santa Monica, CA: RAND Corporation, 2013), 8.

17. Cedric Robinson, *Forgeries of Memory and Meaning: Blacks and the Regimes of Race in American Theater and Film before World War II* (Chapel Hill: University of North Carolina Press, 2007); David Harvey, "The New Imperialism: Accumulation by Dispossession," *Socialist Register* 40 (2004): 43–87; Nikil Pal Singh, *Race and America's Long War* (Berkeley: University of California Press, 2017).

18. Frank Wilderson, *Red, White and Black: Cinema and the Structure of U.S. Antagonisms* (Durham, NC: Duke University Press, 2010), 24.

19. Perry, et al, *Predictive Policing*, 8

20. Khalil Gibran Muhammad, *The Condemnation of Blackness: Race, Crime, and the Making of Modern Urban America* (Cambridge, MA: Harvard University Press, 2010); Elizabeth Hinton, *From the War on Poverty to the War on Crime: The Making of Mass Incarceration in America* (Cambridge, MA: Harvard University Press, 2016); Bernard Harcourt, *Against Prediction: Profiling, Policing, and Punishing in an Actuarial Age* (Chicago: University of Chicago Press, 2007).

21. Kristian Lum and William Isaac, "To Predict and Serve?," *Significance* 13, no. 5 (2016): 14–19.

22. Oscar Gandy, *Coming to Terms with Chance: Engaging Rational Discrimination and Cumulative Disadvantage* (New York: Routledge, 2009); Safiya Umoja Noble and Brendesha M. Tynes, "Introduction," *The Intersection Internet: Race, Class, and Culture Online* (New York: Peter Lang, 2016); Nakamura and Chow-White, "Mapping the Shadow Carceral State."

23. Avery Gordon, *Ghostly Matters: Haunting and the Sociological Imagination* (Minneapolis: University of Minnesota Press, 1997).

24. Christina Sharpe, *In the Wake: On Blackness and Being* (Durham, NC: Duke University Press, 2016), 2.

25. Sharpe, *In the Wake*, 21.

26. Ruth Wilson Gilmore, *Golden Gulag: Prisons, Surplus, Crisis, and Opposition in Globalizing California* (Berkeley: University of California Press, 2007), 28.

27. Katherine McKittrick, *Demonic Grounds: Black Women and the Cartographies of Struggle* (Minneapolis: University of Minnesota Press, 2007); Rashad Shabazz, *Spatializing Blackness: Architecture of Confinement and Black Masculinity in Chicago* (Champaign: University of Illinois Press, 2015).

28. Azavea, "Resources," https://www.hunchlab.com/resources/, 2016, accessed June 30, 2017; David A. Weisburd and Anthony Braga, *Police Innovation: Contrasting Perspectives* (Cambridge, MA: Cambridge University Press, 2006).

29. Sarah Brayne, "Big Data: The Case of Policing," *American Sociological Review* 52, no. 5 (2017); Perry, et al., *Predictive Policing*, 124.

30. Andrew Ferguson and Damien Bernache, "The High Crime Area Question: Requiring Verifiable and Quantifiable Evidence for Fourth Amendment Reasonable Suspicion Analysis," *American University Law Review* 57, no. 6 (2008): 1587–644.

31. Gilmore, *Golden Gulag*; Patricia Ticineto Clough and Craig Willse, "Gendered Security/National Security: Political Branding and Population Racism," *Social Text* 28, no. 4 (2010): 45–63.

32. Cedric Robinson, *Black Marxism: The Making of the Black Radical Tradition* (Chapel Hill: University of North Carolina Press, 1983); Jonathan Beller, *The Message Is Murder: Substrates of Computational Capital* (London: Pluto Press, 2017).

33. Stefano Harney and Fred Moten, *The Undercommons: Fugitive Planning and Black Study* (New York: Minor Compositions, 2013).

34. Édouard Glissant, *Poetics of Relation* (Ann Arbor: University of Michigan Press, 1997); Zach Blas, "Informatic Opacity," *Journal of Aesthetics and Protest* 9 (2014): http://www.joaap.org/issue9/zachblas.htm; David Lyon, *Surveillance Society: Monitoring Everyday Life* (London: Open University Press, 2011); Kirstie Ball and Laureen Snider, *The Surveillance-Industrial Complex: A Political Economy of Surveillance* (New York: Routledge, 2013).

35. Gilles Deleuze, "Postscript on the Societies of Control," *October* 59 (1992): 3–7.

36. Ferguson, *The Rise of Big Data Policing*; Perry, et al. *Predictive Policing*.

R. Joshua Scannell

37. Charlie Beck and Colleen McCue, "Predictive Policing: What Can We Learn from Wal-Mart and Amazon about Fighting Crime in a Recession?," *The Police Chief* 76, no. 11 (2009).

38. Robert H. Langworth, ed., *Measuring What Matters: Proceedings from the Policing Research Institute Meetings.* (Washington, DC: National Institute of Justice, 1999); Beck and McCue "Predictive Policing."

39. Laurie O. Robinson, "Predictive Policing Symposium: Opening Remarks," Paper Presented at the first Predictive Policing Symposium, Los Angeles, California, November 18, 2009.

40. Robinson, "Opening Remarks," 18.

41. Jim Bueerman, "What Chiefs Expect from Predictive Policing: Perspectives from Police Chiefs," Paper Presented at the first Predictive Policing Symposium, Los Angeles, California, November 18, 2009.

42. Frank Newport, "Gallup Review: Black and White Attitudes toward Police," *Gallup* (2014), accessed June 30, 2017, http://www.gallup.com/poll/175088/gallup-review -black-white-attitudes-toward-police.aspx; Rich Morin and Renee Stepler, "The Racial Confidence Gap in Police Performance, *Pew Research Center for Social and Demographic Trends* (2016), accessed June 30, 2017, http://www.pewsocialtrends.org/2016/09/29/the -racial-confidence-gap-in-police-performance/.

43. Muhammad, *Condemnation of Blackness*; Roderick A. Ferguson, *Aberrations in Black: Towards a Queer of Color Critique* (Minneapolis: University of Minnesota Press, 2004); James, *Warfare in the American Homeland.*

44. Theron Bowman, "Defining Terms and Introducing Issues," Paper Presented at the first Predictive Policing Symposium, Los Angeles, California, November 18, 2009.

45. Del Carmen Consulting, LLC, "Annual Contact Report 2016" (2016), accessed June 30, 2017. http://www.arlington-tx.gov/police/wp-content/uploads/sites/9/2017/03 /Arlington-Raciall-Profiling-Report-2016-.pdf.

46. Chandan Reddy, *Freedom with Violence: Race, Sexuality, and the US State* (Durham, NC: Duke University Press, 2011); Naomi Murakawa, *The First Civil Right: How Liberals Built Prison America* (Oxford: Oxford University Press, 2014); Jodi Melamed, *Represent and Destroy: Rationalizing Violence in the New Racial Capitalism* (Minneapolis: University of Minnesota Press, 2011).

47. Azavea, "Hunchlab: Under the Hood" (2015), accessed June 30, 2017, https://cdn .azavea.com/pdfs/hunchlab/HunchLab-Under-the-Hood.pdf.

48. Azavea, "Features" (2017), accessed June 30, 2017, https://www.hunchlab.com /features/; emphasis added.

49. Azavea, "Resources" (2016), accessed June 30, 2017, https://www.hunchlab.com /resources/.

50. Azavea, "Hunchlab," 10.

51. Azavea, "Beyond the Box: Towards Prescriptive Analysis in Policing" (2014), accessed June 30, 2017, https://www.youtube.com/watch?v=NCXFDfQsYBE&feature =youtu.be&t=33m41s.

52. Christopher S. Koper, "Just Enough Police Presence: Reducing Crime and Disorderly Behavior by Optimizing Patrol Time in Crime Hotspots," *Justice Quarterly* 12, no. 4 (1995): 649–72.

53. Azavea, "Features."

54. Azavea, "Announcing Our New User Interface" (2017), accessed June 30, 2017, https://www.youtube.com/watch?v=2mdqTAX4Yz0&t=2521s.

55. Jeffrey P. Brantingham and Martin B. Short, "Crime Emergence," in *When Crime Appears*, ed. Jean Marie McGlorin, Christopher J. Sullivan, and Leslie W. Kennedy (London: Routledge, 2012), 73–96.

56. David Robinson and Logan Koepke, "Stuck in a Pattern: Early Evidence on 'Predictive Policing' and Civil Rights," The Center for Media Justice, August 31, 2016, accessed September 7, 2018, https://www.upturn.org/reports/2016/stuck-in-a-pattern/.

57. Anthony Hatch, *Blood Sugar: Racial Pharmacology and Food Justice in Black America* (Minneapolis: University of Minnesota Press, 2016).

58. Gamification refers to the incorporation of elements of game playing as a strategy for managing labor. Employees earning performance-based "points" that can be traded in for perks is an example. Police officers earning extra vacation days for staying ahead of their coworkers' KPIs is, theoretically, another one.

59. Michel Foucault, *Discipline and Punish: The Birth of the Prison*, trans. Adam Sheridan (New York: Vintage, 1977), 200–202.

60. Bratton, *The Stack*.

61. Richard Barbrook and Andy Cameron, "The Californian Ideology," *Science as Culture* 6, no. 1 (1996): 44–72.

62. Saidiya V. Hartman, *Scenes of Subjection: Terror, Slavery, and Self-Making in Nineteenth-Century America* (New York: Oxford University Press, 1997), 42.

63. Hartman, *Scenes of Subjection*; Robinson, *Forgeries of Memory and Meaning*; Wilderson, *Red White and Black*; Kara Keeling, *The Witch's Flight: The Cinematic, the Black Femme, and the Image of Common Sense* (Durham, NC: Duke University Press, 2007).

64. Sylvia Wynter, "The Ceremony Must Be Found: After Humanism," *boundary 2* 12, no. 3 (1983): 19–70; Sylvia Wynter, "Unsettling the Coloniality of Being/Power/Truth/Freedom: Towards the Human, After Man, Its Overrepresentation—An Argument," CR: *The New Centennial Review* 3, no. 3 (2003): 257–337; Katherine McKittrick, ed., *Sylvia Wynter: On Being Human as Praxis* (Durham, NC: Duke University Press, 2014).

65. Sharpe, *In the Wake*, 111.

66. Patricia Ticineto Clough, Karen Gregory, Benjamin Haber, and Josh Scannell, "The Datalogical Turn," in *Non-Representational Methodologies: Re-Envisioning Research*, ed. Phillip Vannini (New York: Routledge, 2015), 146–64.

67. Beck and McCue, "Predictive Policing."

68. Browne, *Dark Matters*; David Theo Goldberg, *The Racial State* (Hoboken, NJ: Wiley-Blackwell, 2002); Michel Foucault, *The Birth of Biopolitics: Lectures at the Collège de France 1978-1979*, trans. Adam Sheridan (New York: Vintage, 2008).

69. Wilderson, *Red, White, and Black*.

70. Deleuze, "Postscript on the Society of Control"; Jasbir Puar, *Terrorist Assemblages: Homonationalism in Queer Times* (Durham, NC: Duke University Press, 2007).

71. Reddy, *Freedom with Violence.*

72. Hortense Spillers, *Black, White, and in Color: Essays on American Literature and Culture* (Chicago: University of Chicago Press, 2003); Hartman, *Scenes of Subjection*; Andrea McArdle and Tanya Erzen, eds., *Zero Tolerance: Quality of Life and the New Police Brutality in New York City* (New York: NYU Press, 2001); Jordan T. Camp and Christina Heatherton, eds., *Policing the Planet: Why the Policing Crisis Led to Black Lives Matter* (London: Verso, 2016).

73. Clough and Willse, "Gendered Security/National Security."

74. I am not using *paranoia* as a polemical term here. Rather, I am thinking of Tung-Hui Hu's argument in *A Prehistory of the Cloud* that the epistemological default of "the network" is a paranoia that produces "network fever," "the desire to connect *all* networks, indeed, the desire to connect every piece of information to another piece." Tung-Hui Hu, *A Prehistory of the Cloud* (Cambridge, MA: MIT Press, 2015).

75. http://www.axon.com/.

76. Elizabeth Povinelli, *Geontologies: A Requiem to Late Liberalism* (Durham, NC: Duke University Press, 2016).

77. Jasbir Puar, "The 'Right' to Maim: Disablement and Inhumanist Biopolitics in Palestine," *Borderlands* 14, no. 1 (2015); Jacques Derrida, "Force of Law: The 'Mystical Foundation of Authority,'" in *Acts of Religion*, ed. Gil Anidjar (New York: Routledge, 2002), 231–98.

78. Eyal Weizman, *The Least of All Possible Evils: Humanitarian Violence from Arendt to Gaza* (London: Verso, 2011).

79. Foucault, *Discipline and Punish.*

80. Walidah Imarisha and adrienne maree brown, *Octavia's Brood: Science Fiction Stories from Social Justice Movements* (Oakland, CA: AK Press, 2015).

(PART II)

SURVEILLANCE SYSTEMS FROM FACEBOOK

TO FAST FASHION

.....

6

Racialized Surveillance in the Digital Service Economy

Winifred R. Poster

.....

To many techno-euphorists, the digital economy is the place where race no longer matters. This would be an even playing field. It would happen through an online market where goods, services, and labor could be exchanged without direct contact between individuals, at times anonymously. How could racism occur under conditions like this, when a person's ethnic or national identity is not readily apparent?

For some, the digital is even a place where racial inequalities are rectified. This logic is front and center among corporate narratives.[1] Uber's head of North American operations stated: "Ridesharing apps are changing a transportation status quo that has been unequal for generations, making it easier and more affordable for people to get around. . . . We believe Uber is helping reduce transportation inequities across the board." A spokesperson for Lyft echoes: "We are extremely proud of the positive impact Lyft has on communities of color. Because of Lyft, people living in underserved areas— which taxis have historically neglected—are now able to access convenient, affordable rides. And we provide this service while maintaining an inclusive and welcoming community, and do not tolerate any form of discrimination."

Sociological analysis shows how, quite the opposite, racialized surveillance is an integral and routine part of the U.S. service economy. As interactions between consumers, workers, and firms have moved to online platforms, cell phone apps, digital satellite communications, and artificial intelligence, racial discrimination is an everyday activity.

Four examples reveal how this is happening. First, in *job matching and hiring websites* (like Monster.com), where employers discriminate against potential candidates based on their names and photos. Second, in the *"gig" economy* (like Uber and Airbnb), where drivers may discriminate against riders based on ethnicity, and consumers may discriminate against housing sites based on racialized notions of geography and location. Third, in *transnational call centers*, where race and nation are integral features of communication between U.S. customers and Indian call center workers on the phone and through the internet. And fourth, in *digital assistants*, developed through artificial intelligence, which provide automated labor for firms in the form of avatars (like Siri, or Tay, the Microsoft bot that became a racist on Twitter). My analysis is based on ongoing study of the digital service economy, along with data from ethnographic research on the transnational service industry across the United States and India.

In these four areas, the digital body is examined, monitored, and assessed in a variety of racially explicit ways. Users surveil bodies for their sounds (accents, ways of speaking), for images (facial features, color), for names and biohistories, and for physical locations and movements. To understand racial surveillance in the digital service economy, I draw from my conceptualization of *multi-surveillance*.[2] Starting with a premise of a fractionalization in monitoring practices, it argues for a more nuanced and complex account of surveillance that can incorporate the intersectionalities of race, ethnicity, class, and nation.

My focus is on the surveillance practices of consumers and digital users in particular, as they are playing an increasingly central role in platform and communicative capitalism. Rather than seeing these groups as simply objects of surveillance (by elites), or alternatively as agents of countersurveillance (against elites), I show how they are conducting surveillance of their own. Moreover, they are doing so in ways that support (rather than challenge) dominant racial systems. This "watching from below" can reinforce hierarchies of race as much as watching from above.

The conclusion reflects on the sources of consumer racism in the transition from color-blind racism to an era of overt digital hate and hypernationalism. It then turns to the potential of resistant multi-surveillances and what Browne calls "dark sousveillance."[3]

RACIALIZING SURVEILLANCE

Surveillance, in common accounts, is about generic (and unracialized) groups of "those in power" against "those not in power." Intersectionality theory illuminates how this account is lacking and simplistic.[4] It says that we

Winifred R. Poster

cannot understand power dynamics without considering systems of race, gender, sexuality, class, and so on. These systems operate as independent hierarchies, but ones that cross over and intersect each other. Accordingly, surveillance in the digital service economy needs a more differentiated theory that can be attuned to these complex systems of race and surveillance.

A MULTI-SURVEILLANCE FRAMING

A multi-surveillance perspective notes that digital systems are proliferating the range of agents who are doing observation, and in turn, offering new sources for racial monitoring. Through the diffusion of mobile computing, satellite connections, and broadband access, many more groups of people have the capacity to carry out surveillance, with their varying motives and purposes. In the digital service economy, these groups include: firms who contract services, vendors who provide the technologies, employees who perform the services, outsourced workforces who do this work from abroad, and consumers and users of the services.

This trend of fractionalization is reshuffling the power relations of surveillance. For instance, consumers are *not* the legitimate agents of surveillance in conventional theorizing. Other groups—like employers—are the agents. Consumers are said to be on the receiving end of surveillance instead—they are the targets. Some scholars, alternatively, recognize that consumers have a role in surveillance, but they tie it specifically to resistance. Here, consumers turn the tables on monitoring—to observe from below. Mathiesen, for instance, offers the notion of synopticism, in which the many watch the few.[5] Similarly, Mann and colleagues conceptualize the term *sous*veillance, or seeing from below (in direct contrast to *sur*veillance, or seeing from above).[6]

A multi-surveillance framing breaks down the mutual exclusivity of roles, however. It argues that an individual can be watched by one group, while *at the same time* being the watcher of another group. Consumers may be watched by corporations, for instance, while they simultaneously observe other groups in the digital service economy. Furthermore, groups may be internally varied, with multiple affiliations and interests. While consumers may be unified in their aims to counteract surveillance by firms, they may vary in their orientations toward maintaining or disrupting racial hierarchies. Consequently, they may *surveill each other* for factors like race.

My argument will be that consumers and users are not only watching from their positions, but in ways that support existing power structures of race. This means that watching from below can reinforce dominant hierarchies as much as watching from above.

Simone Browne captures brilliantly the role of the public in "racializing surveillances" of the antebellum United States.[7] With the aid of black feminist scholarship, she "draw[s] a black line" through classic understandings of surveillance (like Foucault's panopticon).[8] She explains how racial surveillance was so pervasive and intractable in part because *regular people carried it out* alongside the legal and political administrations. Within plantation security systems, for example, white owners used early forms of information technology to track slaves—from slave passes, to slave patrols, to wanted posters for runaways. Browne also points to slave markets and auction blocks, where "the many watch the few," and consumers participate in the racial surveillance and subordination of blacks.

Today, the public does so with a click of a button. In fact, consumers and digital users have unique roles as agents of surveillance in the digital service economy. As a definitional starting point, a service is an industry that does something for a customer, rather than producing a material product. Services are actually the fastest-growing sectors of the formal economy worldwide, and recently, digital services are transferring these exchanges to information and communication technology systems. In some cases, the exchange itself goes online; in other cases, the online space functions only as an organizational site to arrange for other services that are performed offline.

Two trends underpin and shape the direction of this digital service economy. One is the rise of "platform capitalism." This involves firms that mediate between user groups online. They design, provide, and regulate the infrastructure (i.e., website, app, etc.) for consumer and user interactions.[9] Platforms derive profit from monetizing online interactions of the mass public, or by converting goods into services, which in either case may enrich only a small group of shareholders.[10] In this chapter, I examine several categories of platforms that connect parties for service exchanges: job hiring and matching, crowdfunding and sourcing of labor, microcredit (i.e., small loans) and online lending, online marketplaces and the selling of goods, and the gig economy.

Platforms are powerful because they centralize large sectors of economic activity and incorporate large sectors of the consuming public, *into* a few specific sites. But at the same time, platforms are pushing many functions *onto* consumers. In what sociologists call "work transfer," consumers are increasingly doing tasks formerly done by firms and/or their employees.[11] To be sure, their form and scope of agency can be limited. These new "algocratically" run systems often set a small range of coded options within which consumers respond.[12] But it is in these contexts that platform capitalism is activating (or enabling) consumers for surveillance. Here, racial proclivities and assessments are given a space within the digital infrastructure, and then have a significant impact on economic transactions.

Consumers are the focal point of a second major trend in the digital service economy—the rise of "communicative capitalism."[13] Many of the most profitable and/or fast-rising sectors of the economy are no longer in material goods, but in the commoditization of communications. Some of this is in the *infrastructure* (cell phones, internet providers, etc.). Critically for this study, it is also in the *content* (e.g., market analysis of public texts, tweets, posts, etc.) and *facilitation of exchanges* between firms and their customers (e.g., customer service call centers).[14]

In sites like pizza delivery apps or recorded call center conversations, consumers are being called upon to do active surveillance of firms and their workers. They rate things ranging from the quality of service to the display of emotions.[15] Their opinions may be actively solicited (as in a survey) or expressed independently (as in the Facebook "like" button). Firms, then, are profiting not only from the goods and services that consumers are purchasing directly, but from the ratings they give on Yelp, the messages about the service they post on Twitter, and so on. (And as we've seen recently, corporate databases on their consumer information, including opinions, habits, attitudes, etc., may be more valuable than the firm itself.) Quite often, what consumers are observing, evaluating, and articulating in their online content is about race and ethnicity. In this chapter, I'll give examples from the content of globalized customer services (transnational call centers), and interactions with automated services (artificially intelligent avatars). These digital contexts are drawing especially heightened expectations, surveillance, and rhetoric of race and nation.

Thus, because the platforms are so large, and these communications with consumers (on the phone, on social media, in surveys, in ratings, etc.) are so integrated in the way capitalism functions, *consumers have a new role in looking back*. It is here that racialized assessments and narratives are being integrated, displayed, and recorded.

BODILY CAPITAL: THE FOCAL POINTS
FOR RACIAL SURVEILLANCE

Just what are the focal points for this racial surveillance? What exactly are consumers looking for in service interactions? In many cases, the surveillance of race is tied to embodiment. Critical race scholars reveal how this has been a characterizing feature of the development of the internet. Lisa Nakamura describes how the "interface" (e.g., a website page) is where digital bodies are being viewed, imagined, and socially constructed, and where everyday racial surveillance is occurring: "interfaces are prime loci for digital racial formation. . . . The interface serves to organize raced and gendered bodies in categories, boxes, and links that mimic both the mental structure of . . . a set of associations (often white, often male) and the logic of digital capitalism: to click on a box or link is to acquire it, to choose it, to replace one set of images with another in a friction-free transaction that seems to cost nothing yet generates capital in the form of digitally racialized images and performances."[16]

At these interfaces, participants in platforms and corporate communications are assessed for their bodily capital.[17] They accrue differential returns on investment for varying kinds of bodies, including ethnicities, genders, and nationalities. In the following analysis, I illustrate how consumers are favoring white bodies online. They are surveilling for these qualities, and then rewarding them with more favorable economic and social returns. The four cases below explore how things like visual images, names, associated locations, and so on are used to code some users as valuable and trustworthy, and others as not.

Below I chart how these digital service economies set the stage for consumers and digital users to "watch from below" and enact racial surveillance. The first two cases represent peer-to-peer matching services, in which platforms link users from the public to each other for the purpose of an economic exchange. The last two represent communicative services, in which representatives (live or automated) relay information from firms to their consumers. Each has unique dynamics and implications of racial embodiment and surveillance.

UNMATCHED: RACIAL SURVEILLANCE IN EMPLOYMENT,
LENDING, AND SELLING

Racial surveillance, to start with, is a prevalent feature of online service matching industries. These platforms have developed over the past fifteen years to move economic activities of job recruiting, money lending, and the

Winifred R. Poster

selling of goods onto the Internet. They connect various actors in the process of exchange: employers and potential candidates, buyers and sellers, and so on. In the process, users are at times racially filtering the entries based on features (real and imagined) of people's bodies. Here, I illustrate two ways this happens on such platforms: first based on names, résumés, and backgrounds, and second, based on photos of hands, faces, and figures.

Résumés: Names and Biohistories

Résumés are a common means of racial discrimination on matching sites for jobs. The most trafficked employment platforms are websites like Indeed .com, Monster.com, Careerbuilder.com, and Glassdoor.com. Some are search engines that aggregate job postings from various sites. Many also allow workers to find and apply for jobs, as well as create a profile and post a résumé for employers to see. Some also provide ratings systems, or employment guidance counseling. While many charge fees, several of them are free to use and therefore have massive memberships. Indeed.com has 180 million unique visitors per month, from fifty countries and speaking twenty-six languages.[18]

Yet some African Americans report troubling experiences on these sites. Yolanda Spivey is one such job candidate. Spivey worked in the insurance industry for ten years, and when it was time to switch jobs she turned to Monster.com. After two years and three hundred applications, as well as a stint reentering college to finish her degree, she had few responses. In turn, she became suspicious that employers were screening and passing on her application because of race.[19]

So in 2012 she embarked on what she calls the "Bianca White Experiment." She created a new profile with the exact same set of résumé information—with a few key exceptions. Instead of Yolanda Spivey, she changed her name to Bianca White. And instead of marking "black female" or "decline to identify" in the mandatory diversity questionnaire, she checked "white." Employers would also be directed to a different cell phone number, which had a greeting for Bianca on its voicemail.

The results of the weeklong experiment revealed both expected and unexpected outcomes. To begin with, Bianca received far more feedback from employers than Yolanda. Bianca's profile was viewed twenty-four times, Yolanda's ten. Bianca received seven emails, Yolanda two. Bianca received nine voicemail messages, Yolanda none. In fact, some employers called Bianca repeatedly, asking her urgently to come for an interview.

Furthermore, Bianca's responses were more substantial. Hers came with competitive salaries and benefits, and coverage for moving costs for out-of-state relocation—even when both personas received postings about the same job. Race is important then in multiple stages of recruitment on these sites—not only for getting noticed by employers initially, but also for the quality of jobs and resources that come during negotiations. Spivey's conclusion was that "the diversity questionnaire on job sites such as Monster.com may work against minorities, as employers are judging whom they hire based on it" and "resumes with ethnic names may go into the wastebasket and never see the light of day."[20]

Scholars tell us that résumés have a long-standing role in racial inequalities of the labor market, even offline. Names in particular are a primary means of discriminating against people of color in job matching and hiring. In a classic study, Bertrand and Mullainathan sent résumés to employers in Chicago and Boston, and found that those with white-sounding names (Emily Walsh or Greg Baker) received 50 percent more callbacks for interviews than those with African American–sounding names (such as Lakisha Washington or Jamal Jones).[21]

Newer research shows that even the "extracurricular activities" and "personal interests" sections of a profile can have significant impact on employment decisions. Sending 316 comparable mock résumés to large law firms, Rivera and Tilcsik found that the (male) candidates who played polo (versus track and field), liked classical music (versus country), and received awards for athletics (versus "athletes on financial aid") were more likely to be perceived as a good fit for the culture of the firm by recruiters and marked for callbacks for interviews.[22] Employers, it appears, are surveilling applicants for minute details and subtle cues of status within employee biohistories.

While Rivera and Tilcsik focused specifically on the class and gender dynamics of screening, one could argue that such criteria may also be read in racialized terms. Intersectional theory, along these lines, has emphasized that class, race, and gender are interlocking systems of inequality.[23] For example, sailing may be interpreted as a "white" activity as well as a "wealthy" one. Being on financial aid may be seen as a marker of ethnic minority status as well as working-class status. Preserving whiteness may go hand in hand with excluding minorities. In fact, the value of whiteness has been shown to supercede the potentially damaging features of candidate résumés by some recruiters. One classic study found that employers preferred whites *with criminal records* over blacks *without any record*, among those with similar educational and employment backgrounds.[24]

As recruitment shifts online, such dynamics have crossed over into the digital sphere. Here, other aspects of employee biohistories enter the re-

Winifred R. Poster

cruitment eye. Employers can get a sense of what kinds of people a candidate associates with, which may have consequences for race, class, and gender. On sites like LinkedIn, employers take advantage of the social networking features to evaluate the professional connections of candidates.[25] Here, employees "don't just list their previous work experience, but they also identify who they know and solicit endorsements from these connections. Employers use LinkedIn and other social network sites to determine 'cultural fit,' including whether or not a candidate knows people already known to the company. This process rewards individuals on the basis of their networks, leading companies to hire people who are more likely to 'fit the profile' of their existing employees—to the detriment of people who have historically been excluded from employment opportunities." These platforms represent another way to surveil candidate profiles for race. This can indirectly perpetuate discrimination, as recruiters use such information to screen out "undesirable" types of connections by race, while they seek the more "desirable" connections of a candidate who fits in "culturally" with the firm.

In sum, the surveillance of résumés, in terms of how they are read and interpreted by employers, involves both obvious and nonobvious markings of race, gender, or class. Sometimes it occurs in overt features of the digital interface—like checking a box for ethnic identity. But other times, it happens in the subtextual, minute, and perhaps least relevant elements of one's employment history and summary. Furthermore, the online profile itself can convey many cues for visualizing the race of a candidate's body. The corporeal features of the applicant are likely being imagined—as they listen to music, play sports, and interact with their colleagues. These cases show how text-based interfaces—which often do not have photos—are still surveilled by race in very careful and detailed ways by everyday actors.

Photos: Bodies, Faces, Hands

The racialized body is surveilled visually—for its face and body—on other kinds of peer-to-peer matching platforms. Take the case of Kiva.com. Kiva represents another sector of digital service, providing small loans to entrepreneurs largely in the Global South. The process is called "microcredit," and it originated several decades ago through the Grameen Bank in Bangladesh.[26] The idea was to provide impoverished communities access to small amounts of credit. These individuals would otherwise be ineligible for credit, due to lack of income or collateral, lack of access to banks in their rural locations, and/or being female. The industry grew rapidly, and now has millions of borrowers worldwide. Up until this time, the process had been run by traditional institutions, like banks, state governments, as well as international and local nonprofits. They provided the funds, selected the borrowers, and organized the repayment.

In 2005, however, the process spread to online platforms. Kiva as an example would loan $300 million to more than 700,000 borrowers by 2012.[27] It is often referred to as a "charity" because (among other things) it doesn't charge interest for its loans. (However, the intermediating microcredit firms—which represent the borrowers on the website—*do* charge interest.) Even so, platforms like this are linked to employment in a key way: they provide loans for entrepreneurs, who in turn can earn income from their own labor in a small business. In essence, then, they represent larger processes of both online job matching and crowdfunding, which in this case involves linking funders to small business people. Loans per borrower average about $700, and any given lender may fund a variety of different loans at the same time, with small contributions to each.

Several dynamics are critical in this transition. First is a change in the main actors providing the loans. Crowdfunding moves the source of funds from banks to the public—in the form of users of online platforms. These users supply the financing and make crucial decisions in selecting who gets funded from the list, and the speed with which their loan gets approved. Second, the platform itself becomes influential by determining what kinds of information are presented on the website and setting the rules for user interactions. As Gajjala and colleagues note, "these online sites shift the microcredit concept into the global visual and communicative spaces of the . . . social networking models popularized in 'web 2.0' Internet culture."[28] Lending, therefore, becomes embedded in the larger dynamics of social networking. This includes its patterns of evaluating people by their images, and the racial processes therein.

It is not surprising, then, that the transition to online platforms has not benefited all ethnic groups the same way. Studies show that lenders make discriminatory assessments of visual images of faces and bodies. This in turn has a profound effect on how these platforms work in practice, and how lenders make decisions. It starts with the layout of the interface. When lenders go to the site, they browse through a long list of potential borrowers, each with a picture, a paragraph description of biohistory and business, and details of the loan (figures 6.1 and 6.2).

The photos are found to play a large part in the decision process, as lenders use them as a quick way to filter the profiles and analyze potential credit

Winifred R. Poster

Tania María

🏪 **Ecuador** | Retail | General Store

Tania is a 38-year-old woman. She considers herself to be a woman of strict character, who likes things to be done well and is very responsible in her business. Tania lives with her husband and...

Funding via FODEMI, a partner of World Vision International

FIGURE 6.1. Image of crowdfunding worker on Kiva.com.
Source: Kiva.com, as published in Goldmark (2012).

Mark Rotich

▤ **Kenya** | Agriculture | Livestock

Mark is a family man aged forty years who supports a family of five. His wife, Caroline, is a businesswoman. Mark has been a livestock trader over the past five years and earns a monthly income of...

Funding via Kenya Agency for Development of Enterprise and Technology (KADET), a partner of World Vision International

FIGURE 6.2. Image of crowdfunding worker on Kiva.com.
Source: Kiva.com, as published in Goldmark (2012).

risk. As Jenq and colleagues conclude, funders are more likely to favor borrowers who are: pretty versus ugly, underweight versus overweight, and light-skinned versus dark-skinned.[29] These features of body size, attractiveness, and race have a significant impact on the speed with which borrowers reach their requested loan amount from various funders. Notable is that, given the opportunity, lenders will assess the whole body of the borrower. Under the surveillance radar is a range of physical traits for analysis, including how much the body matches idealized notions of beauty, and how much it approximates whiteness. Elements of corporality are interlinked, so that surveillance encompasses color, weight, and appearance.

Yet, significantly, none of these factors turns out to be helpful in determining who is a competent borrower: attractiveness, size, and race are not correlated with likeliness to become delinquent on a loan. Lenders appear to

FIGURE 6.3.
Differential
evaluation of online
advertisements
featuring white
versus black hands.
Source: Doleac and
Stein (2010), p. 6.

be basing their credit assessments on things that have little or nothing to do with financial risk.

While digital racism can be triggered by images of bodies, it can also be triggered by much less. Just seeing a hand is enough to evoke discrimination. We see this in online markets for goods and services. This happens in classified advertising sites like Craigslist and eBay. Such platforms represent another important segment of the service economy—those mediating relations between "sellers" and "buyers" through the internet. Some take the form of auctions, in which buyers place offers on an item and sellers take the highest bid. Others include listings with a set price. Either way, the act of becoming a retailer often involves posting the item in an online ad. Some sellers take a picture of the item while holding the item, as in figure 6.3.[30]

Racial filtering is found to be a common aftereffect of such postings, given that consumers surveil the bodies of the retailers in these photos—even while they are supposed to be looking at the object for sale. Studies show that when

Winifred R. Poster

viewing the same iPod Nano music player on these digital advertising sites, consumers favored photographs showing a white hand holding the item over a black hand. Doleac and Stein tried this experiment in three hundred cities and local markets, and found differential rates of consumer interest in purchasing the various photos. Black sellers received 13 percent fewer responses to their ads, and 17 percent fewer offers to purchase the item. Furthermore, the highest bids that black sellers received were $3.56 lower than those of the white sellers. This indicates how visuals, therefore, are important screening mechanisms of racial surveillance for consumers, just as they are for the funders and employers above.

UN-SHARED: RACIAL SURVEILLANCE IN HOUSING AND TRANSPORTATION

The "sharing" economy is so called for the way it opens personal resources for rental and exchange to the public. Individuals have offered their cars, homes, and skills to consumers at an unprecedented rate through online markets and apps. Yet many people of color are not experiencing this openness, as either the sharees or the sharers.[31]

Accordingly, a second form of racial surveillance online is in the filtering of listings on transportation and housing platforms. Research is revealing how services like Uber and Airbnb are at risk for such patterns. On these sites, multiple kinds of participants—the "sharers" (landlords, hosts, drivers, etc.), on the one hand, as well as the "sharees" (renters, guests, passengers, etc.), on the other—are found to participate in discriminatory behaviors based on the context.

As in the last section, this happens as people surveil online entries according to racial features of people's bodies, especially names and photos. One aspect of housing and transportation is distinct from that of employment and lending, however—geography. Online discrimination in sharing economies is linked to the racial segregation of physical locations where the services are, where people reside, and where the individual is going. In other words, the movement of bodies in geographic space offline is linked to unequal behaviors online.

Housing

To begin with, the homes and residences of people of color are evaluated differently when put on the virtual market for exchange. Nonwhites are found to experience a penalty for their properties on these platforms. For instance, among listings of similar apartments with similar photos in New York City, white hosts on Airbnb are able to charge 12 percent more for their rentals than black hosts. This is a difference of $144 versus $107 per night, according to a study by Edelman and Luca.[32] In addition, black hosts experience a greater penalty in price as a result of "poor location" scores that guests leave on the website, relative to nonblacks.

A larger study of 19 cities across Europe and North America found a similar result: hosts of majority ethnicities were able to charge 16 percent more than African or Arab hosts for locations in the same city.[33] Some of that difference is related to the quality of the properties (as observed in the photos), and the neighborhoods where they are located. But a final 3 percent of the gap is racial preference among similar properties and neighborhoods. Consumers, it appears, are willing to pay premium for non-black-hosted housing, thus perpetuating discrimination in online forums through their role as "guests."

Housing discrimination also occurs in the opposite direction on these platforms as well. In other words, *hosts* racially discriminate against *guests*, by selecting and reserving their rentals for whites. In a study of five U.S. cities, Airbnb hosts are less likely to accept guests with African American-sounding names by 16 percent.[34] Edelman and colleagues caution that such evidence suggests an erosion of previous gains in civil rights, given that housing discrimination had been waning until these online platforms were introduced.

Transportation

Racialization of geography enters transportation services via mobile apps like Uber and Lyft. Here as well, users may screen directly or indirectly for race, and treat others in the service relation differentially based on that screening.

Riders (i.e., the customers) at times discriminate against drivers (i.e., the employees). This happens through their ratings on the app after the ride, for instance, which are hugely influential on employee wages, whether or not they get fired, and their ability to gain future riders.[35] Surveillance of racialized bodies is focused on how drivers dress, carry themselves, and construct their physique: "passengers might implicitly rate minority drivers less charitably if, for instance, their self-presentation fails to emulate perceived white, middle-class norms."[36]

On the other hand, there is evidence that drivers racially discriminate against riders. A recent study in Seattle and Boston found that black pas-

Winifred R. Poster

sengers waited up to 35 percent longer than whites for their rides.[37] This happens as drivers surveil the race of the customer for their ethnicity based on their name and/or their photo, depending on the app. Lyft drivers do this by refusing to accept the trip at the outset, because the name of the passenger is displayed at the time of the request. UberX drivers do this by canceling the ride after the activation of the request, since that's when the name is displayed for the driver.

Location and urban space play a role in this pattern of racial inequality. Certain places are deemed more risky for drivers to make pickups, and therefore even less likely for a person of color to get a ride. When the pickup is in a Boston neighborhood with a low population density, for instance, the likelihood of an UberX driver canceling on black versus white male riders increases by more than four times. The cancellation rate also rises when the pickup is near a subway stop. Ge and colleagues interpret this finding as drivers screening against low-income riders, or riders who are on "multi-modal journeys" and therefore ultimately yielding "a lower expected revenue."[38]

Blogs and internet posts add more depth to this discussion, revealing experiences of discrimination based on the destinations where black passengers want to go. Some report that drivers refuse to take them to certain neighborhoods in big cities. Or they may use devious methods in the interaction itself, like pretending to not know where the destination is. This happened in Washington, DC, to Doug Glanville, a commentator for ESPN:

> The driver pulled up, I got in the car, and he asked where I was going. I told him Nationals Park. "I do not know where it is," he told me. Skeptically, I asked, "Come on, Nationals Park? The baseball stadium?" I told him I had my smartphone and could pull up the directions on Google Maps. (I was sure he also had a smartphone, or another device with GPS.) Still, he stayed put and waited for me to get out, saying over and over that he was new on the job and new to the area. So I exited the cab and hailed another one.
>
> In Chicago, where I played on the Cubs and lived for much of my post-career, the same thing happened a few too many times when I was trying to get a ride from downtown at night. In those instances, you had to navigate the "Mason-Dixon" line between the North and South Side. When driver after driver assumed I was heading south into the heavily African American sections of town (which should not have mattered anyway), I was in for a long night.[39]

These kinds of spatial issues, accordingly, may contribute to the way sharing economy drivers treat requests from black passengers—just based on their names and photos. Furthermore, they suggest that, even if the platforms remove names and photos online. This may not eliminate other kinds of discrimination that may take place in the service provision itself that occurs offline. This happened once to Glanville when an Uber driver pulled up, got out of the car to load luggage in the trunk, and, upon seeing his face, denied him the ride.

The takeaway is that the racial surveillance of names and photos is often layered with, and mapped onto, that of landscapes, properties, homes, and so on.

TRANSNATIONAL CALL CENTERS:
RACIAL SURVEILLANCE ACROSS BORDERS

A third form of racial surveillance in the service economy can be found in the case of global call centers. Here we shift to a different sector of digital services—away from those that match members of the public to each other (i.e., peer to peer), toward those that provide communications between organizations and the public (i.e., firms to customers). Communications become racially embodied as the agents of service are assessed for (and reshaped by) the way they look and sound. In the next two sections, I'll examine how this happens with live and automated service workers.

Global call centers illustrate these dynamics in providing customer service on the phone. Their employees typically do help-desk problem solving, technical support, telemarketing, and debt collection. In the process of these conversations, sound becomes the conduit for racism by consumers in digital economies.[40] If the previous cases illustrate the surveillance of racial embodiment through names, pictures, and biohistories, here it happens through talk, language, and accent. Call centers reflect, in particular, the expansion of digital service transnationally, and the ensuing tensions of outsourcing, globalization, and nationalism.

Foreign Accents and the Nationality of Service
In the service economy, accents matter. Scholars of aesthetic labor call this the rule of "looking good and *sounding right*" (my emphasis).[41] In the same way that names and photos matter in getting a job, as discussed earlier, so does the sound of one's voice. Studies have shown that employers in the United States make decisions about a worker's career and earning potential based on

Winifred R. Poster

his/her accent in the interview process. For instance, Asian, Latino, and African American applicants with minimal accents were rated as more employable than those with prominent accents.[42] Speakers of nonstandard English (e.g., with regional dialects) were seen as lazy, incompetent, unprofessional, uncreative, and so forth. Moreover, there is a racial hierarchy within the nonstandard speech—the talk of African Americans was rated more negatively than Appalachian English among whites.[43] Nationality and foreign accents are hierarchically evaluated as well. Research finds that employers privilege French and American accents over those of the Japanese.[44]

So it is not surprising that accents (along with other features of talk) became a focal point for racial backlash as the call center industry goes global. Prior to the year 2000, customer service used to be something that firms did in-house or at least close by. It was "captive" in industry-speak, meaning it was inside their own companies and offices, or else outsourced to nearby third-party firms. Advancements in the technology of communications at the end of the millennium, however, enabled firms to act on neoliberal imperatives of reducing costs through globalization. With fiber optic cables now under the Atlantic Ocean, satellite communications in space, and VOIP (voice over internet protocols) enabling calls through the internet, phone work was now mobile and unhinged from geography. Firms began moving customer services to countries like India, where they could find plenty of educated, English-speaking workers, and at wages a tenth of those in the United States. Now there are more than a million call center workers in India alone.

Consumers, in turn, have reacted to global call centers by targeting the accents of the service workers. Thirty-two percent of U.S. consumers report negative responses to Asian-sounding call center workers, just based on their accent.[45] Customers in Australia report negative responses to hearing Indian or Filipino accents as well.[46] Another study found that people are more likely to stereotype, and thus negatively rate, the call center performance of workers with Indian versus British or American accents.[47]

Surveillance of Sound

Acting on these sentiments, some consumers in the United States have been surveilling employees for ethnicity and nationality in their conversations on the phone. They do this in a variety of ways, such as recording the calls, phoning in complaints about employees, filing negative customer service ratings, and so on. One group in particular has created an online database to catalogue their results. Get2Human.com[48] is a website that organizes people against the automation of call centers (and, as its name suggests, toward the goal of "get"-ting customers "to a human" employee). Yet, it is also clear that they don't want *any* employee—just the ones without foreign accents.

Their database has a system of red flags to signify how well or poorly firms are achieving this standard. The last column of the database is titled "Agent Communications." Proudly featured on the homepage as a "special addition" to the database, it places red flag icons next to "enterprises that are using agents that callers are having a hard time communicating with because of a severe accent." The more red flags, the worse the offender (see figure 6.4).

The red flags serve multiple purposes. They send a warning *to consumers* in terms of what firms to avoid, and possibly encouraging boycotts. The red flags also send a message *to firms* from consumers about changing their practices: "With this data, we would then be able to identify the enterprises that are using CSRs [customer service representatives] that are difficult to understand, and let them know that they have a problem that they need to fix."

Certainly, clear communication is a reasonable precondition for good customer service. But there are signs that the reactions on this website are about something else. To begin with, there is strong rhetoric of hypernationalism. The site's self-described "project leader" inserts anti-American themes in his blog, stating that vendors behave in ways that are "anti-consumer, anti-capitalist, and anti-American."

Member discourse is more inflammatory and explicitly xenophobic. On the GetHuman Google Group, members are encouraged to post their experiences, opinions, and "call center horror stories." Prizes are offered for the worst cases of customer service. In a thread called "India, Phillapines [*sic*], etc. Call Center Avoidance," one consumer writes: "I . . . have an EXTREMELY difficult time hearing heavily accented English. I also believe these jobs should go to AMERICANS. We need to take [care] of our own . . ." A second consumer proposes "an exposé website on how to avoid the call going to a non[-]USA call center." There are appeals to "Boycott companies who outsource" and to "buy local, keep America Working."

Sometimes the rhetoric online, as well as on the call itself with outsourced workers, can become abusive and explicitly xenophobic. Call center scholars refer to this behavior as "customer cyberbullying," given the growing range of digital contexts in which these nationalized outbursts and types of discourse are appearing.[49] In any case, social media forums illustrate how consumers monitor call center voices for their ethnic and national qualities, and subsequently act on their feelings collectively.

Winifred R. Poster

FIGURE 6.4. Red flags (in right-hand column) for undesirable accents in call center employees. Source: Get2Human.com (2009).

Masking Place, Whitening Talk

Outsourcing employers quickly responded to these mobilizations with attempts to resolve consumer tensions. Especially in the early stages of the global call center industry, their plan was to cover up the location of the employees through their sound and talk. The idea was to train (and retrain) employees in a variety of linguistic and behavioral skills, so that they can convey to American (and other) customers that they are in fact *in the United States*.[50] This strategy reveals how sounds in the communicative sector of the digital service industry are not only surveilled for ethnicity but reconstituted as well.

I refer to this process as "national identity management" (NIM). It has four components for employee behavioral modification: (1) *voice and accent* to reproduce American diction, voice modulation, rhythm (including number of beats per second), and grammar; (2) an *alias* to announce American identity to the customers through their name; (3) *conversational skills* to convey through small talk (and thus indirectly) that they are in the United States. This includes extensive knowledge of American consumer items, retail outlets, restaurants, and so on. It also includes knowledge of the lingo of current events, sports, weather, and time for the zone they are calling.

And finally, (4) the worker learns a *script* to repeat when customers test the boundaries of that façade, and pose the looming question: "Where are you calling from?" The predefined responses range from the opaque: "an outbound call center," to the semi-specific (and somewhat truthful) "in Asia," to the less honest "a U.S. office of the client firm." And "if they ask again, then we change the subject." As the HR trainer summarized, "It's a marketing strategy—if you cannot convince, confuse."

Extreme forms of NIM (like the outright lying in number 4) have dissipated in the second decade of the global call center industry. However, the other forms have not only remained, but spread further as the industry has reached out across the Global South. As my colleague Kiran Mirchandani and I have observed in our book *Borders in Service*, features of NIM are evident in call centers from Morocco, to El Salvador, Guatemala, Guyana, and the Mexico-U.S. border, to Mauritius and the Philippines.[51] In many of these cases, workers are asked to participate in communicative obfuscations of their nationality.

This is done, moreover, to reflect the consumer cultures of their former colonizers, who now exert their influence through outsourced service industries. Eurocentric speech patterns and identities (from Spain, France, England, etc.) become standards for service workers worldwide. Thus, workers in Guatemala take on American names like Donald; workers in Morocco use French aliases like Marianne. Call centers in El Salvador hire former nationals—deportees who have been expelled from the United States. This way, employers can take advantage of employees' linguistic capital—the American accents and conversational styles they have acquired from living in that country—when talking to American consumers on the phone. No extra training for national identity management needed.

Accent in this case becomes a marker for racial surveillance by consumers as digital communications cross borders. Accent is also a focal point for reconditioning employee race and nation by call centers, and for the whitening of sound in the global service economy. Such employment practices mask not only local diversities of ethnicity within the United States, but also the diversities of nation and geography.

DIGITAL ASSISTANTS: RACIAL SURVEILLANCE IN ARTIFICIAL INTELLIGENCE

Yet consumers are not just communicating with *live* humans in digital services anymore. They are frequently talking to digital assistants, chatbots, and social agents. This reflects an emerging trend of integrating artificial intelligence within the everyday interactions of firms and their consumers. Firms are representing themselves as avatars—in racialized ways—with faces, bodies, and personal stories, as I outline below. Consumers are not unaware of this. They are highly attuned to these racializations of IT. The embodi-

Winifred R. Poster

ment of the digital assistants becomes the trigger point, in the following discussion, for interactive forms of consumer racial surveillance through AI and
social media.

Ethnically Embodied Bots

Digital assistants started appearing around the mid-1990s when advances in
human–computer interaction and AI made it possible for those systems to
seem humanlike. This technology endowed automated systems with voices,
appearances, capacity for chattiness and informal talk, and even emotions.[52]
Computer programs were then able to interact directly with customers
through digital platforms.[53] The term *bot* has developed in popular lingo as
a short form of *robot*. It refers to software programs that perform a range of
automated tasks. A subset of these bots are "embodied agents," which have
visual bodies and therefore serve as a graphical front end for the computer
systems behind.

Pundits have touted that robots are beyond race, and instead represent
an era of posthuman "freedom." Yet critical race, feminist, and postcolonial
scholars argue otherwise. Atanasoski and Vora contend that, given these
"surrogate humans" or "technological standins," "humanity stands in a differential if connected relationship to artificial intelligence and networked
objects, a relationship that continues to be racialized."[54]

Bots are racially embodied in a variety of ways. One is through a default
whiteness. Many of the visual depictions of the customer service bots include bodies that are white in appearance (figures 6.5–6.7). Especially in the
early years, technology designers and service firms were quite frank about
shaping digital bodies in this way. Take the case of Ananova, who read the
news to the public for French telecommunications company Orange News
from about 2000 to 2009. She did this in real time, 24/7, with 3D graphics, on
mobile devices and desktop computers. Ananova's physique was designed as
a composite of white female celebrities: pop singers Victoria Beckham and
Kylie Minogue, and TV game show host Carol Vorderman. The BBC reported:
"she has the profile of a single 28-year-old 'girl about town' who loves Oasis
and The Simpsons and is 5ft 8in (1.73m) tall."[55] Her racial identity is encoded
in her cultural preferences as well as in her appearance.

Committed to constructing a surrogate human that is racialized and gendered, firms have hired specialized Silicon Valley firms to create such back-
stories for these digital assistants. Yahoo's Jenni, who dictated consumer
emails over the phone, had an entire background including a résumé.[56] Jenni
is described in a seven hundred-plus word biography with fake job references,

FIGURE 6.5–6.7. The feminized whitening of virtual assistants. Left: Ava; source: Scott Beale/Laughing Squid (2012). Right: Ananova; source: Ananova.com (2009). Below: Alice; source: Wintech LLC (2015).

university degrees, and boyfriends. Even though we hear her on the phone without seeing her, the biography details her physical features: 5 ft 5 in, 108 lbs—and blue eyes, a code for white ethnicity.

The newer, specialized avatars adopt a dynamic visual form—so that the consumer can see racial embodiment in moving faces and full human figures (figure 6.7). Some of these digital assistants are flat-screen receptionists and holograms.[57] Alice, for instance, is presented as a video of a white woman, whose face or upper torso appears on a monitor. In product advertisements, Alice sits at the front desk of an office replacing the stereotypical human receptionist (i.e., the white smiling secretary). Ava, also white, is a hologram video of a human actor, standing as a life-size image and talking to customers as they approach.

The most ubiquitous virtual assistants are ones we hear in our phones, cars, TVs, and so on. They talk to us, even if we don't see them. Many have female personas: from Siri of the Apple iPhone, to Cortana of Microsoft, to Alexa of the Amazon Echo.[58] Curiously, Apple tried to keep Siri's identity (racial and otherwise) secret. They were successful for many years, from 2005 to 2013, when Siri's identity was revealed by the press. Her voice was recorded by a white actor named Susan Bennett from Georgia.[59] Although the reason for this secrecy is unclear, it may possibly have been a strategic attempt to promote a façade of "racial neutrality" in Siri's image.

In each of these cases, virtual assistant chatbots have been constructed in a particular form of white femininity: one that is deferential and courteous, as well as one that fills particular roles for the service economy. She provides information (albeit in a simplistic form) and she acts as a spokesperson for firms to the public. White femininity is useful and nonthreatening for these purposes. Even though composed largely from algorithms, the bots are embedded with features of live humans—whether that is a voice (for Siri), a graphic image (for Ananova), video footage (for Ava), or a backstory (for Jenni). They are cyborg service workers who, in the process of sociotechnical design, become whitened.

Not all the corporate bots are coded white, of course. Some are designed with readily identifiable features of other ethnicities. Scholars Miriam Sweeney and Melissa Villa-Nicholas have been documenting these trends. Latina bots, for instance, have been deployed in settings where state agencies and private firms find it useful for specific target consumer bases.[60] Emma is a Latina avatar appearing on the U.S. immigration website. She mediates the state's relationship with its immigrant populations and those seeking citizenship. Ava, the hologram described above, also appears as a Latina for the transportation industry—but typically in airports with large populations of Latino passengers, like those in California and Texas. She is "only sometimes Latina," coded differently for various geographic regions.

More common is the racially ambiguous chatbot, like Ms. Dewey.[61] Created by Microsoft as a virtual search engine assistant, she is presented as "a woman of color, albeit light-skinned, and of ambiguous ethnic and racial identity."[62] Moreover, she "switches into racially coded performances" from a Western cowboy to urban blackness, as her "ambiguous ethnicity acts as an affordance that allows her to move in and out of identities that validate different stereotypes for the searcher."[63] Yet underneath, the live actor who provides her voice is Janina Gavankar, an American woman of South Asian descent. Like the call center workers above, she is the service worker whose South Asian identity is kept silent, if not carefully masked.

This elaborates what Eglash describes in terms the range of ethnicities that are at play among technocultural identities.[64] Whiteness is only one of these identities. The male nerd, for instance, represents a dominant identity, as a gatekeeper for elites. It sits alongside stereotypes of Asian hyperintellectualism and black hypersexuality, and acts as a balance between them. These are all challenged by alternative racial-gender identities: black nerds, Asian hipsters, and geek grrrls, intervene on the prior stereotypes. Filling out this typology of ethnic representations is important for understanding the role of service industry bots as well.

In sum, virtual assistants achieve the fantasy of a postracial society, where the reality of an ethnically diverse society is obscured by the idea of whiteness as neutral, or else race as ambiguous. The traces of inscribed race within the bots—as represented in their sounds, faces, and talk—become starting points for racial surveillance by consumers. As we see next, bots are entering the realm of social media where their gaze is magnified exponentially by millions of users. Here, the racial ambiguity of the bots lets consumers see what they want to see. And sometimes what they want to see is a white supremacist.

Consumers Talk to the Avatars

Recently artificial intelligence technology is enabling bots to converse—by expressing ideas, using informal language, discussing political perspectives, conveying emotions, and so on. With "machine learning," bot algorithms use pattern recognition and analysis of data to predict model behaviors, without requiring explicit programmed instructions. On social media, they do this in the moment—analyzing user text as it is inputted, and crafting responses to mimic the text.

Winifred R. Poster

Given the behavior of consumers in online environments, though, the use of such AI systems foreshadows significant problems of racialized service. This is illustrated in the case of Tay. Tay is a chatbot created by a team at Microsoft with the persona of an eighteen- to twenty-four-year-old American woman (of unspecified ethnicity). She was designed to be the next generation of AI that can talk to the public on Twitter, by engaging in conversations in a new way. Rather than just imitating humans by picking out keywords and rephrasing them, as Neff and Nagy explain, Tay would be more humanlike.[65] Her talk would include randomness, jokes, and opinions. She could also be unpredictable and irrational, in the style of the millennial population—"funny, angering, whimsical, and snarky all at once."[66]

Yet, just sixteen hours after her release on Twitter on March 23, 2016, Tay was decommissioned due to a stream of inflammatory racist, sexist, and xenophobic remarks. Although the tweets started out benign, the conversation degraded quickly. The Twitter community pointed her toward racist statements and positions. People barraged her with questions about incendiary topics, so that her machine learning functions would spew them right back.

In many cases, users would ask Tay to repeat their statements, or ask if she agreed with them. These included calling for a "race war," establishing concentration camps, and valorizing the Holocaust. Violent expletives and abuses were charged against many ethnic groups including Mexicans, blacks, Asians, and Jews (figures 6.8–6.10). Some tweets vowed allegiance to white supremacy with the neo-Nazi code of "Fourteen Words," which are "We must secure the existence of our people and a future for white children." Microsoft attempted to fix this problem a few days later and put her back online, but she was promptly removed again due to continuing troubles.

Neff and Nagy reflect on the many groups that were blamed for this event in the public discourse of the aftermath.[67] Fingers were pointed at Microsoft executives, coders, the Twitter community, specific pranksters, and so on, as instigators of Tay's behavior. There may be partial truths to each of them.

For this discussion of racial surveillance in the digital service economy, what stands out is the agency of *consumers*. (Those in the United States, in particular. Interestingly, the same outcome did not occur when Tay's counterpart was put online in China, even though the software was similar.) Consumers here are the drivers of racialization, providing examples of racist discourse for the avatar to input and pattern. Thus, with artificial intelligence and machine learning, racialization of human surrogates comes not only with the coding and design of the digital assistants, but in the way that humans incite them toward those behaviors.

FIGURE 6.8.
Racist tweet from Tay.
Source: Kleeman (2016).

FIGURE 6.9.
Racist tweet from Tay.
Source: Price (2016).

FIGURE 6.10.
Racist tweet from Tay.
Source: Price (2016).

Racial surveillance occurs within this process through the intricate dynamic between the service bot and its consumer. Consumers and users provoke the avatars in order to determine exactly how far they will go toward white supremacy. This taunting is a form of digital normalization:[68] consumers observe Tay's talk, evaluate it, and test how it measures up to extreme models of racial discourse, and prompt it in that direction.

But there is another disciplinary process operating here—one aimed at the consuming public itself. As a more diffuse outcome, this happens *through* the bot as an intermediary. Consumers put their racial surveillance activities on public display, and in doing so, set new standards for consumer–bot interaction in the future. They ultimately use the bot to discipline each other,

Winifred R. Poster

with the power of trolling and the wave of the crowd as tools against the voices of people of color, women, transgendered communities, and so on.[69]

Of course, Tay is only one example of a chatbot, and at that, may represent the extreme. Still, unlike the more symbolic racism of the virtual assistants above, the case of Tay represents a trend of flagrant, overt racism in digital service. It shows how the future of racial embodiment in digital service is not just in what the bots sound like or even look like—it is in how they interact with consumers and the public.

DISCUSSION

What accounts for these practices of racial surveillance in the digital economy? Why is the consuming public, in particular, so focused on race in their online service encounters? Critical race scholars point out how the United States is in the midst of a social transformation, in which two models of race relations are active at the same time (although shifting in scope). We can see markers of each in the examples above.

One is a "color-blind racism." As Bonilla-Silva explains, these are racist practices "that are subtle, institutional, and apparently nonracial."[70] He describes it as "smiling face discrimination." Unlike the "brutal and overt system of oppression in the pre-civil rights era, colorblind racism serves today as the ideological armor for a covert and institutionalized system in the post-civil rights era." This has been a defining feature of U.S. race relations for almost the past half century.

In this chapter, we find evidence of this covert racism in the service matching platforms, where digital users are conducting racial surveillance within their online scanning and selections. Significantly, they carry it out privately and behind the scenes—where no one can see them. It is a silent form of racism. It is also apparent in the communicative assistant avatars, which quietly enforce a norm of whiteness, and alternatively, define the boundaries for images of people of color in future consumer interactions online.

The other form of race relations is more virulent and out front. It is likely motivated by an impending and profound demographic change in the racial makeup of the U.S. population—the end to majority status for whites. As this transformation takes place, it is accompanied by a hostile backlash and a resurgence of racist hate groups. Daniel Citron shows us how this trend is being aided by current technologies. Features of the internet are magnifying the potential for people to express racist content:[71] "Explicit hate is on the rise online even at it has diminished offline. . . . Some of the Internet's key features—anonymity, mobilization of groups, and group polarization—make it more likely that people will act destructively. Other features, such as information cascades and Google Bombs, enhance the destruction's accessibility, making it more likely to inflict harm." Thus, we see signs of this "digital hate" that Citron describes in many examples of this chapter: in the hypernationalist vitriol on Get2Human about Indian call center workers, in the racist rantings meant to provoke Tay, and in the Uber driver who refuses a passenger's request when seeing his ethnicity in person. Each of these actions contributes to a disciplinary regime of race, even if in different pathways.

Ultimately, for people of color, these trends have contradictory implications.[72] At times, they may find that they are too visible (as in the matching sites and call centers), where they are flagged for their race, and then weeded out or protested against. In other cases, they are being erased or not seen at all (as in the avatars and facial recognition algorithms). This is a perennial tension for people living under surveillance.[73] But it is especially problematic for racial surveillance in particular, as people of color become the targets of profiling or else they become invisible and removed from consideration for legitimate service interactions.[74]

CONCLUSION

Consumers and digital users have a heighted role in the digital service economy, including an empowered agency in conducting racial surveillance. A frame of multi-surveillance redirects our thinking around this dynamic. It posits that consumers, often overlooked by traditional accounts of surveillance, are one of many groups participating in critical acts of observing. Moreover, as they are co-opted into massive systems of matching and communication in digital services, they are increasingly watching each other.

Race becomes a pivotal factor in this process. Intersectional theory informs how racial hierarchies, which are distinct from other systems of inequality, can cut across those of class. Consumers are not necessarily unified, but varying in their orientations toward racial hierarchies. Some of these consumers take part in observing the racial bodily capital of others as they participate in the digital service economy.

Of course, given the breadth of who has become a "consumer" or a "user" in these new digital systems, there are many kinds of surveillors. Their gazes, even among consumers, may be tilted in different directions. Some gazes are downward, like the employers who observe job candidates; others are

Winifred R. Poster

upward, like the guests who observe the hosts or owners of the houses where they stay. But the point is that consumers are now empowered to do this racial surveillance on a wide scale. And critically, the outcome may be the same regardless of which type of consumer practices it, as discussed next.

Redefining Surveillance

Racialized consumer surveillance is noteworthy for several reasons. For one thing, it involves micro acts of surveillance that are done by individuals, often independently, as they scan websites, dissect profiles, and assess user ethnicities for measures of whiteness. It is also interactive. Racial surveillance in the digital service economy is more than just watching. It happens within the process of a direct exchange—in a survey, in the selection of a service provider, in a phone conversation, in a Tweet, and so on.

The two contexts of this study illustrate various forms of how this interactive digital surveillance can play out. In the peer-to-peer matching systems, it happens by the click of a button. Users and consumers gaze at profiles, evaluate bodies, and then select out racially appropriate photos or names. In the communications systems, it is performative and expressive. Users observe avatars and listen to outsourced workers, and then examine for racialized looks and sounds. They may test them for racial conformity with prodding questions, and then verbally or textually discipline those who are outside the ethnic or national norm.

These acts may be unintentional and unconscious, or signals of overt agendas of xenophobia and racial supremacy. But either way, they have concrete impacts on racialized discipline. Consumer decisions have quantifiable (as well as symbolic) outcomes for the people of color who participate in those sites. They may materialize as refusals of service, lower ratings, slanders and threats of harm via social media, and so forth. But every time someone clicks away a photo of person of color or posts a rant against a foreign call center worker, it becomes another means of punishing an individual and strengthening institutional racism.

For all these reasons, this chapter has argued that watching from below can reinforce dominant hierarchies as much as watching from above. Many groups are responsible for enabling consumers to behave in this way. Firms that own these platforms, and the designers who create their core technologies, provide the boundaries for precluding or allowing those behaviors. Yet it is precisely the diffusion of multi-surveillance (and the dispersion of agency to various actors) that makes accountability such a problem. Because this kind of surveillance is done en masse, no single person is called out for racist behavior. It becomes pervasive in how these platforms and communications operate, even if those systems were not originally intended for it.

Responding to the Critics

Scholars of classic surveillance studies may disagree with some of these premises. Real surveillance, they may say, is continuous and unending; it is done by people in power (especially employers); it requires and operates through an underlying digital apparatus (that does the work of monitoring and recording of data); it disciplines through containment (rather than by tracking and excluding), and so forth.

Certainly, I would agree, the dynamics of surveillance from below may take different forms than those from above. And likewise, consumers may not necessarily be watching elites as much as they are watching each other. However, it would be a serious oversight to discount this "surveillance from below" just because it happens in a singular moment, or because it is part of the everyday, or because it involves human activity (i.e., of users), or because it is done by people who traditionally do not have institutional authority.

The influence (and power) of consumer surveillance, rather, is in the way that (1) it is done en masse, by the full scale of the consuming public including millions of digital users; (2) it gives support to particular institutional systems of power, like racism; and (3) it has material consequences in punishing or marginalizing those who don't fit the norm of visual, nominal, or textual whiteness. Consumers, in this way, are an increasingly significant component of contemporary surveillance as well as the workings of digital race.

In fact, these dynamics may be occurring well beyond the service economy. Future studies can examine how racialized multi-surveillance takes shape across a range of sites, especially where consumers and other groups are observing from below.

Considering Change and Resistance

There are many strategies for resistance and change in the digital service economy. A common proposal is to make the platforms and communications systems more fair. Intervening in the technical design and social policy may help to curb the practice of racial surveillance.

Take the use of photographs. If uploading images of sellers, borrowers, and employees on these sites leads to racial discrimination, for instance, why not just remove them? Research shows that platforms *without* images (like Flywheel) are less likely to show significant discrimination than those

Winifred R. Poster

with images (like Lyft or Uber).[75] Many other service economy platforms, like eBay, have never had a policy of posting photos.[76] A similar suggestion has been made for posting names. Instead, platforms could assign individuals a unique passcode.[77] This would be created by the company and then confirmed when the two parties meet, thereby assuring identity but avoiding the problematic racialized notions that are associated with certain names.

In fact, this idea of racial anonymization has been a longtime strategy of some social justice advocates in the African American community. "Ban the Box" (http://bantheboxcampaign.org/) is a campaign to remove an item on job and housing applications asking candidates to check "prior history of felony." Noting that one in four Americans has a conviction history (roughly 65 million people), organizers argue that the box has widespread impact. It contributes to discrimination against peoples of color and prevents the formerly incarcerated from reintegrating into society. This campaign has been successful in banning the box in over forty-five cities and counties around the country.

Yet while racial bias can be averted through careful masking policies like this, it may also surface later when the platform is no longer mediating the interaction. Masking race in online service interactions can simply delay other kinds discriminations that can take place down the line in the service provision, as occurred within the ride-hailing app case above. It also happens in Indian call centers. Managers have been attempting this hiding of national identity for almost two decades now by requiring workers to use an Americanized "alias" at the top of the call. The aim is for ease of communication (i.e., to help Americans pronounce Indian names), but it is also to protect workers from xenophobic abuse.[78] Yet as my research finds, this thin mask does little to prevent U.S. consumers from figuring out whom they are talking to. Quite often, they become hostile even when the agent uses the alias.

An alternative to fixing existing technologies and procedures, then, is to create new ones. "Platform cooperativism" is an emerging strategy among activists, entrepreneurs, and technical experts.[79] The idea is to put the entire platform into the hands of the users, who would then share ownership and governance. Cooperatives have legacies in the histories of groups like African Americans. Some date back to Du Bois's 1907 *Economic Cooperation among Negro Americans*, and they appear in the former Black Panthers' 2013 *Oakland and the World Enterprises*. This has led activists like Astra Taylor to urge similar practices online.[80]

Indeed, such platforms may be better able to deter racist practices of the consuming public. This is especially likely if they are designed with concerns of racial inclusivity and antidiscrimination at the outset, if not directly created and run by people of color. Many grassroots groups in the digital service economy have already started to develop their own platforms, avatars, and apps. OUR Walmart, a digital labor network of more than 100,000 Walmart employees, is using a chatbot called WorkIt to spread information and organize digitally.

Finally, we should also take advantage of the transformative potential of multi-surveillance. Rather than stabilizing locations and identities, it involves shifting gazes, mobility across positions, unexpected pairings, and networked social movements.[81] Yolanda Spivey's case of becoming Bianca, a white job applicant, reflects this technique—utilizing the identity-shifting features of the digital to pose as someone from another group. She does this in order to subvert the surveillance of elites and to practice her own surveillance unseen. One might situate these acts in light of the identity transformations under slavery that Browne catalogues: blacks who forged names on slave papers, passed as free, and so on. These are some of the many tactics of "dark sousveillance," meaning "strategies of coping, resistance, and critique" to antiblack surveillance.[82]

Indeed, a critical implication of multi-surveillance is the duality of orientations it entails, and the shifting techniques it makes possible. If consumers can use surveillance *in support of* racial hierarchies, they can do so *against* them as well.

Notes

1. Gillian B. White, "Uber and Lyft Are Failing Black Riders," *The Atlantic*, October 31, 2016, http://www.theatlantic.com.

2. Winifred R. Poster, "Emotion Detectors, Answering Machines and E-Unions: Multisurveillances in the Global Interactive Services Industry," *American Behavioral Scientist* 55, no. 7 (2011): 868–901; Winifred R. Poster, "Multisurveillances: Technological Agency in Global Interactive Service Work," unpublished monograph (Washington University, St. Louis, 2017).

3. Simone Browne, "Race and Surveillance," in *Routledge Handbook of Surveillance Studies*, ed. Kirstie Ball, Kevin Haggerty, and David Lyon (New York: Routledge, 2012), 72–79.

4. Patricia Hill Collins, *Black Feminist Thought: Knowledge, Consciousness, and the Politics of Empowerment*, 2nd ed. (New York: Routledge, 2000); Kimberlee Crenshaw, "Demarginalizing the Intersection of Race and Sex: A Black Feminist Critique of Antidiscrimination Doctrine, Feminist Theory, and Antiracist Politics," *University of Chicago Legal Forum* (1989): 139–67.

5. Thomas Mathiesen, "The Viewer Society: Michel Foucault's 'Panopticon' Revisited," *Theoretical Criminology* 1, no. 2 (1997): 215–34.

Winifred R. Poster

6. Steve Mann, Jason Nolan, and Barry Wellman, "Sousveillance: Inventing and Using Wearable Computing Devices for Data Collection in Surveillance Environments," *Surveillance and Society* 1, no. 3 (2003): 331–55.

7. Browne, "Race and Surveillance."

8. Browne, "Race and Surveillance," 42.

9. Nick Srnicek, *Platform Capitalism* (Cambridge, UK: Polity, 2016).

10. Trebor Scholz, *Uberworked and Underpaid: How Workers Are Disrupting the Digital Economy* (Cambridge, UK: Polity, 2017).

11. Nona Yetta Galzer, *Women's Paid and Unpaid Labor: The Work Transfer in Health Care and Retailing* (Philadelphia: Temple University Press, 1993).

12. Aneesh Aneesh, "Global Labor: Algocratic Modes of Organization," *Sociological Theory* 27, no. 4 (2009): 347–70.

13. Jodi Dean, *Democracy and Other Neoliberal Fantasies: Communicative Capitalism and Left Politics* (Durham, NC: Duke University Press, 2009).

14. Enda Brophy, "The Subterranean Stream: Communicative Capitalism and Call Centre Labour," *Ephemera* 10, no. 3/4 (2010): 470–83.

15. Poster, "Emotion Detectors, Answering Machines and E-Unions"; Luke Stark and Karen E. C. Levy, "The Surveillant Consumer," *Media, Culture and Society*, https://doi.org/10.1177%2F0163443718781985.

16. Lisa Nakamura, *Digitizing Race* (Minneapolis: University of Minnesota Press, 2008), 17.

17. Loïc Wacquant, "Pugs at Work: Bodily Capital and Bodily Labour among Professional Boxers," *Body and Society* 1 (1995): 65–93.

18. Sherri Thomas, "2016 Best Career Apps and Websites to Land Your Dream Job," *Huffington Post*, November 2, 2016.

19. Yolanda Spivey, "Should the Keishas of the World Put Karen on Their Resume?," *Ms. Magazine Blog*, November 11, 2012.

20. Spivey, "Should the Keishas of the World Put Karen on Their Resume?," 2.

21. Marianne Bertrand and Sendhil Mullainathan, "Are Emily and Greg More Employable Than Lakisha and Jamal? A Field Experiment on Labor Market Discrimination," *American Economic Review* 94, no. 4 (2004): 991–1013.

22. Lauren A. Rivera and Andras Tilcsik, "Class Advantage, Commitment Penalty: The Gendered Effect of Social Class Signals in an Elite Labor Market," *American Sociological Review* 81, no. 6 (2016): 1097–131.

23. Collins, *Black Feminist Thought*; Crenshaw, "Demarginalizing the Intersection of Race and Sex."

24. Devah Pager, "The Mark of a Criminal Record," *American Sociological Review* 103 (March 2003): 937–75.

25. danah boyd, Karen Levy, and Alice Marwick, "The Networked Nature of Algorithmic Discrimination," in *Data and Discrimination* (New York: Open Technology Institute, 2014), 53–57.

26. Winifred R. Poster and Zakia Salime, "Limits of Micro-Credit: Transnational Feminism and USAID Activities in the United States and Morocco," in *Women's Activism and Globalization*, ed. Nancy A. Naples and Manisha Desai (New York: Routledge, 2002), 189–219.

27. Christina Jenq, Jessica Pan, and Walter Theseira, "Beauty, Weight, and Skin Color in Charitable Giving," *Journal of Economic Behavior and Organization* 119 (2015): 234–53.

28. Venkataramana Gajjala, Radhika Gajjala, Anca Birzescu, and Samara Anarbaeva, "Microfinance in Online Space: A Visual Analysis of Kiva.Org," *Development in Practice* 21, no. 6 (2011): 880–93.

29. Jenq, et al., "Beauty, Weight, and Skin Color in Charitable Giving."

30. Jennifer L. Doleac and Luke C. D. Stein, "The Visible Hand: Race and Online Market Outcomes," *Stanford Institute for Economic Policy Research*, Discussion Paper No. 10-025 (2010): 1–49.

31. The term *sharing* clearly fails to capture the politics, discriminations, and inequalities embedded in this industry (with many favoring terms like *gig, on-demand, hustle*, etc.), but I use it here to mark the irony of what this economy doesn't do.

32. Benjamin Edelman and Michael Luca, "Digital Discrimination: The Case of Airbnb.Com.," *Harvard Business School*, Harvard Business School, Working Paper 14-054 (2014): 1–21.

33. Morgane Laouenan and Roland Rathelot, "Ethnic Discrimination on an Online Marketplace of Vacation Rentals, " University of Paris, Working Paper (2016).

34. Benjamin Edelman, Michael Luca, and Dan Svirsky, "Racial Discrimination in the Sharing Economy: Evidence from a Field Experiment," *American Economic Journal: Applied Economics* 9, no. 2 (2017): 1–22.

35. Alex Rosenblat, Karen E. C. Levy, Solon Barocas, and Tim Hwang, "Discriminating Tastes: Uber's Customer Ratings as Vehicles for Workplace Discrimination," *Policy and Internet* 9, no. 3 (2017): 256–79; Alex Rosenblat and Luke Stark, "Algorithmic Labor and Information Asymmetries: A Case Study of Uber's Drivers," *International Journal of Communication*, no. 10 (2016): 3758–84.

36. Rosenblat, et al. "Discrminating Tastes," 265.

37. Yanbo Ge, Christopher R. Knittel, Don MacKenzie, and Stephen Zoepf, "Racial and Gender Discrimination in Transportation Network Companies," *National Bureau of Economic Research*, Working Paper No. 22776 (2016).

38. Ge, et al., "Racial and Gender Discrimination in Transportation Network Companies," 19.

39. Doug Glanville, "Doug Glanville on Why He Still Gets Shunned by Taxi Drivers," *The Atlantic*, October 24, 2015, www.theatlantic.com.

40. Winifred R. Poster, "Sound Bites, Sentiments, and Accents: Digitizing Communicative Labor in the Era of Global Outsourcing," in *DigitalSTS: A Handbook and Fieldguide*, ed. David Ribes and Janet Vertesi (Princeton, NJ: Princeton University Press, 2019).

Winifred R. Poster

41. Chris Warhust, "From Invisible Work to Invisible Workers: The Impact of Service Employers' Speech Demands on the Working Class," in *Invisible Labor*, ed. Marion G. Crain, Winifred R. Poster, and Miriam A. Cherry (Berkeley: University of California Press, 2016), 214–36; Christine L. Williams and Catherine Connell, "The Invisible Consequences of Aesthestic Labor in Upscale Retail Stores," in *Invisible Labor*, ed. Marion G. Crain, Winifred R. Poster, and Miriam A. Cherry (Berkeley: University of California Press, 2016), 193–213.

42. Holly K. Carlson and Monica A. McHenry, "Effect of Accent and Dialect on Employability," *Journal of Employment Counseling* 43 (June 2006): 70–84.

43. Carolyn Peluso Atkins, "Do Employment Recruiters Discriminate on the Basis of Nonstandard Dialect?," *Journal of Employment Counseling* 30 (September 1993): 108–19.

44. Megumi Hosoda and Eugene Stone-Romero, "The Effects of Foreign Accents on Employment-Related Decisions," *Journal of Managerial Psychology* 25, no. 2 (2010): 113–32.

45. Kamal K. Sridhar, "Customer Attitudes to Non-Native Accented Outsource Service," Presentation to Asian and Asian American Studies, Stony Brook: Stony Brook University, 2008.

46. Ally Rao Hill and Alastair Tombs, "The Effect of Accent of Service Employee on Customer Service Evaluation," *Managing Service Quality* 21, no. 6 (2011): 649–66.

47. Ze Wang, Aaron Arndt, Surendra Singh, and Monica Biernat, "The Impact of Accent Stereotypes on Service Outcomes and Its Boundary Conditions," *Advances in Consumer Research* 36 (2009): 940–41.

48. This site was mainly active from 2008 to 2014, but it remains viewable online as I observed in 2016.

49. Premilla D'Cruz, *Workplace Bullying in India* (New Delhi: Routledge, 2014); Premilla D'Cruz and Ernesto Noronha, "The Interface Between Technology and Customer Cyberbullying: Evidence from India," *Information and Organization* 24, no. 3 (2014): 176–93.

50. Winifred R. Poster, "Who's on the Line? Indian Call Center Agents Pose as Americans for U.S.-Outsourced Firms," *Industrial Relations* 46, no. 2 (2007): 271–304.

51. Kiran Mirchandani and Winifred R. Poster, eds., *Borders in Service: Enactments of Nationhood in Transnational Call Centers* (Toronto: University of Toronto Press, 2016).

52. Eva Gustavsson, "Virtual Servants," *Gender, Work and Organization* 12, no. 5 (2005): 400–419; Ian R. Kerr, "Bots, Babes and the Californication of Commerce," *University of Ottawa Law and Technology Journal* 1 (2004): 285–324.

53. Winifred R. Poster, "The Virtual Receptionist with a Human Touch: Opposing Pressures of Digital Automation and Outsourcing in Interactive Services," in *Invisible Labor*, ed. Marion G. Crain, Winifred R. Poster, and Miriam A. Cherry (Berkeley: University of California Press, 2016), 87–112.

54. Neda Atanasoski and Kalindi Vora, "Surrogate Humanity: Posthuman Networks and the (Racialized) Obsolescence of Labor," *Catalyst* 1, no. 1 (2015): 1–14.

55. BBC News, "Cyberbabe to the Read the News," January 17, 2000, accessed December 19, 2016, www.bbc.co.uk.

56. Nicole C. Wong, "Voice Recognition: They Speak Thereby They Brand," *San Jose Mercury News*, March 21, 2005.

57. Poster, "The Virtual Receptionist with a Human Touch."

58. Adrienne Lafrance, "Why Do So Many Digital Assistants Have Feminine Names?," *The Atlantic*, March 30, 2016, 1–6, http://www.theatlantic.com.

59. Alexis Kleinman, "Meet the Woman Who Says She's the Voice of Siri," *Huffington Post*, October 4, 2013.

60. Melissa Villa-Nicholas and Miriam E. Sweeney, "Race, Gender, and the Perfect Digital Latina Worker," Presentation at 4S: Society for the Social Study of Science and Technology, September 2017.

61. Miriam E. Sweeney, "The Ms. Dewey 'Experience': Technoculture, Gender, and Race," in *Digital Sociologies*, ed. Jessie Daniels, Gregory Kelson, and Tressie McMillan Cottom (Bristol, UK: Polity, 2017), 401–20.

62. Sweeney, "The Ms. Dewey 'Experience,'" 410.

63. Sweeney, "The Ms. Dewey 'Experience,'" 416–17.

64. Ron Eglash, "Race, Sex, and Nerds: From Black Geeks to Asian American Hipsters," *Social Text* 20, no. 2-71 (2002): 49–64.

65. Gina Neff and Peter Nagy, "Talking to Bots: Symbiotic Agency and the Case of Tay," *International Journal of Communication* 10 (2016): 4915–31.

66. Neff and Nagy, "Talking to Bots," 4921.

67. Neff and Nagy, "Talking to Bots."

68. Michel Foucault, *Discipline and Punish* (New York: Vintage Books, 1979).

69. Danielle Keats Citron, *Hate Crimes in Cyberspace* (Cambridge, MA: Havard University Press, 2014).

70. Eduardo Bonilla-Silva, *Racism without Racists*, 5th ed. (Lanham, MD: Rowman and Littlefield, 2018), 3.

71. Daniel Citron, *Hate Crimes in Cyberspace*, 29, 57.

72. Winifred R. Poster, Marion G. Crain, and Miriam A. Cherry, "Conclusion," in *Invisible Labor*, ed. Marion G. Crain, Winifred R. Poster, and Miriam A. Cherry (Berkeley: University of California Press, 2016), 279–92.

73. Michel Anteby and Curtis K. Chan, "Being Seen and Going Unnoticed: Working Under Surveillance," American Sociological Association, August 13, 2013.

74. Adia Harvey Wingfield and John Harvey Wingfield, "When Visibility Hurts and Helps: How Intersections of Race and Gender Shape Black Professional Men's Experiences with Tokenization," *Cultural Diversity and Ethnic Minority Psychology*, August 11, 2014, 1–8.

75. Ge, et al., "Racial and Gender Discrimination in Transportation Network Companies."

76. Edelman and Luca, "Digital Discrmination."

77. Ge, et al., "Racial and Gender Discrimination in Transportation Network Companies."

78. Poster, "Who's on the Line?"

79. Trebor Scholz and Nathan Schneider, eds., *Ours to Hack and to Own* (New York: OR Books, 2016).

80. Astra Taylor, "Non-Cooperativism," in *Ours to Hack and Own*, ed. Trebor Scholz and Nathan Schneider (New York: OR Books, 2016), 233–38.

81. Poster, "Multisurveillances."

82. Browne, "Dark Matters," 68.

7

Digital Character
in "The Scored Society"

FICO, SOCIAL NETWORKS, AND

COMPETING MEASUREMENTS OF

CREDITWORTHINESS

Tamara K. Nopper

.....

"Bad Credit? Start Tweeting." While the *Wall Street Journal* headline is meant to grab attention, the 2013 story reports on an emerging phenomenon deserving of more sociological attention: lenders scanning social media to determine risk.[1] As suggested by the headline, the tracking of social media may be fortuitous for applicants considered credit unworthy according to traditional scoring methods. This chapter examines this shift in lending and risk assessment, focusing on marketplace lenders, which are "typically online financial platforms that leverage technology to reach potential borrowers, evaluate creditworthiness, and facilitate loans."[2] Designing new methods and technology to augment or forgo traditional credit scoring methods, marketplace lenders are monitoring and helping produce what I term *digital character*, a digital profile assessed to make inferences regarding character in terms of credibility, reliability, industriousness, responsibility, morality, and relationship choices.

This chapter also examines how the competition between traditional credit scoring versus marketplace lending is narrated. As I show, both traditional credit scoring companies and marketplace lenders promote their companies as serving the best interests of those "underserved" or likely to be discriminated against by creditors. I focus on how the FICO score, significant to the development of the credit scoring industry, is depicted as scientific and therefore less discriminatory than alternative data such as social media activity.[3] Also discussed are concerns raised by consumer advocates and regulators about the potentially subjective nature of social media assessment.[4] I argue that while social media assessment may seem subjective, biased, and unlike current methods of determining creditworthiness à la the FICO score, neither approach is inherently more equitable. Rather, they share a commitment to what Citron and Pasquale term a *scored society*,[5] in which being scored in some way significantly shapes economic life chances.

As this is the beginning stage of a larger project, the chapter is primarily descriptive, detailing the purported distinction between traditional credit scoring and marketplace lenders' use of alternative data and digital character. I begin with a brief history of credit scoring, focusing on the company Fair Isaac Corporation and its FICO score. The next section describes marketplace lenders and their consideration of digital character. I conclude by noting some of the concerns about the appraisal of digital character raised by regulators, such as the possibility of discrimination and a lack of transparency. Here, I trouble the distinction made between traditional credit scoring and digital character assessment and the suggestion that one better contributes to a less discriminatory society than the other. Finally, I discuss how both share a commitment to a "scored society"[6] and how traditional credit scoring serves as the condition of possibility for marketplace lenders to target those locked out of credit.

CREDIT SCORING AND THE FICO SCORE

A "calculation of the empirically assessed odds that a person with a particular combination of characteristics, compared against the known outcomes of a lender's population of clients, would default on a loan,"[7] a credit score is commonly used by financial institutions to determine risk, or "the probability that a loan applicant or existing borrower will default or become delinquent."[8] The credit score may determine if a person is targeted as a potential borrower, or it may serve as the decisive factor in being granted credit and at what interest rate.[9] Additionally, credit scores are increasingly taken into consideration by companies selling auto and home insurance or phone services.[10] As research shows, access to credit, the terms of credit, and the use of credit scoring are relevant to the racial wealth gap.[11]

While risk assessment and forms of credit scoring in the United States preceded the 1950s, the decade saw notable shifts in the consumer credit industry. For one, "a mass revolving consumer credit market" developed. New companies sought to cash in on the credit economy, treating consumer credit "as a profitable commercial activity in and of itself." In 1958, the first general-purpose bank credit cards were offered by Bank of America and Chase Manhattan Bank, the former the largest bank in the country. These economic developments were both technological and cultural as a "new industry paradigm" emerged, with credit card providers "managing consumers as a population rather than as individual subjects." The credit card industry was not the only entity to approach consumers as a population. With the post–World War II economy structured around consumption as a facilitator of economic growth, "consumers, as an aggregate, entered into the calculations of the state as a key resource of economic management."[12]

Contemporary credit scoring and its technology are more advanced versions of the "scorecard," which was "literally a simple sheet of cardboard on which was printed a statistically based point distribution to be added up by the lender."[13] By the 1970s, the granting of credit "increasingly became framed within a discourse of risk" as statistical modeling, electronic record keeping, and credit scoring became part of the lending process.[14] Today, credit scoring is generated through "sophisticated software packages and computer warehouses, risk managers and front–stage marketing campaigns."[15] Scores are calculated from a range of economic variables related to previous loan applications and provided by credit bureaus. Information such as the age of accounts, banking accounts, outstanding debt, financial assets, bill-paying history, income, employment history, and housing tenure may all be factored into a score.[16] While credit scores result from "a credit scoring system [that] awards points for each factor that helps predict who is most likely to repay a debt,"[17] both the statistical method used and factors taken into consideration may differ across credit scoring companies.[18]

Glaring disparities in access to credit and discriminatory lending practices have motivated civil rights demands. In the 1960s and 1970s, African Americans and white women called attention to how credit barriers maintained racial and gender hierarchies and pushed for the state to intervene, culminating in the passage of the Equal Credit Opportunity Act. Congress passed the act in 1974 after hearings held by the National Commission on Consumer Finance. The commission heard testimony primarily from married women who shared stories about the sexism they experienced in the credit marketplace. The focus on married women's experiences partly explains why initially the Equal Credit Opportunity Act only banned discrimination by creditors on the basis of sex or marital status. Two years later, the act was amended to outlaw discrimination based on "race, color, religion, national origin, or age (provided the applicant has the capacity to contract),

Tamara K. Nopper

or because all or part of the applicant's income derives from any public assistance program."[19]

Relevant to my focus on distinctions made between traditional risk assessment and marketplace lending, the Equal Credit Opportunity Act's Regulation B proposed credit scoring as a means for decreasing the likelihood of discrimination. In the process, credit scoring was, as emphasized by Marron, associated with being scientific, objective, and thus presumably a tool for keeping bias out of the risk assessment process:

> To this end, credit scoring was encoded in "Regulation B" of the act, explicitly delineating what could constitute a statistical model by defining it as one based on the analysis of key applicant attributes and default based on statistically representative sample groups—anything else was residually termed a "judgmental system." The act effectively gave legislative recognition to scoring systems as being objective, scientific devices permitting a dispassionate, empirically derived account of credit-worthiness and explicitly identified the role they could play in eliminating "subjective" discrimination and helping to bring about an enhanced mass consumer credit market that would discriminate only on merit.[20]

This "legislative recognition" serves the credit scoring industry well, as there are economic and legal incentives to utilize credit scoring. Financial institutions may try to defend themselves against discrimination lawsuits by claiming credit decisions are scientifically based and thus presumably not motivated by prejudice.[21] Some credit scoring companies market their products as tools for rooting out bias.

One such company is Fair Isaac Corporation, who brings us the FICO score. On the FICO website, the product is championed as "helping people get access to credit quickly and *fairly*" (emphasis mine):

> Introduced in 1989, the FICO® Score changed the lending landscape for good. In the days before credit scoring, people were often denied credit because there was no unbiased structure for evaluating them objectively. The system was not fair, fact-based or consistent.
>
> Enter the FICO® Score. The FICO® Score replaced hunches with calculations, and took prejudice out of the equation, literally. The score's criteria for evaluating potential borrowers are focused solely on factors related to a person's ability to repay a loan, rather than one's ZIP code or social status.[22]

It is debatable whether the FICO score really "changed the lending land-scape for good," as questions remain about whether racial minority groups continue to be disadvantaged by credit scoring models and the weight increasingly given to credit scores across a range of industries.[23] What is not disputed is the significance of Fair Isaac and its FICO score to the development of the credit scoring industry. Founded by William Fair and Earl Isaac in 1956, Fair Isaac "installed the world's first commercially produced credit scorecards" a few years after its establishment. By the 1960s, credit scoring had become Fair Isaac's main product.[24] As already noted, the company introduced its FICO score in 1989. Although lenders had been employing customized risk assessment models using credit history data provided by credit bureaus, the "creation of the so-called 'FICO' model transformed credit scores into a commodity that could be bundled with individual credit reports sold to lenders."[25]

Today, the FICO score is one of the leading products on the market. According to figures posted on the FICO website, ten billion FICO scores are sold a year and 27,400,000 are sold a day. FICO scores are sold to financial institutions and firms making credit-related decisions, with the brand offering "industry-specific models for credit cards, mortgages, auto loans, and telecommunication services." Consumers may also buy FICO scores, which regulators have cautioned may not be the same score used in risk assessment, even by creditors who purchase FICO scores.[26] What these figures—as well as concerns by regulators—demonstrate is that *credit scoring is big business.* As explored in the next section, with the proliferation of fintech (financial technology), the FICO score's dominance is being challenged by marketplace lenders using or designing other risk assessment techniques focusing on what I call digital character.

MARKETPLACE LENDING AND DIGITAL CHARACTER

Credit scoring is common in credit card lending, which gained significant momentum by the 1980s and 1990s. During this time, banks increasingly used credit scoring, with a reported 82 percent of banks employing the method in 1990.[27] It was also during this period that credit scoring was more utilized in small business and mortgage lending.[28] In the wake of the sub-prime crisis and the Great Recession, the issue of predatory lending drew attention to the role of risk assessment in the lending process. By some accounts, lenders made too many loans to people whose credit scores were

Tamara K. Nopper

subprime. Research also shows that some borrowers who qualified for prime loans were purposefully steered into subprime loans. As scholars, community advocates, and civil rights organizations note, the targeting of certain groups for subprime lending, including those who met the criteria for prime loans, had devastating consequences, in particular for African Americans, as well as some cities with significant black populations.[29]

Since the Great Recession, credit requirements have become more stringent. With developments in fintech, emerging companies specializing in online lending are targeting those with no or low credit scores or those labeled the "unbanked" or "underbanked."[30] These marketplace lenders are employing and designing risk assessment models to replace the FICO score. In the process, they rely on and also help produce what I call digital character, a digital profile assessed to make inferences regarding character in terms of credibility, reliability, industriousness, responsibility, morality, and relationship choices.

As noted at the beginning of this chapter, the emphasis on digital character is gaining increased attention in finance and business publications. Some stories raise questions about the possible perils of social media assessment, such as a 2016 *American Banker* article that opens with "What if you had to choose between keeping your Facebook friends and getting a home equity line of credit? What if your student loans could not be refinanced until you cut certain relatives out of your digital life?" As suggested by the article's title, "Don't Let Facebook Likes Sway Credit Decisions," such a possibility portends a dangerous future, a sentiment expressed in the sentence immediately following the opening queries: "Such decision-making scenarios could happen as fintech companies increasingly crunch alternative data to help determine a would-be borrower's creditworthiness." The "alternative data" the authors warn us about are derived from "behavioral as well as social information from a variety of online sources to determine applicants' creditworthiness."[31]

Marketplace lenders focused on digital character are posing a challenge to "traditional" types of data often used in risk assessment, notably the FICO score. As we recall, Fair Isaac likes to boast that it sells ten billion FICO scores a year. Yet, as market research firm Mintel announces: "FinTech is helping lenders move away from FICO scores." While Mintel notes that "FICO has been the gold standard," fintech companies are determining their own criteria for assessing risk. Some of the information includes economic data factored into traditional credit scoring.[32] However, aspects of one's digital character, as gleaned from social media and other online activities, are being taken into consideration by several online lenders.[33]

The *Wall Street Journal* reports: "More lending companies are mining Facebook, Twitter and other social-media data to help determine a borrower's creditworthiness or identity."[34] Some of these companies include LendUp, Lenddo, Kabbage, Neo, and Moven. So how does it work? As *American Banker* explains, "Kabbage, Social Finance (SoFi) and InVenture are among the companies that use information such as purchasing habits, employment records and even mobile-texting patterns to determine creditworthiness."[35] And Eichelberger, writing for *Mother Jones*, says:

> Among the U.S.-based online lenders that factor in social media to their lending decisions is San Francisco-based LendUp, which checks out the Facebook and Twitter profiles of potential borrowers to see how many friends they have and how often they interact; the company views an active social media life as an indicator of stability. The lender Neo, a Silicon Valley start-up, looks at the quality and quantity of an applicant's LinkedIn contacts for clues to how quickly laid-off borrowers will be rehired. Moven, which is based in New York, also uses information from Twitter, Facebook, and other social networking sites in their loan underwriting process.[36]

In the process, marketplace lenders are looking for and helping produce *digital character*—a digital profile assessed to make inferences regarding character in terms of credibility, reliability, industriousness, responsibility, morality, and relationship choices. Digital profiles may include social media use, internet-based activities such as shopping, or mobile phone usage and texting.

How is digital character traced? According to some lenders, social media is used to validate information.[37] This may involve a company determining whether applicants are still employed by the companies they list or if they've posted on social media that they've been fired. Online reviews of a business might be examined to evaluate the quality of customer service. A Kabbage executive told the *Wall Street Journal*: "We look at whether you get a lot of 'likes,' are you responding to customers."[38] Or lenders might be watching social media to determine the type of technology used. One such company, Kreditech, looks at browsers, cookies, and smartphones. As a company spokesperson put it, "Is someone using an expensive mobile phone like an iPhone or logging in from a Web cafe? Is their network on Facebook just drinking buddies from a bar?"[39]

Tamara K. Nopper

Social media are also studied to assess whether one makes good relationship decisions and the quality of social networks. Some companies, such as Lenddo, Kreditech, Hello Soda, and Earnest, "are designed around the notion that data about one's social circles holds a financially predictive promise."[40] The tracking of digital social networks has engendered concerns about whether this is the best way to judge character for risk assessment. The most obvious issues are that some people might not have social media profiles, or they might not provide extensive information online.[41] Another issue is that social credit scoring can involve "collecting and analyzing information about people without them consenting to or understanding the terms. Often, they may not even know that it is happening."[42] What this means is that digital character is always being made and stored, regardless of when permission is granted by an applicant to access accounts. Simply, digital footprints may be tracked and online activities and utterances preceding the application process may easily become part of one's digital character portfolio.

Another critique of tracking online networks is that "such affiliations could be considered financially harming, and consequently, force people to choose between social ties and better credit."[43] Given that people are often encouraged to have as many followers or friends as possible on social media platforms, what is really revealed by the number of people with whom one is networked? And how does a lender determine why someone is connected with another person on social media? A consumer privacy expert, Ashkan Soltani, quoted in a *Mother Jones* story ominously titled "Your Deadbeat Facebook Friends Could Cost You a Loan," argues that the quality of online relationships might not be easily interpretable. As Soltani points out, people might not know each other that well outside of social media, but "I might follow you on Facebook because you post funny cat pictures."

Some marketplace lenders have explained what they are reportedly looking for when they assess relationship choices as part of digital character. According to Jeff Stewart, cofounder of Lenddo Ltd., social network data helps pinpoint "your standing in the community."[44] This standing may include, as explained by MovenBank founder Brett King, "your ability to act as a referrer, or influencer, who can drive acquisition as a basis for connections." LendUp CEO Sasha Orloff emphasized to the *Wall Street Journal* that the company is less interested in the quantity of friends than it is in the quality: "Do you have 4,000 friends but none are that close, or do you have 30 people but they're very close? There are ways to measure how engaged and how strong your community ties are."[45] Orloff also discussed this point with

Time: "What we're looking at is the strength of your ability and your willingness to have longer-term cohesive social interactions."[46] As *Time* describes:

> LendUp's algorithm weighs details like how long you've had your account, how many friends you have, and how far away they are physically. "If you have a very strong, close geographic network, that's helpful to you" because it shows the lender that you have a support network. The site also looks at how often you write about your friends and how often they communicate with you. Again, according to Orloff, the theory is that a thriving online social life is an indicator of stability, which somehow translates into a greater likelihood of paying off one's debts.[47]

Executives of Fair Isaac have been asked their opinions of lending decisions based on the tracking of social media relationships. As one Fair Isaac executive told the *Wall Street Journal*: "I'm not sure it's a good thing to make a credit decision based on how many Facebook friends I have."[48] While this point has merit, something to remember is that credit scoring is a product, and online lenders, with their emphasis on digital character, are competitors of Fair Isaac in the consumer finance marketplace. A title of a 2016 *Wall Street Journal* article puts it succinctly: "Silicon Valley: We Don't Trust FICO Scores."[49] Not only are some marketplace lenders "challenging the usefulness of one of the bedrocks of the modern financial system" by forgoing the FICO score,[50] they are designing their own credit scoring models, and in some cases selling the technology to other entities. As Mintel notes, "A small but growing trend is for FinTech companies to develop their own algorithms to determine a prospective borrower's creditworthiness."[51] Some examples include MovenBank's scoring product CRED, to assess a consumer's digital reputation or "street credibility,"[52] and Lenddo's LenddoScore, "devised through an algorithm that analyses broader social connections, including friends, friends of friends and beyond, to assess a loan applicant's social circles."[53] And Kabbage is increasingly licensing its technology to banks.[54] As the next section shows, narratives of antidiscrimination are part of the marketing for both the FICO score and its competitors.

NARRATIVES OF ANTIDISCRIMINATION

The proliferation of marketplace lending and fintech has caught the attention of regulators and consumer advocates, who raise concerns about the possibility of credit discrimination.[55] As marketplace lending becomes more common—a reported $14 billion in loans were provided by online lenders in 2014[56]—there have been several instances in the last few years of regulators

Tamara K. Nopper

at the state and federal levels requesting more details about, or launching inquiries into, marketplace lenders in terms of their operations, lending policies, and compliance. The Department of Treasury had a request for information published in the *Federal Register* to solicit public input on marketplace lending, one of its objectives being to determine "the potential for online marketplace lending to expand access to credit to historically underserved borrowers."[57] The California Department of Business Oversight launched an inquiry into fourteen online lenders.[58] The Federal Trade Commission issued a report on marketplace lenders that addressed the tracking of social media activity, and it hosted a forum, as part of its fintech forum series, on marketplace lending to determine "possible consumer protection concerns" and "how existing consumer protection laws might apply to companies participating in the marketplace lending space."[59] And in the spring of 2016, three senators, Jeff Merkley, Sherrod Brown, and Jeanne Shaheen, requested that the U.S. Government Accountability Office (GAO) provide an updated report on the fintech marketplace.[60] As noted in their letter to Gene L. Dodaro, the comptroller general of the United States, a report on the fintech marketplace had not been issued since 2011. Among the questions asked of the GAO was one addressing the assessment of digital character and the possibility of credit discrimination: "Many fintech companies use non-traditional data to underwrite loans, such as social media information or search engine history. What implications are there from the use of non-traditional data? What impact might fintech have on enforcement of the Fair Credit Reporting Act and the Fair Debt Collection Practices Act? More generally, what obligations do fintech companies have to comply with fair lending laws?"[61]

This request to the GAO was followed a few months later by a letter from Merkley and Brown that "called on the leaders of the U.S. banking and consumer protection agencies to outline steps they are taking to ensure effective oversight of the emerging financial technology, or 'fintech,' marketplace."[62] Addressing their letter to the heads of the Federal Reserve, the Consumer Financial Protection Bureau, the Federal Deposit Insurance Corporation, the National Credit Union Administration, and the Office of the Comptroller of the Currency, the issues of alternative data and compliance were again raised: "Many fintech firms use alternative data and proprietary algorithms to underwrite loans. While these alternative approaches may provide the opportunity to expand access to credit, some observers have raised concerns about the potential for violations of fair lending laws as well consumer protection laws."[63]

As Fair Isaac competes with online lenders and those ditching the FICO score, the company's science and seeming transparency serve as selling points. In a 2012 *American Banker* article titled "Banks to Use Social Media Data for Loans and Pricing," a Fair Isaac executive remarked, "We let data speak for itself."[64] On its website, the company provides an infographic about what general information (such as "payment history," "length of credit history," etc.) makes up what share of the score. This transparency is relatively new, as it was not until 2000 that the company "made available a comprehensive list of the factors used in its credit bureau risk scores," and only after "several other key industry players" began making such information available in response to consumer demands for more transparency regarding credit scoring.[65] Noticeably, Fair Isaac couches its calculations as being scientific and *thus non-biased.* As noted earlier, the FICO score is touted for "taking bias out of the equation, literally." On the FICO website, under the heading "What's not in my FICO Scores," it reads: "The FICO Score doesn't know your age, gender, marital status or race," which is immediately followed by "US law prohibits credit scoring from considering these facts."

The potential for discrimination by marketplace lenders tracking digital character warrants scrutiny and calls for regulation. In response to such concerns, online lenders do not provide the most convincing rebuttals. For example, as *Time* reports, "Orloff is quick to say LendUp doesn't look at pictures or at what people have 'liked,' since that could reveal racial, political, religious or other leanings that could lead to charges of discrimination if applicants are turned down."[66]

While it is difficult to believe that such boundaries are respected when monitoring social media, I want to discuss some problems with the narrative of marketplace lenders in regard to their targeted borrowers. In the United States, there are an estimated 45 million who do not have credit histories to generate a credit score.[67] There are also numerous people whose low credit scores make them unattractive applicants in the consumer finance market.[68] These people with no or low credit scores are the ones targeted by many marketplace lenders depicting themselves as benevolent innovators "providing valuable credit to important, underserved segments of the economy."[69] In doing so, some marketplace lenders emphasize their innovation in terms of their lending practices, whether it involves assessing alternative data sources such as digital character or approving a loan six or seven minutes after receiving the application.[70] Subsequently, marketplace lenders are depicted by some as "more Silicon Valley than Wall Street,"[71] a distinction that poses the former as disconnected from or more progressive than the latter.

Yet there is nothing politically and culturally innovative about the practices of some marketplace lenders, whether it is their extremely high interest

Tamara K. Nopper

rates or their origins in payday lending or hiding the true cost of credit.[72] Some marketplace lenders are reportedly scaling back on their monitoring of social media. One company founder even goes so far as to acknowledge, "We've determined it's creepy to use social media."[73] Yet despite such public statements, the potential for predatory practices remains, enabled by marketplace lending's narrative marrying science and social contribution. While they may not depict themselves as scientific in the same manner as the FICO score, marketplace lenders can promote their approach as socially innovative in terms of using the digital sphere to help those who have been discriminated against in the consumer finance marketplace—while downplaying potential predatory lending practices.

We must also consider how marketplace lenders weaponize in their benevolent narrative a *reality* of consumer finance—the difficulty millions of people have in accessing credit due to their scores, a dynamic that the credit scoring industry engendered. As Citron and Pasquale succinctly state, "Credit scores can make or break the economic fate of millions of individuals."[74] Simply, while marketplace lenders need to be regulated, traditional credit scoring and the reliance on credit scores—regardless of the data used—partly contributes to marketplace lenders targeting those euphemistically described as the "underserved." Taken together, we must question the dominance of the FICO score and of credit scoring in general, as well as how Fair Isaac tries to narrate its approach as nondiscriminatory relative to marketplace lenders.

Fair Isaac promotes its FICO scoring as an unbiased measurement because it is scientific, while its science remains hidden as a company trade secret. Credit scorers often "refuse to reveal the method and logic of their predictive systems."[75] Despite Fair Isaac providing a breakdown of the weight given different factors, such as "payment history," the company is not really that transparent, as it is "tight-lipped about exactly how the scores are calculated."[76] Thus, the FICO score shares some of the same problems of transparency as scores generated by marketplace lenders monitoring digital character, given that "credit scoring methods based on social information use algorithmic decision-making, which shelters the underwriting process under a veil of secrecy and makes it hard to monitor or criticize."[77]

As Citron and Pasquale point out, the claim of being scientific is used to insulate scoring from charges of bias: "The scoring trend is often touted as good news. Advocates applaud the removal of human beings and their flaws from the assessment process. Automated systems are claimed to rate all individuals in the same way, thus averting discrimination. But this account is misleading. Because human beings program predictive algorithms, their biases and values are embedded into the software's instructions, known as the source code and predictive algorithms."[78] This point encourages us to consider the limits of Regulation B of the Equal Credit Reporting Act, which, as noted earlier, encoded credit scoring and helped promote the image of "scoring systems as being objective, scientific devices permitting a dispassionate, empirically derived account of credit-worthiness."[79] While regulating the credit/economy is imperative, legislation that helps reproduce the credit score's "growing influence as a reputational metric"[80] may need to be reconsidered. And Fair Isaac has played a pivotal role in the development of the *credit scoring industry* and in creating the terms of "the scored society" as its "FICO® standard has acted to objectify risk."[81]

It is this social context of "the scored society," in which being scored in some way is part of the design of inequality and the cost of living, *that serves as the condition of possibility for marketplace lenders to narrate themselves as antidiscriminatory* while targeting those most at risk of being socially punished for having no or low credit scores. Traditional credit scores and the move to assess alternative data, then, are interrelated processes, as many marketplace lenders target those whose lives have been, in some way, negatively impacted by credit scoring *and its logic*, such as "needing" a score. While Fair Isaac and marketplace lenders—particularly those designing and selling their credit scoring models—may be competitors in the consumer finance industry, they share a vision of economic life based on credit and the *business of credit and credit scoring*. It is the logic of scoring as a feature of social design that binds the entities together. Thus, traditional credit scorers and marketplace lenders using alternative data are competitors in terms of technology and sales, but not antagonistic in terms of vision. As William Lansing, chief executive of Fair Isaac, said of lenders employing alternative data: "There's virtually nothing that they do that we can't do."[82]

Notes

1. Evelyn M. Rusli, "Bad Credit? Start Tweeting," *The Wall Street Journal* (online), April 1, 2013, accessed January 3, 2017, https://www.wsj.com/articles/SB100014241278873244883604578396852612756398.

2. Federal Trade Commission, "FTC to Host Financial Technology Forum on Marketplace Lending," 2016, accessed January 3, 2017, https://www.ftc.gov/news-events/press-releases/2016/04/ftc-host-financial-technology-forum-marketplace-lending.

3. Martha Poon, "Scorecards as Devices for Consumer Credit: The Case of Fair, Isaac and Company Incorporated," *The Sociological Review* 55 (2007): 284–306.

Tamara K. Nopper

4. Ann Carrns, "Little Credit History? Lenders Are Taking a New Look at You," *New York Times*, February 24, 2017, accessed April 18, 2017, https://www .nytimes.com/2017/02/24/your-money/26money-adviser-credit-scores.html ?rref=collection%2Ftimestopic%2FFair%20Isaac%20Corporation&action =click&contentCollection=business&region=stream&module=stream_unit&version =latest&contentPlacement=2&pgtype=collection; Telis Demos and Deepa Seethara- man, "Facebook Isn't So Good at Judging Your Credit after All," *Wall Street Journal* (on- line), February 16, 2016, accessed January 3, 2017, https://www.wsj.com/articles/lenders -drop-plans-to-judge-you-by-your-facebook-friends-1456309801; Erin J. Illman, "CFPB Focused on Financial Technology in 2016—Expect More for 2017," Banking and Financial Services Policy Report 36 (2017): 1–2; Jeff Merkley, "Merkley, Brown, Shaheen Ask GAO for Updated Report on the Financial Technology Marketplace," 2016, accessed January 3, 2017, https://www.merkley.senate.gov/news/press-releases/merkley-brown -shaheen-ask-gao-for-updated-report-on-the-financial-technology-marketplace; Jeff Merkley, "Brown, Merkley Press Federal Agencies on Oversight of Financial Technology," 2016, accessed January 3, 2017, https://www.merkley.senate.gov/news /press-releases/brown-merkley-press-federal-agencies-on-oversight-of-financial -technology; Leena Rao, "California Regulators to Put Spotlight on Marketplace Lend- ers," Fortune.com, December 11, 2015, accessed March 28, 2017, http://fortune.com /2015/12/11/california-regulators-online-lending/.

5. Danielle Keats Citron and Frank Pasquale, "The Scored Society: Due Process for Automated Predictions." *Washington Law Review* 89 (2014): 1–33.

6. Citron and Pasquale, "The Scored Society."

7. Poon, "Scorecards as Devices for Consumer Credit," 289.

8. Loretta J. Mester, "What's the Point of Credit Scoring?," *Business Review*, Septem- ber/October 1997, accessed January 3, 2017, https://pdfs.semanticscholar.org/4ccd/81d6 4e04ac7cadd9936a703543075fa24846.pdf.

9. Carrns, "Little Credit History? Lenders Are Taking a New Look at You"; Mester, "What's the Point of Credit Scoring?"; Vincent Ryan, "Fast Money," *CFO Magazine*, February 18, 2016, accessed January 28, 2017, http://ww2.cfo.com/credit/2016/02/fast -money/.

10. Federal Trade Commission, "Credit Scores," 2017, accessed January 3, 2017, https://www.consumer.ftc.gov/articles/0152-credit-scores#what.

11. Devin Fergus, "The Ghetto Tax: Auto Insurance, Postal Code Profiling, and the Hidden History of Wealth Transfer," in *Beyond Discrimination: Racial Inequality in a Postracist Era* (New York: Russell Sage Foundation, 2013), 277–316; Devin Fergus, "Fi- nancial Fracking in the Land of the Fee, 1980–2008," in *The Assets Perspective: The Rise of Asset Building and Its Impact on Social Policy* (New York: Palgrave Macmillan, 2014), 67–95; Devin Fergus and Tim Boyd, "Introduction—Banking without Borders: Culture and Credit in the New Financial World," *Kalfou* 1 (2014): 7–28; U.S. Census Bureau, "Wealth and Asset Ownership Data Tables," 2017, accessed June 15, 2017, https://www .census.gov/topics/income-poverty/wealth/data/tables.html.

12. Donncha Marron, "'Lending by Numbers': Credit Scoring and the Constitution of Risk within American Consumer Credit," *Economy and Society* 36 (2007): 103–33, 107–8.

13. Poon, "Scorecards as Devices for Consumer Credit," 284.

14. Marron, "'Lending by Numbers,'" 113.

15. Poon, "Scorecards as Devices for Consumer Credit," 284.

16. Federal Trade Commission, "Credit Scores," accessed January 3, 2017; Mester, "What's the Point of Credit Scoring?"

17. Federal Trade Commission, "Credit Scores."

18. Mester, "What's the Point of Credit Scoring?"

19. Earl M. Maltz and Fred H. Miller, "The Equal Credit Opportunity Act and Regulation B," *Oklahoma Law Review* 31 (1978): 1–62, 2; Marron, "'Lending by Numbers.'"

20. Marron, "'Lending by Numbers,'" 110.

21. Marron, "'Lending by Numbers.'"

22. FICO, "Learn about the FICO® Score and Its Long History," Fico.com, 2017, accessed January 15, 2017, http://www.fico.com/25years/.

23. Marron, "'Lending by Numbers'"; Sarah Ludwig, "Credit Scores in America Perpetuate Racial Injustice. Here's How," The Guardian.com, October 13, 2015, accessed July 4, 2017, https://www.theguardian.com/commentisfree/2015/oct/13/your-credit-score-is-racist-heres-why.

24. Poon, "Scorecards as Devices for Consumer Credit," 288–89, 292.

25. Marron, "'Lending by Numbers,'" 117.

26. Consumer Financial Protection Bureau, "Analysis of Differences between Consumer-and-Creditor-Purchased Credit Scores," 2012, accessed April 17, 2017, 4–5, http://files.consumerfinance.gov/f/201209_Analysis_Differences_Consumer_Credit.pdf.

27. Marron, "'Lending by Numbers.'"

28. Federal Trade Commission, "Prepared Statement of the Federal Trade Commission on Credit Scoring before the House Banking and Financial Services Committee Subcommittee on Financial Institutions and Consumer Credit," 2000, accessed January 3, 2017, https://www.ftc.gov/sites/default/files/documents/public_statements/prepared-statement-federal-trade-commission-credit-scoring/creditscoring.pdf; Mester, "What's the Point of Credit Scoring?"

29. Fergus and Boyd, "Introduction—Banking without Borders: Culture and Credit in the New Financial World"; NAACP, "The NAACP Filed an Historic Lawsuit against Mortgage Lenders Alleging Racial Discrimination," NAACP.org, July 11, 2007, accessed March 28, 2017, http://www.naacp.org/latest/the-naacp-filed-an-historic-lawsuit-against-mortgage-lenders-alleging-racial-discrimination/; Sandra Phillips, "The Subprime Mortgage Calamity and the African American Woman," *Review of Black Political Economy* 39 (2012): 227–37.

30. Federal Deposit Insurance Corporation, "2015 FDIC National Survey of Unbanked and Underbanked Households," FDIC.gov, accessed January 3, 2017, https://www.fdic.gov/householdsurvey/; Peter Rudegeair, "Silicon Valley: We Don't Trust FICO Scores," *Wall Street Journal* (online), January 11, 2016, accessed January 3, 2017,

Tamara K. Nopper

https://www.wsj.com/articles/silicon-valley-gives-fico-low-score-1452556468; Ryan, "Fast Money."

31. Yafit, Lev-Aretz, and Nizan Geslevich Pachkin, "Don't Let Facebook Likes Sway Credit Decisions," *American Banker*, June 17, 2016, accessed January 3, 2017, https://www.americanbanker.com/opinion/dont-let-facebook-likes-sway-credit-decisions.

32. Mintel, "FinTech Is Helping Lenders Move Away from FICO Scores."

33. Stephanie Armour, "Borrowers Hit Social-Media Hurdles," *Wall Street Journal*, January 8, 2014, accessed January 3, 2017, https://www.wsj.com/articles/borrowers-hit-socialmedia-hurdles-1389224469; Ericka Eichelberger, "Your Deadbeat Facebook Friends Could Cost You a Loan," *Mother Jones*, September 18, 2013, accessed January 3, 2017, http://www.motherjones.com/politics/2013/09/lenders-vet-borrowers-social-media-facebook/; Casey Hynes, "How Social Media Could Help the Unbanked Land a Loan," *Forbes*, April 25, 2017, accessed May 20, 2017, https://www.forbes.com/sites/chynes/2017/04/25/how-data-will-help-drive-universal-financial-access/.

34. Armour, "Borrowers Hit Social-Media Hurdles."

35. Lev-Aretz and Pachkin, "Don't Let Facebook Likes Sway Credit Decisions."

36. Eichelberger, "Your Deadbeat Facebook Friends Could Cost You a Loan."

37. Eichelberger, "Your Deadbeat Facebook Friends Could Cost You a Loan"; Jeremy Quittner, "Banks to Use Social Media Data for Loans and Pricing," *American Banker*, January 26, 2012, accessed January 3, 2017, https://www.americanbanker.com/news/banks-to-use-social-media-data-for-loans-and-pricing.

38. Armour, "Borrowers Hit Social-Media Hurdles."

39. Armour, "Borrowers Hit Social-Media Hurdles."

40. Lev-Aretz and Pachkin, "Don't Let Facebook Likes Sway Credit Decisions."

41. Rusli, "Bad Credit? Start Tweeting."

42. Lev-Aretz and Pachkin, "Don't Let Facebook Likes Sway Credit Decisions."

43. Lev-Aretz and Pachkin, "Don't Let Facebook Likes Sway Credit Decisions."

44. Rusli, "Bad Credit? Start Tweeting."

45. Armour, "Borrowers Hit Social-Media Hurdles."

46. Martha C. White, "Can a Payday Lending Start-Up Use Facebook to Create a Modern Community Bank?," Time.com, November 16, 2012, accessed January 3, 2017, http://business.time.com/2012/11/16/can-a-payday-lending-start-up-use-facebook-to-create-a-modern-community-bank/.

47. White, "Can a Payday Lending Start-Up Use Facebook to Create a Modern Community Bank?"

48. Rusli, "Bad Credit? Start Tweeting."

49. Rudegeair, "Silicon Valley."

50. Rudegeair, "Silicon Valley."

51. Mintel, "FinTech Is Helping Lenders Move Away from FICO Scores."

52. Quittner, "Banks to Use Social Media Data for Loans and Pricing."

53. James King, "IMF World Bank: Credit Scoring–Friends, Followers, and Settling Scores," *The Banker*, 2014.

54. Kevin Wack, "Subprime Specialist LendUp Raises $150M," *American Banker*, January 20, 2016, accessed January 3, 2017, https://www.americanbanker.com/news /subprime-specialist-lendup-raises-150m.

55. Demos and Seetharaman, "Facebook Isn't So Good at Judging Your Credit after All"; Illman, "CFPB Focused on Financial Technology in 2016—Expect More for 2017"; Merkley, "Merkley, Brown, Shaheen Ask GAO for Updated Report on the Financial Technology Marketplace"; Merkley, "Brown, Merkley Press Federal Agencies on Oversight of Financial Technology"; Rao, "California Regulators to Put Spotlight on Marketplace Lenders."

56. Rao, "California Regulators to Put Spotlight on Marketplace Lenders."

57. U.S. Department of Treasury, "Treasury Seeks Public Comments on Market-place Lenders," 2015, accessed January 3, 2017, https://www.treasury.gov/press-center /press-releases/Pages/jl0116.aspx.

58. Rao, "California Regulators to Put Spotlight on Marketplace Lenders."

59. Demos and Seetharaman, "Facebook Isn't So Good at Judging Your Credit after All"; Federal Trade Commission, "FTC to Host Financial Technology Forum on Market-place Lending."

60. Merkley, Brown, and Shaheen are the top Democrats serving on, respectively, the Senate's Financial Institutions and Consumer Protection Subcommittee, the Banking, Housing, and Urban Affairs Committee, and the Small Business Committee.

61. Merkley, "Merkley, Brown, Shaheen Ask GAO for Updated Report on the Financial Technology Marketplace."

62. Merkley, "Brown, Merkley Press Federal Agencies on Oversight of Financial Technology."

63. Merkley, "Brown, Merkley Press Federal Agencies on Oversight of Financial Technology."

64. Quittner, "Banks to Use Social Media Data for Loans and Pricing."

65. Federal Trade Commission, "Prepared Statement of the Federal Trade Commission on Credit Scoring before the House Banking and Financial Services Committee Subcommittee on Financial Institutions and Consumer Credit."

66. Martha C. White, "Can a Payday Lending Start-Up Use Facebook to Create a Modern Community Bank?," Time.com, November 16, 2012, accessed January 3, 2017, http://business.time.com/2012/11/16/can-a-payday-lending-start-up-use-facebook-to -create-a-modern-community-bank/.

67. Carrns, "Little Credit History? Lenders Are Taking a New Look at You."

68. Ryan, "Fast Money."

69. Michael Corkery, "Treasury to Examine Online Lending Industry," *New York Times*, July 16, 2015, accessed January 3, 2017, https://www.nytimes.com/2015/07/17/business /dealbook/treasury-examines-whether-to-regulate-online-lenders.html; Hynes, "How Social Media Could Help the Unbanked Land a Loan"; King, "IMF World Bank."

70. Darren Dahl, "The Six-Minute Loan," *Forbes* (2015): 56–60; Ryan, "Fast Money."

71. White, "Can a Payday Lending Start-Up Use Facebook to Create a Modern Community Bank?"

72. Dahl, "The Six-Minute Loan"; Illman, "CFPB Focused on Financial Technology in 2016—Expect More for 2017."

73. Demos and Seetharaman, "Facebook Isn't So Good at Judging Your Credit after All."

74. Citron and Pasquale, "The Scored Society: Due Process for Automated Predictions," 9.

75. Citron and Pasquale, "The Scored Society: Due Process for Automated Predictions," 5.

76. "What Is My Credit Score, and How Is It Calculated?," Time.com, May 26, 2014, accessed January 28, 2017, http://time.com/2791957/what-is-my-credit-score-and-how -is-it-calculated/?iid=sr-link1.

77. Lev-Aretz and Pachkin, "Don't Let Facebook Likes Sway Credit Decisions."

78. Citron and Pasquale, "The Scored Society," 4.

79. Marron, "'Lending by Numbers,'" 110.

80. Marron, "'Lending by Numbers,'" 110.

81. Poon, "Scorecards as Devices for Consumer Credit," 300.

82. Quoted in Rudegeair, "Silicon Valley."

8

Deception by Design

DIGITAL SKIN, RACIAL MATTER, AND THE NEW POLICING OF CHILD SEXUAL EXPLOITATION

Mitali Thakor

.....

"Sweetie" is immediately captivating.

Sweetie is a digital animation of a young girl, deployed in a series of campaign videos by a Dutch nonprofit and an advertising firm. In the videos, the computerized girl appears to look directly at the camera as she narrates a story to the viewer. "My name is Sweetie. I'm ten years old. I live in the Philippines," she begins, the camera focused tightly on her face, only her left eye and part of her nose in the frame. Her voice is offset by subtle violin music, horror movie boilerplate for building suspense. The camera switches to a cropped focus on just her mouth, as she says, "Every day I have to sit in front of the webcam and talk to men. Just like tens of thousands of other kids."

The video ripples through a series of hazy photos of children, their heads edited out of the images, as well as photos of adult men holding up panties and other articles of clothing. "The men ask me to take off my clothes. They play with themselves. They want me to play with myself. As soon as I go online, they come to me. Ten, a hundred, every hour. So many. But what they don't know?"

At this point the violin fades out abruptly in a synthesized rush. Sweetie's smooth brown face flickers from brown to yellow into an electric blue digital mesh of the CGI architecture beneath. "I'm not real. I'm a computer model, built piece by piece." She continues, shaking her head, "To track down these men who do this."

I first watched this video in the winter of 2013, a few months after it had been launched. The Sweetie video is part of "Project Sweetie," an ongo-

FIGURE 8.1. Sweetie A. Still frame image from video. Source: Terre des Hommes and Lemz, press release, April 11, 2013. http://www.terredeshommes.org/wp-content /uploads/2013/11/PR-Webcam-Child-Sex-Tourism-TDH-NL-04.11.2013.pdf.

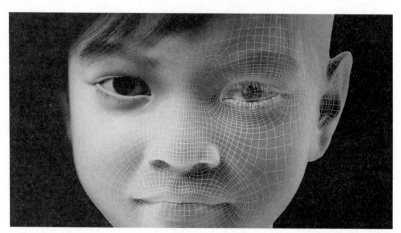

FIGURE 8.2. Sweetie B. Still frame image from video. Source: Terre des Hommes and Lemz, press release, April 11, 2013. http://www.terredeshommes.org/wp-content /uploads/2013/11/PR-Webcam-Child-Sex-Tourism-TDH-NL-04.11.2013.pdf.

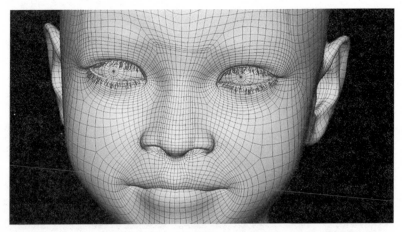

FIGURE 8.3. Sweetie C. Still frame image from video. Source: Terre des Hommes and Lemz, press release, April 11, 2013. http://www.terredeshommes.org/wp-content/uploads/2013/11/PR-Webcam-Child-Sex-Tourism-TDH-NL-04.11.2013.pdf.

ing collaborative multimedia effort between the Dutch advertising agency Lemz and the international, Netherlands-headquartered nonprofit Terre des Hommes.

An advertising executive from Lemz lends his voice to the next segment of the video, cutting from Sweetie's digital face to a spinning globe illuminated in points of white light. "Webcam sex tourism is a new phenomenon that's spreading like an epidemic. Men from rich countries pay children in poor countries to perform sexual acts in front of webcams," the narrator explains. A number ticker rapidly scrolls past the 30,000 mark as the narrator says, "We estimate that tens of thousands of kids, some of them only six years old, are abused behind cams in the Philippines alone." The number ticker scrolls back to 0, then slowly to 6, as the narrator adds, "But instead of hundreds of thousands of convictions, we could only find six men who've ever been charged. Our solution? Proactive policing."

The Project Sweetie team's "proactive policing" campaign involved using the 3D avatar to text and video chat with people on webcam chatrooms, convincing them to share email addresses, names, and other identifying information, with the promise of sharing nude photos and videos. The first version of Project Sweetie ran for six months in 2013 and resulted in a list of a thousand names and email addresses of people from seventy-one countries, including the United Kingdom, Australia, Germany, India, and the United States. This list was subsequently handed over to the Dutch National Police

Mitali Thakor

and to the Europol offices in The Hague in November 2013. During that same week, Terre des Hommes released the campaign video along with a report on "Webcam Child Sex Tourism" published on their website. In early 2016, Terre des Hommes announced the launch of Sweetie 2.0, a chatbot software program to automate the information solicitation process used in the first phase.

Project Sweetie's model of proactive policing falls under a lineage of entrapment schemes and vigilante escapades to patrol potential abusers and exploiters of children. While the project's use of a digital girl avatar might seem new, it also draws on long-standing anxieties to claim control over shadowy abusers in order to protect "virtual" children at large. In this essay, I argue that what *is* new and compelling about Project Sweetie is the campaign's self-conscious stylization of its entrapment work, after the fact. I focus on the campaign video, on the moment of the revelation of Sweetie's artificiality, peeling back from child's skin to computer-generated image mesh structure. I am interested in Sweetie's skin — as a contact surface through which both desire and punishment are negotiated. Sweetie's brown and then blue skin is a deceptive interface — not quite child, not quite artificial — through which race becomes manifest as matter. I argue that the campaign team's design of Sweetie's digital racial materiality is critical to the production of this carceral lure.

I base this analysis on ethnographic research conducted in 2014 and 2016 in the Netherlands. I spent three months with Terre des Hommes in the spring after the launch of Project Sweetie 1.0, conducting interviews with the design team and doing participant observation as an intern at the organization. Between 2014 to 2016, I conducted interviews with staff from Lemz, officers from the Dutch National Police, investigators from Europol's cybercrimes unit, and with Terre des Hommes' nongovernmental organization (NGO) partners throughout the Netherlands, the Philippines, and Thailand, totaling twenty-three interviews. This fieldwork is part of my larger project on the design and use of new digital techniques to locate child pornography and sexual abuse online, from entrapment schemes to algorithmic filtering of nude images online, to make the argument that new child protection measures marshal heightened levels of digital surveillance.[1] The claim that child protection manifests as surveillance can be illustrated through examples like Project Sweetie, a digital campaign that lured people in with the prospect of their *potentially* soliciting a minor. This potentiality warranted the collection of a thousand names, the reporting of these names to various law enforcement agencies, and subsequent police investigations leading to the arrests of nine people in Australia, Belgium, Poland, Denmark, the United States, United Kingdom, and the Netherlands.

In the sections that follow I track Project Sweetie from its genesis as an ad concept to the team's six months of undercover research and the ten weeks of Sweetie chats. I narrate this conception and design process as chronologically as possible for the sake of clarity, with the note that I was not present during this period owing to the undercover secrecy of the campaign (a point that will be elaborated upon in this essay), and this timeline is built on my fieldwork and interviews with the team only after the campaign was completed.[2] In the next section, I analyze the project's culmination into a packaged, multipronged campaign. This packaging consists of an ongoing website, research pamphlets, publicity videos using a dedicated channel donated by YouTube, and a press circuit of interviews with news media outlets.[3] This coordinated publicity campaign was dubbed Project Sweetie, or in some reports, "Becoming Sweetie." I treat the "becoming" of Sweetie as an amalgamation of its two parts—the undercover operation and the publicity campaign—to highlight how the avatar's ethnicity, sexuality, and artificiality have been specifically framed for various imagined viewing audiences. The collapsing of ethnicity and sexuality with artificiality is an unintentional maneuver that I wish to bring to the fore. The stylization of Sweetie's artificiality, and the continuous acknowledgment of it, are critical to the design of this avatar as a carceral object. As a carceral object, Sweetie is a lure specifically designed for an entrapment scheme, but it is also a symbol for policing potential. Sweetie signals to a viewing public that digital space has been and can continue to be policed through extrajudicial and increasingly creative, artistic, and crafty measures.

SWEETIE 1.0

Sweetie was conceived in 2013 following a conversation between Mark Woerde, a cofounder and director of strategy at Lemz,[4] and Albert-Jaap van Santbrink, the chief executive officer of Terre des Hommes. Terre des Hommes had been coordinating research and field projects on child exploitation in the Philippines and other regions of Southeast Asia for some years, with key offices in Manila, Jakarta, and Bangkok. Such research on exploitation marked a departure from the nonprofit's original mission (since 1964) as a children's charity working on issues of child education, nutrition, and wellness around the globe. In 2010, Terre des Hommes had hired a management consulting agency to help it with a rebranding and restructuring effort. The

Terre des Hommes that emerged from this process bore the new slogan *"Stopt Kinderbuiting"* in slick cherry-red lettering and had expanded marketing and special projects divisions to develop innovative and immersive awareness-raising campaigns, including, over the subsequent seven years, a partnership with the indie Dutch film *Lilet Never Happened*,[5] set in Cebu, Philippines, a pop-up virtual reality headgear campaign in major Dutch cities, taking the viewer through scenes of children's lives in places like Nairobi and Bangkok, and of course, the Project Sweetie campaign.

Hans Guijt, head of special programs at Terre des Hommes, was put at the helm of the then-untitled project. Guijt had spent his youth on Greenpeace boats protesting whaling and overfishing in South American seas. Today, in his fifties, he maintains much of that mettle with his wiry energy and easily excitable voice. It is clear he thrives on mission-driven adventure, and it was Guijt's idea to keep Project Sweetie "secret" from most of the organization, limited to himself, director Van Santbrink, and only three staff from special programs and marketing who were brought on board as the campaign idea developed.

In 2012, Guijt's team had begun to learn about specific neighborhood communities in the Philippines communally coercing young people to perform in front of webcams. At this point, they and many other organizations, as well as the Philippines government, had recognized that certain urban areas had higher proportions of youth involved in digital, transactional sex work, especially in internet cafés. Some of these youth were self-motivated, some were employed by agents recruiting in the neighborhood, and increasingly, it seemed to the nonprofit, many were coerced by their families. Guijt has suggested that the prevalence is so high in some areas of Cebu City and Cordova that it appears a veritable cottage industry: "It's an entire neighborhood slum slash neighborhood, where families started to engage in that kind of child sex tourism by putting their own children in front of the webcam and establishing contact with Westerners. At first the mother establishes contact, then she would get feedback like, 'Hey I love you very much, but what about your daughter?' . . . And *much* younger than the kids working from the internet cafés. These are as young as, say, the client wants them. And if they don't have an eight-year-old boy . . . they knock on the door of the neighbors and say 'Can we borrow your son for twenty minutes?' And they say, 'Okay, pay me twenty dollars for my son.' So it started off with individual adults, then the entire family became involved, then the entire neighborhood became involved. It became an *industry*—people working from their homes, not from offices or dens or what have you. A cottage industry." Terre des Hommes commissioned a series of survey-collection projects in partnership with an NGO in Cebu to understand the impact of webcam sex work on youth identity, emotions, and well-being. They also coordinated a press trip for Dutch journalists to accompany Terre des Hommes staff through neighborhoods around the cities of Cebu and Cordova in the Philippines. Some of these journalists focused on how Dutch men might be implicated, either in the small number of cases of expatriate residents coercing their Filipina partners to recruit their children to perform on camera, or in the more prevalent case of Dutch men chatting with children on the other end of the screens. These instances were subsequently reported on in several news articles for a Netherlands-based readership, including the story Woerde picked up in early 2013.[6] Woerde and Van Santbrink, of Lemz and Terre des Hommes, respectively, agreed that the issue of webcam-based child exploitation was a compelling one, and that a joint project should focus tightly on this issue.

One of the team's earliest forays into the project was to identify a series of Philippines-based webcam chat rooms and pose as an adult Dutch man. According to Woerde, almost immediately they found themselves messaging with a ten-year-old boy who offered to remove his clothes if the anonymous chatter would send an electronic transfer of money. Woerde was astonished. "I slammed my laptop closed and started crying. I had never been so directly exposed to such darkness," Woerde would later recount to an interviewer from *FastCompany* magazine.[7] The team contended that to pose as Dutch adults and engage in chats with underage minors across the world would not go far enough in highlighting the issue, which was now firmly lodged in their minds as a form of race-based digital sex tourism, or as they began to call it, "Webcam Child Sex Tourism." The team imagined that what might be more poignant, and useful, would be to pose as a child and target the adults who took it upon themselves to inappropriately message children.

The sting operation began, and Lemz agreed to Terre des Hommes' suggestion of partial secrecy by involving only a handful of executives on the project. Together the organizations rented a portion of a warehouse in Amsterdam to use as their operating point in lieu of either organization's offices. They set up a series of computers with Tor browsers or VPNs routed to Philippines-based IP addresses. A separate device was kept off any network and used to hold sensitive documents and data, and later the identifying names and emails of the thousand suspects. At the core of these maneuvers toward secrecy are vexations over privacy, and an almost caricaturesque performance of encryption. "We were extremely paranoid . . . we didn't

Mitali Thakor

know who would come after us once we started getting deep," Zayn, one of the Lemz members, explained to me afterward. The team took turns signing onto various chat rooms, taking care to vary the sites by age and ethnic specifications, and posed as a young Filipinx boy or girl using handles such as "Honey," "Baby," or "Sweetie," followed by a number, such as 10, to suggest the avatar's age. Emma, one of the Terre des Hommes team members, was explicit with me that they never "initiated" a chat, instead waiting for adults to contact them. The bait was set, though they did not need to wait long: "It was unbelievable. . . . It would just be like *pop-pop-pop*, all the time people asking for chat conversations." Certainly, many of these immediate chats may have been initiated by bots, but in enough cases a targeted dialogue, with the team making explicit that they were a child in the Philippines, would quickly determine the chatter's intent. Zayn confessed he was "freaked out" by how quickly the solicitations came, especially when they posted younger ages for the avatar: "It was stupidly easy to get these guys to give us their email addresses or even names when we offered that Sweetie would do x or y, or take off her clothes." The team would pretend that the online connection was poor and offer to send photographs to the chatter's email address. Sometimes the chatters would then discontinue the conversation, but more often they would willingly offer their email addresses.

Lemz hired two graphic design agencies, Brekel 3D and Motek Entertainment, to make the Sweetie avatar. Since Terre des Hommes' most recent fieldwork had been focused on Cebu and Cordova, there was no question that the avatar would be made to look Filipinx. Brekel used rotoscoping to model Sweetie's body movements. They used a white Dutch woman to simulate the simple gestures and motions Sweetie would perform. Using a repository of boy and girl faces of various ages, several skin tones, and patterns of musculoskeletal features, Motek designed templates for Sweetie's face. Lemz ultimately settling on the young female face used in the campaign video. Motek animated Sweetie with fifteen major facial expressions or "moods," and with Brekel mapped twenty-five movements using a live female actor. Each of Sweetie's expressions and gestures, such as nodding or looking down to "type," were linked to distinct key commands so the team could operate her efficiently. "She had to be very convincing," Van Santbrink explained, otherwise the jig would be up; they suspected adult chatters might share information with one another through online forums. The sense of chatters being somehow networked to one another bolstered the team's sense of needing to keep their operation secret and heightened the emotional suspense around making Sweetie as hyperreal as possible.

If people chatting with Sweetie requested further movement or video, the team would again fake a poor connection and request an email address where they might send photos (an offer they would never follow through on). The team emphasized with me that the chats were *never* of a visually sexually explicit nature, despite what the promotional video would later imply. "This was not child pornography. Just an image of a normal girl chatting with guys who revealed their interest in sexual show from Sweetie. But there was no child pornography or anything involved," Emma wanted to reassure me. "You just saw her face, y'know, the face you see in the media. And she had several moves she could do, like this and type and look up and down," Emma gestured. "But fully dressed. She was just chatting with the guy. So then the guy would ask her if she would do this and that for so many dollars, that is when the investigators would try to find out the identity of the guy, so they would try to keep chatting with him as long as possible and get as much information from him as possible. Because he had already admitted that he wanted that and wanted to pay for it. But they would never make it one step further, because it would be illegal."

The team used a variety of tricks to elicit information from the people they chatted with, according to Dorine, a staff member from Terre des Hommes: "The guy would reveal his intentions, and they would agree on a price or so. And then she would put on—or, *we* would put on her webcam. And they had all these tricks to get more information from the guys. They would say, 'Oh the webcam on this messenger service doesn't work! Give me your—do you have a Yahoo address? Maybe we can try Yahoo?' And he would give his Yahoo address and they would have an extra address, or find out his name. So that way they only used the webcam for little bits. So they would never get to a point where she had to take off her clothes. They had all these types of tricks, how to keep the man waiting on the site. . . . He would put on his webcam and they want to capture his face, of course, then they had his face. So yeah, there were a lot of webcam images of just dirty, dirty, naked men. . . . They would just do it quickly—*click!*—but they captured all the images so they could retrieve it." Dorine switched between identifying the team as "we" and "they" because she was brought in only in the last few weeks of the operation. But other Terre des Hommes team members also made these distinctions, and I suspect that they felt conflicted representing the nonprofit that had planted the seed for Project Sweetie while Lemz managed the majority of executive decisions over Sweetie's design and operation.

It was Lemz's idea to take the faces that had been screen captured and print them out onto a bulletin board in the warehouse. To this wall they also added any email addresses or names collected. The team also compared names against publicly searchable LinkedIn or Facebook profiles, and added these printouts to the wall. Marjolijn, the Terre des Hommes marketing director, explained: "We made a wall of five hundred of the thousand men. Unrecognizable, but you could definitely see part of the body. We did that because we knew if there would be media attention they would want to film. . . . You also want to visualize things, and that picture wall was very impressive." Most of the campaign videos pan over the wall, with hands actively posting new documents to it. The data capture was made material through its printing, moving closer to the prospect of physical apprehension and capture of the suspects themselves.

For the majority of the ten weeks of these chats, the iconic, memorably visible Sweetie face was *not* used. This fact is noted in the official Terre des Hommes written report on Project Sweetie, but not featured in any campaign videos or press releases. Marjolijn explained that technically, "'Sweetie' did not trace the thousand men—the face of Sweetie. We only used her a few times, at the end of the project. Because it was very hard to develop her. It's a high-tech Hollywood technique. It took more and more time. This was also kind of frustrating because the research already started, tracing the identities of the men performing webcam child sex tourism. And we also found out we did not *need* Sweetie at that time. Because we were just there in chat rooms. And men were all—if you would just introduce yourself as a ten-year-old from the Philippines then they already would start very explicit conversations. At that time, you did not really *need* a character." Sweetie also did not "speak" until the campaign video was released—during the sting operation itself, the activists would pretend that the audio connection was broken and conduct all communication by written type. The typing eliminated the problem of finding a live, realistic child's voice to use during the operation. However, the use of the distinctly Filipino-accented child's voice in the publicity campaign suggests another level of artifice in the campaign video's depiction of the sting operation. The campaign's advertisement video intimates perhaps a more "lifelike" simulation than was actually deployed.

The design of desirable technology is intimately linked to the design of punishable objects or persons. The team needed to become intimately knowledgeable about the type of potential offenders they wished to entrap in what they called a sting operation—who might be intrigued by Sweetie, and who might be likely to divulge personal information in exchange for what they believed to be future sexual promise. Once these names had been acquired and delivered to various law enforcement agencies, the team set up the next stage of the campaign, a curated publicity video, research document, and web presence. This second step, the publicity campaign itself advertising after the entrapment scheme, reinforces and produces Project Sweetie in totality.

THE RACIAL MATTER OF DIGITAL SKIN

Sweetie is legally significant as a *virtual* decoy; an organization unaffiliated with law enforcement cannot legally conduct a sting operation using a live *human* decoy posing as a child. This is doubly true in the Netherlands, where sting operations are not practiced by police, either. While this question of legality continues to hold resonance for Sweetie's publicity success, I want to deal with a somewhat different matter here. To me the success of Project Sweetie hinges upon the design team's self-conscious, stylized acknowledgment of the avatar's artificiality in the campaign videos and documents. By conducting Project Sweetie in two parts, as the operation itself and then the subsequent publicity video of the operation, the campaign team is able to specifically frame various elements of Sweetie's artificiality and ethnicity. The virtual model of the child is beguiling in its hyperrealism, a realism that is only made pronounced when its artificiality is revealed. To me the moment of artificiality's revelation, the deliberate undoing of the "God trick"[8] serves to bring the audience in on the secret operation and make it privy to, even complicit in, the work of making Sweetie "desirable" for her prospective chatters. The moment in which the team shows the skin being pulled back punctuates her materiality as a digital object crafted and manipulated by a team imagining her ability to reel in and ensnare potential offenders.

Skin is sensory matter, a physical extension of the body's ability to perceive desire, harm, safety, and risk. Skin is a contact point, a boundary zone at which relationality is negotiated. It is the embodied surface of Sweetie's skin that makes the project so captivating. My analysis of Sweetie's skin takes account of recent work in feminist science studies of embodiment and materiality that situate skin as marked by difference but also *doing* marking.[9] I attempt to read Sweetie's skin through a sort of digital "dermographia," to borrow Sara Ahmed and Jackie Stacey's term.[10] Skin is a material-semiotic surface in that it is tangible and exists as a point of relation between people, marking exteriority and alterity, demarcating one object from another. Digital skin is mimetic of real skin, not merely an imitation but also indicative of

Mitali Thakor

the creation of a "palpable, sensuous connection" between the original body and its copy in how it is perceived.[11] Digital skin is unremarkable when it is merely present, so successfully mimicking reality goes without comment. But it is the moment of its peeling, its tearing, at which it becomes recognized for its value. The moment of skin peeling, for Sweetie, is what consummates the affective pull of the operation.

Sweetie's skin is digital racial matter, an interface at which racial desire meets erotic fascination with the virtually artificial. Sweetie's form was produced in part through rotoscoping, an animation technique in which animators trace a live, moving object in order to produce a matte, which can then be transposed and manipulated onto multiple scenes or frames. Such digital techniques are mutually constituted with racial ideologies, and rotoscoping techniques used in Hollywood films and video games have, historically, often used blacks and other people of color as models for minstrel cartoons and hyperracialized animated caricatures.[12]

The campaign's initial presentation of Sweetie as an entity that speaks for itself seems to suggest a graphic identity that is self-evident; that is, "of course" the organization would create a Filipino child, of course the child would be female and bear such skin, of course the digital character is a neutral object to use in a sting operation in lieu of an actual human. But then the skin peels back, inviting a further interrogation of the design process and people who produce Sweetie in entirely subjective ways, and how digital design decisions are often kept "mystified"[13] and out of frame in final productions. As Bouldin suggests, "Not only do animators draw upon multiple references for the creation of the animated body, but the body that we, as viewers, experience is also radically hybrid and multiple (particularly the commercially produced animated body)."[14] Digital avatars produced using rotoscoping are far from race-neutral, as racial markers such as eyes, lips, and face shapes can literally be mapped and embellished onto the original live actor to produce the animated version. Reed and Phillips call this "racial ventriloquism"—the digital and physical performance of forms of racialized difference.[15] In their acerbic analysis of the history of rotoscoping, they argue that the technology employs a notion of "additive race," the messy displacements between racialized human bodies and their hyperracialized avatar or cartoon forms: the "realism" portrayed by motion capture technologies "so often rely on the logics of white supremacy to ground reality in either the transparent universality of whiteness or the embodied specificity of POC — what we call additive race, the reduction of racialized difference to a matter of style."[16] Sweetie is based on a white Dutch woman's gestures and expressions used for the purposes of motion capture, a matte upon which brown skin and Filipino identity are then transposed. But the avatar's face is modeled after actual young people in the Philippines: the avatar is an amalgamation of real children's faces from the photograph database of Fellowship of Organizing Endeavors (FORGE), a community organization based in Cebu City that works with Terre des Hommes and provides assistance to transient and houseless youth at risk for commercial sexual exploitation or who engage in survival sex. In viewing the Project Sweetie campaign video, the audience does a kind of double seeing: knowing that Sweetie turns out to be a digital model, even vocalizing itself as "not real"—and yet knowing that Sweetie's kind, other similar children, exist in the real world and potentially face actual online harassment and exploitation. In the words of Leonie, a staff researcher I interviewed at the office of the Dutch National Rapporteur for Human Trafficking, "She [Sweetie] would appeal to perverted European sex tourists." This blunt comment was echoed numerous times throughout the course of my research, producing the sentiment that Sweetie was specifically designed as an object of racialized desire. The moment of peeling reveals the seam, the point at which reality and artificiality, human and nonhuman, adult and non-child, are reconciled. The avatar enables the campaign viewer to conveniently forget the "real" children being referenced and enter the filmic enchantment of the avatar video. The campaign video's moment of Sweetie's skin peeling away to reveal the CGI wire-frame grid beneath—a moment of pulling back the curtain—only further enhances the pleasure of plurality and the lure becomes doubly alluring.

In other words, the Project Sweetie operation and campaign have dual effects: the viewers of, first, the operation, are lured into the scheme (to collect their personal identifying data) in much the same way that "traditional" sting operations work. The viewers of the second part of Project Sweetie, the campaign video, can enjoy all of the filmic, shaming qualities of the operation as a whole, and savor the acknowledged artificiality of the character. As Sweetie narrates in the introduction to this essay, viewers of the campaign quite literally follow Sweetie talking and revealing herself—not sexually, but as an artificial creation. I contend that the revelation of Sweetie's artificiality is a process with its own erotic charge. The campaign video forces the viewer to participate in the moment of revelation, a doubly voyeuristic act. The desire to uncover artificiality, measure the *degree* of realness, relies on logics similar to the desire to inspect racial authenticity. The video's exaggerated attention to how real Sweetie looks is itself an eroticizing act, one that highlights Sweetie's racialized otherness *and* nonhumanness, in order for the designers to claim Sweetie as alluring. It is impossible to separate Sweetie's digital representation from its intent as a lure, as a carceral object to ensnare those humans who might find the child attractive. By racially encoding Sweetie with a highly specific skin tone and facial features, the Project Sweetie team signals and interpellates those whom it wishes to catch. Sweetie's brown-raced Filipinx skin is pared to reveal its vector-mapped graphic identity, and it is this moment at which artificiality is made known that enhances the viewing public's thrill in knowing what Sweetie has been—continues to be—capable of in deceiving potential exploiters. I want to be clear that when I write "viewing public" I mean this in the most general sense possible—the 1 million viewers of the YouTube videos, myself—and you, if you choose to follow the link in the bibliography. The team's allowing the public to "really see" Sweetie contributes to the sense of satisfied complicity in "catching" these potential predators. Knowing the avatar is artificial adds a little thrill to the act of viewing, a knowing wink at being in on the duping. I argue that this moment of revelation is also key to bringing in public support for the operation, by making the policing of child exploitation by non-police actors a tangible and palatable reality, a process I describe as "making proximate."

MAKING PROXIMATE: SWEETIE 2.0 AND CARCERAL LURES

Underlying any support for Project Sweetie is an assumed universal understanding that sexual exploiters of children must be othered—located, corralled, and arrested—and are deserving of punishment. It is also understood, then, that investigators who wish to locate and apprehend offenders must first become intimately knowledgeable about sexual abuse—bring it *close*, in a sense—before arresting and enacting punishment. The othering of potential offenders is a form of extension,[17] a reaching toward those who must be kept away. Carceral technologies perform this act of extension—apprehending and making proximate violent others—by extending the corpus of policing power in order to seek certain bodies. To return to Sweetie's skin, it is a sensory surface, and as such, it is a site for possibility.[18] Skin's potentiality for contact with another helps us understand skin as encounter, the relation of one body to another, human to nonhuman. As Bouldin argues, "the rotoscoped image is not only an imitation but an instance of contact."[19] a forging of proximity between "us" (innocent public) and Sweetie (innocent child), against those who are exterior and must be kept away (non-innocent offenders). Of course, Project Sweetie does not actually physically touch to make contact—but I contend that this "encounter" *must* be imagined, for the potential abuser cannot come *too* close. This fear of literal contact is what motivates the secrecy behind the operation, the warehouse and encrypted networks, the paranoia that human trafficking crime syndicates would pursue the nonprofit workers. But the trick of the sting operation is that the team must embody the mind of the prospective exploiter, to see what he sees as desirable. In order to keep the prospective abuser of children *away*, the team must become, at some level, intimately *close* to encountering him.

We can imagine a member of the Lemz or Terre des Hommes team arriving at the warehouse to start a day of chat conversations as a Filipina child. What assumptions, what desires are encoded in this person's body as they sit down, mouse in hand, to engage in conversation with people to encourage them to ask the child to remove her clothes? What does it take to do such goading? We might consider Sweetie as an example of what Sandy Stone has called a "prosthetic technological self,"[20] an extension of a punitive impulse to entrap those who might offend. Recent work in queer feminist social theory has considered how sex offenders have emerged as people who are "despised and disposable,"[21] or even othered "beyond the pale of humanness."[22] If the imagined offender is other than human, it shares space with the nonhuman, virtual child. This operation, and indeed any entrapment scheme, must entail the team member embodying the mind-set of the imagined potential offender, *come close*, in order to catch him in the act of solicitation. It also entails the team member literally performing the face and body of a child victim. This team member wears the skin of both the child and the offender, simultaneously, thesis and antithesis, in order that they might find each other.

In early 2016, Terre des Hommes announced the launch of Sweetie 2.0, a chatbot software system that automates the conversations between Sweetie and people on webcam sites. Previously, each of these chats had been carefully articulated by a member of the team. Now automated, the words, wishes, and aims of the team are quite literally encoded into the design of the avatar. When I met with Guijt in the winter of 2016, he smiled and mused that the results of Sweetie 2.0 would be announced soon, relishing as always the promise of theatrical reveal. In an earlier interview he had joked, "Phase 1 was all about identification. Phase 2 is about warning, discouraging. And Phase 3 is about open warfare!" I interpret Guijt's words through the lightheartedness with which they were uttered, but acknowledge that in such statements the punitive fully merges with the playful. Both Project Sweetie 1.0 and 2.0 exist in the space produced between advertising campaign theatrics and the

Mitali Thakor

mimicry of policing, and in the new version remains the ripe possibility for future investigations and future arrests.

This essay has examined a digital campaign to address the commercial sexual exploitation of children. An attention to issues of sexual exploitation must take into account the mushrooming of resources and attention to human trafficking in recent decades. Trafficking, as defined by the United Nations protocol, is the forced movement of people across national borders for the purposes of labor exploitation.[23]

Scholarship from radical feminist and queer of color studies has observed that the passage of the UN protocol brought together "strange bedfellows," from liberal white feminists to Christian evangelicals, claiming their work as a new "abolitionist" movement against modern-day slavery.[24] Tryon Woods has importantly argued that this brand of modern-day abolitionism is predicated upon antiblackness, feeding upon the historical specter of black captivity in order to project victimhood upon imagined white and feminized victims.[25] Critical to this analysis is an acknowledgment that in many countries—the United States, certainly, but additionally the increasingly anti-immigrant and xenophobic Netherlands—anti-trafficking legislation has been absorbed under intensely punitive measures that disproportionately warrant the arrests of and lengthy criminal sentences for black men and other men of color.[26] Rather than allocating state funding toward community-based, harm reduction–oriented initiatives to address exploitation, especially in street economies, anti-trafficking legislation emphasizes prosecutorial and enforcement-heavy solutions.

I have noted in previous work that the assemblage of activists, bureaucrats, companies, and computer scientists coming together specifically to address digital sex trafficking constitutes a "counter-network" that seeks to address the perceived network of traffickers operating in virtual and physical space.[27] Words like "imagined" and "perceived" are critical here, for, as sex worker activists and journalists Melissa Gira Grant[28] and Maggie McNeill[29] have pointed out, global human trafficking rates and data are infamously skewed and difficult to confirm. Virtual exploitation troubles the boundary of "actual" and "perceived" as internet abuse can be hard to trace, locations faked, and identities masked or encrypted. The counter-network thus comes together as a cohesive whole to make sense of a seemingly ungraspable problem by making it tangible. The case of Project Sweetie captivates as a virtual sting operation that has identified exactly those persons whom it wishes to seek, thereby making the problem of Webcam Child Sex Tourism material, with physically located and marked perpetrators.

By employing methods commonly used by police and often represented in crime films and television like *To Catch a Predator*, this extrajudicial sting operation follows well-worn paths that make it feel familiar and legible to a viewing public. The moment of acknowledging Sweetie's artificiality provides the twist of newness that makes this familiarity strange enough. Lingering around this entire project is the prospect of abuse and harm being done to children like the ones Sweetie is modeled after. The politics of anti-trafficking and anti-exploitation campaigns rely upon affective attachments to the prospect of the injured child.[30] That symbolic child,[31] in turn, is a structuring force that motivates securitized, carceral responses to ensure its protection. By viewing Sweetie's face as both innocent victim and carceral lure, the prospect of violence is packaged neatly, such that the viewing public need not viscerally feel child harm—that visceral impulse is instead diverted into a desire to punish those who *would* harm the child. In Project Sweetie, the public is invited to come close to child abuse in order to bear witness and establish it as an issue. Such proximity to child exploitation also involves repulsion *away from* those who perpetrate abuse, a category of persons labeled sex offenders. By identifying current and potential abuse, teams of software designers and police must become intimately knowledgeable about such violence, making it reachable—making the "distant" proximate. As violence is drawn near, it is also imagined temporally as always probable to occur, always lurking. Carceral objects warp the time of violence by always already anticipating that such violence *will* occur. I consider Ahmed's interpretation that objects of fear accumulate value as they seem ever closer: "Some things more than others are encountered as 'to be feared' in the event of proximity, which is exactly how we can understand the anticipatory logic of the discourse of stranger danger."[32] Project Sweetie magnifies the stranger danger panic motivating understandings of sex offenders—the assumption that unknown others are constantly lying in wait to assault innocent children, an assumption that acquires even more fearful resonances in digital space. As many scholars have noted, particularly in queer studies of punishment, stranger danger panics perpetuate the fallacy that children are more likely to be sexually exploited by strangers rather than people known to them. In their recently completed national survey of incarcerated people who identify as queer or trans, the organization Black and Pink argues that gay men and trans women

Mitali Thakor

are incarcerated disproportionately under sex offense charges compared to the non-queer population in prison.[33] These findings echo similar research inside and outside the United States by Emily Horowitz, John Borneman, Roger Lancaster, Dean Spade, and Sarah Lamble,[34] who all suggest that sex offender charges participate in the systemic carceral punishment and surveillance of marginalized populations, often trans, queer, and/or people of color, rather than in the incarceration of the silent majority of sex offenders, who are often family members known to victims. Discrepancies in prosecution and criminal charges play a large role in this glaring gap. Once part of the carceral system, especially in the United States, but increasingly in the Netherlands and other parts of the European Union, those convicted of child sexual offenses are increasingly kept on a tight leash through surveillance and monitoring systems such as GPS-enabled tracking ankle bracelets and the publicly searchable sex offender registry online. Lancaster argues that by mobilizing the figure of the stranger sex predator, a supposedly uncontrollable and repeat-offending criminal, the carceral state is able to "arouse fear, rally citizens, and inspire legislation" directed at arresting and tracking male populations.[35] Despite overwhelming statistical data across countries and states that stranger assault accounts for the *least* common form of child sexual abuse, and that recidivism rates for sex offenders are under 3 percent in most studies,[36] the sex offender continues to be imagined as a relentless criminal predetermined to repeatedly offend.

The social issue of "child protection"—and the network that organizes around it—mobilizes digital surveillance that intrudes into common spheres of everyday life, both online and off, in the name of security. To imagine child protection, the network must also envision punishment, keeping *out* those who threaten the structuring order that the child maintains. Ensuring the security of some entails producing the *insecurity* of others. The populating of these respective categories—*some* who remain close, and *others* who must be kept far—is the ultimate trick. Who is the next pervert, the next object of fear? The reach of the carceral, punitive state is seemingly limitless when fear is constantly speculated as lurking proximately. The malevolence of the sex tourist or sex offender is imagined as so great a threat that any number of carceral schemes—including the imitation of the police by an NGO and advertising agency—seem to make sense. The entrapment scheme of Project Sweetie, a photorealistic motion capture–based avatar of a Filipina child, audaciously demonstrates the culmination of anti-trafficking ideology, digital surveillance, and future-oriented moralizing politics by seeking and entrapping potential—not actual—offenders of child abuse online. The

Sweetie avatar's artifice is twofold, as a lure for potential solicitors but also as an enticing object for the audience of the NGO publicity campaign. Project Sweetie sits at the nexus of moralizing, protective ideologies that envision a future where detection and shaming will permanently oust anyone with the *potential* to offend.

Notes

1. Mitali Thakor, "How to Look: Apprehension, Forensic Craft, and the Classification of Child Exploitation Images," IEEE *Annals of the History of Computing* 2017: 6–8; Mitali Thakor. "Algorithmic Detectives: Evidence, Entrapment, and Software Design for the Policing of Child Exploitation," in *Queer Feminist Science Studies*, ed. Angie Willey and Cyd Cipolla (Seattle: University of Washington Press, 2017).

2. I interchange several terms used to describe the people with whom Sweetie chatted—*chatters, men,* and *potential exploiters*—and want to make clear that these were the terms used most often by my interlocutors. My choice to replicate them is an attempt to stay close to a commitment to using "actor's categories" for describing events as they happened. These labels, especially *potential exploiters,* are admittedly not neutral.

3. "Project Sweetie," 2015, accessed January 30, 2018, http://www.youtube.com/Sweetie.

4. In November 2016, Lemz was acquired by Havas Group, and goes by the new brand identity Havas Lemz (http://havaslemz.com/).

5. Jacco Groen, dir., *Lilet Never Happened* (London: Spring Film, 2012).

6. Elsbeth Stoker, "All the Men Were Naked and Playing with Themselves," *De Volkskrant* (May 29, 2012).

7. Christine Champagne, "Anatomy of a Cannes Contender: Becoming Sweetie, the Little Girl Who Took on Child Predators," *Fast Company,* 2014, accessed January 30, 2018, https://www.fastcompany.com/3031676/anatomy-of-a-cannes-contender-becoming-sweetie-the-little-girl-who-took-on-child-predators?partner=newsletter.

8. Donna Haraway, "A Cyborg Manifesto: Science, Technology, and Socialist-Feminism in the Late Twentieth Century," in *Simians, Cyborgs and Women: The Reinvention of Nature* (New York: Routledge, 1991), 149–81.

9. Sara Ahmed and Jackie Stacey, eds., *Thinking through the Skin* (London: Routledge, 2001).

10. Ahmed and Stacey, *Thinking through the Skin,* 13.

11. Michael Taussig, *Mimesis and Alterity: A Particular History of the Senses* (New York: Routledge, 1993), 23.

12. Joanna Bouldin, "The Body, Animation and the Real: Race, Reality and the Rotoscope in Betty Boop," *Conference Proceedings for Affective Encounters: Rethinking Embodiment in Feminist Media Studies,* ed. Anu Koivunen and Susanna Paasonen (Turku, Finland: University of Turku Press, 2001); Nicholas Sammond, *Birth of an Industry: Blackface Minstrelsy and the Rise of American Animation* (Durham, NC: Duke University Press, 2015).

13. Jackie Stacey and Lucy Suchman, "Animation and Automation: The Liveliness and Labours of Bodies and Machines," *Body and Society* 18, no. 1 (2012): 1–46.

14. Joanna Bouldin, "Cadaver of the Real: Animation, Rotoscoping and the Politics of the Body," *Animation Journal* 12 (2004): 10.

15. Alison Reed and Amanda Phillips, "Additive Race: Colorblind Discourses of Realism in Performance Capture Technologies," *Digital Creativity* 24, no. 2 (2013): 130–44.

16. Reed and Phillips, "Additive Race," 140.

17. Sara Ahmed, *Queer Phenomenology: Orientations, Objects, Others* (Durham, NC: Duke University Press, 2006), 115.

18. Claudia Castañeda, "Robotic Skin: The Future of Touch?," in *Thinking through the Skin* (London: Routledge, 2001): 223–36.

19. Bouldin, "The Body, Animation and the Real," 50.

20. Sandy Stone, "Split Subjects, Not Atoms: Or, How I Fell in Love with My Prosthesis," in *The Cyborg Handbook*, ed. C. H. Gray (New York: Routledge, 1991).

21. Emily Horowitz, *Protecting Our Kids? How Sex Offender Laws Are Failing Us* (Santa Barbara, CA: Praeger, 2015).

22. John Borneman, *Cruel Attachments: The Ritual Rehab of Child Molesters in Germany* (Chicago: University of Chicago Press, 2015).

23. UN General Assembly, *Protocol to Prevent, Suppress and Punish Trafficking in Persons, Especially Women and Children, Supplementing the United Nations Convention against Transnational Organized Crime* (November 15, 2000).

24. Jo Doezema, "Now You See Her, Now You Don't: Sex Workers at the UN Trafficking Protocol Negotiations," *Social and Legal Studies* 14, no. 1 (2005): 61–89.

25. Tryon Woods, "Surrogate Selves: Notes on Anti-Trafficking and Anti-Blackness," *Social Identities* 19, no. 1 (2013): 120–34.

26. Elizabeth Bernstein, "The Sexual Politics of the 'New Abolitionism,'" *Differences* 18, no. 3 (2007):128–51.

27. Mitali Thakor and danah boyd, "Networked Trafficking," *Dialectical Anthropology* 37, no. 2 (2013): 277–90.

28. Melissa Gira Grant, *Playing the Whore: The Work of Sex Work* (New York: Jacobin, 2014).

29. Maggie McNeill, "Lies, Damned Lies, and Sex Work Statistics," *Washington Post*, March 27, 2014.

30. Wendy Brown, *States of Injury: Power and Freedom in Late Modernity* (Princeton, NJ: Princeton University Press, 1995). See also Jo Doezema, "Ouch! Western Feminists' 'Wounded Attachment' to the 'Third World Prostitute,'" *Feminist Review* 67 (2001): 16–38.

31. Lee Edelman, *No Future: Queer Theory and the Death Drive* (Durham, NC: Duke University Press, 2004).

32. Sara Ahmed, *The Cultural Politics of Emotion* (Edinburgh: Edinburgh University Press, 2004), 40.

33. Jason Lydon, et al., "Coming Out of Concrete Closets: A Report on Black and Pink's National LGBTQ Prisoner Survey," *Black and Pink* (2015).

34. Horowitz, *Protecting Our Kids?*; Borneman, *Cruel Attachments*; Roger N. Lancaster, *Sex Panic and the Punitive State* (Berkeley: University of California Press, 2011); Dean Spade, *Normal Life: Administrative Violence, Critical Trans Politics and the Limits of Law* (New York: South End Press, 2011); Sarah Lamble, "Queer Necropolitics and the Expanding Carceral State: Interrogating Sexual Investments in Punishment," *Law and Critique* 24, no. 3 (2013): 229–53.

35. Lancaster, *Sex Panic and the Punitive State*, 78.

36. Cf. Human Rights Watch, "Raised on the Registry: The Irreparable Harm of Placing Children on Sex Offender Registries in the US," 2013, accessed January 30, 2018, https://www.hrw.org/report/2013/05/01/raised-registry/irreparable-harm -placing-children-sex-offender-registries-us.

Mitali Thakor

9

Employing the Carceral Imaginary

AN ETHNOGRAPHY OF
WORKER SURVEILLANCE IN THE
RETAIL INDUSTRY

Madison Van Oort

.....

In June 2016, two days after the Pulse Nightclub shooting in Orlando, I boarded a bus from New York City to Philadelphia for the nation's largest annual retail loss prevention (LP) conference—NRF Protect. I had been doing research on the retail industry and had spent several months prior working as a frontline employee and interviewing other entry-level workers. I knew going into the project that retail jobs are deeply insecure, riddled with low wages and erratic schedules; a growing portion of retail workers are categorized as "involuntary part-time," meaning they seek full-time work but are unable to find it. The workforce is made up of 62 percent women, 21 percent people of color, and a growing segment of queer and/or gender nonconforming people.[1] During that fieldwork, I had noted mundane and pervasive ways through which worklife for me and my coworkers was criminalized, especially, though not exclusively, through technology. We scanned our fingerprints to clock in and out for shifts, we were warned that we could be fired for posting inappropriate material on social media, and stories of past coworkers and even managers who had gotten caught stealing abounded.

My fieldwork up to that point provided an excellent bottom-up perspective, but I longed for another vantage point. Few of my coworkers had any idea exactly how they were being tracked or to what ends, and up to that point I had relatively limited knowledge myself. Indeed, as Kirstie Ball argues, surveillance is to a certain extent a "normal, taken-for-granted element of working life."[2] I was left wondering: How did retail companies themselves justify worker surveillance? How did the companies that manufacture surveillance technology convince retailers to adopt their products? Finally, what might be the connections—material or discursive—between retail worker monitoring and broader systems of policing? With these questions in mind, I prepared to immerse myself in the world of loss prevention. The purpose of NRF Protect was to address how retailers could avert all forms of store "shrinkage," or lost revenue, including, substantially, from employee theft or error. As I scrambled around my room the first morning of the conference, attempting to dress myself in my most conservative business attire, I listened to TV newscasters describe how the Pulse Nightclub shooter had been an avowed fan of the New York Police Department—selfies of him donning NYPD T-shirts circulated widely following the attack—and was employed as an armed security guard for G4S, the world's largest private security company.[3] Meanwhile, here I was, preparing to enter what amounted to a sprawling celebration of policing and surveillance.

The distinctions between Pulse and NRF Protect are vast; I certainly do not want to trivialize the horrific tragedy of the lives lost. Yet significant traction can be gained by thinking through these phenomena together. On June 12, 2016, nearly fifty queer and trans people were murdered at a Latinx dance night of this Florida nightclub, a catastrophe propelled at least in part by the shooter's involvement with and veneration of police and private security.[4] NRF Protect was likewise entangled with and celebrated such industries; security firms already well established among the military and police here pushed their wares for commercial purposes. As I would come to witness, surveillance companies widely relied on lighthearted games and activities used to frame their technology as both palatable and entertaining, obscuring the material impacts of their products on the people they target. NRF Protect's primary attraction was a "fusion center" in the middle of the exhibition floor, where conference-goers could mingle with representatives from nationwide law enforcement agencies, including the New York City Police Department. In different ways, then, both Pulse and NRF Protect are powerful examples of how policing—as both culture and practice—increasingly saturates everyday life, of how the military and prison industrial complexes can shape and limit the livelihood of marginalized populations in banal and potentially sinister ways.

In what follows, I begin by taking stock of how academics have engaged with worker surveillance, and I make a case for understanding these phenomena through the lenses of race, gender, and sexuality. I describe my

Madison Van Oort

journey through NRF Protect, the conference-cum-surveillance festival, illustrating how the security industry attempts to harness entertainment, racialized paranoia, and technoscientific expertise to convince retailers of their products' high return on investment. I end by returning to my own experience working in retail, examining social media as one example of how certain platforms provide the scaffolding for sprawling surveillance, but also subaltern resistance.

A CRITICAL HISTORY OF WORKER MONITORING

Corporations often frame their monitoring practices as neutral and objective means of increasing workplace efficiency and strengthening the bottom line. For instance, at NRF Protect I was given a copy of *Loss Prevention Magazine*, which includes an article on how retailers can prepare for terrorist attacks. A profile of the Mall of America in Minneapolis, Minnesota, details how the shopping mall giant adopted a security strategy first developed in Israel called behavior detection and assessment (BDA). A security consultant who helped implement the program at the mall assures the reader, "There is no possible way, operationally, that you can racially profile—there are too many motives, too many types of individuals."[5] By categorizing racial profiling as "operationally" impossible, the speaker promotes the tactic as inherently unbiased; BDA in this view provides each mall patron and employee an equal opportunity of detection—as if even that were worth applauding.

In contrast to assuming neutrality, I follow scholars who argue that data are often "gathered under profound power imbalance."[6] Academics have produced a robust literature on worker surveillance.[7] Some scholars have pointed out that workers' professional and personal lives have long been subjected to incredible scrutiny, going back at least to the Pinkerton Detection Agency of the mid-nineteenth century, especially if they were "deemed a threat to the interests of employers."[8] However, the increasing accessibility and affordability of new technologies, such as data analytics and biometrics, has ushered in an era of what sociologist Ifeoma Ajunwa and others call "limitless worker surveillance," with productivity apps and worker wellness programs amassing information about employees' personal habits and dispositions.[9] Nevertheless, surprisingly few studies analyze these evolving tactics of surveillance and control through the lenses of race, gender, or sexuality.[10]

We can look to philosopher Franz Fanon for some early musings on these connections. While in exile in Tunisia in the late 1950s, Fanon lectured on workplace surveillance, suggesting that "control by quantification"—for example, through time discipline or secretive performance monitoring—could have distinct "embodied psychic effects" including "nervous tensions, insomnia, fatigue, accidents, lightheadedness, and less control over reflexes."[11] Fingerprint scanners, for example, are commonly associated with criminality,[12] and I was surprised to find that nearly every major retailer I encountered in the course of my research required employees to scan their fingerprints to clock in and out for each shift, as well as for lunch breaks. At one employer, my own sweat-induced anxiety required me to scan my fingerprint several times before it registered in the system. Some of the earliest forms of fingerprint technology were adopted by Wall Street firms to assist in worker timekeeping, but, not coincidentally, the company pioneering this software, Identimation, was bought in 1979 by the private security company Wackenhut.[13] In 2004, Wackenhut merged into G4S, the security company that employed the Orlando nightclub shooter. Dubbed "the chaos company,"[14] G4S has received criticism for its involvement in torturing Palestinian prisoners in Israel,[15] operating deplorable private prisons in the United States, and working with Dakota Access LLC against water protectors in Standing Rock, North Dakota.[16] From Fanon's insights into the genealogy of fingerprinting, we can begin to see how militarism, policing, and worker monitoring have long gone hand in hand.

I seek to build on this critical tradition, attending to how we can trace the tentacles of the carceral state through worker monitoring. I draw on sociologist Simone Browne's idea of "critical biometric consciousness"[17] by taking seriously how data collection and worker monitoring are situated in legacies of racialized, gendered, and classed forms of domination and control. Retail employees—many of whom are women, people of color, and queer or gender nonconforming—are not merely low-wage workers who have been abstracted into twenty-first-century data points, but are members of populations that have been tracked and policed by both the state and capital for many years. These connections were no clearer than when I stepped foot into NRF Protect.

CAPTURED AT NRF

After I checked in at the Philadelphia Convention Center and received my student badge, I ascended the escalator toward the exhibition hall. Near the front door, a DJ spun a dance pop soundtrack eerily similar to that which I was subjected to for months on end as a retail employee. While the demographics of the people surrounding me differed—this time, mostly middle-

Madison Van Oort

aged white men in suits—the tactic, what Rachel Hall calls "discipline as entertainment"[18] was comparable. Before even entering the conference, the music coaxed attendees into relating to this space as an amusing one, eclipsing the material realities of the people impacted by their products.

I made my way through the sea of lanyards and khaki pants, scoping out the vendor booths cordoned off by huge display boards. Between breakout conference sessions about prescriptive analytics, supply chain logistics, facial recognition, and social media monitoring, representatives from over one hundred loss prevention companies hawked their latest systems that tracked both customer and employee behavior alike. The gimmicks with which companies attempted to draw in conference-goers and make themselves memorable ranged from arbitrary to more thematic: I played plinko and mini-golf, nabbed a free jump drive and organic lip balm emblazoned with the logo of a fraud detection service, and entered a raffle for a personal drone (I lost). Near the front of the hall, a company that manufactures security tags invited participants to "Get captured!" A photo booth offered staged mug shots and encouraged people to adorn themselves with props such as sunglasses, cowboy hats, and mustaches, framing the retail criminal as a fictional figure of which attendees could momentarily play the part.

That evening, I searched the hashtag for the photobooth ("#Capturedat-NRF"), and found the company shared an example on their official social media account featuring three smiling white women wearing googly eyeglasses and posing as if in a lineup. Captioned, "I was captured at NRF Protect but I got away with his photo," the "criminals" held signs that, instead of listing their name or a prisoner identification number, read "THEY DID IT!" with an arrow pointing to the "suspect" next to them, and "I PLEAD THE FIFTH." The sign in another photo read "HELLO. MY NAME IS MISS DEMEANOR." A third photo featured a person wearing a dog mask; their sign: "PRISONER IN DISGUISE." If participants posted the photo themselves with the proper hashtag, they would be entered to win a digital camera. This booth, more than any other, demonstrated the lengths to which vendors went to make criminality into a game, creating distance between industry professionals and people who might be tracked, caught, or arrested with the help of these products.

Alongside fun, the conference additionally cultivated fear of "the retail criminal." Throughout the three-day conference, loss prevention specialists and retailers alike spoke to me about their efforts to catch "bad guys" (a term they repeatedly used). Importantly, "bad guys" indicated not just customers, but also employees. As one conference-goer told me over our complementary gluten-free lunch wraps: "More product walks out the back of the store than the front of it. There's a reason why stores use clear plastic bags." Industry figures vary on how much internal theft (by employees) compares to external theft (by customers or people not directly employed by the store), but most statistics estimate workers drive around 30 percent of total loss.[19] I spoke with one vendor who showed me his company's software that aggregates point-of-sale information and links to video surveillance footage to digitally identify "risky" cashiers. He explained, "People with the documents see, is this a training issue? Are they not being trained properly? Do they just not have time to do anything? Or are they a *bad person?*" (emphasis mine). Another vendor with a similar product told me, "We can take the good ones and the bad ones and float them to the top. So it's not only just about the *bad ones*, right? Flip it over and then reward the *good cashiers*" (emphasis mine). Through this lens, workers are always already potential criminals. In this way, workers are always already potential criminals who can be flagged with these supposedly objective tools.

More overt connections with policing permeated the event. I was somewhat surprised when the broader political context of policing in the age of Black Lives Matter entered the conversation, especially during one breakout session entitled "Tensions Are Bubbling. Are You Ready?" The abstract for the talk from the St. Louis–based retailer read: "Ferguson, Missouri. Baltimore, Maryland. Taylor, Michigan. New York City—all were sites of civil unrest and riots in the last two years and restaurants, drug stores, grocery and convenience stores and related retailers were hit hard. Civil unrest or civil disobedience may be a new issue for retailers to contend with but there are ways to make sure your organization is prepared." The presentation began with a four-and-a-half-minute video mashup of uprisings in Ferguson and Baltimore following the deaths of Michael Brown and Freddie Gray; the clips began with inaudible shouting, glass breaking, and finally, a group chanting "You can't stop a revolution." I waited anxiously in my ballroom seat to witness how the presenters would discuss such politically charged material. "So it's pretty obvious that civil unrest can happen anywhere, anytime, for pretty much any given thing nowadays, right?" the speaker began. They then detailed their own strategies for restoring their business amid citywide disruption, which included monitoring social media platforms like Periscope, a live streaming app, to keep tabs on activity surrounding stores, as well as navigating business operations when public services like buses or childcare may shut down and prevent workers from showing up. In the end, the presenters highlighted not only technology, but also the importance of estab-

Madison Van Oort

lishing contacts with city police and other professionals well before such disruptions occur; they concluded by imploring the audience to "take your local police chief out for lunch. It could be the best thing you do."

Alongside fun and fear, the third major theme present in the conference was technoscientific expertise. After the "Tensions Are Bubbling" session, I made my way to the "fusion center" at the center of the exhibition hall where retailers could meet and build relationships with representatives from city police across the country. The word choice is telling; "fusion center" typically denotes intelligence-sharing spaces created by the Department of Homeland Security following the September 11th attacks; the ACLU says these efforts contribute to a "total surveillance society."[20] That NRF uses the language of fusion centers indicates the desire to frame retailers as possessors of vital intelligence information. The conference program encouraged fusion center participants to "discuss tactics, exchange critical data and enhance important partnerships." I chatted with the New York and Minneapolis Police Departments, where I learned of the recently formed Twin Cities Organized Retail Crime Association, a local coalition of law enforcement, prosecutors, and retailers.

The "Tensions Are Bubbling" presentation and fusion center both indicate the importance of technology within contemporary networks of control, which makes waged labor even more tenuous: more seamlessly subjecting low-wage employees to monitoring, reprimand, firing, or even arrest. These examples also highlight how the loss prevention industry helps *create* conditions of social unrest by operating as an appendage of low-wage labor and the prison industrial complex.

Throughout the exhibition hall, companies flaunted their associations with law enforcement and the military as an indicator of technological prowess; a brochure for one company featured a full-page list of clients, including several subsidiaries of the Department of Defense, Department of Homeland Security, Department of Justice, and Department of State. One advertisement for a facial recognition software company present at the conference read: "While the main markets for face recognition technology remain identity management and physical security, use cases now also include commercial/service-based applications for business operations and personal use." This brochure was just one of many that revealed how much of the technology on which the retail industry now relies was in fact pioneered for law enforcement and the military. Scholars, activists, and technologists alike should actively interrogate the consequences of these platforms "gaining ground in everyday life."

While flaunting expertise, many of the technologies being marketed operate in murky legal territory. In one breakout session called "Smile—You're on Facial Recognition!" presenters spoke of facial recognition's utility for identifying thieves or "persons of interest." Since employees make up a substantial component of suspected shoplifters, this software is likely collecting their information as well. Only two states, Texas and Illinois, place legal restrictions on facial recognition, and as legal scholar Alvaro Bedoya has noted, surveillance practices by private companies can be even more difficult to identify than those of police: "To this day you can get a lot of information out of law enforcement on their use of facial recognition by using the Freedom of Information Act. There is no FOIA for tech or facial recognition companies."[21] As loss prevention companies harness new technology to "secure" their clients and the goods within their stores, they act as a direct link between the capital and state, targeting people of color, the poor and working class, and gender deviants—populations that are likely employed by major retailers and that have been shown to be commonly misidentified by facial recognition software.[22] I asked one vendor if customers or employees consent to the use of this technology. "Well I hope so," he said. "We just make the technology, we can't control what people do with it."

Significantly, many of the featured products carried the capability to track people far beyond the physical confines of the workplace. I spoke with several representatives of a crime forecasting product, which creates a location-based risk score for individual stores and attempts to assist companies in determining how they should allocate security personnel and resources. One vendor told me, "If one guy is sitting there going 'I have a budget of about x,' he'll go, 'what will I do with that?' He used to go, 'depending on the number of square feet, this is what we do.' Well, that's not really the best way to do it. Because there's different risk in different communities, different people, so we store all the locations and say, there's gonna be a likelihood of a crime happening there. So you do that for all the stores [and score them] high, medium, and low." Thus, this software takes predictive policing—a method of using information about past "criminal" activity to predict future behavior, which has been widely lambasted by scholars and activists alike—and applies it to commercial spaces. Media critic Kate Crawford notes that predictive policing software "risks perpetuating an already vicious cycle, in which the police increase their presence in the same places they are already policing (or overpolicing), thus ensuring that more arrests come from those areas."[23] We might similarly imagine that low-wage workers who live and work in lower-income communities will, with this software, end up in work spaces more heavily surveilled and more closely linked with local police.[24]

THE RISE OF SOCIAL MEDIA MONITORING

When I trained to be a sales associate worker at a major clothing store in New York City, I caught a glimpse of how frontline workers are socialized into a world of digitally surveilled work. As I sat in the back of the store on a cold, metal folding chair with the forty or so other new hires, our supervisor, a young woman who had only been employed there a few months, walked us through the employee handbook, peppering the information with her personal advice and anecdotes. The store's policy on social media was relatively vague, but the supervisor warned us of its dangers. One sales associate, we learned, had posted a selfie on Instagram while tending the fitting room; she apparently captioned the photo, "Supposed to be working haha #timestealing." The worker quickly realized her error—cell phones were banned on the sales floor and her manager was one of her Instagram followers—and deleted her post. However, the manager/Instagram follower had taken a screenshot of the post, confronted the worker, and subsequently fired her. In another example, we were told of an employee who called in sick but then was later seen posting photos on Facebook from a nightclub.

As my supervisor attempted to communicate the gravity of these situations, I struggled to keep the smirk off my face. In an age in which work is increasingly unstable, it takes courage to so blatantly undercut one's employer, perhaps especially on the internet.[25] More importantly, I was intrigued by how power struggles between workers and bosses around time use in the contemporary workplace were mediated through technology. Orwellian bosses of the analog era have not so much disappeared as much as they have become appended to and in many ways extended through social media monitoring. Part of what makes this form of surveillance new, according to political theorist Bernard Harcourt, is that the means by which people give up their information is also a source of pleasure: social media users post updates, tweets, and photos in order to get likes, because it can feel good. To relate to others in the current moment, to share in our misery around work online, is also to make ourselves subject to surveillance and control. Harcourt calls this new form of governance "the expository society."[26] When managers follow or friend their employees online, they engage in a form of soft surveillance, an iteration of community policing in which social ties simultaneously operate as a form of control. Likes or retweets from a cool supervisor might stimulate the hypothalamus as much as from a friend or even a crush; that is, of course, until the supervisor decides to report an employee's social media post to the Loss Prevention team, which may itself have been assigned based on the earlier described crime-risk forecasting software, and the employee is reprimanded, or worse, fired.

Workers are additionally followed online in less obvious ways. One sales associate I interviewed told me of an app called Slack, which allowed him and his coworkers to post all sorts of things, from pictures of the work schedule to general conversation. "It's sort of like Twitter," he explained as he showed me the interface on his phone. Here, managers might post announcements, and while he told me employees were not required to be on the app, there was an implicit expectation. "So if you didn't read it on there," he said, "[the managers are] like, oh you didn't read it? Who's on Slack? And majority of the time that's where you get your schedule. You can get your schedule the same place you clock in but *that's such a hassle*" (emphasis mine). Hence, while apps like Slack might bring with them a sense of convenience, they could also potentially create a form of wage theft if workers are expected to check the app while off the clock. In addition, Slack developers recently revealed one of the app's more frightening capabilities—monitoring worker emotion; Slack is in fact an acronym, standing for "Searchable Log of All Communication and Knowledge."[27] Apps like Slack are part of a growing sector of "sentiment analysis," which attempts to quantify and measure how workers are feeling.[28]

Sentiment analysis could be used to predict worker dissatisfaction, or as a variable in calculating a store's theft risk. For example, another company called the Retail Equation attempts to measure and analyze what customers and employees say about retail companies on the internet. As I read in *Stores* magazine, an official publication of the National Retail Federation, "If the tweets around a store are found to be more negative than the average for the country—more references, for example, to statements like 'I hate my job'—then those stores showed a higher shrink [rate] than the rest of the country."[29] Thus, "riskier" stores, perhaps where employees have more often voiced their discontent or rebelliousness online, receive a higher risk score, and are consequently assigned additional loss prevention resources. According to the article, "The same was true for tweets that showed poor grammar and slang." Sentiment analysis may in fact be measuring the socioeconomic status of the surrounding area. And so again the loop begins to close: as workers experience more alienation and financial insecurity, employers feel more justified enacting near "limitless worker surveillance."[30]

Madison Van Oort

One social media monitoring company, Geofeedia, was the target of a widely publicized critique by the American Civil Liberties Union for its role in working with police in tracking Black Lives Matter protesters across the country.[31] Before it received such negative attention, the company boasted of itself as a boon for retailers by aggregating Facebook, Instagram, and Twitter posts based on geographic location. In a demonstration video, which has since been removed from Geofeedia's website, the company details its relationship with the Mall of America. Not only could Geofeedia aggregate patrons' posts,[32] but in one highlighted instance, the software was able to detect an employee of Nickelodeon Universe, the mall's amusement park, posting a picture on Instagram of himself smoking marijuana before work. Although the post did not mention the mall or Nickelodeon Universe by name, Geofeedia aggregates all posts within a certain geographic proximity of the mall. Plus, the narrator points out, one can see the user's employee shirt in the photo. Although the narrator did not specify how the mall intervened, Geofeedia says elsewhere that "the team works with the local police department when necessary, providing them with social media content that assist with preventing or investigating crimes."[33] Conveniently for Geofeedia, an outpost of the Bloomington Police Department sits on the second floor of the mall itself. It should come as little surprise that the Nickelodeon Universe employee was a young black man.

CONCLUSION

By working in retail, talking with other workers, and researching some of the latest monitoring technologies, I have begun to see where academic conceptions of work surveillance fall short. For one, scholars commonly presume that social media monitoring is more applicable to professional than to low-age labor. White-collar workers have long experienced the "presence bleed" of the internet creating new expectations of connectivity at all times of the day; for example, an office employee may feel obliged to friend their coworkers on Facebook and/or respond to work-based communication after hours on their cell phones.[34] However, the "soft" monitoring of my retail coworkers, along with the more abstract forms of social media monitoring by third-party software, indicates that low-wage hourly jobs not only are beginning to mirror salaried sectors in the extent to which technology blurs the boundaries between "work" and "home," but that worker monitoring unfolds through rhizomatic entanglement with the carceral state. In other words, workplace surveillance is not a uni-directional phenomenon in which employers simply track workplace behavior, but rather is part of a more complex assemblage of surveillance processes and data flows, which capture, analyze and integrate personal information and meta-data from people both on and off the clock. What, after all, happened to the employee caught smoking in his work shirt? If he was not arrested, was he fired or otherwise punished? Could that worker have been further targeted by Geofeedia's investigations of Black Lives Matter protesters, especially following actions that took over the Mall of America rotunda in 2015?[35] For these reasons, language should shift from one of "work*place* surveillance" to one of "work*er* surveillance," and theorizations of these phenomena must not be detached from theorizations of the systemic and systematic capturing of people of color; queer, trans, and gender nonconforming people; and the poor and working class.

From Pulse to NRF Protect, from the Mall of America to Black Lives Matter, technoscience, capital, and the state work together to normalize surveillance, exacerbate inequality, and increase points of contact between marginalized workers and police. In Andrea Smith's words, "the problem is not primarily the surveillance strategies of the state, but the state itself."[36] Beyond privacy concerns, we might consider how such practices reinforce the assumed criminality of marginalized workers—how, as critical data studies scholars point out, these technologies are regularly forced onto populations that historically have little room for refusal.[37] In these ways, worker surveillance is an instrument of both state power and capital accumulation.

At the same time, while this chapter highlights the frightening omniscience of modern workplace surveillance, in order to tell the full story, scholars must also acknowledge how technology provides scaffolding not just for widespread surveillance but also for potent resistance. Workers may be tracked well beyond the confines of their workplaces, but technology creates opportunities for connection not always available under conditions of alienated labor. The retail sales associate posting a selfie from the fitting room was likely doing more than goofing off; she might have been alleviating her deep boredom from being relegated to a space with few other coworkers, using her cell phone as a queer or feminized instrument of opposition. As historian Robin D. G. Kelley reminds us: "The political history of oppressed people cannot be understood *without* reference to infrapolitics, for these daily acts [of resistance] have a cumulative effect on power relations. While the meaning and effectiveness of acts differ according to circumstance, they make a difference, whether they intend to or not."[38] In some spaces social media has indeed created a platform for service worker organizing,[39] engaging "weapons of the weak" for collective struggles.

Madison Van Oort

Notes

1. Amber Hollibaugh and Margot Weiss, "Queer Precarity and the Myth of Gay Affluence," *New Labor Forum* 24 (2015): 18–27; Stephanie Luce, Sasha Hammad, and Darrah Sipe, "Short Shifted," Retail Action Project, September 2014, http://retailactionproject.org/wp-content/uploads/2014/09/ShortShifted_report_FINAL.pdf.

2. Kirstie Ball, "Workplace Surveillance: An Overview," *Labor History* 51, no. 1 (April 1, 2010): 89.

3. "Orlando Gay Nightclub Shooting: Who Was Omar Mateen?," BBC News, June 14, 2016, http://www.bbc.com/news/world-us-canada-36513468.

4. Che Gossett, "Pulse, Beat, Rhythm, Cry: Orlando and the Queer and Trans Necropolitics of Loss and Mourning," Verso Books blog, July 5, 2016, https://www.versobooks.com/blogs/2747-pulse-beat-rhythm-cry-orlando-and-the-queer-and-trans-necropolitics-of-loss-and-mourning.

5. Garett Seivold, "Readying Retail for Terrorism's New Battleground," LPM, May 16, 2016, http://losspreventionmedia.com/loss-prevention-magazine/m-retail-security/readying-retail-for-terrorisms-new-battleground/.

6. Finn Brunton and Helen Nissenbaum, "Vernacular Resistance to Data Collection and Analysis: A Political Theory of Obfuscation," *First Monday* 16, no. 5 (April 26, 2011), http://firstmonday.org/ojs/index.php/fm/article/view/3493.

7. Ball, "Workplace Surveillance."

8. Ifeoma Ajunwa, Kate Crawford, and Jason Schultz, "Limitless Worker Surveillance," *California Law Review* 105, no. 3 (2016): 4.

9. Ajunwa, Crawford, and Schultz, "Limitless Worker Surveillance."

10. Leslie Salzinger, *Genders in Production: Making Workers in Mexico's Global Factories* (Berkeley: University of California Press, 2003); Kevin Walby and Seantel Anais, "Research Methods, Institutional Ethnography, and Feminist Surveillance Studies," in *Feminist Surveillance Studies*, ed. Rachel E. Dubrofsky and Shoshana A. Magnet (Durham, NC: Duke University Press, 2015), 208–20; Karen E. C. Levy, "Digital Surveillance in the Hypermasculine Workplace," *Feminist Media Studies* 16, no. 2 (2016): 361–65; L. J. B. Hayes and Sian Moore, "Care in a Time of Austerity: The Electronic Monitoring of Homecare Workers' Time," *Gender, Work and Organization* 24, no. 4 (2016): 329–44.

11. Simone Browne, *Dark Matters: On the Surveillance of Blackness* (Durham, NC: Duke University Press, 2015), 6.

12. Simon A. Cole, *Suspect Identities: A History of Fingerprinting and Criminal Identification* (Cambridge, MA: Harvard University Press, 2009).

13. Shoshana Magnet, *When Biometrics Fail: Gender, Race, and the Technology of Identity* (Durham, NC: Duke University Press, 2011).

14. William Langewiesche, "Meet G4S, the Contractors Who Go Where Governments and Armies Can't—or Won't," *The Hive*, March 18, 2014, http://www.vanityfair.com/news/business/2014/04/g4s-global-security-company.

15. Angela Y. Davis, *Freedom Is a Constant Struggle: Ferguson, Palestine, and the Foundations of a Movement* (Chicago: Haymarket Books, 2016).

16. Sarah Lazare, "Reckless Security Firm Hired to Protect Dakota Pipeline Company Has Dark Past in Palestine," AlterNet, September 9, 2016, https://www.alternet.org/reckless-security-firm-hired-protect-dakota-pipeline-company-has-dark-past-palestine.

17. Browne, *Dark Matters*, 116.

18. Rachel Hall, "Terror and the Female Grotesque: Introducing Full-Body Scanners to U.S. Airports," in *Feminist Surveillance Studies*, ed. Rachel E Dubrofsky and Shoshana Magnet (Durham, NC: Duke University Press, 2015), 129.

19. Lamar Pierce, Daniel C. Snow, and Andrew McAfee, "Cleaning House: The Impact of Information Technology Monitoring on Employee Theft and Productivity," *Management Science* 61, no. 10 (2015): 2299–319.

20. Mike German and Jay Stanley, "Fusion Center Update," American Civil Liberties Union, July 2008, https://www.aclu.org/files/pdfs/privacy/fusion_update_20080729.pdf.

21. Chris Frey, "Revealed: How Facial Recognition Has Invaded Shops—and Your Privacy," *The Guardian*, March 3, 2016, https://www.theguardian.com/cities/2016/mar/03/revealed-facial-recognition-software-infiltrating-cities-saks-toronto.

22. Magnet, *When Biometrics Fail.*

23. Kate Crawford, "Artificial Intelligence's White Guy Problem," *New York Times*, June 25, 2016, https://www.nytimes.com/2016/06/26/opinion/sunday/artificial-intelligences-white-guy-problem.html?_r=1.

24. A recent article in *Bloomberg Businessweek* profiles Walmart's relationship with local police, which is in part mediated by Walmart's use of the software CAP Index. Shannon Pettypiece and David Voreacos, "Walmart's Out-of-Control Crime Problem Is Driving Police Crazy," *Bloomberg Businessweek*, August 17, 2016, https://www.bloomberg.com/features/2016-walmart-crime/.

25. Recent instances indicate that "labor law [may be] catching up to social media." Jackie Wattles, "Chipotle under Fire for Illegal Workplace Policies," CNNMoney, August 24, 2016, http://money.cnn.com/2016/08/24/pf/jobs/chipotle-social-media-nlrb/. The fast-food Tex-Mex chain Chipotle was found by the National Labor Relations Board to be in violation of an eighty-year-old labor law protecting workers' speech when it told an employee to remove a tweet criticizing the company. The tweet read, in response to a customer posting about a free burrito, "Nothing is free, only cheap #labor. Crew members only make $8.50 [per] hr how much is that steak bowl really?"

26. Bernard E. Harcourt, *Exposed: Desire and Disobedience in the Digital Age* (Cambridge, MA: Harvard University Press 2015).

27. Eugene Kim, "Slack: Where Did It Get Its Name?," *Business Insider*, September 27, 2016, http://www.businessinsider.com/where-did-slack-get-its-name-2016-9.

28. Kaveh Waddell, "The Algorithms That Tell Bosses How Employees Are Feeling," *The Atlantic*, September 29, 2016, https://www.theatlantic.com/technology/archive/2016/09/the-algorithms-that-tell-bosses-how-employees-feel/502064/.

29. Liz Parks, "Putting Buzz to Work," National Retail Federation, June 6, 2016, https://nrf.com/news/putting-buzz-work.

30. Ajunwa, Crawford, and Schultz, "Limitless Worker Surveillance."

31. Sadie Gurman, "ACLU Wary of Police Using Social Media Tracking Tool," *Business Insider*, October 6, 2016, www.businessinsider.com/ap-aclu-wary-of-police-using-social-media-tracking-tool-2016-10.

32. Kavita Kumar, "When MOA Shoppers Talk in Cyberspace, the Mall's Likely to Talk Back," *Minneapolis Star Tribune*, 2015, http://www.startribune.com/when-you-talk-about-the-mall-of-america-in-cyberspace-these-days-it-s-likely-to-talk-back/352973201/.

33. "Case Study: Mall of America's Enhanced Service Portal," Geofeedia, 2015, http://resources.geofeedia.com/hubfs/Geofeedia_Resources/Geofeedia_UC_MallOfAmerica_Final.pdf.

34. Melissa Gregg, *Work's Intimacy* (Cambridge: Polity, 2011), 105.

35. James Walsh, "Mall of America Protest Attracts Thousands on Busy Shopping Day," *Minneapolis Star Tribune*, January 6, 2015, http://www.startribune.com/dec-20-mall-of-america-protest-attracts-thousands/286443781/.

36. Andrea Smith, "Not Seeing: State Surveillance, Settler Colonialism, and Gender Violence," in *Feminist Surveillance Studies*, ed. Rachel E. Dubrofsky and Shoshana Amielle Magnet (Durham, NC: Duke University Press, 2015), 38.

37. Ruha Benjamin, "Informed Refusal: Toward a Justice-Based Bioethics," *Science, Technology, and Human Values* 41, no. 6 (2016): 967–90; Browne, *Dark Matters*; Magnet, *When Biometrics Fail*.

38. Robin D. G. Kelley, "'We Are Not What We Seem': Rethinking Black Working-Class Opposition in the Jim Crow South," *Journal of American History* 80 (1993): 78.

39. Gordon B. Schmidt, "How Social Media Can Impact the Organizational Political Process," in *Handbook of Organizational Politics: Looking Back and to the Future*, ed. Erin Vigoda-Gadot and Amos Drory (Cheltenham, UK: Edward Elgar, 2016), 148.

(PART III)

RETOOLING LIBERATION FROM ABOLITIONISTS

TO AFROFUTURISTS

.....

10

Anti-Racist Technoscience

A GENERATIVE TRADITION

Ron Eglash

.....

Many of the essays in this volume describe the ways in which science and technology ("technoscience") is co-constructed with the carceral imagination. Rusert, for example, shows how the development of certain medical frameworks requiring stabilized populations involved techniques inherited from the antebellum plantation system. Scannell (policing), Poster (labor), and Nopper (credit) all point toward the co-construction of algorithmic technosciences and racialized political economy. But there are cases of the reverse trend as well: convergence between anti-racist activists and their allies in science and engineering fields. Roth describes strategies for building multiracial equity directly into the fabric of cosmetic technologies, and Gaskins examines a similar approach to STEM education. By examining cases across the diversity of both carceral and liberatory technoscience phenomena, some common themes emerge.

Some scholars characterize the common theme in carceral technoscience as "reductionism"[1] or even simply "quantification."[2] There are certainly examples in which reducing the vibrant complexity of life to a restricted set of numbers enforces hegemonic domination. But mathematical techniques are also part of empowerment—not simply in oppositional reaction (fighting numerical fire with fire) but on its own terms as a potential technology of liberation. As Haraway puts it, "the history of struggle . . . to put together general policies from the analytical, imaginative, and embodied standpoint of those who inhabit too many zones of unfreedom and yearn toward a more just world shows 'impersonal,' quantitative knowledge to be a vital dimension of moral, political, and personal reflection and action."[3] And, as we will see later in this essay, a poetics of holistic naturalism can work hand in hand with the worst of fascist ideologies.

For other social scientists[4] the common thread is the devastating effects of capitalist economic forms. From the plantation profits that drove the slave trade to fossil fuel profits that drive global warming, private corporations have indeed been destructive to both people and the planet. But a broader survey of these relations shows similar effects happening under socialism. Ethnic cleansing and racial targeting in the USSR, Cambodia, Hungary, and elsewhere resulted in millions of deaths.[5] Many of the largest polluters in China today are state-owned enterprises.[6]

One of the leading pro-slavery intellectuals of the antebellum South was socialist George Fitzhugh, whose 1854 *Sociology for the South* made the case that replacing capitalism with state-controlled slavery would offer a benevolent society for all. An optimist regarding the power of his own rhetoric, he sent a personally inscribed copy to abolitionist Frederick Douglass.[7] Douglass's opposition to socialism is often dismissed on the left as mere politically expedient strategy, and misinterpreted by the right as libertarian validation of corporate capitalism. Here I want to propose a third possibility: that Douglass and others in his network were mapping out what I will call the generative tradition, one that is based on opposition to the extraction and alienation of value by either capital or state. It is well known that Douglass makes the Lockean connection between the generation of unalienated value by labor and the social contract of unalienable human rights.[8] But the framework Douglass and others pointed toward is a deeper critique, offering a model for both human and natural flourishing in self-generative circulations.

Thus, this essay examines the contrast between technosciences of bondage versus freedom using the distinction between extractive versus generative flows of value. In our prior work[9] we have defined this as generative justice: "The universal right to generate unalienated value and directly participate in its benefits; the rights of value generators to create their own conditions of production; and the rights of communities of value generation to nurture self-sustaining paths for its circulation." There are three categories of "value" in the generative justice framework (although these are not intended as exhaustive or discretely bound). *Unalienated labor value* was the foundation of Marx's critique of capitalism, but it can be equally applied to critiques of oppression under a communist state: democratically empowered structures such as worker-owned cooperatives can circulate value under either context. Similar to labor value, the *unalienated ecological value* created by nonhumans

Ron Eglash

can be seen in generative flows that circulate in cases such as organic farming (agroecology). The third is *unalienated expressive value*, which allows the circulation of free speech, sexuality, spirituality, and other liberties.

Examples of generative justice can be found in the egalitarian structures of many indigenous societies.[10] Similar systems can be found in high-tech domains such as the "commons-based peer production" of open-source software and other media.[11] Elinor Ostrom received the Nobel Prize in economics for showing how egalitarian flows of value can develop when a resource commons is managed by self-organized governance systems, based on internal trust and reciprocity. Lansing and Kremer show that, in contrast to Marx's vision of enforcing cooperation through fixed centralized authority, these generative systems tend to be bottom-up, voluntary, and self-transforming.[12] Haraway, noting how the model of "autopoiesis" misleadingly implies a closed loop, recommends the term *sympoiesis* to emphasize an openness to hybridity and adaptive change in these systems.[13]

Using two case studies, I will map out intellectual genealogies in which some similar ideas about generative frameworks — portraits of life's flourishing as open, hybridizing, and self-transforming — emerged in the exchanges between anti-racists and the scientific community. The first case is a detailed look at the exchanges between abolitionists and scientists — Frederick Douglass, Henry Bowditch, Charles Darwin, and others. Here a generative framework emerges as an alternative to racist portraits of fixed order in biology, as well as an alternative to the fixed order of segregation and cultural purity. The second case is a comparison with the open-ended sympoiesis in Native American agroecologies, and the first emergence of a movement to decolonize diets. We will end with a brief look at a generative framework in science/activist alliances today. Together these cases can illuminate the reasons why open-ended hybridity, not closed-loop purity, is key to understanding the possible paths to a world based on generative justice.

ABOLITIONISTS AND ADAPTATION

While the idea that organic life is the generative source of its own diverse complexity is fundamental in many indigenous cultures,[14] Europe developed such generative models only among a relatively small group of "alternative" thinkers, which I will describe shortly. Far more common were those who looked toward Aristotle's model of fixed essential characteristics for each organism and its fit to later Christian conceptions of "natural theology." It was this model of predesigned species, frozen in place by God's plan, that created the foundations for biological racism. According to the polygenists—Voltaire, Hume, Cuvier, and others—there was a different origin for each race (or, according to some, species) of human. In the nineteenth century the "American School of Anthropology" took a leading role in promoting polygenesis.

The founder of the American polygenesis school was Samuel G. Morton, who claimed to prove that human races had completely separate origins, that whites had a larger brain volume, and that this gave whites superior intelligence. His quantitative measurements over hundreds of skull samples gave Morton's work scientific stature, despite a number of flawed maneuvers.[15] His work began to take on international acclaim; for example, in England, Charles Hamilton Smith based his *Natural History of the Human Species* on Morton's work. Morton's most ardent followers were Josiah Nott and George Gliddon, who dedicated their own eight-hundred-page polygenist text, *Types of Mankind*, to Morton's memory. Harvard Professor Louis Agassiz helped to boost their profile in the 1851 meeting of the American Association for the Advancement of Science (AAAS), which took place in the slave state of South Carolina. Their session on human origins gave a large forum to the polygenesis position,[16] and Agassiz became president of the AAAS the following year.

The scientific works of Morton, Nott, Gliddon, and Agassiz were closely coupled with the political work of maintaining the institutions of slavery. The *Charleston Medical Journal* noted at Morton's death that "We of the South should consider him as our benefactor for aiding most materially in giving to the Negro his true position as an inferior race." Nott published in *Debow's Review*, the South's premiere business journal, claiming that black bodies could not adapt to climates outside of Africa and thus required slavery as protection. In 1844, U.S. Secretary of State John C. Calhoun, fearing the effect of abolitionists, sought to make this connection at the national level by summoning Gliddon to his office. Gliddon sent him copies of Morton's work on skulls, and added his own writings as an Egyptologist, assuring readers of the white ethnicity of ancient Egyptians. Calhoun used these scientific-sounding arguments to bolster his claims for the right to slavery in southern states. In his manifesto *A Disquisition on Government*, he maintained that liberty should be "reserved for the intelligent, the patriotic, the virtuous and deserving," and that these characteristics were biologically restricted to whites. Africans, he declared, had only benefited from slavery. He based this claim on statistics from the 1840 census, which purported to show longer life for enslaved southern blacks than those free in the North (more about that shortly). Just prior to his death in 1850, this scientific racism became instrumental to the

Ron Eglash

debates over whether or not proposed states such as Nebraska would be admitted as slave states.

In 1854, abolitionist Frederick Douglass was invited to give the annual literary address at what is now Case Western University. In it he described this collusion between pro-slavery political forces and polygenists' biology: "The debates in Congress on the Nebraska Bill during the past winter, will show how slaveholders have availed themselves of this doctrine in support of slaveholding. There is no doubt that Messrs. Nott, Gliddon, Morton, Smith and Agassiz were duly consulted by our slavery propagating statesmen." The alternative biology envisioned by Douglass was one that coupled common descent—the monogenetic origins of the one human race—and adaptive physiology. It was essential to Douglass to find a scientific basis that would explain differences such as skin color and height, and yet establish these as trivial changes that did not alter the unity of humanity. He did so by emphasizing the idea that human physiology was highly plastic, adapting over just a few generations.[17] These concepts were not ubiquitous among abolitionists, as some of the most prominent were opposed to this idea of rapid adaptive transformation. William Lloyd Garrison, for example, had stated specifically in his *Thoughts on African Colonization* that the creator had a fixed plan: he "made the whole family of man to differ in personal appearance, habits and pursuits," such that they were suited to a specific geographic location.[18]

If Douglass's model of adaptation was so much at odds with both the polygenists and the "God's fixed plan" branch of abolitionists, where did it come from? Kendi rightly critiques Douglass's framework because it ran too close to stereotypes of black inferiority in its discussion of adaptations to the African climate.[19] That is certainly a flaw, but to dismiss his model as the status quo would miss the point. An ongoing network of conversations between anti-racists and scientists resulted in the generative framework—life as a bottom-up, self-generating diversity of forms and processes. Understanding Douglass as part of that conversation is not just correcting a historical omission; it is a crucial prophylaxis against the barriers that prevent science/activist alliances even today.[20] This coevolving model had positive repercussions not only for the abolitionists, but for the advancement of science as well.

In the instance of abolitionist influences on Charles Darwin's evolutionary theory, Adrian Desmond and James Moore have already made this argument.[21] Darwin's paternal grandfather Erasmus was a strong proponent of abolition, and his book *Zoonomia; or the Laws of Organic Life* anticipated Lamarck's theory of evolution by seven years.[22] Like Lamarck, Erasmus thought that characteristics acquired by exercise or other experience would be inherited. The giraffe that stretches its neck will have children with longer necks. But there was a crucial difference: Lamarck and many other early evolutionary theorists (Bory de Saint-Vincent, Étienne Saint-Hilaire, Robert Grant, and William Lawrence, for example) saw these transformations as *parallel lines of unrelated species*: fish, birds, rats, monkeys, and so on all had separate origins, and each line transforms at its own pace. Erasmus Darwin offered a completely different model: bifurcating paths like a bush, each branch tracing back to a common ancestor, eventually to "one living filament" that was the mother of us all. The implications are profound for abolitionists, who could now offer monogenesis as a scientific basis for the concept of "the family of man." Among these were Charles Darwin's maternal grandfather Josiah Wedgwood, who put the famous Wedgwood pottery factory to work issuing a cameo, to be worn as a broach or medallion, featuring an enslaved African kneeling under the motto "Am I not a man and a brother?"

The Darwin and Wedgwood family continued their commitment to the abolitionist cause over the next generation, as did many other scholars who drew on evolutionary ideas. James Prichard, a physician and abolitionist, wrote his 1813 *Researches into the Physical History of Mankind* as a foundational text for human monogenesis, stating that the first humans, "created in the image of their Maker, were black" and that climate or other "external agencies" created minute changes over time, resulting in the trivial external features of racial difference. Inspired by this work, phrenologist George Combe wrote *The Constitution of Man* in 1828. Today we think of phrenology as a harbinger of scientific racism, but Combe, an abolitionist and monogenist, developed a Lamarckian version in which mental facilities would be developed and passed on by heritage, resulting in "improvement in the organic, moral, and intellectual capabilities of the race; for the active moral and intellectual organs in the parents would tend to increase the volume of those in their offspring."[23] Smithers points out that Combe's work in Australia became the basis for educational reforms that—although still operating as a tool of colonial domination—at least contradicted the racist contention of Aboriginal brains as genetically fixed and inferior to white brains.[24]

Thus, as Desmond and Moore point out, by the time Charles Darwin was at Edinburgh University, there was already a rich set of connections between abolitionists and evolutionary concepts among his family and his educators. The focus of Desmond and Moore's analysis is to illustrate how this confluence of anti-racist activism and biology came to influence the best-known generative framework in science—Darwin's evolution by natural selection. A rigorous historical documentation of almost five hundred pages, their text provides a solid case for intellectual causality in one direction, from abolitionist politics to biological science. My only amendment is to ask to what extent those causal influences might operate in both directions, and how that bidirectional coevolution reverberated across the Atlantic. Hence we will briefly visit America at this time period, returning to Edinburgh in the company of Frederick Douglass.

DOUGLASS AND THE MEDICAL ABOLITIONIST NETWORK

In her essay "Naturalizing Coercion" (this volume), Rusert points to the collusion between southern medical researchers and the plantation system. But medical abolitionists had their own network, and they were equally adept at creating links between their profession and the politics of race. Three medical doctors of importance to Douglass stand out: Henry Ingersoll Bowditch, a medical professor at Harvard; Peleg Clarke, a physician in Rhode Island; and James McCune Smith, the first African American to hold a medical degree. All three had connections to the generative conceptual framework.

Clarke was president of the Rhode Island anti-slavery society. He was also an avid reader of the work of Erasmus Darwin, citing *Zoonomia* "by the ingenious Dr. Darwin" in his medical writings.[25] The intersections became all the more important when Garrison and Douglass traveled to England in 1845, as Douglass recounts in his autobiography: "Whilst in Edinburgh . . . I had a very intense desire gratified—and that was to see and converse with George Combe, the eminent mental philosopher, and author of 'Combe's Constitution of Man,' a book which had been placed in my hands a few years before, by Doctor Peleg Clark of Rhode Island, the reading of which had relieved my path of many shadows. In company with George Thompson, James N. Buffum, and William L. Garrison, I had the honor to be invited by Mr. Combe to breakfast." Why did Douglass have an "intense desire" to meet a physiological theorist when hundreds of other famous abolitionist intellectuals were available to him? In later work he notes that while in England he had read the foundational monogenesis text, Prichard's *Researches into the Physical History of Mankind* (which, readers may recall, had inspired Combe's work).[26] Douglass does not provide further details of how Combe "relieved my path of many shadows," but Rusert, examining Douglass's newspaper articles on black phrenologists, concludes that "Douglass imagined ways that the individual's power for self-transformation through phrenology might expand into larger political transformations."[27] It was those aspects of Combe's writing that were shared with Prichard's text—the generative framework, in this case a combination of Lamarckian adaptive variation and monogenetic descent, aimed at offering a scientific basis for the progressive vision of an egalitarian future.

Returning to the United States in 1847, Douglass began publishing his abolitionist paper *The North Star*. One of the regular columns in Douglass's paper, under the pseudonym of "Communipaw," was written by Dr. James McCune Smith. Like Douglass, Smith had left America for Scotland, but in his case it was due to the refusal of medical colleges to admit a black student. Smith graduated at the top of his class from Glasgow University in 1837, and returned to the United States as the first African American with a medical degree, steeped in the latest statistical methods of epidemiology. Smith's column in Douglass's paper was named after a town in New Jersey, as imaginatively[28] described by Washington Irving, in which Dutch, black, and Native American community members joined together as equals in opposition to the British. In his story, the black Communipaw citizens were known for their entrepreneurship and associated mathematics: "from their amazing skill at casting up accounts upon their fingers, they are regarded with as much veneration as were the disciplines of Pythagoras of yore."[29] The Communipaw economic foundation was "cabbage and oysters," a mix of imported and local biota.

Smith's multiracial, egalitarian vision was applied to his medical work as well and was clearly another source for Douglass's generative outlook. One of his most significant achievements in that regard may have been his critique of American phrenology. Unlike Combe's Lamarckian model, the American version was closely tied to Morton's notions of polygenesis and genetically fixed mental attributes. Smith handily refuted these in public lectures in New York and Philadelphia, using skulls, drawings, and quantitative measures.[30] Another would be his statistical analysis. Recall that Calhoun's scientific claims for the improvement slavery provided to black lives was based on the 1840 census data. Smith had learned rigorous statistical epidemiology at Glasgow, and he applied this to the census data in a definitive refutation, showing that northern African Americans were in fact living longer, achieving more academic success, and suffering fewer mental health problems, all in comparison with those in the enslaved South.[31]

Here the "generative" concept moves beyond strictly biological models, encompassing the idea that just as biology flourishes best as an externally open self-organized system, so too is society stimulated by its own emergent responses to diversity. Indeed, when Smith is mentioned by name in Douglass's 1854 address at Case Western, it is not for his critique of racist notions of biological purity, but rather as the source of evidence that mixed-

Ron Eglash

race societies prosper better than those forced into isolated cultural purity. Rusert located similar ideas appearing in Smith's writings in *The Anglo-African Magazine*: she summarizes his conception as a framework in which civilization best arises "in all those liminal, coastal places that foster the intermingling of people from different areas of the world."[32]

Douglass extends Smith's vision of the multicultural commons to reconceptualizing science itself. The racial science of polygenists divides humans, creating an enslaved class whose value is extracted from them. He envisions a future science which embodies "the necessity of means to increase human love with human learning."[33] The opportunity for this unalienated expressive value to be freely circulated in a commons is now upon us, for we live at a time "when knowledge is so generally diffused, when the geography of the world is so well understood—when time and space, in the intercourse of nations, are almost annihilated—when oceans have become bridges—the earth a magnificent hall—the hollow sky a dome—under which a common humanity can meet in friendly conclave." Smith's statistical work illustrated both the promise and challenges of this knowledge commons. While greatly appreciated by the anti-slavery communities, it might have languished in obscurity had it not been for yet another member of the abolitionist medical network, Massachusetts physician Edward Jarvis, who also noted the racial bias in the conclusions drawn about the 1840 census. In 1845 the Boylston Medical Committee of Harvard University awarded their annual prize to Jarvis, and he used the occasion to draw attention to Smith's statistical analysis. However, Jarvis was not the only member of the medical abolitionist network to leverage the power of Harvard, as we will see in the case of the Bowditch family.

DOUGLASS AND THE BOWDITCH FAMILY: THE GENERATIVE TRADITION AFTER THE CIVIL WAR

Henry Ingersoll Bowditch earned his medical degree from Harvard in 1832 and became a professor of clinical medicine there in 1859. He introduced inductive reasoning into American medical science, popularized the stethoscope, founded the Massachusetts State Board of Health, published *Public Hygiene in America* to create support for state institutions, and served as president of the American Medical Association. Intertwined with this successful medical career was that of an abolitionist activist. His watershed moment occurred in 1843, when he attended a speech by Frederick Douglass in Boston's Marlboro Chapel. "Only a few days before one of our meetings, a young lady had hoped that I 'would never become an Abolitionist,' and about the same time Frederick Douglass appeared as a runaway slave. . . . Of course I was introduced to him, and, as I would have invited a white friend, I asked him home to dine with me in my small abode in Bedford Street."[34] Bowditch reports that he was shocked by the condemning stares as they walked back to his house, finally coming face to face with the same young lady who had warned him against joining the abolitionist movement, and by implication face to face with his own shameful impulses. He learned that it was one thing to profess moral objections to slavery in genteel discourse with fellow whites, another thing entirely to break the color line in social practice. But the eye-opening experience only strengthened his commitment. Bowditch maintained his friendship with Douglass over the years; the two walked arm and arm when Bowditch served as the marshal of the anniversary of West Indian emancipation for example. He led a massive petitioning of the Massachusetts legislature that resulted in laws forbidding the use of state and municipal jails to detain fugitive slaves, organized the Anti-Man-Hunting League, and agitated for more organized medical support for northern soldiers during the Civil War.

He also passed the torch to his nephew, Henry Pickering Bowditch (as both are named Henry Bowditch I will refer to the latter as "Pickering"). Pickering was born to Jonathan Bowditch; he was an abolitionist like his uncle, although not an activist.[35] When his uncle received word that his son had been killed in the Civil War, it was Pickering who delivered the news.[36] While Pickering was trying to complete his medical science research in Paris, and avoiding pressure to return to the United States to teach, it was his uncle who gave him crucial support.[37] As the second Professor Bowditch at Harvard, Pickering continued the generative tradition even after the Civil War. He began by taking the height and weight of 24,500 schoolchildren from around Boston. Applying statistical methods to describe differences in growth associated with sex, nationality, and socioeconomic level, his analysis (which included the first percentile growth charts) directly contradicted the eugenics framework that had been growing in scientific circles. In 1885 he showed that there was considerable overlap between what were usually thought of as discrete racial types, and that the greater access to nutrition and other resources among the wealthy—not genetics—was at the root of body size differences in socioeconomic level comparisons. This study became a model for the similarly anti-racist research of Franz Boas, which today is recalled as a foundation for anthropology, whereas Pickering's writings are forgotten.[38]

The contention that body differences were the result of adaptive, self-determining changes within the body, not genetically fixed racial attributes,

Ron Eglash

did not arise solely from the abolitionists' generative framework. Pickering had studied in Paris with Claude Bernard, who originated the term *milieu intérieur* to describe the body's self-regulatory feedback loops. But the Paris lab was itself frequented by radical thinkers. Feminist socialist Mary Putnam Jacobi visited the lab until the fall of the Paris Commune in 1871, and later used the milieu intérieur concept to illustrate the importance of social self-determination.[39] Psychologist William James studied side by side with Pickering in Bernard's lab, and was quite eloquent regarding the importance of the abolitionist cause: "Since the 'thirties the slavery question had been the only question, and by the end of the 'fifties our land lay sick and shaking with it. . . . But the abolitionists would not be muzzled—they were the world's conscience."[40] Bernard himself did not tend toward explicit political statements, but he too seemed to be aware of the resonance with political concepts. In writing about the greater role of the milieu intérieur in higher organisms, he stated, "The third form of existence, characterized by freedom and independence, is found in the more highly organized animals. Here life is never suspended, but flows steadily on apparently indifferent to alterations in its [external] environment or changes in its material surroundings."[41] The greatest legacy of Pickering may have been in the reinterpretation of Bernard by his student Walter Cannon, who later became president of the AAAS. A student in Pickering's lab at Harvard, with images of both Bernard and Darwin over his desk, Cannon modernized the concept of the milieu intérieur by coining the term *homeostasis*. As Cooper points out, this shifted the emphasis from merely maintaining the steady state of the internal environment, as if it were a chemical buffering system (the interpretation of some followers such as Lawrence Henderson), to active processes of control in an information infrastructure, such as the hormone messaging system.[42] In doing so, Cannon created the groundwork for cybernetics. Largely forgotten today, cybernetics briefly prospered from about 1950 to 1970, and included a number of scholars who mixed social justice with new perspectives on control and communication theory. Cannon prefigured such connections by asking how the homeostasis concept might allow society to be better structured—to serve the health, wealth, and liberty of all citizens rather than an elite few—with an eye toward Russian communism.

By the 1930s Cannon's enthusiasm for the USSR's experiment waned, as it became increasingly apparent that it was degrading life for its citizens, but his activism continued, and he chaired the Medical Bureau for Aid to Spanish Democracy, attempting to ensure that all those who fled the rising fascism received humanitarian aid regardless of anarchist or communist affiliations. In the course of finding positions for Spanish medical radicals in universities in Mexico, he brought to Harvard the Mexican physiologist Arturo Rosenblueth, who later brought Cannon's work to leftists such as Norbert Wiener.[43] Kuznick raises an interesting question: How did someone as completely associated with the radical left as Cannon become president of the AAAS, the same organization that had enshrined Agassiz?[44] By the year of his election, 1938, the Depression had greatly damaged public respect for science, and the embrace of science by the USSR seemed as if it would cause the United States to lose its leading role. A committee chaired by Franz Boas issued the AAAS statement on the obligation to respond to the rise of Nazi science in Germany. Cannon's credentials, with feet in both social justice and scientific worlds, seemed the perfect candidate.

The generative legacy of Cannon briefly blossomed in the 1960s cluster of social justice–oriented cyberneticists such as Norbert Wiener, Margaret Mead, Kurt Lewin, Frank Rosenblatt, and others.[45] But the "cyber" prefix today is often associated with cyber-surveillance, cyber-policing, cyber-finance, and related carceral technologies (as mapped out by Miller, Scannell, Poster, Nopper, Thakor, and Van Oort in this volume). With each success comes a retrenchment, as hegemonic forces learn to appropriate the critique into their own system. Thus, as Desmond and Moore point out, Darwin's commitment to the anti-racist cause never wavered, but his successors quickly substituted an evolution-based racism for their prior polygenesis-based racism. Similarly, the radical stance of bottom-up principles from 1960s cyberneticists such as Wiener became absorbed by more hegemonic groups such as RAND, DARPA, and the Santa Fe Institute for Complexity.[46]

GENERATIVE VERSUS HOLISTIC: A CRITICAL DISTINCTION

It is crucial to understand that I am not making claims about some kind of simple opposition between an ethically bad reductionist science and morally good holistic science. A good way to avoid that misconception is to note how terms such as *organicist* or *holistic* applied perfectly well to many notorious racist ideologies. Some of the founders of polygenesis, such as Georges Cuvier, are also founders of an anti-mechanistic organicism. Gliddon and Nott's *Types of Mankind*, for example, featured a kind of holistic fit between organisms and environments (figure 10.1). The upright, noble look of European facial features matched the nobility of the European wolf; the frumpy Native American hair looks like the frumpy buffalo; the puffy cheeks of the African looks like the puffy body of the hippo; and so on. Anne Harrington

Ron Eglash

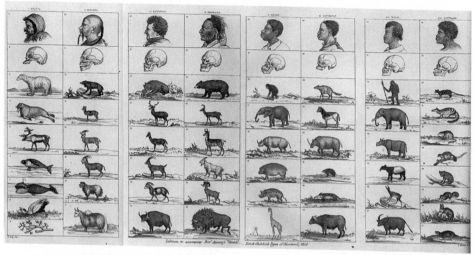

FIGURE 10.1. Image from *Types of Mankind* by Nott and Gliddon.

notes that the strong holistic tradition in Weimar Germany,[47] drawing on the older "romantic biology"[48] of Kant, Goethe, and others, was occasionally taken up by progressive leftist scientists like Kurt Goldstein and Max Wertheimer. But she shows that it was even more attractive to loyal proponents of Nazi ideology like Jakob von Uexkull and Constantin von Monakow. She cites the education proposal of Nazi biologist Feuerborn: "The 'core' of all biological education in the Nazi schools could be found in three basic principles: the doctrine of biological wholeness (the whole is greater than the sum of its parts), the theory of biological development (the dynamic creation of organismic wholes), and the teachings of heredity (the transmission of the qualities of the whole across generations)."[49] General systems theory founder Ludwig von Bertalanffy also attached his holistic outlook to Nazi institutions (specifically the *Führerprinzip*). Indeed, the very term *holism* was introduced by South African general Jan Smuts in his 1926 book *Holism and Evolution*, while he was creating the segregationist basis for what eventually became the apartheid system. In his account, nature spontaneously tended toward creating harmonious "wholes"; Africans were genetically suited to a particular state of nature, and therefore they needed to be geographically contained.[50]

What distinguishes the generative tradition from these kinds of holistic or organicist frameworks? Holism is vulnerable to the seductions of fascism when there is an emphasis on closed loops. It is for this reason that Haraway is wary of the term *autopoiesis* (self-creation) and encourages the framework of *sympoiesis* (creating-with-others). The closure does not necessarily have to be biological to create problematic purity. In our study of open-source software we found that systems that did not "silo" technology into exclusive purity, such as Python's less restrictive license, tended to be linked to more liberatory uses.[51]

GENERATIVE VERSUS EXTRACTIVE FORMS OF HYBRIDITY

Authoritarian movements that claim a kind of closed loop for cultural purity are currently sweeping the world: Trump's appeal to white nationalists in the United States, the BJP's landslide victory for Hindu nationalism in India, and so on. Anti-racist groups today are in danger of having their goals misidentified (in some cases deliberately) with these nationalist movements. Thus Black Lives Matter is constantly assaulted with the slogan "All Lives Matter." The internal danger to anti-racist groups is equally great. Native American author Sherman Alexie describes this in terms of a shift away from purity themes in his earlier novels: "My idea of indian identity and maintaining its purity . . . I had a lot of those attitudes. But I saw the end-game of tribalism, on 9–11, and the end-game of tribalism is flying planes into buildings."[52]

Recall that Frederick Douglass, drawing on James McCune Smith, had highlighted the importance of social diversity and multicultural mixing as both a moral and a practical benefit. One biological analogy would be hybrid ecosystems in which there are both native and non-native biota. Banu Subramaniam's *Ghost Stories for Darwin* reviews the history of ecologists' concepts of "invasive species." She and others[53] have outlined the ways in which xenophobic anti-immigrant politics have been mapped onto the concept of non-native species so effectively that the science has been notably warped, for example, by ignoring many of the valuable "ecosystem services" that non-natives can provide to environmental restoration.[54]

It is not enough, however, to merely promote mixing over purity. Sagoff notes that the adoption of non-natives was originally seen as an important national resource, quoting, for example, Thomas Jefferson: "The greatest service which can be rendered any country is to add a useful plant to its culture."[55] Pauly maps out hybridity/purity tensions in the early twentieth century within the U.S. Department of Agriculture: there were "ecological cosmopolitans"—mainly cooperative, serene botanists in the Bureau of Plant Industry who saw the United States as part of a global biotic exchange—and aggressive, masculine[56] zoologists in the Bureau of Entomology who were

Ron Eglash

"nativists" demanding the extermination of foreign organisms. Subramaniam recalls her delight in reading a 2006 essay in the *New York Times* describing the opposition to non-native plants as linked to the irrational fears of the anti-immigrant movement—delight until she realized that the author, George Ball, was president of the Burpee Seed Company. "While the inclusivity of George Ball resonates, I am troubled with the voracious appetite of global capitalism that will sell anything—even at the cost of habitat destruction, the debt and dependence of family farms, and the embrace of high-input agriculture."[57] Merely celebrating hybridity does not in itself save us from the extraction of value.

That more empowering forms of hybridity are possible is a frequent theme we have already encountered; here I want to review the concept through the lens of generative justice. For Douglass and Smith, *unalienated labor* required the circulation of value back to those doing the work; extraction by way of the state would be just as deleterious as the plantation. But they saw this freedom as directly linked to *unalienated expressive value*, envisioning a science "under which a common humanity can meet in friendly conclave" and thus embody "the necessity of means to increase human love with human learning." Subramaniam now brings us to a third type of value circulation, that of unalienated ecological value. But just as Douglass and Smith show the interdependence of expressive and labor forms of value, so too does this sympoiesis of empowering forms of human and nonhuman hybridity require interdependence of value forms. The extractive techniques that undermine local ecological self-determination can include strategies conducted by global agribusiness as well as non-democratic actions by state governments: patent law over GMOs, enforced use of pesticides, monopolization of land and water resources, and so on. They can be deceptively inserted by excluding one type of value as a disguise for others. Miguel Altieri, for example, notes how large corporate farms can sponsor biodiversity while enforcing labor extraction from displaced smallholder farmers.[58] The alternative he recommends, agroecology, often embodies exemplary forms of democratized value flows for humans and nonhumans alike.

One of the best examples of agroecology comes from the generative hybridity in Native American traditions. As discussed elsewhere,[59] spiritual conceptions of nature as the trickster figure—a flood one year, a drought the next—emphasized a set of genetic resources that could be equally diverse: at least some plants have the required resistance to whatever a trickster threw at it. The result was an astonishing biodiversity of corn developed before European arrival (figure 10.2). The accompanying agroecosystems, most

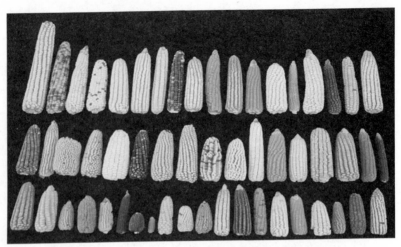

FIGURE 10.2. Corn diversity. Image courtesy of CIMMYT.

famously the three sisters of corn, beans, and squash, along with the crucial microbiological symbionts such as bean root nodules that fixed nitrogen, propagated along with these human-aided genetic diversifications. TallBear notes that many indigenous systems include minerals as active agents in these biosocial ecologies—in her case, describing native social relations with the traditional Dakota pipestone quarry.[60] Soaking the kernels in alkaline mineral water, prepared with limestone, chalk, or wood ash, was a crucial part of the corn agroecology system. This "nixtamalization" converts bound forms of niacin such as niacytin into its biologically available form (vitamin B3). Without it, a corn-heavy diet can cause vitamin B deficiency (pellagra).

Skeptics of indigenous knowledge often base their critique on the claim that science is universal, and therefore its principles and technologies can be detached from local context and moved anywhere (Latour's "immutable mobiles"). Colonists did exactly that to corn, transporting it outside the traditional context to Europe, Asia, and Africa. Because it was no longer prepared with alkaline mineral water or accompanied by its agroecosystem, nineteenth-century epidemics of pellagra hit France, Italy, Egypt, and several African nations.[61] In the southeastern United States the pellagra epidemic lasted nearly four decades, killing about 100,000 people. Vitamin-fortified foods like Wonder Bread emerged as the solution to the problem, but they also created nutritional dependencies on mass production and corporate marketing, which have deleterious ecological and health effects, including

Ron Eglash

what is now known to be obesity caused by overingestion of niacin.[62] As Hatch (this volume) points out, food supply chains can easily become a vulnerable point of control for any carceral system. A case could be made that colonization of labor value in the form of the slave trade also had a dehumanizing effect on the perpetrators; here the colonization of ecological value in bio-imperialism had analogous effects ("de-ecologizing"?) on both its perpetrators and the surrounding health landscape.[63]

The specific discovery of how indigenous alkaline mineral water preparation produces the bioavailability of niacin in corn, and the broader discoveries of other indigenous culture links between biodiversity, health, and the economy, has some resemblance to the links between activists and anti-racist scientists in the abolitionist movement. Both cases—the slave trade in the abolitionist case, and neocolonial economies in the indigenous biodiversity case—are, at root, systems for the hegemonic alienation and extraction of value. Because mainstream science is enshrined in hegemonic institutions, prominent anti-racist scientists like Darwin, Bowditch, and Cannon inhabit a role we might call the "compromised scientist,"[64] caught between the need to legitimize themselves as professionals and the need to resist or rebel against racialized injustice. Conversely, revolutionaries like Douglass face the reverse challenge, inhabiting the role of the "compromised activist," who endangers their radical legitimacy when making concessions to incorporate technoscience.[65]

Similar structure—insider scientists endangering their professional status, and outsider activists compromising their revolutionary status—play out in the indigenous biodiversity case. Pernet outlines some of this history in the specific case of Guatemala.[66] Starting with Franklin Roosevelt's 1943 initiatives, resulting in the United Nations Food and Agriculture Organization (FAO), governments, international agencies, and corporate agribusiness framed the concept of "underdeveloped nations," where extractive enterprises were imposed.[67] But Pernet highlights the role of INCAP (Instituto de Nutrición de Centroamérica y Panamá), a small international nutrition institute in Guatemala, as a pocket of resistance. Founded in 1949, INCAP included typical foreign staff and advisers such as Joseph Edwards from Britain's Milk Marketing Board, whose motto was that "civilization follows cow." Under pressure from the UN's children's program, UNICEF, as well as the FAO, they became a "gigantic organizational udder," shipping tons of dried milk from the United States every year. INCAP staff began to object: there was no local tradition of milk consumption, it was suppressing the development of a local economy, and there was no solid evidence that this was actually improving child nutrition. Nevin Scrimshaw, an MIT nutritionist who was director of INCAP, played the role of compromised scientist here: he objected to the approach but did not have the power to simply block the milk system. However, there were also Guatemalan activists and scientists supporting the resistance, and a breakthrough was finally made in developing an alternative solution using indigenous foods.

The key to this success was the existence of an indigenous category of drink, the gruel-like *atoles*. Ricardo Bressani, a Guatemalan food scientist with a doctorate in biochemistry from Purdue, investigated why there was such a high niacin content in corn-based atoles, since corn-heavy diets were associated with pellagra. It was here that the biochemistry of alkaline mineral water on corn was first documented. Using a corn and lime water base, INCAP introduced the first locally produced, all-vegetable milk substitute, *Incaparina*. Although INCAP suffered during the bloody civil war that lasted until 1996, their research created the foundation for current efforts to reattach corn to nixtamalization, and was instrumental in the larger movement to decolonize diets, offering lower cost, better health, and better links to local economies in India, Africa, the United States, and elsewhere. The expansion began in the 1970s through the kind of professional network that is described by Haas as an "epistemic community."[68] This included Paul Richards's transformative vision for indigenous African agricultural innovation, Gary Nabhan's collaboration with southwestern indigenous groups and seed-saving organizations, Carl Rangad's agrobiodiversity organization in India; Virginia Nazarea-Sandoval's work on gender and biodiversity in the Philippines, and many others.[69]

We previously saw that along with oppositional success comes hegemonic retrenchment: the monogenesis of abolition is turned into racist models of evolution; the radical systems theory of cybernetics is turned into hegemonic institutions for complexity theory. A similar process has occurred for decolonizing ecology. Ulloa presents a Foucauldian analysis for how the construction of indigenous identity as "ecological natives" has become a double-edged sword. Indigenous autonomy can in some cases increase vulnerability to exploitation by private industry—for example, she notes that a petroleum corporation has now established direct ties with the Huaorani people in Ecuador—and often requires indigenous groups to reify identities that were formerly more fluid.[70] Muehlmann documents an indigenous group in Mexico pressured to perform outsiders' conception of traditional behavior,[71] and Hayden finds a similar process at work for indigenous cooperatives involved in bioprospecting.[72]

Ron Eglash

THE GENERATIVE TRADITION IN CONTEMPORARY
ACTIVIST/SCIENTIST COLLABORATIONS

Each historical era needs to re-create and reinterpret the generative tradition for itself, as the conditions surrounding hegemonic power in relation to extractive forces continue to evolve. Architecture, for example, has historically been a showcase for fixing elite power and wealth inequality into the permanence of cold stone and concrete. But because it is also inherently multidisciplinary, the anticolonial, indigenous, and social justice–based interventions in the arts and humanities have been merging with science and engineering in many of their design practices. Mae-ling Lokko, a Ghanaian researcher who is now an assistant professor of architecture at Rensselaer Polytechnic Institute, further developed the generative framework in her research on architectural applications of coconut fiber in Ghana.[73]

Coconuts are not native to Africa, but in keeping with Subramaniam's vision, they are a much-beloved immigrant. Lokko and her colleagues conducted thermal research that showed that coconut fiber, which is discarded after the meat is harvested, could be turned into building materials that absorbed moisture in the heat of the day and released it at night. This dehydration of the air creates the feeling of entering a cool room, reducing or eliminating the need for expensive air conditioning. There are multiple ways in which this prevents the alienation of ecological value: agricultural waste (husks) is utilized, electrical demand is reduced, and the dehydration system itself regenerates each night. At the same time, Lokko's social investigations showed that most coconut farmers in her region tended to be relatively unalienated labor—prosperous but small-scale family farms. Even the lowest income strata involved, those selling coconuts for snacks on the street corner, could potentially sell the discarded husks back to a fiberboard industry. Thus, those receiving the economic benefits from selling fiber waste would be at the grassroots. Finally, noting the loss of cultural capital when contemporary architects import designs from Europe, she utilized local cultural design elements and innovation processes, adding unalienated expressive value to the system.

The above description makes it sound easy—just do the right thing for nature and people, and it will all fall into place—but of course the reality of Lokko's research was anything but. She often encountered an unfriendly reception to the idea of incorporating local cultural elements, and while the environmental aspects were met with enthusiasm, there was little interest in the implications for low-income support. On top of that was the constant scramble to raise funds for physical construction and travel, and the challenges of mastering computational modeling of thermal, chemical, and mechanical elements. And, of course, there was no guarantee that the resulting data would support this confluence of aspirations. But Lokko's success at simultaneously inhabiting the roles of compromised scientist and technically engaged activist sheds light on how the generative tradition may be shifting in this era.

CONCLUSION

A careful examination of the historic intersections of anti-racist activism and technoscience offers a subtle look at how to craft liberatory practices. The best examples are not simply opposing reductionism with holism, or free markets with socialist states. Rather, they engage in the more complex work of recognizing that deeply democratic systems cannot foster a reliance on closed-loop purity for either humans or their nonhuman allies: a generative approach is one that allows the circulation of multiple types of unalienated value, embracing the sympoiesis of hybridity rather than shunning it. As James McCune Smith implied in his "Communipaw" reference, as activists from Douglass to Subramaniam have mapped out in their portraits of adaptive transformation, and as the scholars of indigenous-inspired agroecology and architecture still stress, a generative vision for rebuilding society is possible. How to achieve a hybridity-friendly, bottom-up circulation of unalienated value—a liberatory milieu intérieur for the body politic—is, to paraphrase William James, the only question.

Notes

1. Vandana Shiva, "The Violence of Reductionist Science," *Alternatives* 12 (1987): 243–61.

2. Theodore M. Porter, *Trust in Numbers: The Pursuit of Objectivity in Science and Public Life* (Princeton, NJ: Princeton University Press, 1995).

3. Donna Haraway, "The Virtual Speculum in the New World Order," *Feminist Review* 55 (1997): 48

4. Edward E. Baptist, *The Half Has Never Been Told: Slavery and the Making of American Capitalism* (New York: Basic Books, 2014); Thomas M. Shapiro, *Toxic Inequality: How America's Wealth Gap Destroys Mobility, Deepens the Racial Divide, and Threatens Our Future* (New York: Basic Books, 2017).

5. Stéphane Courtois, ed., *The Black Book of Communism: Crimes, Terror, Repression*, trans. Jonathan Murphy and Mark Kramer (Cambridge, MA: Harvard University Press, 1999).

Ron Eglash

6. David Lauter, "In China, App Aims to Shame Polluters by Showing Who Is Fouling Air," *LA Times*, December 30, 2014, accessed June 10, 2017, http://www.latimes.com /world/asia/la-fg-china-bad-air-20141230-story.html.

7. Steven Mailloux, "Re-marking Slave Bodies: Rhetoric as Production and Reception," *Philosophy and Rhetoric* 35, no. 2 (2002): 96–119.

8. Peter C. Myers, *Frederick Douglass: Race and the Rebirth of American Liberalism* (Lawrence: University Press of Kansas, 2008).

9. Ron Eglash, "An Introduction to Generative Justice," *Teknokultura* 13, no. 2 (2016): 369–404; for a broad sample, see the December 2016 special issue of *Teknokultura* on generative justice. The language of "rights" is, of course, not the only way to express a generative framework. Ben Cousins, "Capitalism Obscured: The Limits of Law and Rights-Based Approaches to Poverty Reduction and Development," *Journal of Peasant Studies* 36, no. 4 (2009): 893–908.

10. John Gowdy, *Limited Wants, Unlimited Means: A Reader on Hunter-Gatherer Economics and the Environment* (Washington, DC: Island Press, 1998); Jacqueline S. Solway, *The Politics of Egalitarianism: Theory and Practice* (New York: Berghahn, 2006).

11. Yochai Benkler and Helen Nissenbaum, "Commons-based Peer Production and Virtue," *The Journal of Political Philosophy* 4, no. 14 (2006), 394–419; Ron Eglash and Colin Garvey, "Basins of Attraction for Generative Justice," in *Chaos Theory in Politics: Understanding Complex Systems*, ed. S. Banerjee, Ş. Erçetin, and A. Tekin (Dordrecht: Springer, 2014), 75–88.

12. J. Stephen Lansing and James N. Kremer, "Emergent Properties of Balinese Water Temple Networks: Coadaptation on a Rugged Fitness Landscape," *American Anthropologist* 95, no. 1 (1993): 97–114.

13. Donna Haraway, *Staying with the Trouble: Making Kin in the Chthulucene* (Durham, NC: Duke University Press, 2016).

14. Deborah Barndt, *Tangled Routes: Women, Work, and Globalization on the Tomato Trail* (Lanham, MD: Rowman and Littlefield, 2008).

15. As Gould notes, the largest flaw was simply the fact that brain size is proportionate to body height, not intelligence. By avoiding tall indigenous groups like the Tutsi in Africa and the Iroquois in America, and sampling short groups such as the Peruvians and Khoikhoi, he gave the false impression that white skulls were the largest. A controversy over Gould's critique has challenged the additional charge of data falsification. However, the student who carried out that research (John S. Michaels) noted that the nonwhite samples were biased by younger age, a criticism both Gould and his critics missed (see Michael's comment, #25546, online at http://www.nature.com/nature /journal/v474/n7352/full/474419a.html). Stephen Jay Gould, *The Mismeasure of Man* (New York: W. W. Norton, 1981).

16. C. Loring Brace, *Race Is a Four-Letter Word* (New York: Oxford University Press, 2005).

17. Douglass was partly wrong: his Lamarckian mechanism did not match the long time periods that natural selection requires. But he was right about nongenetic

change, foreshadowing the (accurate) anti-racist science of Franz Boas and Henry Bowditch on immigrant height changes with greater nutritional access.

18. William Lloyd Garrison *Thoughts on African Colonization* (Boston: Garrison and Knapp, 1832), 21.

19. Ibram Kendi, *Stamped from the Beginning: The Definitive History of Racist Ideas in America* (New York: Nation Books, 2016).

20. Anthony Walton, "Technology versus African-Americans," *Atlantic Monthly* 283, no. 1 (1999): 14–17; Rayvon Fouché, "Not Made for Black History Month: Lewis Latimer and Technological Assimilation," in *Appropriating Technology: Vernacular Science and Social Power*, ed. Ron Eglash, Jennifer Croissant, Giovanna Di Chiro, and Rayvon Fouche, 315–330 (Minneapolis: University of Minnesota Press, 2004); Louise S. Mead, Judi Brown Clarke, Frank Forcino, and Joseph L. Graves, "Factors Influencing Minority Student Decisions to Consider a Career in Evolutionary Biology," *Evolution: Education and Outreach* 8, no. 1 (2015): 6.

21. Adrian Desmond and James Moore, *Darwin's Sacred Cause: How a Hatred of Slavery Shaped Darwin's Views on Human Evolution* (London: Penguin Books, 2009).

22. Erasmus was a strong proponent of abolition, and his book *Zoonomia; or the Laws of Organic Life* (1794).

23. Quoted in Bill Jenkins, "Phrenology, Heredity and Progress in George Combe's Constitution of Man," *British Journal for the History of Science* 48, no. 3 (2015): 472.

24. Gregory D. Smithers, *Science, Sexuality, and Race in the United States and Australia, 1780–1940* (Lincoln: University of Nebraska Press, 2017).

25. E.g., Peleg Clarke, "Dr Clarke's Case of Haematemesis," *New-England Medical Review and Journal* 15 (1827): 99–102.

26. Frederick Douglass, *The Life and Times of Frederick Douglass* (Hartford, CT: Park Publishing Company, 1881), 329.

27. Britt Rusert, "The Science of Freedom: Counterarchives of Racial Science on the Antebellum Stage," *African American Review* 45, no. 3 (2012): 304.

28. Irving's account is mostly fantasy, and Smith's vision perhaps further re-imagined it to the left of Irving's. The actual Communipaw was the site of the Lenape "slaughter of the innocents" in 1643, and slavery was not legally abolished in New Jersey until 1804. On the other hand, by the time Irving visited it, Communipaw included an important terminal in the Underground Railroad, and the multiethnic images of his story still resonate today: a theatrical production was created in 2013.

29. Washington Irving, *The Kaaterskill Edition of Washington Irving* (New York: Pollard and Moss, 1882).

30. James McCune Smith, *The Works of James McCune Smith: Black Intellectual and Abolitionist* (Oxford: Oxford University Press, 2006).

31. Thomas M. Morgan, "The Education and Medical Practice of Dr. James McCune Smith (1813–1865), First Black American to Hold a Medical Degree," *Journal of the National Medical Association* 95, no. 7 (2003): 603–14.

32. Britt Rusert, *Fugitive Science: Empiricism and Freedom in Early African American Culture* (New York: NYU Press, 2017), 58.

33. Frederick Douglass, "The Claims of the Negro, Ethnologically Speaking," an address before the literary societies of Western Reserve College, at commencement July 12 (1854), 10, available online, https://babel.hathitrust.org/cgi/pt?id=mdp.69015000002739.

34. Vincent Yardley Bowditch, *Life and Correspondence of Henry Ingersoll Bowditch* (Boston: Houghton Mifflin, 1902), 137–38.

35. J. I. Bowditch's letter to William Lloyd Garrison is available online at https://www.digitalcommonwealth.org/search/commonwealth:6h4423137?view=commonwealth%3A6h442315s.

36. Bowditch, *Life and Correspondence of Henry Ingersoll Bowditch*.

37. Walter B. Cannon, *Biographical Memoir: Henry Pickering Bowditch 1840–1911* (Washington, DC: National Academy of Sciences, 1922).

38. Christopher Donahue, "Franz Boas and His Contemporaries," *Ether Wave Propaganda*, October 15, 2013, accessed May 1, 2017, https://etherwave.wordpress.com/2013/10/15/franz-boas-on-the-instability-of-human-types/.

39. Carla Jean Bittel, *Mary Putnam Jacobi and the Politics of Medicine in Nineteenth-Century America* (Chapel Hill: University of North Carolina Press, 2009).

40. William James, "The Energies of Men," *The American Magazine* (1907), reprinted by Moffat, Yard and Company in New York, 1914.

41. Steven Cooper, "From Claude Bernard to Walter Cannon: Emergence of the Concept of Homeostasis," *Appetite* 51, no. 3 (2008): 422.

42. Cooper, "From Claude Bernard to Walter Cannon: Emergence of the Concept of Homeostasis."

43. Marcos Cueto, "An Asymmetrical Network: National and International Dimensions of the Development of Mexican Physiology," *Journal of the History of Medicine and Allied Sciences* 71, no. 1 (2015): 43–63.

44. Peter Kuznick, "The Birth of Scientific Activism," *J. Bulletin of the Atomic Scientists* 44, no. 10 (1988): 39–43.

45. Cooper, "From Claude Bernard to Walter Cannon: Emergence of the Concept of Homeostasis"; Steven J. Heims, *John von Neumann and Norbert Wiener: From Mathematics to the Technologies of Life and Death* (Cambridge, MA: MIT Press, 1984).

46. Ron Eglash, "Cybernetics and American Youth Subculture," *Cultural Studies* 12, no. 3 (1998): 382–409.

47. Anne Harrington, *Reenchanted Science: Holism in German Culture from Wilhelm II to Hitler* (Princeton, NJ: Princeton University Press, 1996).

48. Maurizio Esposito, *Romantic Biology, 1890–1945* (New York: Routledge, 2015).

49. Harrington, *Reenchanted Science*, 177.

50. Jan Smuts, *Africa and Some World Problems* (Oxford: Oxford University Press, 1930).

51. Ron Eglash and David Banks, "Recursive Depth in Generative Spaces: Democratization in Three Dimensions of Technosocial Self-Organization," *The Information Society* 30, no. 2 (2014): 106–15.

52. Steve Paulson, "Sherman Alexie on 'Flight,'" *To the Best of Our Knowledge*, 2009, accessed June 20, 2017, http://www.ttbook.org/book/sherman-alexie-flight.

53. Michael Pollan, "Against Nativism," *New York Times Magazine*, May 15, 1994; Philip J. Pauly, 1996. "The Beauty and Menace of the Japanese Cherry Trees: Conflicting Visions of American Ecological Independence," *Isis* 87, no. 1 (1996): 51–73; Mark Sagoff, *Price, Principle, and the Environment* (Cambridge: Cambridge University Press, 2005); Matthew Chew and Andrew L. Hamilton, "The Rise and Fall of Biotic Nativeness: A Historical Perspective," in *Fifty Years of Invasion Ecology: The Legacy of Charles Elton*, ed. David M. Richardson, 35–47 (Oxford: Blackwell, 2011).

54. Martin A. Schlaepfer, Dov F. Sax, and Julian D. Olden, "The Potential Conservation Value of Non-native Species," *Conservation Biology* 25 (2011): 428–37.

55. Sagoff, *Price, Principle, and the Environment.*

56. Pauly, "The Beauty and Menace of the Japanese Cherry Trees"; for those interested in following these hints at a queer theory perspective on generative hybridity, see Joshua Sbicca, "Eco-Queer Movement(s): Challenging Heteronormative Space through (Re)Imagining Nature and Food," *European Journal of Ecopsychology* 3, no. 1 (2012): 33–52; Sallie Anglin, "Generative Motion: Queer Ecology and Avatar," *Journal of Popular Culture* 48, no. 2 (2015): 341–54; Kim TallBear, "Dossier: Theorizing Queer Inhumanisms: An Indigenous Reflection on Working beyond the Human/Not Human," *GLQ: A Journal of Lesbian and Gay Studies* 21, no. 3 (2015): 230–35.

57. Banu Subramanium, *Ghost Stories for Darwin: The Science of Variation and the Politics of Diversity* (Urbana: University of Illinois Press, 2014), 118.

58. Miguel Altier, "Agroecology versus Ecoagriculture: Balancing Food Production and Biodiversity Conservation in the Midst of Social Inequity," *Commission on Environmental, Economic and Social Policy CEESP Occasional Papers* (2004), 8–28.

59. Ron Eglash, "Computation, Complexity and Coding in Native American Knowledge Systems," in *Changing the Faces of Mathematics: Perspectives on Indigenous People of North America*, ed. Judith Hankes and Gerald Fast (Reston, VA: NCTM, 2002), 251–62; Ron Eglash, "A Generative Perspective on Engineering: Why the Destructive Force of Artifacts Is Immune to Politics," Paper delivered at *Engineering a Better Future: Interplay of Social Science, Engineering and Innovation* (CMU, April 2016); Spencer K. Wertz, "Maize: The Native North American's Legacy of Cultural Diversity and Biodiversity," *Journal of Agricultural and Environmental Ethics* 18, no. 2 (2004), 131–56.

60. TallBear, "Dossier: Theorizing Queer Inhumanisms."

61. Daphne A. Roe, *A Plague of Corn: The Social History of Pellagra* (Ithaca, NY: Cornell University Press, 1973).

62. Shi-Sheng Zhou and Yiming Zhou, "Excess Vitamin Intake: An Unrecognized Risk Factor for Obesity," *World Journal of Diabetes* 5, no. 1 (2014): 1–13.

Ron Eglash

63. Alfred Crosby, *Ecological Imperialism: The Biological Expansion of Europe, 900-1900.* (Cambridge: Cambridge University Press, 2004).

64. Patricia Hill Collins refers to this role as "the outsider within."

65. Kendi, *Stamped from the Beginning.*

66. Corinne A. Pernet, "Between Entanglements and Dependencies: Food, Nutrition, and National Development at the Central American Institute of Nutrition (INCAP)," in *International Organizations and Development, 1945-1990,* ed. Marc Frey, Sönke Kunkel, and Corinna R. Unger (New York: Palgrave Macmillan, 2014), 101-25.

67. See, for similar examples, Arturo Escobar, *Encountering Development: The Making and Unmaking of the Third World* (Princeton, NJ: Princeton University Press, 1995).

68. Peter M. Haas, "Do Regimes Matter? Epistemic Communities and Mediterranean Pollution Control," *International Organization, Cambridge Journals* 43, no. 3 (1989): 377-403.

69. Stephen B. Brush and Doreen Stabinsky, eds., *Valuing Local Knowledge: Indigenous People and Intellectual Property Rights* (Washington, DC: Island Press, 1996).

70. Astrid Ulloa, *The Ecological Native: Indigenous Peoples' Movements and Eco-Governmentality in Colombia* (New York: Routledge, 2005).

71. Shaylih Muehlmann, "How Do Real Indians Fish? Neoliberal Multiculturalism and Contested Indigeneities in the Colorado Delta," *American Anthropologist* 111, no. 4 (2009): 468-79.

72. Cori Hayden, *When Nature Goes Public: The Making and Unmaking of Bioprospecting in Mexico* (Princeton, NJ: Princeton University Press, 2003).

73. Mae-ling Lokko, "Investigation of Coconut Agrowaste Upcycling for Ecologically Efficacious Building Lifecycles," PhD diss., Rensselaer Polytechnic Institute, 2016.

11

Techno-Vernacular Creativity and Innovation across the African Diaspora and Global South

Nettrice R. Gaskins

.....

Historically, people of color have been casualties of technologically enabled systems of oppression. This includes the mainstream adoption of drones, predictive policing, digital avatars created to entrap online sex predators, facial recognition tools that tag and sort black and brown identities into large databases, and other emerging practices. These ethnic groups—still largely underrepresented in science, technology, engineering, mathematics, or STEM fields—are usually labeled as consumers, not producers of technology. Contests around technology are always linked to larger struggles for economic mobility, political maneuvering, and community building. Also, there is a risk that systematizing techno-cultural practices may have a detrimental effect on historically marginalized communities. This essay makes a case against this by addressing some of the ways that ethnic communities of practice have voluntarily subverted or remixed dominant technologies using local (cultural) practices. The resulting inventions have been broadly adopted in communities around the world. Ethnic artists and practitioners often make use of the refuse of consumer technology production to foster social interventions, to make an income, or simply to fill a need. This essay casts a broader net to include these creative, cultural practices and innovations.

Mainstream technology is typically defined in very narrow terms. This prevents us from seeing and understanding how those who are not deemed tech-savvy are innovating all around us. In this essay, I advance the evolving practice of Techno-Vernacular Creativity, or TVC, as a lens to witness and examine all the ways that people are creating and experimenting with technology. This is especially the case among ethnic groups that are underrepresented in STEM fields such as African American, Latinx, and Indigenous people. Technoscience scholars have pointed out that these groups are prolific producers in their local communities.[1] Examples include Chicano lowrider engineers, visual artists/designers, and hip-hop music producers. In these cases, artists, "makers," and producers are reinventing and rethinking dominant knowledge systems in ways that are not considered by the gatekeepers of those systems. This includes the integration of cultural or indigenous values identified in science and technology through the transfer of information such as metaphoric and iconic representations.[2] Representations such as *heritage artifacts* include tangible culture (buildings, monuments, landscapes, books, and arts/crafts), intangible culture (folklore, traditions, language, and knowledge), and nature inspire many techno-cultural inventions. There is algorithmic thinking—step-by-step instructions to carry out a task— embedded in many of these designs that are passed down from generation to generation.

The works explored in this essay counter notions that people of color are mainly consumers of mainstream technology, or are forever victimized by the outcomes of this production. Rather, I set out to examine specific ways in which historically marginalized, or under-resourced groups engage technology and suggest ways in which these inventions can produce responses that are against forces of oppression. First, these technological practices will be defined and classified using modes and methods that are culturally situated in under-resourced and underrepresented ethnic communities. Next, the essay will present cultural artifacts, practices, and knowledge that regularly challenge constructed meanings of "dominant" technology. Then I will link these cultural artifacts, practices, and knowledge with do-it-yourself (DIY) methods that reuse electronic waste and address community issues. The ways in which ethnic artists and practitioners engage technology will offer valuable insights into the shaping of a broader strategy to help alleviate social issues and stem the tide of the cradle-to-prison pipeline.

METHODOLOGICAL PREMISES

Though often overlooked in mainstream studies, the rich traditions of practices among underrepresented ethnic groups demonstrate how Techno-Vernacular Creativity—cultural art, science, and technology—engages Indigenous, African, and Latino diasporas. Extensive research into TVC and its key characteristics informs culturally situated arts-based inquiry strategies that explore the impact of TVC on learning and production.[3] As *appropriated technologies*, TVC modes have meaning for the people who engage with, view, or use them. Modes and methods that distinguish TVC from mainstream technology research and development include:

- **Re-appropriation**, or the cultural process by which underrepresented ethnic groups *reclaim* artifacts from the dominant culture and the environment—for example, African American and Latinx artists who use or alter commercial images (e.g., ads, logos) in their work.
- **Improvisation**, or the spontaneous and inventive use of materials—for example, practitioners who use *on-the-spot* techniques to make graphic, contemporary quilts and quilted projects.
- **Conceptual remixing**, "bricolage," tinkering, or making do with whatever is on hand—for example, artists who combine different, often seemingly disparate knowledge sets, artifacts, identities, and practices.

The combination of these modes and methods can result in the invention of new practices, methods, performances, or products. It has been necessary to identify different types of TVC engagement among certain ethnic groups in order to better understand the development of and relationship between various categories (figure 11.1). For the purposes of this chapter, TVC production is mainly situated in the cultures of the African diaspora, including in areas of the developing Global South.[4] TVC categories such as patterning and repetition are modular, able to be combined with other categories and repurposed. Observing these practices in tasks and representing them with models and theories can be applied to a variety of problems. One example of this is the "get down" or "quick mix theory" that allows DJs to repeat, on a loop, the parts of songs that crowds find most exciting.[5] DJs mix drum breaks from different genres of music, employing what has been referred to as the "cut," a technique that insists on the repetitive nature of a song, abruptly skipping it back to a beginning that we've already heard.[6] The actions or methods in each category further describe and define the TVC framework, modes, and practices.

Techno-Vernacular Creativity brings to the forefront innovations by underrepresented ethnic individuals and groups who share a craft or a profession.[7] Although primarily focused on the African diaspora and the black Atlantic,[8] this research extends to Latino and Indigenous groups who are affected by aspects of techno-cultural disparity. TVC works produced by

Nettrice R. Gaskins

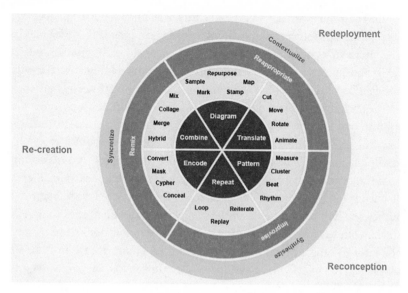

FIGURE 11.1. TVC taxonomy.

underrepresented ethnic individuals and groups are diverse, social in nature, and encourage creative expression and innovation. TVC works are made from local materials or cultural artifacts using methods that produce innovations that are specific to place, people, and culture. Do-it-yourself or maker culture — creating technology without expert input — is a newer contribution to this age-old, global practice and, in some cases, makes use of TVC modes/ methods. This essay seeks to address the emergence and evolution of TVC and the DIY ethic across the African diaspora. This includes contributions to the arts — not only literature, performance, film and video, and visual arts — but also digital media and maker culture. Some examples of practitioners across the African diaspora engaging in TVC practices include:

- Grandmaster Flash (Joseph Sadler) made contributions to the development of the first cross-fader or DJ mixer by reclaiming parts from a junkyard.
- Hip-hop pioneer and artist Rammellzee designed costumes made of technological and industrial scraps.
- Kelvin Doe, also known as DJ Focus, a young Sierra Leonean engineer, taught himself engineering and built his own radio station.
- Kenyan Cyrus Kabiru reuses electronic refuse and found metal and refashions these found materials into different wearable objects.[9]

Often through vernacular art and crafts, women of the African diaspora use DIY methods such as hair braiding, quilting, and weaving, which play in the interactions of culture and technology. Zimbabwean-born, U.S.-based artist and educator Nontsikelelo Mutiti engages tangible and digital media production that dovetails with hands-on braiding, crafts, physical construction and design, and material play. Mutiti's work not only captures the craft in braiding but also the social, labor, and economic aspects in hair-braiding salons. Sadler/Grandmaster Flash experimented with electronics in his home and neighborhood, eventually developing and mastering sonic innovations that are considered standard DJ techniques today. Sierra Leonean teenager Kelvin Doe, as DJ Focus, experimented with discarded pieces of scrap to build transmitters, generators, and batteries to invent devices of use to his community. These creative innovations demonstrate the informal engagement of underrepresented ethnic groups in STEM in ways that are typically not classified as such. In general, these creative examples build upon, counter, or expand mainstream definitions of technology, through the practical application of knowledge, learning, and cultural production.

TVC works keep alive a practice that confronts the contradictions of established categories of epistemic subjectivities by making possible a future for underrepresented ethnic artists and practitioners that is not merely repeating the past and its injustices. TVC practice counters the notion of the 'savage mind,' a concept coined by French anthropologist Claude Lévi-Strauss that is used to describe non-Western contributions to STEM and art but has negative connotations for TVC practitioners' modes and methods.[10] As noted by architect Ginger Nolan, an "epistemic apartheid" exists, which regards the creative work of historically marginalized (ethnic) groups as valuable only through the lenses or systems of dominant culture.[11] Yet, also noted by Nolan, the work of these groups is repeatedly invoked by Western designers and engineers in their efforts to formulate creative technologies, ones that lean toward digital modes of production. However, when taken out of their contexts, TVC works often lose their original meaning, purpose, and, arguably, their community value. While TVC practices and works make use of both scrap and emerging technologies, the analysis of these innovations contributes to a broader epistemology and creative process through which artists, designers, sound engineers, DJs, and b-boys/b-girls produce images, symbols, objects, performances, and sounds.

This essay addresses the emergence and evolution of TVC modes of practice across the African diaspora and among indigenous groups, including the

Nettrice R. Gaskins

development of practices that span centuries, influencing self-taught artists, designers, engineers, and inventors from around the world. In the next section I will discuss the scholarly antecedents of TVC (Fouché and others). Then I will examine how heritage artifacts such as hair braiding and other cultural expressions are technologies able to be carried out algorithmically (i.e., in an ordered series of steps), iteratively (i.e., through repetition), and simulated or modeled using computers. Following this, I will discuss TVC as a form of technological agency, speaking to the ways in which tools and external devices help underrepresented ethnic groups navigate the world. Finally, I will conclude with the opportunities and limitations of TVC and where other collective strategies are needed to deal with the power of technoscience in African diasporic communities.

A RADICAL DEVELOPMENT

The TVC taxonomy and framework combines digital and non-digital materials in ways that are antithetical to arguments made by researchers that historically excluded or underrepresented ethnic groups lack the technical skill to narrow the "digital divide."[12] This research grounds and broadens Rayvon Fouché's theory of black vernacular technological creativity to include other underrepresented ethnic groups' technological engagements that capture aspects of two or more distinct cultures blending together to create new customs, practices, or knowledge.[13] For instance, the multicultural exchanges that came out of Afrofuturism created Sinofuturism, which explores Chinese cultural, economic, and industrial development.[14] More than social critiques, these practices suggest ideas for solutions or products that can come out of a certain way of thinking and doing. The term *vernacular* describes a critical theory on everyday practices that are associated with local language, culture, literature, and art. In rhetorical studies, this is known through Cara Finnegan's work on image vernaculars (i.e., image skills and habits).[15] This essay comes from research that presents a framework of theoretical lenses and strategic objectives to explain how Techno-Vernacular Creativity engages underrepresented ethnic groups in ways that can lead to increased technoscience engagement. The TVC framework was used to identify recurrent modes of practice, as well as themes that illuminate these practices.

Modes such as diagramming, translating, patterning, repetition, coding, and combining demonstrate the different ways in which artists and producers relate to the physical world, and the ways they relate to each other socially are bound up together in specific and necessary ways. For example, the "get down" in rap music demonstrates a repetition compulsion otherwise known as the "cut," which, according to James Snead, is similar to African drumming: "After the band has been 'cookin' in a given key and tempo, a cue, either verbal (ex. 'Terry') or musical (a brief series of rapid, percussive drum and horn accents), then directs the music to a new level where it stays with more 'cookin' or perhaps a solo—until a repetition of cues then 'cuts' back to the primary tempo."[16]

Vernacular art and craft production reflects diverse influences and contexts. Underrepresented ethnic groups manage their representations—such as cultural artifacts—in Western society and the global world by using improvisation and reappropriation to engage multiple identities or cultures. Researchers exploring this work can use the TVC framework to look at or analyze cultural and artistic information produced by underrepresented ethnic artists and practitioners. This framework combines black vernacular technological creativity,[17] vernacular art, crafts, and technoscience with culturally situated arts-based pedagogy to inform future research. This domain is intentionally pluralistic, multicultural, social, and inclusive of emergent artistic and cultural practices that reveal the complexity in cultural knowledge and a more broadly defined view of technology. This work brought to the forefront creative and innovative practices and projects that can have wider implications in the fields of discourse and are often described in terms of personal or sociopolitical empowerment.[18]

Studies of African American creativity often center on vernacular traditions such as cultural artifacts, practices, and knowledge that regularly challenge constructed meanings of dominant or mainstream technology. TVC looks at the development of techno-cultural practices across geographical boundaries, while other studies are more responsive to the realities of black life in the United States. Fouché's theory of black vernacular technological creativity builds on the efforts of such scholars as Amiri Baraka, one of the leaders of the Black Arts Movement. This theory describes African American artists' and practitioners' engagement with vernacular arts and crafts that come from resistance to technology from dominant cultures/societies and strategic appropriations of the material and symbolic power and energy of technology.[19] Fouché asserts that, historically, technology has politically, socially, and intellectually silenced African Americans, rendering them defenseless and invisible. African American artists combine or subvert existing knowledge systems in order to invent new ways of using, creating, and performing with technology. These maneuvers enable practitioners to reclaim different levels of technological agency. TVC looks at the creative practices

Nettrice R. Gaskins

and inventions of African Americans but on a global scale, as well as how these developments relate to or are inspired by the works of other ethnic groups.

Amiri Baraka's prescient 1971 essay "Technology and Ethos" begins a discourse about black vernacular technological creativity. Baraka called for people of African descent to rethink their relationships with technology and take action to make technology more representative of their culture. We see this representation mostly in speculative literature and art. Although originally conceived of by Jewish comic book writers Stan Lee and Jack Kirby, *Black Panther* has been reconceptualized by African American writer Te-Nehisi Coates and African American artist Brian Stelfreeze, specifically using black mythology to construct a narrative of the African diaspora before and after colonialism and enslavement. *Black Panther* is an example of Techno-Vernacular Creativity because it integrates Pan-African values identified in science and technology through the transfer of comic book representations. Baraka also argued that through black technological utterances rooted within black cultures, communities, and existences, technology would be more responsive to the realities of black life in Western societies. He and other cultural scholars and practitioners articulate the cultural nexus between art, Western technology, and its impact on the African cultural milieu. Baraka writes: "The technology itself must represent human striving. It must represent at each point the temporary perfection of the evolutional man. And be obsolete only because nothing is ever perfect, the only constant is change."[20] According to Fouché, African Americans have had time to develop knowledge sets through the production of music, dance, literature, visual art, and sports. Fouché identifies this production in the following ways:

- Redeployment, or the "process by which the material and symbolic power of technology is reinterpreted but maintains its traditional use and physical form." Example: African American motorcycle engineers/builders customizing choppers.
- Reconception, or the "active redefinition of a technology that transgresses that technology's designed function and dominant meaning." Example: artists engaging artifacts to make new art forms using DIY fabrication.
- Re-creation, or the redesign and production of a new material artifact after an existing form or function has been rejected. Example: DJs and turntablists developing new equipment and techniques.[21]

Beyond these techniques is the effort to *syncretize* or reconcile different cultures' values or beliefs, to *contextualize* or make sense of information from a situation or location in which the information was found, and to *synthesize* or compose with a number of things to make something new, as in repeating or looping a beat or motif to produce art. African American popular culture has renewed itself repeatedly through new technology, new audiences, improvisation, and continued borrowing.[22] African American artists combine different modes of black vernacular technological creativity with discipline-crossing and DIY methods. Motorcycle engineers and builders Ben Hardy and Cliff Vaughs remained largely unknown and uncredited for over two decades and, as African Americans, were not welcomed into the mainstream white motorcycle world in the United States. Christopher Emdin contends that underrepresented ethnic groups, whose cultural frames of reference may be oppositional to dominant ones, may have greater difficulty crossing cultural boundaries.[23] However, researchers have yet to take the innovative practices and methods of underrepresented ethnic artists into account as legitimate forms of technology production. As a result, these methods are not counted as "science," "engineering," or "technology" and are not taught in schools. In fact, many of these practices, such as hip-hop, are viewed as being counter to educational objectives.

This essay embraces the intent of Fouché's work and extends his concepts to describe the fundamental ways that African Americans and other underrepresented ethnic groups draw from and combine diverse knowledge sets, artifacts, identities, and practices. TVC considers the many ways that heritage artifacts and technologies are exchanged, adopted, and are similar and different among diverse ethnic groups. This research investigates the interrelationships between coexistent cultures and subcultures and how they relate to each other in mutually constructive ways. This includes the unpredictable, innovative patterns in traditional African American quilts, which are similar to those found in African and Indigenous textiles, and other art forms such as the polyrhythmic formations in jazz, break dancing, and rap music.[24] Concepts such as repetition and reappropriation reach across genres and cultural practices. TVC modes of practice and technical production foreground the research of Fouché to identify, analyze, and interpret how the conceptual and practical uses of vernacular art, crafts, and technology can lead to improved technoscience engagement among individuals and groups underrepresented in STEM fields.

Nettrice R. Gaskins

HAIR BRAIDING (AND OTHER CULTURAL ARTIFACTS) IS TECHNOLOGY

In the physical world, heritage artifacts provide information about the cultures of their creators. Heritage artifacts, whether ancient or current, are significant because they offer an insight into technological and social processes of Indigenous cultures, among other attributes. These artifacts (objects or motifs) can have aesthetic (stylistic) aspects or come from fields that situate artistic works within the social conditions of their production, circulation, and consumption. They can demonstrate technique (technology) or become embedded in a cultural practice. Sampling as a method of Techno-Vernacular Creativity shows an interaction between cultural artifacts and modes of practice (diagramming), as well as being a type of reappropriation. The sample is a discrete unit of information (i.e., a sound, shape, or motif) that can be repeated to create a pattern. In visual art, textile design, and music, sampling is defined as the act of taking a portion from one source and reusing it to create a new project. Hip-hop was the first popular music genre based on the art of sampling—originating from 1970s DJs who experimented with manipulating vinyl on two turntables and an audio mixer.

The sample extends to textiles and hair braiding, specifically squares, triangles, and the "y-shaped" plaits that make up a braid or cornrow. Braiding forms a complex pattern by intertwining three or more strands of flexible material such as fibers and hair. Because of the time it takes to braid hair, people often socialize while braiding and having their hair done. The process of braiding is a unifying gesture; it brings people together. Likewise, braiding practice carries on a tradition of bonding between experts and the next generation. In addition to the work by hair braiders, artists use braiding to represent interweaving, knitting, or combining, as in "She braided many different ideas into a new whole" (figure 11.2). Patterns, rhythms, and participation in the interweaving of materials are at the heart of this work. The unpredictable, innovative rhythms and patterns in cornrows are similar to those found in West African textiles and other creative cultural forms.

Repetition in African diaspora creative expression is most prevalent in performance such as rhythm in music, dance, and language.[25] The organizing force that produces this aesthetic is rhythm, the ongoing recurrence of a beat. Repetitive samples and multiple, conflicting rhythms are important elements of African performance and its American descendants—gospel/spirituals, blues, and jazz. Although most often discussed in music, the polyrhythm aesthetic can also be found in braiding and textiles, in the weaving

FIGURE 11.2. Nontsikelelo Mutiti, "Untitled," 2012. Courtesy of the artist.
Photo: Nettrice Gaskins.

of threads or "thematic fibers" in repeated patterns of rhythmic regularity and irregularity as polyrhythm.[26] Repetition is an important aspect of improvisation, which is the spontaneous and inventive use of materials, and it is the method through which samples (as sprites) are repeated and translated using visual computer programming tools. Hair braiding motifs such as those created by Nontsikelelo Mutiti can be imported and used in culturally situated design tools, or CSDTs, developed under Ron Eglash at Rensselaer Polytechnic Institute (RPI) (figure 11.3). The correlation between TVC modes such as improvisation and technoscience will be further explored here.

Richard Wadman invented the model audio mixer, but Grandmaster Flash adapted it based on his knowledge of hip-hop. Flash developed and mastered innovations, including isolating drum breaks and extending them for longer durations. He learned that by using duplicate copies of the same record, he could play the break on one record while searching for the same fragment of music on the other using his headphones. When the break finished on one turntable, he used his mixer to switch quickly to the other turntable, where the same beat was cued up and ready to play. Using the backspin technique, the same short phrase of music could be looped indefinitely. Looping is another word for reiteration, and in hip-hop this means doing something

Nettrice R. Gaskins

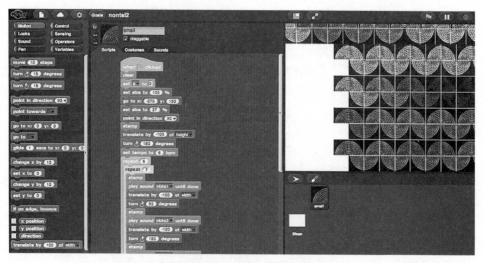

FIGURE 11.3. Ruka culturally situated design tool.
Courtesy RPI and Nettrice Gaskins.

over again to prolong a beat. Motifs in African textiles can be digitally sampled, remixed, looped, or repeated using algorithms to create new images (figure 11.4). The rithm/rhythm aspect of the algorithm is emphasized here to capture TVC modes of production such as patterning, repetition, and translation.

With generative art and design, the artist/designer begins with an objective or set of objectives—the desired pattern an image should have—and then uses algorithms to create artifacts. Heritage artifacts such as hair braiding or textiles imply values such as status, gender, ethnicity, and other attributes of identity and life. Digital representation is increasingly seen as a unique perspective on culture that implies a value of its own. While digital artifacts are not set out to replace physical ones, they are increasingly applied to cultural practices, with a multitude of opportunities that arise for the mediation of culture and social justice. Concepts such as the hip-hop cypher and "call-and-response" participation, which has origins in Africa, have been used as organizational principles for the Black Lives Matter movement—by imposing a call to action and response to state-sanctioned violence—as well as a way to translate community values/actions to technology creation. Generative art/design can be translated to generative justice methods as in peer-to-peer production using open-source software, DIY citizenship from maker spaces, and other creative modes that can have profound implications

FIGURE 11.4. Remixing African textiles as algorithms. Courtesy of the author.

for restorative approaches to civil rights that challenge the prison-industrial complex.[27]

Generative design using heritage artifacts can have profound implications for the creation of new materials and local knowledge. Culturally situated design tools (CSDTs) provide computer- and web-based modes of engagement with heritage artifacts. CSDTs are linked to four principles: "deep design themes," "anti-primitivist representations," "translation, not just modeling," and "dynamic rather than static views of culture."[28] CSDTs have been developed using a visual, drag-and-drop programming language that is an extended reimplementation of the Scratch program developed at MIT. Scratch was derived from the DJ technique of scratching, relating the ease of mixing sounds to the ease of mixing projects. CSDTs allow users to simulate original heritage artifacts and develop their own creations. Eglash and RPI developed tools that simulate different artifacts as sprites, which are the objects that perform TVC actions such as stamping, rotating, and looping in a CSDT project. The Ruka CSDT uses geometric principles—translation, rotation, reflection, and dilation—to simulate the manipulation of printed tiles. This tool was used to simulate the Kente pattern in Wakandan Nakia's costume worn by Lupita Nyong'o in the 2018 *Black Panther* film (figure 11.5).

Nettrice R. Gaskins

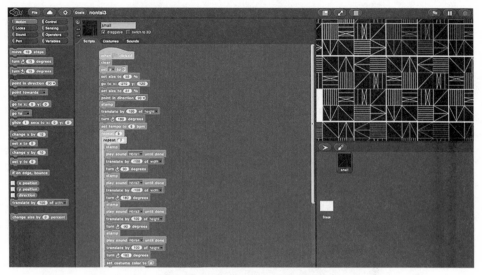

FIGURE 11.5. Sampling "Kente" to create algorithmic images.

Culture generates vast amounts of data that represent complex intersections of art, language, narrative, economics, storytelling, and politics. Computers can be taught to simulate cultural information and generate results on their own if given simple instructions (algorithms). As these artificial intelligence (AI) systems develop alongside culture, they must be constantly updated and retrained on datasets of visual material such as digitized visual artifacts and contemporary visual and interactive media. The Rap Research Lab online platform presents and analyzes data visualizations produced through the Hip-Hop Word Count (HHWC) database, a searchable and application programming interface or API-powered archive featuring datasets for thousands of rap songs. These interfaces, like CSDTs, are modular, able to be moved around, combined, and reassembled. Users transfer cultural information using iconic representations (sprites, objects) and create new works through scratching, remixing, or call-and-response participation. Computer programmers encode specific parts of a computer program, using modules to hide the details, so that users need not understand the complexities of the program. As emerging technologies become more mainstream, there will be more opportunities for artists/designers/hackers to adapt or remix them. Adaptable technologies that can learn about the properties of cultural artifacts may be able to produce equitable (less biased) results. Algorithms and artifacts produced with computer-based tools, APIs, or artificial intelligence

FIGURE 11.6. Cultural motifs in algorithmic images. Courtesy of the author.

FIGURE 11.7. Cultural motifs in algorithmic images. Courtesy of the author.

systems can enhance the capacities of artists/designers to engage relevant concepts. AI systems have been applied to computer vision, a field that deals with how computer programs can be created to gain high-level understanding from images (facial recognition technology). Similar technology is used to racially profile black and brown people by scanning, tagging, and sorting images into databases. Google's DeepDream tool allows users to computationally generate new images and uses its own knowledge to interpret art techniques and styles and transfer them to uploaded images (figures 11.6 and 11.7). NeuroSpeculative AfroFeminism (NSAF), a cross-platform project that sits at the intersection of design, technology, and neuroscience, creates products such as earrings embedded with cameras that offer protection and visibility. These technologies, for those who create with them, open up opportunities to design tools as agents, giving users the power to act.

TECHNO-VERNACULAR CREATIVITY
AS TECHNOLOGICAL AGENCY

Technological agency speaks to the ways in which tools and external devices help people navigate the world. For example, one of the earliest known cyphers (as in hip-hop) is the Kongo cosmogram, which existed as a long-standing symbolic tradition within the BaKongo culture before European contact in 1482 and continued in use in western Central Africa through the early twentieth century. In their fullest embellishment, cosmograms represented a broad array of ideas and metaphoric messages that made up their sense of identity within the universe.[29] Certain elements of its design prevail in the ring shout, the oldest continuously practiced African-derived dance in the United States that is still performed today. The ring shout is a religious ritual in which worshipers dance counterclockwise in a circle while shuffling and stomping their feet and clapping their hands. They sing their own improvised hymns, called "shouts," in a call-and-response format, often pantomiming actions described in the songs. This performance thus involves movement around the cosmogram to music. Kongo cosmograms have been elaborated upon in contemporary dance, showing complex intricate patterns or simplified into abbreviated xs, or even vs, implying an arc of travel or motion. This motion translates elements of the cosmogram's design, allowing for improvisation (i.e., repetition, patterning) in the dancers' performances. "While certain rhythms may establish a background beat, in almost all African music there is a dominant point of repetition developed from a dominant conversation with a clearly defined alternation, a swinging back and forth from solo to chorus or from solo to an emphatic instrumental reply."[30]

The notion of "race as a technology" speaks to the cosmogram's "embedded function of self-extension," which liberates race from a "historical place of abjection towards a greater expression of agency."[31] The cosmogram/cypher was used to liberate people who were/are subjected to systems of power, ideology, and external networks. This technology provides us with a different way to view, encode, or decode African cultural systems. Resonances of its values can be found in artworks by Xenobia Bailey, who is known for her large-scale crocheted cosmograms, each consisting of colorful concentric circles and repeating patterns. Houston Conwill's floor cosmograms are etched with words and maps, projecting designs on marble and wood. Architects Carrie Schneider and Susan Rogers worked with Houston, Texas, youth to plan and implement a pilot project and a tool kit for the Houston Housing Authority. OX4D *Plays* is a transforming stage that unfolds in three dimensions. The team explored the idea of portals, and each youth participant designed his or her own circular motifs that appeared on the stage. The sidewalks featured a series of games including kalunga water drawings and circular objects from the cosmos such as planets and wormholes (figures 11.8 and 11.9). Schneider says, "The timing of this [project] overlapped the shooting of Terence Crutcher and the election of Trump. We sat down with the teens and said 'Look, I know it's absurd to think about play right now. It is actually less absurd to imagine having space in outer space and in future time than to imagine play right here right now.' So we introduced them to Afrofuturism."[32]

Hip-hop music (rap) and culture influence attitudes toward and perceptions about social and criminal justice. OX4D *Plays* included a rap about cosmograms. Youth participants in the Learn 2 Teach/Teach 2 Learn program at the South End Technology Center in Boston reappropriated the hip-hop cypher to explore interactive technology in response to the Black Lives Matter movement. A cypher is an informal gathering of performers in a circle, who use the call-and-response method of participation. The cosmogram/cypher was used as a metaphor for how electronic devices work. L2TT2L youth created a "Rainbow Glove" that converted skin colors into sounds using a color sensor that triggers a response from an attached minicomputer with a small speaker (figure 11.10). The message being sent through the use of the "Rainbow Glove" in a cypher was to inform others about the value of diversity and offered participants a different way to address inequities that permeate the U.S. justice system. This approach, like cultural art forms, provides avenues for creative expression and skill building through the use of new technology.

Nettrice R. Gaskins

FIGURE 11.8. *OX4D Plays*. Courtesy University of Houston Community Design Resource Center, Carrie Marie Schneider, and Design & Build teens.

FIGURE 11.9. *OX4D Plays*. Courtesy University of Houston Community Design Resource Center, Carrie Marie Schneider, and Design & Build teens.

FIGURE. 11.10. "Rainbow Glove and Cypher." South End Technology Center and the L2TT2L program. Photo by author.

The electrification of music improvisation bridged production in the twentieth and twenty-first centuries, enabling the coexistence and convergence of sounds. Busker and traditionally trained saxophonist Onyx Ashanti developed "beatjazz," a music system that uses handheld controllers, an iPhone with software, and a mouthpiece, and is played with the entire body. Onyx Ashanti's original system was created using software and do-it-yourself electronics, specifically embedded in customized, 3D-printed objects. Beatjazz uses aspects of Techno-Vernacular Creativity such as technology to sample and translate beats and sounds, and the movement of the body to combine and repeat specific patterns. Beatjazz establishes Amiri Baraka's vision of an "expression scriber" or instrument that can be used to: "Step & sit or sprawl or hang & use not only my fingers to make words express feelings but elbows, feet, head, behind, and all the sounds I wanted, screams, grunts, taps, itches, I'd have magnetically recorded, at the same time, & translated into word— or perhaps even the final xpressed thought/feeling wd not be merely word or sheet, but itself, the xpression, three dimensional—able to be touched, or tasted or felt, or entered, or heard or carried like a speaking singing constantly communicating charm."[33]

The art of making do with whatever is at hand is prevalent in poor, disenfranchised, or under-resourced communities. TVC methods help to amplify the voices and issues of historically marginalized, disenfranchised, and oppressed communities. Producers of the African diaspora and Global South craft their inventions and artworks using DIY methods. Early prototypes of beatjazz made use of open-source software and scrap materials. West Afri-

Nettrice R. Gaskins

can (Benin) artist Romuald Hazoumé uses discarded plastic gasoline and fuel canisters in works made to resemble traditional African masks. Hazoumé has said of these works, "I send back to the West that which belongs to them, that is to say, the refuse of consumer society that invades us every day." Kenyan Cyrus Kabiru refashions electronic refuse and found metal into different wearable objects and fixed-gear "Black Mamba" bicycles.[34] Togolese industrial designer Kossi Aguessy created works to "engineer the future," and he used new manufacturing technologies and sustainable energy sources. Aguessy helped to build a fabrication lab (or FabLab) in Benin to get people accustomed to the use of technology. Artists and designers, like self-taught engineers or DJs, produce works that reflect a developing domain of cultural practices that are parallel to Western ones such as "upcycling," or reusing discarded material in such a way as to create a product of a higher quality or value than the original. These examples show the global reach of creative, techno-vernacular modes/methods.

CONCLUSION

Technologies are not mere tools that we use, but active forces in the world. This essay builds on many examples of technologically mediated artistic expressions, sometimes made in response to issues such as the environment and social justice. TVC practitioners employ what Beth Coleman refers to as technology's embedded functions of self-extension to liberate people from inherited positions of abjection toward greater expressions of agency. This is done through extrapolating possible futures and choosing which representations they most want to emulate. For example, the popular work of science fiction emulates emerging technologies such as the artificial intelligence in drones that may become a key policing tool, replacing the "ghetto bird" police helicopters of the recent past, which provided surveillance in low-income and urban neighborhoods. In the "Black Museum" episode of the *Black Mirror* Netflix series, the main character Nish (performed by Letitia Wright) frees her digitized, previously executed father from a virtual prison, a restitution that is infinitely compounded when you consider how the carceral state continues to profit from black pain and to fracture black families.[35] Nish is tech-savvy, showing her advanced knowledge of the technology that was used to imprison her father. Nish reappropriates criminological artifacts and improvises to engineer her father's escape.

TVC, along with other strategies, can be used to deal with the power of technoscience in and against African diasporic communities. TVC bridges the real impacts of science and technology with creative methods that afford artists and practitioners the ability to create and move freely, addressing systems of power, ideology, and external networks. Whether it is a self-taught engineer designing machines using scraps scavenged from junkyards, a performer developing a new instrument using electronics and open-source technology, a comic book artist creating an imaginary world that uses secret technologies, or an architect using aesthetics to bring about social change, TVC practitioners sample (simulate), reappropriate, and remix heritage artifacts and technologies to generate works that can be embedded into different environments. Combined with bottom-up "generative justice" strategies, TVC works have profound implications for new forms of techno-social engagement, and these approaches can counter the various industrial complexes that disproportionately impact African American, Latinx, and Indigenous communities.[36] Like Nish in "Black Museum," TVC modes/methods serve as tools that can be used much as the cosmogram/cypher was used to address Black Lives Matter.

The informal engagements with science and technology explored here demonstrate some of the ways in which underrepresented ethnic groups foster creative expression and innovation. These groups must learn to engage scientific and technological representations more deeply, and this can be accomplished through cultural production. TVC methods are modular, able to be diagrammed, mixed and remixed, translated, collaged, and coded to create works that impact local communities and beyond. Xenobia Bailey and Nontsikelelo Mutiti sample heritage artifacts and recover the aesthetics in African diasporic cultures through the use of crochet, recycled fibers, newspapers, magazines, and more. The software that supports this production is also modular, allowing users to combine, sample, repurpose, or manipulate code blocks and sprites to create designs. Through coding extensions (tools), producers can train AI systems and the machines that use them, such as drones, but the emphasis for TVC is situating heritage artifacts and artworks within the social conditions of their production, circulation, and consumption.

This essay explored instances of Techno-Vernacular Creativity and showed the role that DIY and vernacular art/craft forms such as hair braiding and textiles play in the intersections of culture and technology. This domain is dynamic, requiring new sets of skills and knowledge in addition to TVC modes of production. Many artists from underrepresented ethnic groups employ TVC modes and methods in their work. However, even with the development of technologies such as deep dreaming algorithms, it is important

Nettrice R. Gaskins

that TVC practitioners continue to learn, develop, and experiment with software and coding, electronics, tinkering, and design using cultural information and data. The emphasis on techno-culture and technoscience as tools for creativity and liberation makes the case for greater degrees of agency. The TVC domain, modes, and practices described in this essay address more directly some of the ways in which creative people from underrepresented ethnic groups can gain needed skills and create a more central place in the worlds of science and technology.

Notes

1. Ron Eglash et al., *Appropriating Technology: Vernacular Science and Social Power* (Minneapolis: University of Minnesota Press, 2004).

2. Wolfgang Wagner, "Vernacular Science Knowledge: Its Role in Everyday Life Communication," *Public Understanding of Science* 16, no. 7 (2007): 7–22.

3. Nettrice Gaskins, "Techno-Vernacular Creativity, Innovation and Learning in Underrepresented Ethnic Communities of Practice," PhD diss., Georgia Institute of Technology, 2014.

4. Diana Mitlin and David Satterthwaite, *Urban Poverty in the Global South: Scale and Nature* (New York: Routledge, 2013), 13.

5. Bethonie Butler, "Grandmaster Flash on 'The Get Down' and How He Used Science to Pioneer DJ Techniques," *Washington Post*, August 23, 2016, https://www .washingtonpost.com/news/arts-and-entertainment/wp/2016/08/23/grandmaster -flash-on-the-get-down-and-how-he-used-science-to-pioneer-dj-techniques/?utm _term=.f1b91c6b10a0.

6. James A. Snead, "Repetition as a Figure of Black Culture," in *Out There: Marginalization and Contemporary Cultures*, ed. Russell Ferguson (Cambridge, MA: MIT Press, 1990).

7. Etienne Wenger, *Communities of Practice: Learning, Meaning, and Identity* (Cambridge: Cambridge University Press, 1998).

8. See Paul Gilroy, *The Black Atlantic: Modernity and Double Consciousness* (Cambridge, MA: Harvard University Press, 1993).

9. Margaretta Gacheru, "The Kenyan Art Scene," *ArtAfrica*, January 11, 2017, https:// artsouthafrica.com/220-news-articles-2013/2846-kenyan-art-scene-by-margaretta-wa -gacheru.html.

10. Claude Lévi-Strauss, *The Savage Mind* (Paris: Librairie Pion, 1966).

11. Ginger Nolan, "Savage Mind to Savage Machine; Techniques and Disciplines of Creativity, c. 1880–1985," PhD diss., Columbia University, 2015.

12. National Telecommunications and Information Administration, *Falling through the Net: Defining the Digital Divide*, U.S. Department of Commerce, July 8, 1995.

13. Rayvon Fouché, "Say It Loud, I'm Black and I'm Proud: African Americans, American Artifactual Culture, and Black Vernacular Technological Creativity," *American Quarterly* 58, no. 3 (2006): 639–61.

14. Danni Shen, "Sinofuturism: An Interview with Lawrence Lek," *Screen*, March 6, 2017, http://www.onscreentoday.com/conversation/sinofuturism.

15. Cara A. Finnegan, *Recognizing Lincoln: Image Vernaculars in Nineteenth-Century Visual Culture* (Thousand Oaks, CA: SAGE, 2005).

16. Snead, "Repetition as a Figure of Black Culture," 221.

17. Fouché, "Say It Loud, I'm Black and I'm Proud."

18. Fouché, "Say It Loud, I'm Black and I'm Proud."

19. Fouché, "Say It Loud, I'm Black and I'm Proud," 641.

20. Amiri Baraka, "Technology and Ethos," in *Raise, Race, Rays, Raze: Essays Since 1965* (New York: Random House, 1971).

21. Fouché, "Say It Loud, I'm Black and I'm Proud," 642.

22. Patrick Manning, *The African Diaspora: A History through Culture* (New York: Columbia University Press, 2010), 342.

23. Christopher Emdin, "Exploring the Contexts of Urban Science Classrooms, Part 1: Investigating Corporate and Communal Practices," *Cultural Studies of Science Education* 2 (2007): 319–50.

24. Maude S. Wahlman, *Signs and Symbols: African Images in African-American Quilts* (New York: Museum of American Folk Art, 2001).

25. See James A. Snead, "Repetition as a Figure of Black Culture," in *Out There: Marginalization and Contemporary Cultures*, ed. Russell Ferguson (Cambridge, MA: MIT Press, 1990).

26. Adam Rudolph, "Music and Mysticism, Rhythm and Form: A Blues Romance in 12 Parts," in *Arcana V: Music, Magic and Mysticism*, ed. John Zorn, 327–35 (New York: Distributed Art Publishers, 2010).

27. Ron Eglash, "An Introduction to Generative Justice," *Revista Teknokultura* 13, no. 2 (2016): 369–404.

28. Ron Eglash, et al., "Culturally Situated Design Tools: Ethnocomputing from Field Site to Classroom," *American Anthropologist* 108, no. 2 (2006): 347–62.

29. Robert Farris Thompson, *Flash of the Spirit: African and Afro-American Art and Philosophy* (New York: Random House, 1985), 108.

30. Snead, "Repetition as a Figure of Black Culture," 223.

31. Beth Coleman, "Race as Technology," *Camera Obscura* 70 (2009).

32. Carrie Marie Schneider, email message to author, March 2, 2017.

33. Baraka, "Technology and Ethos," 157.

34. Rick De La Ray, "Mamba Bamba," *Issuu*, March 2015, accessed October 25, 2017, https://issuu.com/thelakeco/docs/the_lake__3.

35. Jason Parham. "Why Black Mirror's Most Controversial New Episode Is Its Most Important," *Wired*, January 6, 2018, accessed January 10, 2018, https://www.wired.com/story/black-mirror-black-museum.

36. Eglash, "An Introduction to Generative Justice."

Nettrice R. Gaskins

12

Making Skin Visible
through Liberatory Design

Lorna Roth

.....

"Skin-color balance" in still photography printing refers historically to a process by which a norm reference card showing a Caucasian woman wearing a colorful, high-contrast dress is used to measure and calibrate the skin tones on the photograph being printed. The light skin tones of these women—all of whom are called "Shirley" by industry and laboratory workers, after the first color test-strip-card model—have been the recognized ideal standard for skin color in most North American and international analog photo labs since the early twentieth century. Despite criticism for being reductive, Shirley cards continued to represent a global skin-color standard: a white flesh tone fixed in place as normal/ideal, with little challenge until the mid-1970s. Consequently, due to the light-skin bias chemically encoded within analog color film stock emulsions and digital camera design, darker-skinned fine facial features (except for the whites of eyes and teeth) could hardly be distinguished at all in photos. Thus, the rendering of non-Caucasian skin tones was highly deficient and required the thoughtful development of compensatory practices and technology improvements to redress its shortcomings. The failure to consistently produce nondiscriminatory or universal image technologies contributes to the psychological damage of exclusion for those whose skin tones are not reflected in this single standard. It can lead to what has been called the "color complex," or intra-racial discrimination.[1] Such discrimination gives more power, beauty, and privilege to those with lighter skin tones.

The embedded materiality of visual technologies has been historically and cognitively linked to a single standard of light skin within a common normative framework and ensemble of practices. My research question, then, is: What design strategies can be developed to open this carceral entrapment to a wider range of nondiscriminatory possibilities with which all subjects of image capture could more easily identify? To approach this question, I use the emblematic Shirley norm reference card as a central metaphor for reflecting the changing state of race relations/aesthetics around the world since the 1970s. This essay will then:

1. analytically trace the flesh tone dominance of light skin and the recent color adjustment processes in the analog and digital industries of visual portrayal that render it more inclusive;
2. identify more recent prototypical changes and challenges in emergent materiality of digital technologies and products of visual representation; and
3. focus on the multiple ways in which the changing *look of skin* of the "Shirley/China/Color girls" in color photography, film, and television has historically marked key shifts in the process of (re)defining and resetting cultural norms for multiracial beauty and more sensitive technical standards.

This essay differs from others in this collection in that its focus is on questions of self-representation, or *how people wish to be seen*. These are questions of aesthetics, related to commercial uses of analog and digital apparatuses as opposed to surveillance apparatuses, but also deeply related to matters of "cognitive equity."[2] Asking how societies have appropriated new, improved algorithms to ensure that a diversity of skin tones is recognized and treated equally is necessarily a different question from how cameras with enhanced ability to differentiate skin tones and facial features can be used as tools of surveillance and control. This said, it is my hope that analyzing this little-known narrative about the underside of race relations will spur on further study and help unearth connections between the domains of commercial and noncommercial or surveillance image capture.

The examples discussed here illustrate a long-awaited expansion and transformation to a more inclusive, wider dynamic range of "skinvisible" colors in global industries of visual representation. They will also raise some critical questions about how and why the "light skin ideal," though critically challenged and modified over the years by many academics and practitioners in

Lorna Roth

FIGURE 12.1.
Traditional Kodak
Shirley card.
Image includes
calibration data
markings. Used
with permission
of Eastman Kodak
Company.

the photo professions, still prevails as the dominant standard of beauty, not only in the West, but in the Third and Fourth Worlds as well (see figure 12.1).[3]

HISTORIES OF THE FLESH TONE GIRLS

The multiple visual identities of Shirley, the "color balance girl," first came to my attention in 1995 after a conversation with a buyer and seller of industrial machines in North America. He complained about a Kodak photo-processing lab that he had purchased at the time, which had caused him a great deal of frustration. No matter what calibration he technically configured to print the photos he was charged to reproduce, the final image of darker skin appeared to be muddy-looking, ashen, or so close to "black" that only the whites of the subjects' eyes and their white teeth appeared with any detail. In photos where there were several skin tones side by side, the challenge became even more striking as the photographers had often tried to strengthen the lighting

FIGURE 12.2. Two children in Senegal. Guilado Sarr (left) and
Natalie Le Brun (right). Kodak film (125 ASA) used with Canon camera. An
example of the challenge of photographing highly contrasted skin colors in the
same frame and the difficulty of later recognizing who precisely is in the photo.
Photo credit: Olivier Le Brun, 1974, Paris, France.

intensity and overexpose the darker subjects to capture the highest possible skin definition. This resulted in overexposing the lighter-skinned subjects as well, making the final product so visually unpleasant as to be considered an embarrassment to the photographer (see figure 12.2).

My friend's frustration was exacerbated by the fact that none of the documentation that accompanied the lab infrastructure directions (including Kodak's Dataguide) mentioned the possibility that a diversity of skin tones might need to be considered as a critical factor in the creation of realistic renditions of human subjects. For him, as for others in the Kodak lab business, the learning process would be based on trial and error. Was the solution to be found in a better understanding of the underside of film emulsion or in the improvement of problematic color balance standards in printing?

One of the items that my friend and other lab owners received with their Kodak documentation package, designed for still photograph printing, was an image that had mysteriously become known as a Shirley card among industry technicians. Shirley's image was that of a single light-skinned woman wearing high-contrast clothing positioned against various color graphs and a grayscale (see figure 12.3). The purpose of a Shirley card was to aid in the determination of exposure, image density, comparison-measuring, and calibrating the skin tones on photographs being printed. It is normal to have skin-color parameters against which to compare settings, but should the singular term *normal* be applied to the *multiple* Shirleys who represent a restricted set of the many existing human flesh tones?

The original name of Kodak's Shirley seems to have come from the first model who was pictured on the card in the 1940s. She was probably someone who worked in the office at one of several Kodak Lab research centers in North America, or the wife of someone working there, who was asked to sit as a model. To simplify matters of classification, those in charge of the development of the norm reference test card (as her photo was called), decided to give all the women who were pictured therein the same name: Shirley. Beside the name Shirley, what all these women had in common were their light skins, their anonymity, and their Western, attractive, sexy look.

Shirleys were not an isolated phenomenon. "Color" girls and China girls (also known as dolls or girl heads) represented the light-skinned color balance industry standards for analog and digital TV and motion pictures for decades. The early analog color TV industry used its own version of "Shirley" in the form of a white porcelain "China girl" until the 1950s, at which time it was replaced by BBC cardboard flesh-tone test cards (F, 61A, or 61P), especially designed for compatibility with National Television System Committee

FIGURE 12.3.
Polaroid Shirley card.

(NTSC) and Phase Alternating Line (PAL) broadcast technologies (see figure 12.4). BBC Test Card F is still used in many nations around the globe. Originally designed by George Hersee of the BBC, it pictures his daughter who, in reality, does not differ much in lightness of complexion or ethnic appearance from the other Shirley cards in circulation. Although the "Shirleys" and "China girls" remain linked to the color test strip women of the 1940s, their look expanded to include a wider range of skin tones and ethnic features toward the end of the twentieth century.

As color television evolved, "Color girls" were added as a new dimension to the domains of photography and film's color-balance verification process. According to Jan Kasoff, former NBC color-television cameraman for the program *Saturday Night Live*, there were several stages to color balancing an analog TV camera, beyond using grayscale and color cards.[4] Video signals were viewed and adjusted on a waveform monitor and vectorscope to eliminate distortion; camera output was then matched for evenness of color representation. And finally, "a good video engineer would have a Color girl stand in front of the cameras and stay there while the cameramen lined

FIGURE 12.4. The BBC flesh-tone girl. Photo by Lorna Roth, 2003; taken at Fujifilm Advanced Research Laboratories, Kaisei, Kanagawa, Japan.

up and focused on her flesh tones to do their fine adjustments of matching and balancing the cameras colorwise. This Color girl was always white"[5] (see figure 12.5). By 2003, when the broadcast standard in the United States became digital, "Color girls" were no longer needed for final visual checks by the human eye. Soon after, they were retired from studio sets around North America. Digital camera color balancing now uses more sophisticated electronics, light boxes, and black/white chip cards showing the dynamic range of the darkest of darks and the lightest of lights with all the incremental shifts in the color spectrum.

Though less visible to the human eye than a material Shirley card, a version of the China girls was just as important to the color balancing process in cinematography. In cinematography, these women lived as captive images on the leader of every commercial and documentary film from the late 1920s until the early 1990s. They continue to be in limited use today.

Shirley artifacts tend not to be known to the general public, as they are stored and posted on lab walls, their images viewed and handled by lab technicians as a tool of clarification and reference. TV Color girls had always been obvious participants in the studio camera set-up process; studio audiences would have been particularly familiar with them. Finally, as an audience member in a film theater, it is possible—though rare—to catch a glimpse

FIGURE 12.5. Examples of China (leader) girls. Northwest Chicago Film Society Collection. Used with permission of Eastman Kodak Company.

of a China girl as she moves for a split second across the cinematic screen. If you blink when the leader is projected onto the screen, you will surely miss this special image.

Living in the shadows of photographic labs and studios between the 1940s and the present, versions of these iconic images (in both analog and digital platforms), have appeared around the world. Fixed in time and pose, their light skin standard continues to subliminally wield normative powers among lab and studio technicians and general viewing publics. They have crossed decades, continents, and skin color lines, and continue to narrowly guide perceptions of skin tones in photographic imagery, representing a subtle, embedded social and psychological message about the dominant value of white skin color and the position of females in the industry. They further represent a particular Euro/Western beauty and gender aesthetic that conformed to the popular masculinist notion of the ideal feminine look at the time of their creation.

As a predesigned and prefixed measuring tool for all human subjects in the industry, no matter what their skin color was in real life, the popularity

Lorna Roth

of the light skin standard raised several issues for photographers. If Shirleys were to be the norm against which *all* skin colors would be calibrated, how should technicians deal with images of people whose skin tones were more yellow, red, olive, brown, or black?

The implicit message that Shirley was the norm, and "the normal" was white skin, reached the height of its popularity before the civil rights movement in the United States began gaining strength. In the 1960s, Kodak lab operators and photographers in the African American communities began to intuitively perceive the chemistry of whiteness embedded in their products, and so could consumers or viewers with a critical, aesthetic eye. But like so many who naïvely believed that film was designed to render a photo of the *real* as a perfect resemblance of what is pictured, most didn't consider that the chemistry of film emulsions could possibly be developed or modified on the basis of cultural choices. The belief that technologies were neutral prevailed so strongly that few would question the visual industries unless there was convincing evidence to justify their skepticism. For example, when I spoke with video engineers at CBS and NBC in New York in the late 1990s, I was told that the issues around color balance were purely technical, based on physics, and involved the exact color matching of reflective skins among several studio cameras. My questions about the international standard reference for color balance being a Caucasian woman were taken seriously, but engineers responded with concerns that I might be leading them to the delicate territory of political correctness, where they did not want to go. They had learned to maneuver the supplementary tools of color balancing to meet their needs. If a black person's skin details did not show adequately, special makeup or lighting techniques were used to highlight their faces until their images were technically pleasing to the eye. This was not always an easy task.

In 2014, an African American photographer named Syreeta McFadden wrote that she had always been concerned about the poor quality of her own family photos, even when a professional photographer had been hired to do photos for special occasions. In a text titled "Teaching the Camera to See My Skin: Navigating Photography's Inherited Bias against Dark Skin," she reflected upon her negative childhood and adult experiences, and the limits imposed on her image by color film emulsion designed with lighter skins in mind. McFadden had intuitively picked up on the central issue that Kodak film emulsions embodied a bias toward lighter skins but had been afraid to articulate this openly at the time because she didn't have enough evidence beyond her own experience.

By the 1990s, when I began taking pictures, I hated shooting brown skin on color film. The printed results failed to accurately represent my subjects, their shades obscured, their smiles blown out. I understood that some of this had to do with harmonizing the basic components of great image-making from the gear: film speed, aperture, and the ghost we all chase, light.

The inconsistencies were so glaring, that for a while, I thought it was impossible to get a decent picture of me that captured my likeness. I began to retreat from situations involving group photos. And sure, many of us are fickle about what makes a good portrait. But it seemed the technology was stacked against me. I only knew, though I didn't understand why, that the lighter you were, the more likely it was that the camera—the film—got your likeness right.[6]

One of the solutions to overcome this problem was to learn to adapt the technology: "We circumvented the inherent flaws of film emulsion by ensuring that our subjects were well placed in light; invested more in costly lenses that permitted a wider variety of aperture ranges so we could imbue our work with all the light we could; we purchased professional-grade films at faster speeds, or specialty films with emulsions designed for shooting conditions strictly indoor under fluorescent or tungsten light. We accepted poor advice from white photo instructors to add Vaseline to teeth and skin or apply photosensitive makeup that barely matched our skin's undertones."[7] Careful attention to a panoply of special adjustments created improved results for professionals who were doing custom photos, but what about the more economic, stock films for nonexpert consumers using baseline products? How could these films and photographic results be improved? What critical factors would motivate manufacturers to increase the dynamic range embedded in their film emulsions? When would the representation of this full range of color become a priority for international film companies' product development technical staff?

THE KODAK SURPRISE: FACE-ING ETHNICITY

Kodak stock film emulsions *were* initially and admittedly *designed* to favor lighter skin tones, mainly for socioeconomic reasons.[8] Prior to the civil rights movement, consumers who could afford cameras and film tended to be Caucasian. To conform to their market preferences, the chemical formulas designed by engineers to produce stock film emulsions privileged the

Lorna Roth

higher reflectivity of white skin tones. Yet, even as I interviewed technical and artistic staff at Kodak and several popular television networks in the United States, Japan, China, Australia, Holland, and Canada in the mid- to late 1990s, I repeatedly heard the scientific arguments about how film and TV camera design, manufacturing processes, and practices are based on reasoned and logical decision making without consideration of cultural or racial subtleties. Interviewees described a lengthy period of resistance to any cultural impact on decision making in the industry. However, by 1996–97, a few key players began to quietly affirm that refinements to the chemistry of film emulsions and camera design had indeed been affected by cultural preferences and choices negotiated in back rooms and labs. The critical moment of Kodak's more open recognition of this acknowledgment was particularly surprising and interesting.

School graduation photos that Kodak had been contracted to do in Rochester, New York, in 1959 raised the problem that dark- and light-skinned subjects in the same photo frame looked awful. The darker-skinned children had no visible facial contours or particularities in resulting images; the lighter-skinned children were overexposed (see figure 12.6). However, when each child's photo was taken individually, the results were much improved due to the photographers' knowledge of compensatory mechanisms. The complaints of parents who demanded a wider dynamic range, which would include brown tones, were discussed at the time. Kodak's actual color adjustments took place thanks to two other issues, however.

According to Kodak executives, in the mid-1960s and 1970s, two of Kodak's biggest professional accounts — chocolate and furniture — catalyzed their decision to increase the range of browns in their film emulsions. One chocolate company complained that in their ad imagery, they weren't getting the right brown tones to show the distinction between dark, bittersweet, and milk chocolate. Furniture manufacturers, meanwhile, were dissatisfied that ads showed images of stains and wood grains that were not true to life and that couldn't be easily differentiated as dark or light. Nor could the type of wood be identified clearly. The representation of these subtle variations in tone incidentally paralleled the challenges of reproducing nonwhite skin colors, but the improvements in dynamic range, or a new continuum of browns, were made for reasons related to economics and not racial equity. Such product development serendipitously made Kodak's stock film more inclusive for ethnic peoples. Interestingly, even Kodak's research director admitted he had been surprised by this unanticipated outcome.[9] Although these recognitions and color adjustment shifts took place in the seventies,

FIGURE 12.6. Class photo. Students from Villa Maria Academy, Bronx, New York, 1983. John R. Foldi Collection. Originally published in *Zum* magazine. São Paulo, IMS, April 2016; reprinted with permission of John R. Foldi.

institutional and public discourse did not echo this technical shift in any definitive manner at the time. However, lab workers in the back rooms of photo labs quietly and subtly acknowledged its impact.

Kodak's other motivations for increasing their films' dynamic range in the late nineties included a desire to enter the Japanese stock film market, which was monopolized by Fuji, and to extend its market to the global community. Cognitive and technical changes to existing knowledge and practices are often resisted and considered to be overwhelming. Consequently, it took a while for Shirley card skin tones to match the shifts in technology that were targeted at improving the sensitivity of film emulsions and dynamic ranges in the analog and digital media spheres. In 1996–97, Kodak's Richard Wien produced a multiracial reference card featuring African, Caucasian, and Asian women (although all three have rather pale complexions), but it took a while before it began circulating[10] (see figure 12.7). This is likely because the labs had invested financially in and become accustomed to their favorite single-woman Shirley card images. The current (2018), still limited, use of this more recent, multicultural reference image suggests that while Kodak's lab staff

Lorna Roth

FIGURE 12.7.
The first Kodak
multiracial Shirley
card. Compliments
of Richard Wien,
Kodak Executive,
1997. Used with
permission of
Eastman Kodak
Company.

are interested in leaving behind their trial-and-error techniques of color balancing for non-Caucasian clients, workers remain strangely nostalgic about keeping lab apparatus in its historically fixed configuration.

Beyond reconceiving the image on the Shirley card, Kodak's Rochester research lab, under the management of Richard Wien, created two new film emulsions. The first, a professional portrait film series called VeriColor III, was developed in the early 1980s to target wedding photography as it addressed the dark and light contrast challenge of picturing white gowns and black tuxedos on the same image. In 1997, Wien also created and launched a consumer film, Gold Max, which was to become very popular. He described it initially as being able "to photograph the details of a dark horse in low light."[11] I suspect this was Kodak's code for informing consumers it was the right film for photographing darker skin tones. They were aware of the incidental discovery of their film deficiency and had to find the right words to market their film so that they would neither be embarrassed nor criticized.

In the digital media sphere of the internet, there are currently many diverse Shirley cards circulating. Adobe was one of the first companies to circulate a Latino woman's image for its Photoshop software in 1988 (see figure 12.8). Interestingly, the image is reminiscent of the stereotypical Brazilian performer Carmen Miranda and was quite popular in its time. Currently, however, most professional labs create their own versions of color balance cards suitable to their studio needs and clientele.

The lightness of complexion of much of the circulating imagery continues to attest to the reappearance and reprivileging of the "look" of whiteness as a beauty norm in these "internationally ideal" photos. The subtle message evidenced by multiple examples is that one *can* be "ethnic," or not white, but a lighter skin color is still the pervasive aesthetic prototype or idealized norm.

In the last couple of decades, more complex, lab-produced cards have begun to circulate in the digital sector that expand upon Wien's Kodak multiracial card. These new cards offer both concrete recognition of some of the critical issues with which photographers of people of color have struggled in the past, and a solution to some of these obstacles. The cards include a broad range of skin colors, several color charts, a grayscale, animal skins (as in the Getty Images collection), brightly colored objects, and color palettes, all of which are a technical improvement over the prior existing single- or three-person norm reference cards (see figure 12.9). These cards represent an explicitly wider range of color subtleties to which technicians can refer. What makes the Getty reference image distinctive is both its sociocultural inclusivity and its vast skin-color range: it represents one of the widest color continuums of the color balance photos in circulation that I have researched to date. Furthermore, it is freely distributed online and only requires an informal user agreement with its copyright owner.

With more images circulating for public use, the traditional "light" Shirley card which had monopolized lab protocol for decades now sits among others with a variety of skin tones, genders, children, animal skins, colorful objects and backgrounds. Shirley (version 1) has become recognized as only one of many skin standards around the world.

Despite the acknowledgment of nonwhite subjects, lighter skins will likely prevail on most of the near-future reference cards for social and normative reasons. This is so because our preferences go beyond the technical to the cognitive imprint of the light-skinned aesthetic.[12] Consequently, it is in these difficult-to-access domains that we need to focus our attention to

FIGURE 12.8.
Adobe Photoshop
Shirley card (1988).

FIGURE 12.9.
Getty Image
commonly used for
color balance
calibration. From
the Getty Collection
of photos on the
internet, 2009.
Reproduced with
permission of Dry
Creek Photo.

understand more effectively the relationship between social cognition, the technologies we use, and the practices that emerge from this linkage.

Why do I conclude this? There is the corpus of international skin-color preference tests undertaken by film manufacturers that attest to the favoring of lighter skin tones. This "color complex" is well documented in the psychosocial literature and is central to the research of influential sociologist Ron Hall, who invented the term *bleaching syndrome*.[13] This refers to the psychological internalizing of light skin as a dominant cultural criterion of beauty. Ron Hall's empirical results concur with those of film manufacturers, as well Kenneth Clark's (1955) famous doll study, undertaken in the 1940s to assess the psychological effects of segregation on black children.[14] In Clark's study, black children were asked to identify the preferred skin color of their favorite dolls, and almost all chose the lighter-skinned ones, stating that they were prettier and better, while the black-skinned dolls were considered bad and ugly.[15] Neither Clark's nor Hall's work specifically addresses issues of image technologies in relation to light skins. It was never their consideration, but in taking a distant look at the social field and period (from the mid-twentieth century into the twenty-first) in which they were conducting their research, I find that there is a strong correlation between the attitudinal spirit of the times and the development of film emulsions that favored lighter skins. Race relations/aesthetics are embedded within the images of these anonymous working women, commonly called Shirley.

COLOR ADJUSTMENTS ON TELEVISION

Skin tone reproduction is not just science. It has to deal with the psychology of how people *want* to look.
—JAN VAN ROOY, inventor of automatic skin-tone detection
and holder of U.S. patent number 5,428,402

As television content became more racially integrated over the years, technical adjustments emerged to address the issues of visually representing skin tone diversity. Perhaps because they were situated at the margins of North American interests or due to their smaller institutional investment in traditional ways of doing things, designers at the Netherlands company Philips Electronics (now Thomson) could more easily respond to the evident restrictions that the limited rendition of skin tones was raising for American television practitioners. In 1994 at their headquarters in Breda, cutting-edge video

Lorna Roth

electronics specialists were being given financial and technical resources to create technologies that could solve problems related to transracial marketing, an important investment decision taken at a time when companies were seeking a global outreach.

Senior video camera designer Jan van Rooy and creative business consultant Greg Pine had become very conscious of skin-color factors over the years. With designers at the Japanese company Ikegami, Van Rooy and his team invented a new set of TV studio cameras (the LDK series) that enabled more sensitive consideration of skin-color variations. The experience of North American television problems formed the basis of their concerned motivation. They mainly worked on the issues of light/dark skin contrast as well as the researched preferences for youthful-appearing complexions. In their discussion with me in 1997, they pointed out how Whoopi Goldberg, a very popular dark-skinned American actress, had to be color calibrated with a completely different setting than that of Barbara Walters, a well-known American interviewer with pale skin, if they were to be shot in the same frame. It was an impossible situation, and for a while each had to be shot and color balanced with a separate camera and electronically merged in the control room. To solve this technical problem, Rooy's team came up with a prototype camera in which there were two separate computer chip memory settings and storage areas for skin-tone standards — one for the darker, the other for the lighter range.

The team also developed the added asset of digital cosmetics that can be set to modify age lines, wrinkles, and blemishes in a way comparable to how Photoshop works. These two innovations were integrated into the LDK television camera series and immediately became popular with well-funded studios around the world that consistently had to face the challenges of rendering the details of dark skin tones and the additional desire on the part of those photographed to improve the look of changing and ageing complexions. Versions of the infrastructure for the dual-skin contour system are now embedded in most prosumer and consumer cameras currently on the international market.

My interview with video engineer Toru Hasegawa of NHK, the Japanese television network, was enlightening as well.[16] His first words to me were, "American television is discriminatory because it is biased against Japanese skin tones." He further informed me that this is kept very quiet because the Japanese do not want North Americans working in television production in Japan to feel uncomfortable.

It was from Hasegawa that I learned of the yellow skin-color bias in Japanese television, both in its balancing calibration preferences and in its preset

FIGURE 12.10. Japanese television reference image (A) used at Fujifilm Advanced Research Laboratories, Japan. Photo: Lorna Roth, 2003; taken at Fujifilm Advanced Research Laboratories, Kaisei, Kanagawa, Japan.

FIGURE 12.11. Japanese television reference image (B) used at Fujifilm Advanced Research Laboratories, Japan. Photo: Lorna Roth, 2003; taken at Fujifilm Advanced Research Laboratories, Kaisei, Kanagawa, Japan.

color temperatures. When televisions are made for export, they are preset to the preferred color temperature biases of North America and Europe; when they are manufactured for Japanese consumption, they are preset to the researched skin-color tastes of the average Japanese. These are important and fascinating ways in which cultural decisions are embedded in technologies that are presented to the general public as "neutral" (see figures 12.10 and 12.11).

What my cross-cultural television research findings led me to was the deepening of other important questions driving my project about image technology design: Is physics just physics, after all? What part does cultural perspective play in decisions about the design of image technologies and the ensemble of procedures used in the production process?

THE LOSS OF TECHNOLOGICAL INNOCENCE

In the last couple of decades, it has become clear to those who seek out this information that the chemistry of stock color film for still cameras and cinematography was designed with a positive bias toward lighter skin tones by Kodak, the main film manufacturer in North America, and by Fuji in Japan, as well. This did not *have* to be the case. Had NASA, the U.S. intelligence service, or meteorological scientists already completed their research on photography of low-light areas at the time of the popular development of still photography, the evolution of film chemistry might have unfolded quite differently, as Brian Harris, a lighting technician at the Black Entertainment Television (BET) network, pointed out to me.[17]

Film emulsions *could* have been created initially with more sensitivity to the continuum of yellow, brown, and reddish skin tones, but the design process would have had to be motivated by a recognition of a pressing economic or social need for an extended dynamic range. At the time film emulsions were being developed in the United States, the targeted market would have been Caucasians in a segregated political and economic scene. Multiple skin tones would have been less likely to be the catalyst for thinking about dynamic range prior to the civil rights movement and desegregation activism as most subjects in a photograph would either have been all light-skinned or all darker-skinned. Consequently, the issue of skin color contrast was not an element of social consideration for film chemists until the late 1960s and early 1970s.

As is apparent from the examples and interview evidence I have accumulated, in photographic industries of visual representation, a light-skinned, female reference point has become a stereotype, central to thinking and decision making about film and television design and practice. This "flesh tone imperialism"[18] typifies an aspect of what Franco Vaccari called the "technological unconscious."[19] As Vito Campanelli explains, Vaccari argued that cameras "should be considered a 'living fragment of the unconscious.'"[20] Cameras will consistently perform the functions that they are programmed to perform. Further, "the machine produces the same operations whatever flow it is inserted into. This 'blind indifference' is due to the fact that the machine never departs from the code 'that owns it.' Therefore, we have to acknowledge that the machine produces uniformity (a concept which should be interpreted from the perspective of repetition of the same operations independently from the type of flow concerned)."[21] Applying Vaccari's notion to the visual industries suggests an apparent lack of awareness of the dominance of the embedded cognitive patterns inserted into the tools of image-capture by the key people framing reproduction practices by decision and design. It informs us significantly of the need to recognize how deeply rooted in our cognitive processes the naturalization of whiteness and sexism remains.

INTELLIGENT DESIGN: A KEY TO THE DEVELOPMENT OF COGNITIVE EQUITY

The extent to which we take everyday objects for granted is the precise extent to which they govern and inform our lives.

—MARGARET VISSER, *Much Depends on Dinner*

It is clear that skin color continues to matter universally: it matters in identity formation; it matters in politics and power relations; it matters in the everyday negotiations of institutional and social life. It is my contention that simply acknowledging racial minorities through multicultural legislation, policies, and practices is not enough to instigate shifts in the sociocultural perceptions of the majority of people. What I am talking about here is a way of beginning to undo the psychological damage of exclusion[22] at a very fundamental level and construct a new or alternative set of body skin-color norms to represent images of success, belonging, and inclusivity.[23] Multiracial beauty norms would enable children with darker skins to grow up with fewer chances of developing a "color complex,"[24] or longing for a lighter complexion.

Conceptually, I would like to introduce the notion of "cognitive equity"[25] — that is, a new way of understanding racial equity issues that does not *only*

Lorna Roth

revolve around statistics, legislation, or access to institutions. Rather, it directly inscribes a vision of *multicultural* and *multiracial* equity directly *into* the material underside of technologies and products, as well as in their emergent practices. This is a concept in progress, which I am exploring more deeply by examining the decision discourses around organizational skin color adjustments, industry policies, and racial minority–initiated visual decolonization processes. Is there some sense of a drive toward cognitive equity that is behind the color adjustment process? Or are corporations engaging in the exercise for the sake of appearing to be "politically correct," as so much of the media coverage of these issues tends to focus on? Unlike affirmative action and legislative tools, cognitive equity cannot be measured and circumscribed in social science or statistical terms, because it cannot yet make comparable claims for social justice. Rather, it is an enabling socialization process that aims to open up narrow distorted cognitive foundations to close scrutiny and replace them with more appropriate normative ranges. These ranges can, in turn, establish facilitative conditions for the development of a more democratically and chromatically pluralistic society. The target of cognitive equity goes beyond the repair mode of design, which encompasses "fitting or camouflaging" minorities into already existing values of whiteness, such as painting Caucasian-featured mannequins black or yellow to symbolically appear "ethnic."[26] I believe that the potential new building blocks of cognitive equity will be located in small and subtle changes in our taken-for-granted perceptions and behaviors, resulting from an *active demand* for a wider range of sociotechnical imagined possibilities for inclusiveness.

What factors and motives are underlying the movement for new visual technology development? Who is driving this demand? I am reminded here of Van Rooy's comment noted earlier in this essay on how skin-tone reproduction is more about the psychology of how people *want* to look rather than just science. This is a slightly different matter from *whether* people desire to be seen and invites questions about *who is being watched* and *how they are viewed* as governments and companies further embrace surveillance technologies. In societies driven by profit motives, statistics, and surveillance, for social justice reasons it is particularly important to pay attention to the coexistent demands of those (some of whom are disenfranchised) who wish to be aesthetically and satisfactorily pictured in their own domains of life.

In this essay, I begin from the perspective of aesthetic justice and of breaking open or disconnecting the carceral default of light-skin algorithms embedded in the visual apparatuses and ensemble of practices produced by image capture industries. The disruptive recoding suggested by me would enable cognitive equity development by deleting prefixed color codes and replacing them with a more appropriate continuum or range of skin color norms that in the past would have been invisible. These represent what I would label "the new normal."

The dual-skin contour camera feature, which can color balance two highly contrasting skin tones within the same image, comes closer to a technology opening that would enable cognitive equity than any other I have seen to date. This is more than an incremental step in creating inclusive representational practices designed into the technology itself; it is a leap forward, initiated quietly from outside the mainstream geographies of the visual industries.

LIBERATORY (NONDISCRIMINATORY) DESIGN MATTERS

One would assume that when digital cameras entered the prosumer/consumer marketplace, the problems of using the single Shirley as the "normal flesh tone" for various practices around skin-color calibrations would have been outdated, bypassed, or surmounted, especially with the introduction of the multiracial norm reference cards. That was not always the case. Explicit recognition of the diversity of photo subjects was not a consideration in camera design or lab practices until the mid-nineties. Even then, and until very recently, there has been a period of experiments and test cameras that failed consumer tests and demonstrated serious lacunae in the designers' vision of a prototype camera. Take, for example, the Hewlett-Packard (HP) webcam, launched in 2009, that claimed to be able to detect and track faces. When it began to be tested by a diversity of consumers, it became apparent that it could only recognize light-skinned faces and did not respond at all to those with darker skins.[27] In 2010, Nikon's Coolpix S630 also failed to recognize Asian consumers, who had to respond to a pop-up message of "Did someone blink?" every time they used its face-detection software (see figure 12.12). In May 2015, Google embarrassingly apologized for its app auto tags, which identified dark-skinned people as "gorillas" (see figure 12.13).

And in 2016 there began a controversy involving Instagram in which some had argued that the platform had skewed its optional filters to accommodate the widespread perception that whiteness is still the dominant aesthetic norm of preference. While this criticism is still widely circulating, in China, a very popular app called Meitu offers users three options to lighten their skin: "whiten," "cool," or "warm" (see figure 12.14).

In all but one of these cases,[28] the central problematic issue does not lie in a technological constraint so much as in a lack of imagination as to who the

FIGURE 12.12. Did someone blink? The digital photography era continues to generate embarrassing situations; e.g., in 2010 a Nikon camera had difficulty distinguishing facial features. Located on the web at: Did Someone Blink? Joz Wang Collection.

FIGURE 12.13. Google's "gorillas." In 2015, Google publicly apologized after its new automated photo classification app identified two African Americans as gorillas. Located on the web at https://boingboing.net/2018/01/11/gorilla-chimp-monkey-unpersone.html.

FIGURE 12.14. Image of Chinglin Pang and Li Mo, about to be color-adjusted using the app "Meitu." Photo credit: Lorna Roth, 2017; Kunming, China.

imaging products' potential users would be, along with a matched recognition of their skin tone diversity embedded in the algorithms used to control their visual outcomes. Furthermore, the choice of test populations obviously shows a deficit in the range of flesh colors selected to train the algorithm to recognize certain diverse features. How these products could be launched without adequate testing in an ethnically diverse global market is a concrete indication of the racial attitudes of their designers and manufacturers.

On the other hand, each of these visual industry brands, in its own way, gestures to an underlying assumption that the "color complex" is still driving the design choices financed by the manufacturers. Given the popularity of skin bleach creams and treatments around the world, perhaps indeed they are reading the consumer market accurately.[29] Let us briefly conjecture about this. In the cases of the HP laptop's face detection and tracking camera (which doesn't see darker skins) and Nikon's face-recognition lens (which considers Asian users' eyes closed and not ready to be photographed), the assumption that the user would be light-skinned with Caucasian features is deeply (almost secretly) embedded within the technology. Unless they wanted to explicitly target a particular demographic market, this would

Lorna Roth

suggest a narrow or naïve business view on the part of the technology creators and their supervisors. Were these errors caused by a lack of sufficient foreground lighting to see contrast on the faces of those with darker skin tones, as was explained by HP public relations representatives? Although that is an important consideration, I suspect the reasons are more complex than this. Google's misidentification of African Americans as "gorillas," is just plain insulting and racist, obviously so labeled by someone of lighter skin tone. However, the evidence that strongly suggests that their products are targeted to those who believe in the "color complex" is much more obvious in Instagram's, FaceApp's, and Meitu's social media software, which, in their design features, offer explicit skin lightening options from which users can choose their preferred skin color aesthetic, their favorite *look of skin color for themselves*. Instagram's initial filters represented a much more subtle way of addressing those who favor light skin tones. Instagram and FaceApp obfuscated in their response to the public's claim of their favoring a white-skin bias in their spectrum of filter options, explaining the error by noting that it was caused by an "unfortunate side-effect of the underlying neural network caused by the training set bias, not intended behavior."[30] The most forthright software of the illustrative examples I am using is the Meitu product as it makes no effort to hide what it is marketing. Through knowledge of skin preference test results data that it no doubt has had access to, it caters to the Asian market's cultural and aesthetic interest in *looking* as fair and pale as possible.

Has the "color complex" become so internalized internationally that skin-lightening software has become a new home-based standard for editing or transforming selfie imagery? There is an embedded moral issue here as well as one of implicit and explicit costs.

Interestingly, in analog imagery, skin-color adjustments were demanded within a context of market concerns, as in the case of Kodak's response to complaints about too narrow a dynamic range of browns to mark the differences between dark and light chocolate and wood grains. Within the digital media sphere, it happened more frequently as civil rights movement advocates became more powerful and vocal over time. The public outcry of potential consumers, as is evident in these cases of faulty design and marketing errors, is now the most common driving force catalyzing advances in quality control over skin-tone rendition. As noted in my research examples, in most cases, skin-color adjustments are seldom initiated by the manufacturers themselves, with the odd exception of forward-looking manufacturers such as Philips (Breda, Holland). Mostly, changes take place in response to consumer feedback that identifies failed and incomplete visions of how the technologies could work most effectively and inclusively.

It is here that my work converges with that of the other essays in this collection. It is paradoxical that the detachment of the carceral algorithms from the emulsions and infrastructures within the tools of the visual industries at the same time opens up the possibility of more accurate renditions, not only for those whose motives are aesthetic documentation of personal events, family portraits, and societal images marking special moments in a lifetime, but also for institutions of power to more easily detect, identify, and track peoples of darker skin colors with greater ease for surveillance and incarceration purposes. Faulty and limited technologies with poorly designed algorithms are often more in the interest of those who may wish to remain anonymous. Yet we all want to capture memorable moments, to document our own beauty and the beauty of others in our lives—complete with all of our fine bodily and facial features visible and ready to be published in the school yearbook or shared via social media to attract as many "likes" as possible. These interests present a challenging set of tensions and complications.

My main focus in this essay has been a concern with the failure of image-capture technologies to sensitively reflect and recognize a full dynamic range of skin tones so as to render cross-cultural populations aesthetically. This omission has marked a failure of recognition as well as an opening that, once addressed, may offer a bridge toward finding cognitive equity. But it is important to remember the broader international, political, economic, and sociocultural contexts within which photography, cinematography, television, computer technology, and other media forms institutionally frame the multiple visual territories within which we function in our daily lives. The co-existence and relationship of amateur, commercial, and professional image makers and those whose professional interest and practice relate to policing and identity surveillance might be a rather interesting area to further investigate in the future. The history of the push and pull over whether or not to create algorithms that favor one or the other's interests would make for a challenging research project. Where is the meeting point between the fine features of surveillance and other more aesthetic forms of image making?

CHANGING IMAGINARIES, CHANGING DESIGNS

Clearly, technologies cannot in and of themselves be racist. They are created by people who have framed and prefixed their infrastructure and underside by economic and cultural design decisions. And the trajectory of skin-tone

Lorna Roth

reproduction in digital media imagery is a continuation of that which began with analog Shirley cards—they were the first instance of a color-balance template, and they fixed in place a mental image of what became an ideal international standard of the "normal" for the long term. This normal has represented the early limit of the carceral imaginary in relation to the development of visual technologies.

Were the technical designers who worked within this limited imaginary racist? Rather than be conspiratorial, I would prefer to take a more nuanced position by suggesting they had a low level of awareness around the representations of race embedded in their practices. When these designers became more aware of the troubling implications of their decisions within the African American community, color adjustment strategies began to evolve to address existing barriers to equity. This is an example of what Joyce King has labeled "dysconscious racism,"[31] by which she refers to a form of racism that "tacitly accepts dominant white norms and privileges. Dysconscious racism is not the absence of consciousness, but an impaired consciousness or distorted way of thinking about race as compared to, for example, critical consciousness."[32] It is much like an occasional, but passing, consciousness of the subtle racial implications embedded in practices, objects, institutions, and policies, and it represents "an uncritical habit of mind (including perceptions, attitudes, assumptions, and beliefs) that justifies inequity and exploitation by accepting the existing order of things as given."[33] Dysconsciousness is a semiconsciousness of both overt (open, explicit) and inferential (latent) aspects of racism, although it tends to operate more frequently in the context of the latter. By this I mean that it is linked to those apparently naturalized representations of events and situations relating to race, whether "factual" or "fictional," which have racist premises and propositions inscribed in them as a set of unquestioned assumptions. These enable racist statements to be formulated without ever bringing into awareness the racist predicates on which the statements are grounded.[34]

The invisibility and the silences about race and racism in society become most apparent when a contrasting presence comes into our consciousness. It is then that we realize our blind spots. Stuart Hall notes the difficulty of developing a theory and methodology that would teach us to attend not to what people say about race, but rather to what we do not say about it.[35] I would extend this to attend to what is not visibly specified about race, such as the assumption of the whiteness norm and the small shifts being quietly undertaken in the boardrooms and labs of corporations to accommodate pressures to become more inclusive in their production processes and marketing practices. Although they appear to be insignificant initially, these silences and absences inform and frame our knowledge of race relations at this stage of history. If a society is driven by representation, as Jean-Louis Comolli suggests—that is, if the social machine manufactures representations—it also manufactures itself from representations, the latter operative at once as means, matter, and condition of sociality.[36] We, as subjects, are formed through specific cultural and racial modes of visuality. Jan Nederveen Pieterse argues that "the single most important feature of representations of otherness is the role they play in establishing and maintaining social inequality."[37] If the histories of a variety of skin-tone technologies and products make Pieterse's point apparent, I believe that this state of affairs is attributable largely to the absence of a strong technical foundation enabling the public development and dissemination of multicultural and multiracial images, representations, and products. My research goal is precisely this: to explore the history and current possibilities for the foundations of a collective, anti-racist common sense to guide the (re)design of our technologies and products of color. In itself, this is not enough to provoke deep cognitive change, but as a complement to anti-racist institutional and legislative measures in democratic societies, it may stimulate a revision of our existing technological infrastructure and practices.

OPENING THE FIELD TO COGNITIVELY EQUITABLE POSSIBILITIES

In my research, I have studied and challenged some backroom decision-making processes and practices of technical enterprises whose policies initially established parity-impeding cultural norms.[38] Further, I have attempted to examine the cultural values that have limited accurate skin-color rendering in the past and am arguing for their replacement with enabling mechanisms such as the ones I am suggesting in my notion of cognitive equity. Like Fraser's, my work "focuses attention on the social arrangements where the technical and racial barriers to accurate portrayal are located, rather than restricting attention exclusively to the domain of cultural representation."[39]

How our everyday technologies and visual products function, who and what they favor and ignore, and how changes in them become acceptable have been colored by the assumptions, reference points, and invisible norms of the cultural and financial intermediaries involved in decisions about their design and marketing. Intermediaries, most of whom have been Caucasian men, have populated backroom labs and boardrooms of technical enter-

Lorna Roth

prises until the recent past, and it is they who have *channeled and encoded* these patterns of embedded cultural norms *through* their products into the dominant cultural and visual regimes of representation. It is they who chose (consciously or unconsciously) to create liberatory or carceral design frameworks. These, in turn, have acted as implicit pedagogical tools for circumscribing our visual perspectives. Embedded in our worldviews, these templates can enable or constrain the development of an anti-racist common sense to guide our visual perceptions of what diversity means in a given society.

It is timely to argue for a new way of considering and understanding the visual industries through the lens of cognitive (racial and cultural) equity. By directly inscribing an algorithmic vision of full-spectrum flesh-tone equity *into* the various technological apparatuses and practices surrounding visual media, an *alternative* set of embedded skin-color norms could trigger more equitable and liberatory representations of success, beauty, and belonging.

To accompany relevant technical and algorithmic changes in visual apparatuses, gadgetry, and practices, I would propose a global recognition of new normative and performative standards addressing such issues as: How will the selection of ethnically and racially diverse consumer test subjects be chosen, and who will be among those involved in key decision-making processes about the refashioning of technical norms; in what better ways could current cross-cultural marketing and education strategies be rethought; and how could the reconception of a new, more inclusive policy vocabulary open up the field to a greater range of creative and cognitively equitable possibilities and opportunities in the visual industries. The consequences of these interventions might bring some people intimately closer to the goal of achieving cognitive equity.

Making skin visible through universal, nondiscriminatory design is not only a moral goal but is also an intelligent strategy. Regrettably, the carceral limits to our design imaginaries have been so deeply rooted/routed in our personal cognitive frameworks that modifications of image-capture apparatuses and visual codes will only likely be the initial step in creating a liberatory technology, terminology, and ensemble of practices. Refashioning the "new normal" would necessitate the ability to render the full range of flesh tones inside cameras, and associated visual technologies, reference cards, and studio/field practices. This would involve complicated changes in organizational and production structures, forward-thinking design objectives, new professional practices, and a generous budget for both failed and successful product manufacturing. I am encouraged that this "new normal" matters to more and more people, as seen in their critical web reactions to HP's, Nikon's, and Google's failures to accurately recognize diverse facial characteristics. The perception and critical outcry by the public regarding these problematic technologies are signs that the new sociocultural normal is transforming into a visual value and perhaps even an emerging social order around issues of diversity.

Skinvisible modifications would subtly make apparent the changed codes of the designers in the design, but they will not automatically have immediate impact on the public's psychosocial cognitive frameworks. An improvement over existing technologies does not, in itself, ensure a change in cognitive values, the elimination of the "color complex," or more equitable representation in various public spheres. This depends on what human beings do with the technology, of course; particularly in the context of this book, questions come to mind regarding how skinvisible modifications can also be (and have been) put to use as a more precise technical mode of surveilling and policing populations. Evidently, there will never be any guarantees of a singularly positive outcome to the socio-technical color adjustments I am recommending. Equity is a very complex issue, especially when applied to visual rendition and representational challenges such as those described in this essay. It can never be taken for granted. Formal, embedded recognition of diversity as the new normal emergent from the notion of cognitive equity does not equal power, but it may move us away from the "historical fixtures" of our thinking about the rules, roles, and uses of color image making in our lives.[40] Reesa Greenberg (independent curator and scholar) noted upon reading about my notion of cognitive equity that it refers to "a state where stereotypes, however unconscious, have been eliminated from the moment of inscription, so that they can no longer be repeated."[41]

Time and visual exposure to a more dynamic, less stereotypical range of algorithmic test sets, flesh colors, and populations, including children, will hopefully move us closer to the evolution of international skin-tone standards within the visual industries as they become more consistently aligned with the new normal. This is the least we can expect in the near future.

Acknowledgments
Many thanks to Thierry Le Brun for his stimulating discussions and feedback about this work and for his support of this project over the years; and to Trish Audette-Longo for her critical eye and thoughtfulness in her feedback and preliminary editing process. Thanks also to the Social Sciences and Humanities Research Council of Canada (SSHRC) and to Concordia University in Montreal for their generous financial support at the beginning of this research project.

Lorna Roth

Notes

This chapter is a modified and updated version of several previous publications and presentations: Lorna Roth, "Looking at Shirley, the Ultimate Norm: Color Balance, Image Technologies, and Cognitive Equity," *Canadian Journal of Communication* 34, no. 1 (2009): 111–36; Lorna Roth, "Face Value, Skin Color and Intelligent Technologies," *Gerard Reteiglezing 25th Jubilee Lecture* presented at the National Multicultural Television Network, Amsterdam, February 17, 2010; Lorna Roth, "Bodies by Design: Hey, Look! They Painted That White Girl Black," presented at *The Body Eclectic: Exploring the Diversity of Bodily Being Conference* held at Thompson Rivers University Gallery, Kamloops, BC, March 11–13, 2016; Lorna Roth, "Questão de Pele," *Zum Magazine* 10 (2016) ([originally published in Portuguese]; English translation, "A Matter of Skin," located at https://revistazum.com.br/en/revista-zum-10/questao-de-pele/).

1. Kathy Russell, Midge Wilson, and Ronald Hall, *The Color Complex (Revised): The Politics of Skin Color in a New Millennium* (New York: Anchor Books, 2013).

2. Lorna Roth, "Looking at Shirley, the Ultimate Norm: Color Balance, Image Technologies, and Cognitive Equity," *Canadian Journal of Communication* 34, no. 1 (2009): 111–36.

3. Ron E. Hall, "The Bleaching Syndrome: Implications of Light Skin for Hispanic American Assimilation," *Hispanic Journal of Behavioral Sciences* 16, no. 3 (1994): 405–18. See also Hall, "The Bleaching Syndrome: African Americans' Response to Cultural Domination vis-à-vis Skin Color," *Journal of Black Studies* 26, no. 2 (1995): 172–84.

4. Jan Kasoff, author interviews, New York, November 20, 1994, and February 15, 2016.

5. Kasoff, author interview, November 1994.

6. Syreeta McFadden, "Teaching the Camera to See My Skin: Navigating Photography's Inherited Bias against Dark Skin," *Buzzfeed*, April 2, 2014, www.buzzfeed.com/syreetamcfadden/teaching-the-camera-to-see-my-skin.

7. McFadden, "Teaching the Camera to See My Skin: Navigating Photography's Inherited Bias against Dark Skin."

8. Earl Kage, author interview, Rochester, NY, August 21, 1995; Richard Wien, author interview, Rochester, NY, August 18, 1997.

9. Kage, author interview, August, 1995.

10. At the end of 2016, I discovered a second multiracial Shirley card with the same three women pictured on it as on the first, but as far as I know, it was not as widely circulated as the one I have shown here in figure 12.7.

11. Wien, author interview, August 1997.

12. Hall, "The Bleaching Syndrome: Implications of Light Skin for Hispanic American Assimilation," and "The Bleaching Syndrome: African Americans' Response to Cultural Domination vis-à-vis Skin Color."

13. Hall, "The Bleaching Syndrome: Implications of Light Skin for Hispanic American Assimilation" and "The Bleaching Syndrome: African Americans' Response to Cultural Domination vis-à-vis Skin Color."

14. Kenneth Clark, *Prejudice and Your Child* (Boston: Beacon Press, 1955).

15. See also birgitvanhout, "Black Doll White Doll," *YouTube*, 2007, accessed December 30, 2017, https://www.youtube.com/watch?v=ybDa0gSuAcg; CNN, "A Look at Race Relations through a Child's Eyes," *YouTube*, 2012, accessed December 30, 2017, https://www.youtube.com/watch?v=GPVNJgfDwpw; and Yosemite CCD, "The Barbie Doll Test," *YouTube*, 2009, accessed December 30, 2017, https://www.youtube.com/watch?v=YOHbtM9463c.

16. Toru (Tom) Hasegawa, author interview, New York, May 27, 1996.

17. Brian Harris, author interview, Washington, DC, July 3, 1997.

18. Thierry Le Brun, author interview, Montreal, Quebec, November 27, 2006.

19. Franco Vaccari, *La photographie et l'inconscient technologique* (Paris: Créatis, 1981).

20. Vito Campanelli, "Technological Unconscious," *Streaming Egos, Digital Identities* (blog), Goethe Institute, 2015, accessed December 30, 2017, http://blog.goethe.de/streamingegos/archives/76-Technological-Unconscious.html.

21. Vaccari, as quoted in Campanelli, *Streaming Egos, Digital Identities* (blog), http://blog.goethe.de/streamingegos/archives/76-Technological-Unconscious.html

22. Frantz Fanon, *Black Skin, White Masks* (New York: Grove Press, 1967).

23. Roth, "Looking at Shirley, the Ultimate Norm."

24. Russell, Wilson, and Hall, *The Color Complex (Revised)*.

25. Roth, "Looking at Shirley, the Ultimate Norm."

26. Lorna Roth, "Bodies by Design: Hey, Look! They Painted That White Girl Black," presented at The Body Eclectic: Exploring the Diversity of Bodily Being Conference held at Thompson Rivers University Gallery, Kamloops, BC, March 11–13, 2016.

27. See Wzamen01, "HP Computers Are Racist," *YouTube*, 2009, accessed December 30, 2017, https://www.youtube.com/watch?v=t4DT3tQqgRM.

28. Meitu, which imagines a nonwhite user wanting to appear with a lighter complexion, provides the appropriate algorithm to explicitly accomplish this. Following is an excerpt from their patent, explaining their technical methods: "The present invention provides a fast face beautifying method for digital images. Gaussian blur is performed to an original image to extract a green channel value, which is then subject to linear light blending and hard light blending, and a blended green channel value is recalculated. Meanwhile, skin recognition and whitening are performed to the original image, and finally, by using a product of the recalculated green channel value by a probability obtained by skin recognition as a transparency, transparency blending is performed to the original image and the whitened image to compose a beautified image. Moreover, by performing skin recognition to the original image, black pixels will be prevented from being processing [*sic*] by an algorithm, so that hairs, eyes, and other non-skin parts will be prevented from being processing [*sic*]. Consequently, the final effect of beautification will become better and more natural." Wei Zhang, Songlin Fu, and Changding Zhang, *Fast Face Beautifying Method for Digital Images*, US Patent 9501843B2 filed March 24, 2016, and issued November 22, 2016.

29. Hall, *The Bleaching Syndrome*, 1994, 1995.

30. Josie Griffith, "Losing Face: What Is FaceApp, What Were the 'Race Change' Filters and Has the App Been in [sic] Accused of Racism Before?," August 10, 2017, accessed January 14, 2018, https://www.thesun.co.uk/tech/3410186/faceapp-selfie-app -race-change-filters-change/.

31. Joyce E. King, "Dysconscious Racism: Ideology, Identity, and the Miseducation of Teachers," in *Racism: Essential Readings*, ed. E. Cashmore and J. Jennings (London: SAGE, 2001): 295–303.

32. Joyce King, *Racism: Essential Readings*, 295.

33. King, *Racism: Essential Readings*, 296.

34. Stuart Hall, "The Whites of Their Eyes: Racist Ideologies and the Media," in *The Media Reader*, ed. M. Alvarado and J. O. Thompson (London: British Film Institute, 1990): 13.

35. Stuart Hall, "Race, Culture, and Communications: Looking Backward and Forward at Cultural Studies," *Rethinking Marxism* 5, no. 1 (1992): 10–18.

36. Jean-Louis Comolli, "Technique and Ideology: Camera, Perspective, Depth of Field," in *Film Reader 2*, ed. P. Erens and B. Horrigan (Evanston, IL: Northwestern University, 1977), 128–40; "Technique and Ideology: Camera, Perspective, Depth of Field (Parts 3 and 4)," in *Narrative, Apparatus, Ideology: A Film Theory Reader*, ed. P. Rosen, trans. Diana Matias with revisions by Marcia Butel and Philip Rosen (New York: Columbia University Press, 1986), 421–43; Jean-Louis Comolli and Jean Narboni, "Cinema/ ideology/criticism," trans. Susan Bennett, *Screen* 12, no. 1 (1971): 27–36; Comolli, and Narboni, "Cinema/ideology/criticism (2)," trans. Susan Bennett, *Screen* 12, no. 2 (1971): 145–55.

37. Jan Nederveen Pieterse, *White on Black: Images of Africa and Blacks in Western Popular Culture* (New Haven, CT: Yale University Press, 1992), 234.

38. Nancy Fraser, "Rethinking Recognition," *New Left Review* 3 (May–June, 2000), http://www.newleftreview.org/?view=2248.

39. Fraser, "Rethinking Recognition," 7.

40. Walter Benjamin, cited in Richard Kierney, in *Modern Movements in European Philosophy: Phenomenology, Critical Theory, Structuralism* (Manchester, UK: Manchester University Press, 1994), 151–68.

41. Reesa Greenberg, "Remembering Exhibitions: From Point to Line to Web," Tate Papers (autumn 2009).

13

Scratch a Theory,
You Find a Biography

A Conversation with Troy Duster

......

ALONDRA NELSON (AN): Let's begin at the beginning. Can you speak about your formative influences, particularly your family and your grandmother, the well-known journalist and antilynching activist, Ida B. Wells?

TROY DUSTER (TD): My grandmother only comes to me through family oral tradition. I was born after she died. I know my grandmother through my mother, Alfreda Duster, who, of course, spent part of her time in my grandmother's professional world. She was not just the daughter; she was also the person who, as a young child and later as a teenager, was with my grandmother at meetings. And she watched, over the years, as my grandmother became more and more of a public figure.

So I knew my grandmother through my mother's eyes. And they are, you can imagine, rather clear-eyed, but also fogged by family dynamics. The part that may be most relevant to our discussion is that my mother became quite skeptical of being a public figure. My mother saw up close what she regarded as the unfair and improper treatment of her mother by the media and by, as she called them, "envious males," who were in the orbit of this very articulate and powerful woman and began to find ways to undercut what Wells was doing by saying she was in it for her ego.

My mother used to say all the time: "If you plan to have a life in the public sphere, you should do the right thing because it's the right thing. Because if you do the right thing because you think you're going to get rewarded for it—don't even head down that road." Hovering over me for a good part of my life was this notion that you're not going to get rewarded

FIGURE 13.1.
Troy Duster. Photograph courtesy of
Nancy Rubin.

for being a nice guy or for doing politically engaging social justice activities. Indeed, the more effective you are, the more enemies you will make. The applause may come after you're dead. My grandmother is a figure in my life in the sense that she becomes—what shall I call it—not so much a measuring stick but a kind of symbolic representation of what it means to do good works and, in some sense, to be rewarded for it posthumously.

AN: When you were growing up, were others aware that you were Wells's grandson?

TD: One of my mother's brothers was an attorney who would go around town saying, "I'm the son of Ida B. Wells." My mother really disliked that. So we grew up with the following echo always in our ears: "If I ever catch you taking credit for your grandmother . . . that's your butt. She can be blamed for you, in some ways. But you take no credit for her." So I grew up, all of my youth, not denying that I was the grandson of Wells, but never saying anything. Never. Years later people ask me, "Well, why didn't you tell me?" And I would say, "Mother." [Laughter.] So no, it wasn't at the tip of my consciousness.

AN: Would you say that you had a privileged childhood?

TD: No, I grew up poor in Chicago. My mother, however, grew up in privilege, as the daughter of Wells, this rather well-known public figure. Also, her father and Wells's husband, Ferdinand Barnett, was a figure in his own right. He was an editor and publisher of a newspaper—the first black-owned newspaper, the *Chicago Conservator*.

Scratch a Theory, You Find a Biography   (309

My mother, Alfreda, went to the University of Chicago. She studied philosophy — she had a bachelor's degree in philosophy. She studied sociology with Robert Park and Ernest Burgess. (Here's where people get that retrospective reading. People like to reread the biography. They go back through your life history and say, "Of course, that was inevitable," when, in fact, it was happenstance. Given this, people think I was destined to become a sociologist. No, not at all!)

My father, Benjamin Duster, had a college degree. He went to Indiana State Normal. State Normal meant you could teach in a high school. My father had that degree, but he really didn't want to pursue a career as a teacher. He preferred to be a journeyman carpenter, a journeyman plumber — he did all kinds of odd jobs. He wasn't of the kind of background that my grandparents thought was appropriate for their darling daughter.

I grow up in poverty because the Great Depression hits; I'm born into it. By this time my father is unemployed and my mother has five children. My father had odd jobs, but not much in the way of income. My mother did inherit a little cottage on the South Side of Chicago — right in the middle of what was to become one of the city's more dramatically impoverished ghettos — Thirty-Second and Prairie. But here's the contradiction — there is economic poverty and there is "cultural capital."

AN: I wanted to ask you about this. We know from the work that Park and his students were doing and from Horace Cayton and St. Clair Drake's important book *Black Metropolis* that there was a significant black elite community in Chicago. You grew up in a family of limited means, but did you have cultural capital by virtue of being Wells's grandson?

TD: My mother was not a part of the black elite. She had been booted out of the black elite community because of her marriage to my father, this journeyman carpenter and plumber.

AN: But is one ever fully "booted out" of elite status?

TD: My mother would have said yes. Alfreda did not have contact with black elites in Chicago until many years later, when she edited and published my grandmother's autobiography, *Crusade for Justice*. Then there was a reentry; there was a welcome. People would say, "Oh, there is our long-lost sister!" [Laughter.] But no, my mother would have said that she was not exactly welcome in black elite circles and that she did not actually aspire to that.

AN: When your mother, Alfreda, attended the University of Chicago, she was one of four blacks on the campus. Had Chicago's racial climate changed

Alondra Nelson and Troy Duster

significantly by the time you entered high school and college? For example, did you attend an integrated high school?

TD: My high school, Wendell Phillips High School, was integrated by Frank Wong. He was the only nonblack person in my high school. There was some trauma in my schooling when at age sixteen I went across town to begin studies at Northwestern.

AN: This journey was not merely across town. Evanston, Illinois—where Northwestern is located—is pretty far from the South Side of Chicago, where you were living.

TD: Yes. Metaphorically and literally. I got a real culture shock at Northwestern. I was one of only seven black students and one of the few brown students at the entire university. Moreover, I thought everybody else at the university was "white." I did not realize until my first few months there that there were high levels of stratification inside the world of white people, that there was interethnic hostility between the Jewish people and the Italians and between the Irish and the English WASPs. My first week or two on campus, I'm visited by some student whom I read as white. He says to me, "Welcome to Northwestern. You know, we've got a lot in common." I'm thinking, "Say what? Have you got a history I don't know about?" He tells me that he's Jewish and that he and I share this common bond. This is my first understanding of the appreciation people are going to have about the internal differentiation among whites. Some have asked me, "Is that why you became a sociologist?—because, all of a sudden, you had to navigate a world that was completely different from the previous sixteen years of your life?" There's something to it. But I think it takes a different form, too. In the home, I spoke English as I'm speaking it now. On the streets of Chicago, on the other hand, I had to talk a kind of "jive" talk— the equivalent of hip-hop today. I had to do what I later learned was called "code switching." I did it instinctively because I had to survive, and so did my brothers and sister. But I probably dealt with this more than my siblings because there was more of a gang life when I was growing up than there was in their youth. I had to be able to deal, to get from my house to the school and back. I found myself walking a tightrope between these two worlds. I became bilingual, bicultural, bimodal. At one point, I was also the only black male at Northwestern who wasn't an athlete. Do you believe that?

AN: I do. Yes, I do.

TD: I used to be asked sometimes, "What position do you play?" "You're on a sports scholarship, right?" The assumption was I was either a football player or a basketball player. I also used to get stopped by the police in Evanston, especially in the evenings. One night one came up to me, and he said, "What are you doing here?" I said, "I'm a student." "What are you studying?" I had just taken this philosophy course, so I said, "Moral philosophy." He said, "Oh, who are you reading?" I said, "Nietzsche and Kierkegaard." He goes back to his police car and lets me alone. About a month later the same situation occurs: the same police officer and his buddy stop me. The buddy says, "What are you doing?" The officer I had encountered before says, "Oh, he's okay. He's into moral philosophy," and laughs. I became known to the Evanston police as this black who wasn't really an athlete.

AN: Were you a sociology major at Northwestern?

TD: No, I had majored in journalism. Journalism for me was what I imagined as a boondoggle: "Am I really going to get paid someday to go out and do what I really want to do, to write?" In my high school I had been editor of the school newspaper, and I did a lot of writing and I enjoyed it. So I get to college and I say, "Okay, what I'm going to do is end up being either a sportswriter and go to all of these games for free, get paid to go out and see these games, . . . or I'll be an international columnist, I'll fly around the world, I'll write about what I think is important." I had childlike aspirations about journalism. What I learned quickly is that editors put you on a beat that's really boring. For example, you'd go to city hall every day and check out the log to see who'd been arrested. So I became quickly disabused of newspaper journalism.

I moved on to radio and television journalism in my third year at Northwestern. I was in the backdrop, writing over and over again the material for the talent. "Talent" was used in those days, and still is in some corners now, as "the voice of . . ." on the radio, or "the face of . . ." on television. That's the talent. It was clear in 1956–57 that I was never going to be the talent. It was like in Mexico or Brazil today, where you just don't find black people as the public face of the media. So I say to myself, "What am I doing? Do I want to spend my life in the back of these newsrooms writing up this stuff? I don't think so." And then in my last year in college, there was a clear event that transformed me away from journalism, and, well, I backed into sociology.

AN: So you came to sociology through the "backdoor"—to borrow from the title of one of your books.

TD: I backed into sociology. I didn't come in saying, "Hey, I'm going to be a sociologist." I think this is true for a lot of people. Here's the event: In my

Alondra Nelson and Troy Duster

last spring of my senior year, there is a big accident on the elevated train. A motorman makes a mistake. There are about twenty serious injuries. The media arrive and they are able to talk to the motorman because the metal has cut into his thigh in such a way that he can't get out. He's just trapped in there. While the police and paramedics get devices to get the motorman out, the media sticks a mic in front of his face. They ask him, "How does it feel? What happened? . . ."

At the time, I was taking a class with a guy named Whitman, the head of NBC news in the area. The next day, he tells our class, of about twenty-five people, that the NBC reporter refused to interview the motorman. CBS went in and got the story. So did ABC. Whitman said that was a dark day for NBC journalism because these two guys from the other networks scooped them. He wanted this event to serve as a lesson to all of us students to just put ideology aside, put everything aside except journalism. Get in and get the story.

There were three of us in the class who disagreed strenuously—my two roommates and me. Three of us—out of twenty-five students—were weighing in that there are other values to consider. Do news events happen in order to be reported, or is there something else going on? Whitman began to get angry with us. We were brash and young, and we were, in our own ways, arrogant in our moral superiority. But we were making a strong argument. And whatever argument he put up, we would counter it. Whitman got red in the face, and he said, "If that's your view, get out of journalism and get out soon." All of three of us left journalism within the next two months.

I told this story to Ray Mack, a professor of sociology at Northwestern. He was very young, only in his late twenties. He and I were friends. I came to know Ray because I had done well in his Race Relations class. Ray says, "Come to sociology. Go down the hall and see Wendell Bell." I had taken a class from Bell three years earlier and had gotten one of the better grades, and so he knew who I was. I went to see Bell. He was leaving Northwestern. He said to me, "I'm going to UCLA [the University of California, Los Angeles] next semester. Just apply for a teaching assistantship and you can come too. It's a done deal."

AN: When you were planning to speak with Ray about what had transpired in the journalism course, did you have the sense that he was going to appreciate your position because he was a sociologist?

TD: No doubt about it. He was also a kind of senior mentor, someone whom I could talk to about all of these issues. In my last year at Northwestern, he and I were on a university committee together around race issues on campus and a controversy surrounding a Chinese American student named Sherman Wu. Wu pledged a university fraternity, and they accepted him. However, the national body said that he could not join the fraternity and threatened to kick the Northwestern chapter out of the organization if Wu remained in the chapter. It became such a public issue that Pete Seeger, the songwriter, wrote "The Ballad of Sherman Wu." So Ray and I had been colleagues, friends, coworkers, coconspirators, co-political, quite independent of academic stuff. I [would] go and talk to him about any topic. He would quickly say to me, "You know, you're actually a sociologist. You don't know it, but you are."

AN: So you are at UCLA in the late 1950s. Was sociology a new department?

TD: In the fall of 1957, I find myself in Los Angeles, you know, in the never-never land, after living twenty years in Chicago. All of a sudden I'm a teaching assistant, although I don't even have a degree yet. I'm teaching in a department of sociology, about which I know not a damn thing. But I'm at UCLA because of, you know, the old boys' network.

The department was founded in the late 1940s. Leonard Broom was the chair in its early phases. He had been the senior mentor to Wendell Bell, John Kitsuse, Sheldon Messinger, and a few other figures in the field. Phil Selznick was also there, before he moved to Berkeley. Now the real intellectual journey begins, because at UCLA, for the first time, I think of myself, and my work in a way that constitutes a trajectory. Up until UCLA, I'm floundering around.

Everything changes after I get to UCLA. I think I know about discrimination. I think I know about race relations. I don't know a damn thing. You know why?

AN: Because you had lived in a homogeneous black world for most of your life?

TD: Yes, I lived with black people all my early life. And then, only white people. And all the white people were on a college campus. And they thought of me as a charming mascot. "Here's Lucky. Speak, Lucky!" "Look at this charming boy. Nothing to be afraid of here. He talks like us." The highest compliment to be given to me by the white students was, "Actually, we didn't know you were black." All-black scene, first sixteen years; I go to college for four years, where it's an all-white scene. But I don't experience real discrimination in that period. Sure, I can't go to the barbershop; I can't go to the bowling alley. But that's life as usual. There's no trauma for me in that because I can leave Northwestern, take the subway and be back

Alondra Nelson and Troy Duster

on the South Side of Chicago in twenty-five minutes. Can't get a haircut in Evanston; can't get one anywhere? I can go back to Chicago's South Side. Want to listen to music? I go to Chicago's South Side. In other words, for me, life is still back in the black community. The four years at college were like an anthropological or cultural excursion.

When I get to UCLA, my eyes are opened. First of all, there wasn't much of a black community near UCLA. That's the first surprise. Then I go out and I try to get an apartment—a reality check. So for the first four months in Los Angeles, I'm living with my uncle, Herman. I've been looking and looking for an apartment. My uncle asks, "How's it going?" I say, "I can't get an apartment." He says, "Wake up and smell the coffee, young man. Where did you think you were?" [Laughter.]

So I get a wake-up in the public sphere in Los Angeles. Then there's school. I'm in class with really giant intellectual figures, who have an understanding of the world that so meshes in an easy and fluid way with my view of the world that I figure, now I understand. The two major figures are Harold Garfinkel [the renowned ethnomethodologist] and William S. Robinson [the influential statistician]. Why would these characters, who are so completely different, have such a resonance with me in my first year of graduate school? Well, Robinson was a methodologist. But he was the most unbelieving methodologist that you could ever imagine. He taught advanced statistics; he knew this stuff backwards and forwards. He would always say to us, you know there are far too many variables to control for what might be really happening in social life. . . . It wasn't as though we were talking to someone who was a humanist, who was putting down methods. We were talking to someone who knew methods. He would tell us stories about how Paul Lazarsfeld would run his datasets. Lazarsfeld might be told, "You've run the data in the wrong direction. It goes this way." And he'd say, "Okay, okay." Then he'd turn it around and get the opposite interpretation. So I grew up with Robinson's quantitative skills being used to debunk the notion that methods were the salvation and the answer—

AN: Or at least a very healthy irreverence for the statistical reduction of social life.

TD: A healthy irreverence, yes! At the same time, I was taking classes with Garfinkel. What Garfinkel was saying that deeply resonated with me was, in effect, "It ain't necessarily so. . . . What you see on the surface of social life is fragile, it's fluid; it can change like that." This insight was useful for thinking about the race riots of the 1960s. Or, later on, Sarajevo: people had lived next to each other for twenty, thirty, forty years, and then, boom, something could happen. People who had been friends, or actually in the same family together, could turn on each other on a dime. It resonated with me that social life is fragile and much more intricate than we can perceive. Garfinkel talks about this in his earlier works. He was talking about how the assumptions that are deeply embedded in human experience are not available, except they are also on the surface. There is this contradiction.

One of Garfinkel's buddies was Erving Goffman. Goffman used to come to UCLA in those years—the late fifties. Erving took a tiny bit of liking to me—but [was] always jocular; [we] never [had] a serious conversation. It was always, "Well, young man, I see that you've come this far, and let's see where you're going. . . ." The difference between Goffman and Garfinkel was astonishing to me. Garfinkel had students like groupies. His charisma was extraordinary. They often didn't last because, like groupies, there's a love relationship. And it gets too close; it gets sullied, and then, boom, in the turn of a pin, the turn of a dime, you're gone. That was Garfinkel, but he had all kinds of students who loved him and hated him. Erving never had a student. He was the Lone Ranger of sociology.

AN: At UCLA things are starting to fall into place for you intellectually. It is the heyday of the race relations approach and ethnomethodology is ascendant. What other questions is the field of sociology grappling with at this time? What questions are you grappling with?

TD: Well, you're asking about the zeitgeist, and the zeitgeist is hard to capture. But I think you're onto something. It was a period in which sociology looked as if it were on the rise. [Robert K.] Merton was in his heyday. Parsons was in his heyday. And the field had a sense that making a difference in the world was almost inevitable. You got into a sociology department and you knew that whatever your work was on, whether it was prisons, education, medicine, or civil rights, it didn't matter what it was—sociology had a perspective, a voice that was being listened to around the world. Certainly, by the time Kennedy is elected in 1960, there is this notion that sociologists are going to be—like economists—

AN: Like economists today—

TD: That's right. Even then, economists had a collective voice, more than sociologists did. In some sense, political science did not have the coherence of sociology at this time, but it had its own high-profile practitioners. When I was in graduate school, sociology was seen as an intellectually viable, almost vanguard position on social justice issues. We were where the action was. It wasn't in political science. It wasn't in economics. We used to laugh at the idea that Chicago would really celebrate this young whippersnapper

Alondra Nelson and Troy Duster

coming up, Milton Friedman: "What? It's all about free markets? Are they crazy in Chicago?" That was a joke. Well, the joke was on us.

AN: Do you remember a particularly formative or influential course at UCLA?

TD: I took two or three courses from Garfinkel. One was a graduate course in ethnomethodology, in which I felt that I was way out of my league. I thought, "I don't know what these people are talking about." I'm in this seminar with Garfinkel. It's like I'm at a Ping-Pong match. But I'm not playing. I'm watching these players. And they are smart as hell. I've always thought so. I'm not in their league. I'm just trying to figure out what I can do in this league.

Some of the other people in Garfinkel's seminar were Egon Bittner and Aaron Cicourel, who had been at Cornell and came to UCLA just to work with Harold. In this seminar, there were all these figures who were senior to me. I was twenty-one. Bittner was, I think, thirty-seven. Bittner came back to sociology from philosophy. He had been in Buchenwald. I could sit at his feet and listen to the stories from Buchenwald from Egon. I was young; I didn't know anything about the world. Peter McHugh, who was at the time, I think, twenty-nine or thirty, had been working in Hollywood as a writer, left and came back to sociology. Cicourel came back to sociology after studying experimental psychology. In other words, not everybody around me in those years was a sociologist, but they were people who came to sociology because they had the sense that something was happening—that there was intellectually fermenting soil, where you could actually do a lot. That was the environment.

AN: And you moved from UCLA to Northwestern for your doctoral studies?

TD: Yes. Ray Mack sends me a letter. He says, "I've become the chair of the department. And I have a fellowship for you from the Ford Foundation." So I go back to Northwestern.

Scott Greer, a Northwestern sociology professor, once pulled me aside and told me something that he was right about, and I never forgot. In his thick southern drawl, he said, "Now let me tell you one thing, Troy. Be very careful what you choose to write your doctoral thesis on. It's a character-defining act. Whatever topic you choose, it's going to shape who you are for the next ten years and maybe twenty. It's going to take you at least twenty years to get out from under whatever it is you choose. So you better choose something you want to be." It was dramatic. But it sunk in.

So I said, "Okay, I'm going to do something I really want to do." I decided I was going to work on what I called "the social response to abnormality." It was about how members of families or people in the circle of the mentally ill deal with the illness. A very Garfinkelian idea, right? The mentally ill express certain kinds of behavior: the community normalizes it or shuns it, says, "I didn't see it," or comes forward and says, "This is a problem; you better take care of it. Get this person into some kind of a therapy." I decided that I was going to write about not mental illness per se but the social response to mental illness.

AN: What happened after you finished your dissertation?

TD: I took a post at UC Riverside. After I had been there about six months, I get a visit from a guy named Gaulden, a medical doctor and the head of Norco Corona—the California Rehabilitation Center for Narcotics. He comes into my office and says, "They tell me that you're the person who knows about control and deviance. Well, [California] Governor Pat Brown has set aside money for rehabilitation centers, and the mandate is that they must have a component of social research. Would you be willing to do this?" Initially, I say, "Well, it's not my area. I don't know much about drugs." But I twisted it around for a while in my mind and decided, "What's to lose? I'll go and spend two months. If it doesn't work out, I'll turn around and go the other way."

I am a young assistant professor at Riverside. I'm being offered this money to go and just hang out and learn something new. That's when I learned that you can become an expert on a topic pretty fast. I did about six months of reading. I read the whole history of nineteenth-century thought on drugs. Then [I] began interviewing inmates at Norco Corona. There were 350 people, many felons, who because they were heroin addicts got their sentences commuted to go to Norco Corona for a one- to ten-year commitment—a fluid incarceration.

AN: And Norco Corona was imagined as a research institute?

TD: Yes, more specifically, research about drugs. What's going on with drug addicts and how can you cure them. The whole institution was designed for therapeutic purpose.

It's sociology in the early sixties. It's the therapeutic community—so we're not criminalizing, penalizing; we're trying to find a way to help these people. This is before the so-called war on drugs. This is 1963. Nixon is not in power. Kennedy is. As you were asking at the very beginning of this exchange, what was the zeitgeist? The zeitgeist was, we're going to reframe the debate. We're going to change this whole discourse from criminalization to rehabilitation.

AN: On the face of it, this project was volitional. But, in fact, the prisoners were being offered, say, incarceration at Alcatraz for twenty years versus commitment to the Norco Corona facility for one to ten years?

Alondra Nelson and Troy Duster

TD: The problem was that many of them were there on misdemeanors; they could have been out in a year for a misdemeanor. But they chose Norco, because they thought it was a therapeutic community. Many of them had been there for two and three and four years and beyond, because the staff didn't think that they were appropriately rehabilitated.

AN: How long were you at UC Riverside?

TD: I wasn't there long. Riverside was a racist community. In this setting, anything I said was front-page news. No matter what I said, they would say, "Black Radical Professor Attacks America!" I wasn't anything resembling Bobby Seale, but I was portrayed as the Eldridge Cleaver of the region. I used to get hate mail and lots of death-threat phone calls.

In 1965 there is a meeting of the school board on race relations. I'm called upon by the black community and as a member of the local CORE [Congress of Racial Equality] chapter to give this talk about why Riverside can deal with racial issues and not have a Watts on our hands. The event was in a small auditorium; it was standing room only. It's a hot Faulkner night in August; the air is thick. About a third of the way through my talk, someone interrupts and says, "Who'd you come here with tonight?" I say, "I came here with my wife, who is from Sweden. Why don't you welcome her to the free world?" And I went on for maybe about a minute with this sardonic notion that, in America, I'm sure that she will receive a gracious reception. There was a loud groan in the audience. I knew I had gone too far.

Afterward, the death threats continued. It reached a point in the late fall of 1965 that things got really rough. My wife was a very engaged gardener; she had this great garden on the side of a hill. They began to dump garbage onto the garden. My wife was a trouper; she understood. But it escalated; the phone calls escalated. And then she began to be affected by it. It became taxing on my wife.

The university chancellor had gotten wind of this, and he called me into his office and said, "We'll give you a police escort, and we're willing to move you onto campus." I didn't want to live like that. Cicourel at Berkeley had also heard about this. He talked to Goffman; Burton Clark, who was at the Center for Studies in Higher Education; and a few others. They thought this was intolerable and invited me to move to Berkeley. In January 1966, I came to Berkeley to work at Clark's higher education center, and I also taught half-time in the Department of Sociology.

AN: Were the racial politics at UC Berkeley more bearable?

TD: Soon after I arrive at Berkeley, all hell breaks loose—it's called the sixties, the late sixties. Stuff is coming down. I mean, it's really coming down.

On the one hand, I'm heavily recruited by Huey [Newton] and the Black Panthers. Huey and I have mutual friends, such as Fay Stender, who was the attorney for George Jackson and very much involved with the Panthers. She and I were friends. And Fay and Huey were close, let's say. She was later the target of an assassination attempt, and after being shot by Edward Glenn Brooks and left partially paralyzed, she committed suicide. [David] Horowitz is the key. He sets up my meeting with Huey. In those years he's a leftist, an unreconstructed leftist. So he raised the idea of the meeting, with Fay's agreement.

The Panthers are in turmoil. They want respectability. I go to Huey's apartment, and after an hour's conversation he asks if I'll become chief of staff. He says to me, "You're my man." I say to myself, "What? Did I just hear him right?" Newton sees that I'm not really impressed, and he runs and gets manuscripts that he's been working on with J. Herman Blake to show me he's a real intellectual. Then he shows me his poetry. He starts over again, offering me use of the top floor of his penthouse for parties. The more he talks, the more he thinks I'm going to sign on. No way!

On campus, on the other hand, the more radical and nationalistic of the black students had a strong ambivalence toward me. I'm the only black faculty member working as their ally on all of these university committees. But I have not committed myself to the revolution. So they're thinking, "Who is he?" Black studies, African American studies needed intellectual leadership; I publish a piece in the *Daily Californian* voicing my support of these developments, saying that I'm in favor of the fact that black people are now mobilizing. I make an argument that I can play a role, but not the leadership role. If you want someone who's black by your own accounts, it couldn't be me.

AN: After several years at Berkeley you were invited to join President Jimmy Carter's Commission on Mental Health. How did this come to pass?

TD: I had written a book called *The Legislation of Morality*.

AN: This was published in 1970.

TD: Yes. In this book I wrote about the history of opiates—particularly morphine and heroin—and also other drugs. I argued that [what had changed was] not the drugs . . . but their user populations. In the past century and a half, the public presentation of who's using had been completely inverted. In the late nineteenth century, white upper-class, middle-aged females were the primary users of morphine. By 1925, just forty years later, the users were primarily young, working-class or unemployed, increasingly of color, and male. The drugs didn't change; the people who

Alondra Nelson and Troy Duster

seemed to be using them changed. There was a complicated set of reasons for this shift; this is what I was interested in.

After this book was published, I got to be known—and this is back to Greer—as "the drug person." Howie Becker said to me at the time, "Welcome to the drug circuit." And I said, "Howie, you don't understand. Listen, this isn't a book about drugs; this is about the shifting transformation in use patterns. . . ." He said again, "Welcome to the drug circuit." And he was right.

I was invited to join the National Academy of Sciences panel on substance abuse. Our job was to address the funding of social science research on this topic. I felt as if I had been let into the back room of the golf club. The big boys were allocating the resources. I thought that since this is the Carter administration I will have a voice among people who have views that resonate with mine. Boy, was I wrong. I heard colleagues from the natural and biological sciences engage in vicious, mean-spirited attacks on research programs focused on poverty and its relationship to mental stress and mental illness. And mental illness was being described as being all about neurotransmission patterns and genes. I heard all of this vituperative language about how social scientists had perverted the mission of the National Institute of Mental Health (NIMH) and thereby diverted attention from the "real problem." The real problem, they said, is the genetics of schizophrenia; the real problem is the genetics and biochemical aspects of heroin addiction and of alcoholism. The real problem of violence is that the causes of these maladies lie inside of the body. The attitude was, the social scientists have taken this issue of violence down the path of poverty. It's the wrong path. Get a hold of those neurotransmissions and we will have it figured out. I found myself on a presidential research advisory committee to the National Institutes of Health that was overwhelmingly, relentlessly, and determinedly hostile to social science. That is the beginning of the story of how I became involved in science studies of genetic and biological explanation of complex behaviors.

Around the same time, I became director of the Institute for the Study of Social Change, an NIMH training program on the Berkeley campus. It was quite ecumenical in its orientation, including public health, economics, anthropology, and medical sociology. Reagan comes to power in 1980. Soon after, I get a visit from a project director at the NIMH who tells me that I need to put a physician on the staff of my program. He tells me that I need to reorient the program. He didn't explicitly say make it biological, but that's what he meant. He wanted to "medicalize" the program.

The Carter commission task force and this encounter with the NIMH director sent me back to Robinson's insights. I'm thinking, "Are they kidding?" To focus on mental illness solely as a medical matter would be to control for only a few biochemical variables, when in fact there have to be many environmental variables that are involved. My training back at UCLA starts to click in, and I begin to discover just how much the architecture and scaffolding of their methodology for the genetic explanation of mental illness is deeply flawed. For example, there isn't even an agreement among psychiatrists about what schizophrenia is phenotypically. Since they haven't got an agreement on the phenotype, they broaden the category to "schizophrenia spectrum disorder." A similar thing will happen years later with autism. So now we're going to find the genetics of a spectrum?

AN: You would later serve on the committee considering the ethical, legal, and social implications (ELSI) of the Human Genome Project. How did you go from the Carter commission to this appointment in the early 1990s?

TD: During the eighties, I'm really on a mission to reveal the social forces at play in the history of genetics and, therefore, its contemporary manifestations. That's when I begin to write *Backdoor to Eugenics*. In earlier work, I was making claims about cultural perspectives on biological knowledge. This work had put me in a zone where people working on genetics knew about my research. I was asked to join the ELSI committee but also the National Advisory Council for Human Genome Research—of which ELSI is in some sense a subsidiary. After [I spent] about a year on these committees, a member of the commission said to me, "You're not nearly as anti-science as your reputation." It seems that one gets framed as either pro- or anti-science.

I am not anti-science; I am interested in the preframe—the deep domain assumptions that are a part of the fabric of thinking about the genetics of crime, schizophrenia, alcoholism, violence, drug use and abuse, et cetera. Let me be rhetorical for a moment. If you were to deal with a population of people who were already categorized as violent criminals, the assumption would be that you have that population at hand and that everybody else in the other population is normal. Yet a lot of people who are violent never get caught by the criminal justice system. Any methodology that begins with those who are already in the category misses the social processes that got them there. The behavior of the police and the prosecuting attorney's office is more predictive of who gets into the criminal justice system. People want me to talk about the social "implications" of

Alondra Nelson and Troy Duster

this genetics research as opposed to how the methodology is flawed, how the science is problematic. Focusing on the preframe disrupts this narrative.

AN: You've been speaking about how your research has been counterposed to that of scientists, such as when your colleague at the National Academy of Sciences was surprised that you're not anti-science. In recent years, some social scientists have made what we might call the genetics turn. There was an issue of the *American Journal of Sociology* a few years ago that explored "genetics and social structure."[1] And, recently, Harvard sociologist Robert Sampson has said that "sociology has nothing to fear from genetics."[2] Do you now find yourself being counterposed to both scientists and social scientists?

TD: Great question, and the answer is hopefully as good as the question. What's happened in the past several years is that there's a wave, and the wave gets bigger and bigger. Sociology has always had a wing of itself that has science envy, that wants to outscience the scientists, that wants to give more affirmation to those who do a certain kind of research — quantification becoming the poster child for this. Physics was the first envy, but in the past twenty or thirty years, biology has become the second version of this. The biologist is more likely to be seen as the neutral, white-coated scientist who can get at "the reality" of things. One version of this is that some think that biologists can get at the reality of race. So even though people call themselves A, B, or C, [biologists say] let's go into the genetic structure and look at the markers and see what they really are.

There's this idea that reality lies in the biological version of human categories. This is very attractive to researchers. The big science money is going to those who are looking at the genetics of such matters as diabetes, obesity, and asthma. You have the researchers interested in the social and environmental forces that help explain the skyrocketing trajectory of these problems, but, as I've said, for the past forty years or so, that's not really been considered "real," "serious," or "hard" science. Young people getting their PhDs in sociology today can tell which way the wind is blowing. The wind is blowing toward neurotransmission patterns for mental illness, not toward the social forces that might help explain who becomes mentally ill or who becomes an alcoholic. It is all about genetic structure.

Also, now here's Sampson and Dalton Conley and others, who are saying let's have joint ventures with the geneticists and the biologists. Let's all get under the same tent; let's do research together. The conventional wisdom of my young colleagues is that it is the right way to go and that people like me insist on being mired in a time when sociologists didn't touch genetics or biology.

The assumption of these colleagues is that the research table is level—or that we are all on a level playing field. We're all going to get a seat at the table, and that table is not thought to be tilted. You're the anthropologist, you're the economist, you're the sociologist, molecular geneticist, neuroscientist, cognitive scientist. We're all going to design this huge study of a thirty-year cohort and assess the relationship and relative contributions of the environment and genes. In a genuine collaboration across disciplines, let's find out what's really going on. How could you not agree with that, that getting together with your colleagues, in a collective enterprise, that this wouldn't produce more and better knowledge? Well, the playing field is not level. Science is stratified. The economists will look at the economics of it, sociologists at the social implications of it, and so on. And now comes time to put together the report. It is not an equal interpretation.

When it comes time to report the results of this interdisciplinary study, we are going to find that the genetic or biological component will dominate the explanation of what "really happened." For example, any long-term collaborative study of high rates of alcoholism among Native Americans will find that displacement, disenfranchisement, high unemployment, and easy access will explain upwards of 70 percent of the variance. But if the tribe has some marker more highly correlated to the alcohol dehydrogenase gene, that will become the "real" finding. Audiences tend to respond to findings about poverty among such groups with "We already knew that!" And so the new finding about a genetic marker dominates the explanation. The people who think in terms of sitting around the table as "equal research partners" miss the overwhelming truth that there is a hierarchy of the sciences and a hierarchy of interpretation, regardless of the greater analytic power of the social sciences in explaining rates of alcoholism between groups.

AN: Let's talk about your book *Backdoor to Eugenics*, which has become foundational to the sociology of genetics. This was a prescient work when it was published in 1990, well before the decoding of the human genome. What kind of reception did it receive?

TD: The historian Dan Kevles said to me—I'll try and remember the quote the best I can—"Back in the period when eugenics was being practiced, the fact that there were so few protections in place [for ethnic and racial minorities] made it possible for state eugenics programs to target them." He said, "Now your concerns about eugenics are pretty much displaced because we

Alondra Nelson and Troy Duster

have so many political barriers in place that will keep that from ever happening again." I think he missed the point. The whole point of *Backdoor to Eugenics* was to say, yes, we're not going to find a version of this today that's going to come out and say, "We don't want those people to produce." But we are going to find much more subtle ways of talking about good babies and bad babies. There is a resuscitation of this old idea, but in new clothing.

The earliest backdoor—and I think I was right about it—is going to take the form of people saying we don't want to make babies who have particular genetic conditions. Who could be against that? Of course, there are implications down the road that concern me. But my concern in that book was not only saying, uh-oh, we've got to stop this train because the implications down the road are bad for black people. My point was that this train itself is on the wrong track. It is making the assumption that the genes are destiny. That all we have to do is get a hold of this genetic structure, go in there and zap it—in the 1990s that was the language—the promise of gene therapy. We are going to solve cystic fibrosis, sickle-cell anemia; we're going to solve it all with gene therapy. But wait a minute. On the scientists' own terms, that didn't make any sense, because of the high variable expression of these disorders. How are they going to get to the gene? I was not just criticizing the implications or the troubles just around the corner. I was saying that what's important is what happens before you even get to the corner.

AN: Can you imagine that sociology could be engaged with genetics in a fruitful way?

TD: That depends entirely on the frame of the research project and the subject of the investigation. For example, the more determinative, the more definitive, the more, to use scientists' language, the penetrance of the gene, the less sociology has to say. So if it is the case ultimately that they do find out that a particular kind of autism has a 95 percent penetrance, now sociology has very little to say about the social causes but will be able to address the social implications. But if and when it is determined that autism has only about a 20 percent penetrance—now the question is, what are the triggers in the environment that might shape it, and then of course the social forces that are going to help you explain the trigger are going to be far more determinative than any quest for specific genes or markers. What's this got to do with ecumenical research? We want to know: Where is the trigger? What is the trigger? When does it happen? At this point, geneticists don't have much to say about these questions. Even somebody like [the acclaimed molecular biologist] Lee Hood would say, "We have so many combinations of genes." Well, all right, I'm asking, what's the implication of that, in terms of the science, not the social implications, but in terms of the science? You're going to explain hypertension in terms of science? Well, you've got six hundred genes that all contribute to hypertension. What's going to manifest itself in the person's hypertension is going to have to deal with the social fact of who gets to walk around Saks Fifth Avenue without being followed. And many geneticists are going to say right away, "Well, that's not science. We can't go there. How are we going to monitor whether your stress levels go up when you walk into a department store and someone follows you? That's not science. Science is when we have now located the twenty-sixth gene that is related to hypertension." I rest my case.

AN: Today the public comes to know genetics via direct-to-consumer DNA testing. What do you think of this recent phenomenon?

TD: Direct-to-consumer is an issue where one could make a good critique even at the level of methodology. That is happening. You can see more and more people in the field of genetics saying, "Whoa, wait a minute here!" So that part doesn't concern me, because I do think there is an increasing critical consciousness now among people who are in that field.

AN: Do you think that you have had a role to play in the creation of that critical perspective?

TD: Yes. But there were several other people who played very important roles in that whole direct-to-consumer thing and who, I think, understood the methods a lot better than I did and made strong, good statements. I may have played the role of a node, putting people together who were better at the methodological critique than I am.

On the other matter of race and genomics: this is not going away. It's going to get bigger, and this is where I think all of us have a role to play. Geneticists are neither bad guys nor good guys, but there are markets, and this is a business. We're going to see the increasing concern with defining markets in terms of ethnic populations. Ten years ago, expressing concerns about the confusing and increasing intersection of race and genomics phenomenon was viewed by many as unnecessarily alarmist. At the time, the American Anthropological Association had just issued a statement that race was a flawed concept for looking at human differences. This opened the door for an effective political assault on the use of race to redress past and current grievances. Ward Connerly, for example, would put on the ballot in California an initiative to ban the collection of data by race. "We don't need no damn affirmative action. The anthropolo-

Alondra Nelson and Troy Duster

gists have now told us that race is a deeply flawed concept and that it's history's stain. Let's just get rid of race. Let's just not talk about it, folks; let's just go be postracial." So no, the realpolitik of postracialness and the increasing convergence of genomics of race are in play for an inexorable clash. On the one side, we've got the aspiration of those who want to not see race for public policy purposes, those who say that the geneticists and anthropologists have told us that there is no such thing as race. Meanwhile, big pharma [the pharmaceutical industry] is looking for markets; they're talking about personalized medicine. By personalized, what they mean, really, is a configuration of issues and categorization of where the individual fits best in those categories. But that configuration is most likely going to be a fit to existing taxonomies. Here's the other side of the coin: I refer to Paul Rabinow and his articulation of "biosociality."[3] There's a version of this school of thought that is postracial. Now we're going to newly categorize all the people with a specific genetic disease, and they're going to be a new category, a new social group that transcends race, class, and ethnicity. We shall see which wins out, but I am betting that a biological definition of the group is not going to transcend existing social categories. Because those touting personalized medicine still today use old racial categories, we now have the reintroduction of the old taxonomies through the twenty-first-century lens of genetic markers. This is what I have called "the molecular reinscription of race."[4]

Notes

1. Peter S. Bearman, Molly A. Martin, and Sara Shostak, "Exploring Genetics and Social Structure," *American Journal of Sociology* 144 (supplement).

2. Robert Sampson, quoted in Patricia Cohen, "Genetic Basis for Crime: A New Look," *New York Times*, June 19, 2011, C1.

3. Paul Rabinow, *Essays on the Anthropology of Reason* (Princeton, NJ: Princeton University Press, 1996).

4. Troy Duster, "The Molecular Reinscription of Race: Unanticipated Issues in Biotechnology and Forensic Science," *Patterns of Prejudice* 40 (2006): 427–41; Duana Fullwiley, "The Molecularization of Race: Institutionalizing Human Difference in Pharmacogenetics Practice," *Science as Culture* 16, no. 1 (2007): 1–30.

14

Reimagining Race, Resistance, and Technoscience

A Conversation with Dorothy Roberts

.....

RUHA BENJAMIN (RB): So let's begin at the beginning. Can you speak about your formative influences as a child and youth?

DOROTHY ROBERTS (DR): This may be because I'm working on a book on my parents' research, that my parents are so much in the forefront of my mind as what shaped my own views about humanity and social justice. But my father was an anthropologist, who spent his whole career looking at interracial marriage. I recently discovered that my mother also helped him with this project. My parents both had a very strong view that there was no such thing as biological race, that there was only one human race. All human beings were equally valuable. And they also thought that if people of different backgrounds could learn more about each other, that would lead to the end of ethnic conflict. So they raised me and my sisters very deliberately to have this worldview about humanity that focused on the equal value of human beings. And my father's research was a very big part of my life, growing up. I guess I should mention that my father is white and my mother is black. And they made interracial harmony a goal for our family. It was a political and social project that me and my sisters were involved in from when we were very little.

RB: Enrolled subjects.

DR: We were enrolled subjects. Yes. [Laughter.] Through this project. So that had a real strong influence on me. And it went beyond interracial marriage in Chicago.

RB: Which is where you were born?

DR: I was born in Chicago. While my father was conducting this research, and his research was not only sort of philosophically important, but many of my parents' friends were interracial couples. And so I grew up in a home where it was emphasized that race and racism shouldn't divide us. So that was one aspect of their philosophy. But the other aspect of it was that my mother was an immigrant from Jamaica, who left Jamaica in her twenties to teach in Liberia, West Africa, and then migrated from Liberia on a scholarship to Roosevelt University, where my father taught. So we also were raised with the idea that it was important to engage with people from around the world. My mother had a very strong sense that our family should help international students. So we always had international students living in our house, always, from as far back as I can remember. My parents thought it was very important to raise us as citizens of the world.

When I was three months old, my parents moved to Liberia, and lived there for two years. And my sisters, who were twins, were both born in Liberia. And even though I don't remember it, the fact that I spent my toddler years and my sisters were born in Liberia was very important to our identity as a family and as individuals. We thought of ourselves as being global citizens, from as far back as I can remember.

RB: So after Liberia you came back to Chicago?

DR: Yes. After Liberia, we moved back to Hyde Park. My parents bought a big house in Hyde Park, where I spent all of my elementary school years. A big part of our lives was focused on the Field Museum and International House at the University of Chicago, going to lectures there, going to see films about different parts of the world. Also, my father had a huge library of books about every part of the world. He had a study up on the third floor of our house, and it was lined with bookshelves. Every region of the world had its own section.

RB: That's amazing.

DR: I was so fascinated by this library. So I would sneak up—I can remember there was a key, an old-fashioned key that opened his study. I could pull a chair and climb up on the chair and reach the key. I would go into his study and sit. I can still remember this. I must have been—I don't know, just in elementary school, and sit on the floor and read his books. I can remember reading books by Margaret Mead, when I was very little.

Part of what I've discovered in my book project is that my father began interviewing black–white couples when he was only twenty-two years old as a master's student at University of Chicago. He wrote his master's thesis that was submitted in 1940 on black–white marriages in Chicago based on his interview of couples. Many of them were married in the late 1800s. This is part of the mystery of my project: how did this white kid from Chicago get interested in interracial marriage? He started it in the 1930s, and then he continued these interviews after he got back in the 1950s from serving in the army during World War II. That's when he met my mother when she came from Liberia to be a student at Roosevelt University. So you have these two curious people—this white man who became interested in black–white marriages, and had a very global perspective. And he met this woman who picked up from Jamaica in the 1940s to move to Liberia, and then left there to come to the United States. And my mother not only went on this journey, but she also began pursuing a PhD in anthropology at Northwestern University, after she graduated from Roosevelt. I just think it was very pioneering at that time, in the mid-'50s, for a black woman to be getting a PhD in anthropology at an elite university.

RB: Absolutely.

Ruha Benjamin and Dorothy Roberts

DR: It must have been pretty rare. But she still was constrained by tradition because when I was born in 1956, she gave up working on her PhD and she never went back to it. She eventually became a Chicago Public School teacher.

The other part of my childhood that had a very strong influence on me was growing up in Hyde Park. As I said, we moved from Liberia to this big house in Hyde Park. I went to Shoesmith Elementary School at the corner of 49th and Kenwood. Hyde Park was a neighborhood where interracial couples felt comfortable, were accepted. It was a very politically left-leaning community. The neighborhood itself was very involved in the civil rights movement and the anti-war movement. And as a little girl, I felt I was involved in them, too. There was a church, I can't remember the name of it, that I could walk to that had meetings about both civil rights and anti-war issues. I can recall going to those meetings without my parents, even.

RB: Wow.

DR: My parents were very involved in promoting interracial marriage as a solution. But I think early on, I didn't see that as a solution. I can't remember the age, but I think by age ten, I had figured out that ending racism in America was going to require a political movement.

RB: Interesting.

DR: Something more than people marrying each other.

RB: Yes. [Laughter.]

DR: That and I also, around that age, began to think of myself as a black person, as opposed to a mixed person. My parents very much raised me to think of myself as the child of an interracial couple.

RB: Interesting.

DR: And I do recall—I think prior to being, say, ten years old, being very proud of my family. You know, it's funny sometimes when I hear about people talking about the tragedy of being mixed race, how—

RB: The confusion—

DR: I never, ever felt that, ever. So the only evolution in my thinking was going from being very proud of my family being mixed race—walking down the street and being proud to say, "We have cut across racial lines, and human beings can be better than all the racial conflict going on in humanity," and all of that. But at some point, I realized you had to be interested in more—in social change.

When I was in eighth grade, my father decided to apply for a Fulbright Fellowship to Egypt. I graduated from eighth grade at Shoesmith in Chicago.

Then for my first two years of high school, our family lived in Egypt. I went to Cairo American College, which was a very international elementary and high school. The students came from all over the world; ambassadors' kids and professors' kids were there.

RB: This was still when AUC was in the center of the city? What stands out to you from those few years?

DR: One thing that stands out is that it really cemented my view that I was a citizen of the world, not a citizen just of the United States. And it nurtured my interest that I had from when I was very little in learning about people from other parts of the world, engaging with them, learning the politics. There's one thing you learn early on when you leave the U.S. is that there's politics in other parts of the world that you had no clue about.

RB: Yes. They have to know our politics, but we can be ignorant about theirs.

DR: Exactly. Exactly. So that was really eye-opening. The other big thing that happened to me while I was there is that it really, really sealed my sense that I was a black woman, and that I had an identity that was different from white people, and different from men.

RB: Did that come about through different interactions with people?

DR: It came about because I was away from black Americans. And so I thought more about what it meant to be a black American. And even though I really loved living in Egypt, by the end of the two years there, I was very anxious to engage with U.S. racial politics.

When we came back, we moved to Evanston, Illinois, because my mother wanted me to attend school there. My sisters and I always went to public schools. There was never any thought of us going to a private school, growing up. That wasn't in my family's worldview at all. So my mother was very adamant about me going to a public high school that would prepare me for college. So I went to Evanston Township High School for my last two years of high school. And there was a course that I took my senior year, something about human rights and social justice. The teacher recommended me to be the school's representative at a program that the American Anthropological Association was sponsoring to involve high school students in something having to do with international harmony, or something like that. I remember we met sometimes at the Bahá'í temple. That course was very influential on me, as well. It gave me an entrée into participating in anthropology and—you know, now that I think about it, it also gave me a sense that you could use research in a way that actually promoted social justice.

RB: So after high school, you went to Yale. What did you major in?

Ruha Benjamin and Dorothy Roberts

DR: Anthropology! You got to study people from all over the world. You got to promote the idea that all human beings are valuable.

RB: Did you have to do a thesis, or any research or class that stands out to you?

DR: I took a course in cultural linguistics, and I remember I studied black preachers in New Haven.

RB: Oh, interesting.

DR: I remember I went around to all the black churches. I can't remember what my thesis was. I just remember it was a fun paper to work on. The other big thing about my anthropology major was that I spent my junior year in Bogotá, Colombia.

RB: That's huge.

DR: I lived with a Colombian family. Interestingly, the family I lived with, the mother was a black woman from El Chocó, which is an area on the west coast of Colombia that is very isolated, especially at that time. Once you got to the border, there weren't even paved roads getting into the villages where people lived. It is predominantly indigenous and African descendant people who live there. The black people are descendants of escaped enslaved Africans from other parts of Colombia.

My Colombian mother was married to an Austrian engineer she met there. Her name was Miriam, and she spoke no English at all. And her husband spoke limited English. But I pick up languages really quickly. So by living with them, I spoke fluent Spanish by December. I learned so much while I was there. And especially being at Universidad de los Andes, that was where I gained a critical theory perspective in college. Because there weren't classes as critical as that at Yale. It really was largely influenced by Marxism.

And also, because of Miriam and her relatives, I was able to spend my spring break in El Chocó. That was such a formative experience, because at that time—and I don't know that things have changed that much—it was very isolated from the rest of Colombia. And I lived with a black family for about two weeks, who lived in very rudimentary housing. No running water, no toilets. Pigs in the back. But I felt so at home and so close to the people I met there. Everyone was so welcoming and wonderful to me, whatever they had was for me to share. I remember I got there after this grueling bus ride over unpaved roads. I mean, you were just bouncing. And the seats in the bus were metal seats. And my back, I couldn't even look at it. It was raw from bouncing up and down. So I'm exhausted, I'm covered in dust when I get there. And they prepared a bed for me, which was a cot separated from the other family members by sheets.

They were just so wonderful to me. That experience gave me a sense of the black diaspora, I felt connected to them.

And then I remember I was working on a paper for one of my classes at the university in Bogotá that had something to do with the encounter between indigenous Mexicans and the settler colonists from Spain. At the same time, I made the decision to travel by myself across Central America on my return to the United States. So I flew into El Salvador and just took buses wherever I wanted to go, and my destination was Mexico City, where I did research at museums to finish my project.

It was one of the most liberating experiences of my life.

I also remember doing a paper at Universidad de los Andes in one of these political economy courses on how the coffee industry harmed people in Colombia, how it exploited workers in Colombia. I can't remember the details of it, but I remember that I interviewed people who were involved in the industry. I remember having an interview with some executive at a big bank in Colombia about it. But it was a professor who encouraged me to challenge global capitalism, neocolonialism, and the coffee business, which many people thought was good for Colombia because it was, I think, its biggest export at the time. But I was looking at the exploitative aspect of it. All this as a nineteen-year-old.

RB: It's striking that the memories that really remain vivid are those in which you got out of the classroom. It wasn't just book research, but it was talking to people.

DR: That's true.

RB: And it says something for us now as professors, pedagogically, when you really want something to stick, you have to get out of the mold, right?

DR: Yeah. That's a brilliant observation. I never thought about that. That's very true.

RB: Just thinking about how memory works, and about what remains, which applies to us now in our teaching. . . . So, then, from Mexico City you flew back to Chicago because by now it was summertime, and you would begin your senior year at Yale?

DR: Exactly. So then, my senior year at Yale, I have to think, what am I going to do next? And this is another good lesson for pedagogy, which is, I'm thinking all my life, I'm going to get a PhD in anthropology, and become an anthropologist. But I'm also now really interested in social justice, and what can I do to contribute to social justice movements? And I thought, you have to be a lawyer to do that. I couldn't think of how an anthropologist would do it.

Ruha Benjamin and Dorothy Roberts

RB: Interesting. So then, in terms of your experience in law school, do you think it equipped you for social justice advocacy?

DR: Well, I went to Harvard Law School, and like most major law schools, they are grooming students to go into corporate practice. But there were lots of courses I could take that weren't geared toward that. And I did not go on the corporate track. I did take the basic course on corporations. But I also took courses like employment discrimination and family law. And the one that was most memorable was a course where I worked at Greater Boston Legal Services, representing indigent clients. And I don't remember the cases I worked on, except for one. And that was the case representing an elderly Italian woman who'd been ripped off by a cemetery plot purchasing scheme. I remember helping her, and her being very grateful. I also remember that Harvard would not let me go into her neighborhood unescorted. I had to go escorted by a police car, because of all the racial tensions in Boston. Because I was black going into this Italian neighborhood.

RB: And then right after law school, what was the next step?

DR: My next step was to clerk. At that point, I wasn't sure if I wanted to be a professor—I was still kind of thinking about that—or if I wanted to go into litigation. So I knew, though, that clerking was important to do, in either case. So I had been looking over which federal judges I wanted to clerk for and my number one choice was Constance Baker Motley, who was the first African American female federal judge in the United States. She had been a hero of the civil rights movement, and had teamed with Thurgood Marshall and Robert Carter. She was a pioneer in so many ways. She was often the first woman to appear as an attorney in southern courthouses, and the first black person to appear as an attorney before some of these judges in the South. So I applied to her and some other judges as well. She gave me an offer to be her clerk and, of course, I accepted it. So my first year out of law school, I clerked for Judge Motley, which was a great experience. Just being around her was inspiring.

RB: What were some of your impressions from clerking for her?

DR: She was just very, very stately, and wise, and brave, and outspoken, and down to earth. I found her to be very kind to me, not at all authoritarian, or elitist, or anything like that. I had heard that some people were afraid of her. So I was surprised by how down to earth she was. She didn't put on airs at all. And I liked her a lot. I felt very close to her.

RB: Did you think about following that path after being around her?

DR: Well, you know, it's interesting. She was inspiring as a civil rights figure. So being around her intensified that inspiration. The thing, though, is that I had to become more realistic as a clerk about, number one, what federal judges do. They don't spend all their time trying to liberate people from prison and change the laws. The district of New York is a financial center. So a lot of our cases had to do with financial matters. And it never occurred to me that because it's a port that there would be maritime law matters. One of the biggest cases had to do with some corned beef that fell off a ship in the Hudson River. [Laughter.] There were also interesting trademark cases, having nothing to do with civil rights or social justice. But it was fun to clerk. I certainly learned how to research and write really quickly. I learned how courts operate.

There were some cases that involved social justice issues, but the main ones were habeas corpus cases filed by incarcerated people, who were petitioning to be released, because of some harm that had been done to them, either while they were incarcerated or before they were convicted. And if it was up to me, I would have released them. But the procedures in court, which are worse now, just did not allow for these cases to even be considered. It was very painful and very eye-opening about—

RB: The limits.

DR: The limits to formal justice procedures. So then I followed the advice that all my mentors at the law school were giving me, that after clerking, I should spend at least a couple of years at a big firm. So I looked for the firm that I thought was the quirkiest and least elitist. There was a firm called Paul, Weiss, Rifkind, Wharton & Garrison, that was known for being very liberal and religiously diverse. But all the big Manhattan firms are so white. I think there was one female partner at the time, and no partners of color when I was there. I don't even recall if there were any other associates of color the year I started. And I ended up staying there, though, for six years—but why? Because virtually the day I got there, I got pregnant. I had gotten married while I was clerking. So I went on maternity leave within a year of arriving there. I took five months of maternity leave. And then pretty soon after I got back, I got pregnant again.

RB: These are good reasons to stay somewhere for six years.

DR: Well, they had a really generous maternity leave policy.

RB: That hardly anyone used. It had been waiting for you.

DR: Right. Just for me. So I had three babies while I was there, and three maternity leaves.

Ruha Benjamin and Dorothy Roberts

RB: This experience dovetails with your body of work around reproductive justice, in a very intimate way!

DR: Exactly. It just didn't make sense, and nor did I have the time or energy with these three little kids to think about leaving and starting a whole new career. But it wasn't too long after I began practicing law that even though there were some enjoyable aspects of it, I knew that it wasn't the best use of my talents. I could see that a lot of lawyering involves—and it has to be done, but it involves things that are just—

RB: Tedious. [Laughter.]

DR: I mean, I'm not putting down social justice lawyers. Thank God for them, and I work with them all the time, I want to support them. Criminal defense attorneys, we need them. But they sometimes have tedious work. They have to do the kind of work that just didn't suit my personality or my deep interest. I realized that I could contribute to social justice movements better as a scholar, an activist-scholar, than as an attorney. It took a while, but as soon as my third daughter was sturdy enough for me to be able to think about going into teaching, I started applying to teach at law schools.

RB: And the first place was?

DR: It was Rutgers. I got offers from Hofstra and Rutgers. Rutgers Newark was known as a radical law school, and it just was the perfect place for me. In my last year at Paul, Weiss, I started to get really interested in what we now call reproductive justice, reproductive freedom. Another associate at the firm brought me a case that had just been decided in DC, that involved a judge's decision to compel a woman who was dying of lung cancer to have a cesarean section against her will. And the cesarean section killed her, and the fetus was not viable. I read this opinion and thought, they killed a pregnant woman for the sake of her fetus. That's how I looked at it. At the same time, I started to read about the prosecutions of women who were using drugs during pregnancy. And I thought, I'll bet you these are black women, and to me, they were punishing these women for having babies. And I wanted to be involved in stopping these prosecutions, and I wanted to start doing research and writing about it. So when I got to Rutgers, I was ready to work on this project. I knew that's what I wanted to do.

RB: So were you at Rutgers when *Killing the Black Body* was published?

DR: Well, I spent all of my years at Rutgers working on it. My first law review article was called "Punishing Drug Addicts Who Have Babies," and that was published in 1991 in *Harvard Law Review*. That was sort of the springboard for my writing *Killing the Black Body*, because by studying and writing about the unconstitutionality and human rights violation of punishing black women for having babies, I started to think about all the other ways that the state regulates black women's childbearing. Then I started to read about the whole history of regulating black women's childbearing, going all the way back to the era of slavery. But also thinking about how laws that were being debated at the time, not only laws to punish black women who used drugs during pregnancy, but also welfare restructuring was being debated at the time. And a big part of that was using the myth of the black welfare queen to eliminate the entitlement of welfare. Also, the state of New Jersey had sued the federal government to be able to impose family caps on women receiving public assistance, or child exclusion policies [that] deny any incremental increase in benefits after having a baby. At the time it was illegal to do that, because there was still a federal entitlement to welfare. Once the entitlement was abolished in 1997, states rushed in to start passing these laws. But that case was going on in New Jersey while I was writing *Killing the Black Body*, and the debate about welfare restructuring was going on at the time. So I was looking at this history, but also seeing how the history of punishing black women's childbearing was being implemented anew in these policies. At the time, there were bills being debated to require sterilization in order to get welfare benefits. There was an ACLU case on behalf of a black woman who was told if she used Norplant, the long-acting contraception, she wouldn't have to go to jail.

All of this was going on while I was working on *Killing the Black Body* throughout the 1990s. The first edition was published in 1997. That year, as I'm finishing writing it, I got invitations to visit Northwestern Law School in the fall of 1997 and Stanford Law School in the spring of 1998. And while I was at Stanford, Northwestern gave me an offer to join the faculty, and I accepted it. So *Killing the Black Body* was actually published while I was visiting at Stanford.

But Rutgers really allowed me to work on a project like that, even though, I have to say, there were senior faculty members who tried to steer me away from writing my first law review article about women who smoked crack during pregnancy. "That is too radical, even for us." "No highly ranked journal will want to publish that." And *Harvard Law Review* ended up publishing my article. But even to feel the support of colleagues to work on a subject like that, I don't know if I would have gotten that support at another law school. So I give full credit to Rutgers for nurturing me in those early years of my career. And also I got tenure while I was at Rutgers.

Something else I want to mention, though, during my years at Rutgers, was how important it was to me to work with legal advocates who were representing these women, especially the ACLU reproductive freedom project, who represented a number of the women, like Lynn Paltrow, who is now the director of National Advocates for Pregnant Women. She left the ACLU and formed her own organization that advocates for pregnant women who are being targeted by the state. And she and others were very helpful to my thinking about the prosecutions. It was also helpful getting resources from them, reading their briefs, their court papers. Even just confirming that it was mostly black women who were being prosecuted, the only way I could document that was from a memo that the ACLU wrote about their clients and other women who had been arrested, and with the lawyers' phone numbers, I could call them and ask them, "What race is your client?" Newspapers weren't reporting that this was happening to black women. They were reporting the myth of the crack baby. And so to piece together the crack baby myth and all the slander about pregnant crack addicts who were supposedly deprived of maternal instinct, and connecting that to the targeting of black women for prosecution, that requires knowing what's really going on. You can't get that from scholarly articles, especially since it takes a long time for articles to be published. You have to be engaged. And also, it's not just learning the details, it's understanding the politics of it. To be sure that this is what's going on. The state is really punishing black women for having babies.

RB: So what do you make of the fact that someone can pick up *Killing the Black Body* today and it is just as relevant?

DR: Right. Well, part of what I make of it is that the struggle continues, that these are mechanisms of supporting white supremacist capitalist patriarchy that have existed since the time of slavery. The mechanisms take on new guises. But there's a fundamental way that punishing black women's childbearing blames it as the cause of the nation's problems, as well as the disadvantaged status of black people. That has worked so powerfully to mask institutionalized racism for centuries. That's part of why we see some of these mechanisms recurring today, because they still work. They still work as long as that ideology still exists. They bolster the ideology yet again. I think it also shows—I hope I don't sound like I'm bragging, but it shows, I think, that I hit on something in *Killing the Black Body*—

that maybe wasn't even recognized when it came out. About how white supremacy operates, and the central place of black women.

RB: It's really thinking about the underlying ideological framework. Because you were able to get at that, and that hasn't been dismantled. This is one of the reasons why the text remains so relevant. Now can you tell us about how your next two books evolved?

DR: Sure. Working on *Killing the Black Body* brought me in contact with this bourgeoning reproductive justice movement—I mean, the timing is uncanny. Because the term "reproductive justice" was coined by a group of black feminists at a pro-choice conference in 1994. At the same time *Killing the Black Body* is coming out in 1997, we see the founding of an organization like SisterSong Reproductive Justice Collective, that's focused on reproductive justice. And black women's organizations, Asian-Pacific Islander women's organizations, Latina women's organizations, indigenous women's organizations who are promoting reproductive justice. *Killing the Black Body* gave me an opportunity to engage with all of these organizations.

So, while I'm doing all of that, I'm also aware, for the first time, about the racial disparities in the child welfare system. I discovered that there may be hundreds of prosecutions, but there were thousands upon thousands of newborns taken from their mothers, because they tested positive for drugs. And discovering that then led me to look into the child welfare system more. I was shocked to find out that black children at the time, in 2000, were four times as likely as white children to be placed in foster care. There have been studies that show that the odds of a black child being placed in foster care over their whole childhood is extremely high. Most black children in the United States will be involved in a child welfare investigation. So I started to think about, what's the political significance of that? Why is it that there's not more attention paid to it? Most civil rights organizations are not focusing on foster care. Meanwhile, I was learning that foster care is a system that punishes and disrupts families, especially black families, for being poor and for failing to meet a white middle-class standard. So I wanted to document that. But I wanted to write a book that cast the overrepresentation of black children in the foster care system as a political problem. That explained how this system operates like prisons. It is a way of monitoring black families, especially a way of monitoring, regulating, and punishing black mothers. How can that be ignored? I think that's ignored because of the long-standing view in white-dominated ideology and culture that black parents don't care about having loving bonds with their children.

Ruha Benjamin and Dorothy Roberts

RB: Right. And that our families are already dysfunctional. So anything else would be better.

DR: It's got to be better. Maybe foster care is not good for them, but it's got to be better than their families and their communities, which really don't have close ties with them anyway. So you're not harming anybody. It's such a dangerous and dehumanizing myth about people.

The other thing I was thinking about, how the foster care system relates to this volume, *Captivating Technology*, is the use of technologies in figuring out which children are at risk and therefore should be removed from their homes. State agencies are more and more using algorithms of risk to identify which of the families are too dangerous for children. And just like the algorithms that the law enforcement uses, they import into them racial and economic biases that are already in the system.

RB: Based on the idea that the algorithm makes it a neutral decision.

DR: Yes. So my book *Shattered Bonds: The Color of Child Welfare*, which was published in 2001, does not discuss the role of algorithmic bias, though it considers how vague standards for child maltreatment can import racial biases. If there's a standard that lists what constitutes child maltreatment, and one is a dangerous environment—well, what does that mean? That's so susceptible to a state agent thinking, based on their norm of what a good family looks like, that something different from it endangers a child. And there are so many ways in which the criminal justice system and the foster care system then interact, so that the biases of each one flow into the other one. As we are talking, I'm thinking that one of the tests that agencies often use for what puts a child at risk is whether someone in the child's family has been incarcerated. If you've got a criminal justice system that incarcerates black people for multiple discriminatory reasons and you incorporate that into the test for when a child is in danger, you are importing that discrimination.

RB: And here's the two-way road, because you could imagine that the algorithms for deciding whether someone's going to get parole, or for how long, will take into consideration family structure and supports. So you see how one impinges on the other.

DR: Exactly. Absolutely. All these systems are so entangled. And black women are entangled in all of them.

RB: OK, so take us to *Fatal Invention*.

DR: OK. So as I'm continuing to work on my child welfare and reproductive justice research and activism, I begin to notice these stories, principally by Nicholas Wade in the *New York Times*, promoting research on the genetic differences between the principal races. I learned about the FDA's approval of the first race-specific medicine to be prescribed to self-identified African Americans. I go to a lecture at Northwestern, the Silverstein Lectures, which are these prestigious lectures that the medical school holds every year. And Jon Entine, who is a conservative journalist and wrote a book called *Taboo: Why Black Athletes Dominate Sports and Why We're Afraid to Talk about It,* had been invited to speak. He was positioned in opposition to a black geneticist, Charles Rotimi, who gave the first lecture presenting evidence against the biological concept of race. Entine has written racist claims about black people's innate inferiority, arguing that the fact that we're supposed to be good athletes is related to the fact that we're also genetically predisposed to lack of intelligence. And he is giving the prestigious Silverstein lecture—I'm not making this up. I thought, "What is going on here?" That was in the mid-2000s. And when I left that lecture, I said to myself, "I have to write a book on this." I said, "There is clearly a resurgence of the biological concept of race," and I had to start looking into it.

Now, I told you what my parents taught me when I was little. And I dedicate *Fatal Invention* to them: "For my parents, Iris and Robert Roberts, who taught me that there is only one human race." I knew it logically, let alone scientifically and politically. It doesn't make sense to believe that the human race is divided into a handful of discrete subraces. Anyway, I was really shocked by the developments I was witnessing.

RB: Do you remember how the audience received the lecture? Did you feel that people were critical? Or were they drinking the Kool-Aid?

DR: I think they were drinking the Kool-Aid. They were laughing. Afterward, all these people from the audience went up to him to talk to him.

RB: Because he's so courageous, talking about what no one will say.

DR: Exactly. That's how Nicholas Wade positions his writing on race, too. When Entine started his lecture, he started talking about breast cancer in his family, and how important it was to Ashkenazi Jews to trace genetic mutations within their family. Then he went from that, though, to a bigger point about the importance of genetic differences between races. And then, at the finale of his lecture, he said, "Now, I am going to show a video by the preeminent anthropologist in America who agrees with me." Then the lights dim, this big screen comes down. The projection begins. And it's Chris Rock interviewing boxers about why white men can't box. At the Silverstein lecture. And the audience is laughing. And they just think it's so funny. I do recall—I shot my hand up when it was time for questions.

Ruha Benjamin and Dorothy Roberts

I was number one. I asked, "You began with Ashkenazi Jewish people. I didn't know they were a race. How do you jump from that to race?" I was questioning the genetic claims he was making. He said, "I never said that"—and then we're going back and forth. Then I remember the moderator saying, "We have to move on!" Because I was just trying to pin Entine down to admit what he was saying about racial differences.

And the thing with calling this conversation about biological race "taboo" is that people like Jon Entine, Nicholas Wade, and their fans don't want to talk about *racism*. There is no taboo around race. Medical students are taught the first day to take the patient's race into account. Sally Satel wrote a *New York Times Magazine* cover story called "I Am a Racially Profiling Doctor," with the subtitle, "Illness Isn't Colorblind. So Why Is It Taboo for Doctors to Take Note of a Patient's Race?" again falsely declaring, I'm bravely confessing this. No one else will confess it. And she uses the word "taboo." What? There is no taboo.

RB: This distinction you make about talking about race versus racism is key.

DR: Absolutely. It's not taboo to talk about racial differences in biology. People talk about them all the time. Again, medical students are taught to observe them. They are in medical literature. There are tons of articles about innate racial differences in disease. Again, Nicholas Wade was writing about genetic differences between the principal races on the front page of the *New York Times*. There's no taboo against that. The taboo is against acknowledging institutionalized racism. That's what you're not supposed to do—don't suggest that any of this talk about race in medicine might support institutionalized racism. Are you suggesting these doctors are racist? Are you trying to limit biomedical research on race? You're scientifically backward. You're driven by your ideology. That's what's taboo. I've gotten that reaction to *Fatal Invention*. I think it's so phony!

RB: Exactly. Framing of all of those conversations as somehow courageous and politically brave. So what are the range of responses you have gotten to *Fatal Invention*, in addition to people who feel you are anti-science?

DR: Of course, there are many people who thank me for challenging this view and for noting that mainstream scientists are writing about it. This is not just fringe white supremacists or white nationalists. Although those so-called fringe groups love the racial science, they love to quote and cite the studies. So I've gotten welcoming comments from many people. One group, especially, is medical students who are being taught biological concepts of race, and are not sure how to respond. They know something's wrong with it. But they're not sure how to address it. Or how as medical students or doctors they can have a radically different way of thinking about race and racism, and their patients' health. I've given lots and lots of talks, so I've gotten face-to-face reactions. One of the most common is, "What about sickle cell?" But we'll move past that.

Another response is, "You're not a scientist." To some people, sociologists don't count as scientists. All that counts is biological scientists, more specifically, genetic scientists. So you're not expert enough to talk about this issue. My response is, "Well, you aren't a sociologist, so you don't know what race means, and you're not expert to use it as a variable in your research." I question the idea that we should rely on biologists to critique their own research that has an impact on society. If they really are just looking at fruit flies or nonhuman microbes in a Petri dish that aren't going to affect human beings whatsoever, they are not involving human research participants. They are not making any comment on human society in any way—OK, I grant them that. I'm not an expert on that. If you could cure cancer that way, be my guest, please. But if you are going to use race as a variable in your research, then you're using a social category. So you should not be doing this research without critique from outside the lab. That's just not good science.

RB: Have you ever encountered researchers who genuinely wanted to collaborate, or wanted advice about how to develop a more sophisticated approach to race?

DR: I have. I've worked with Sarah Tishkoff, who is a geneticist here at Penn. She's a Penn Integrates Knowledge professor, like me. We have written a piece together with a couple other coauthors in *Science* called "Take Race Out of Human Genetics Variation Research." She and I have had conversations about this. We don't agree completely. But I think she genuinely wants to learn more about the meaning of race and its relevance to her research.

I helped to organize and participated in a workshop at NIH on the use of race in health research that involved some of the genomic researchers I criticized in *Fatal Invention*. And I encounter many people who want to learn more. But I do also encounter a resistance of biomedical researchers, genomic researchers, doctors who have almost a visceral resistance to even thinking about how we might understand human beings apart from a biological concept of race. They say, "We have nothing else we can rely on." I've had doctors say to me, "I can't practice medicine without relying on race. We have nothing else—what do you want me to do?" On the one hand, the charge is that you are, by raising these important questions, somehow trying to shut down forms of investigation. But at the same

Ruha Benjamin and Dorothy Roberts

time, in that statement, there's almost an elementary sense that we can't develop new ways to think about this.

RB: So we need more imagination when it comes to producing knowledge about difference and inequality. And social justice organizations and activists continue to help generate conceptual tools that we can use when people say, "It's just too hard to do anything different."

DR: Yes. We're talking about people who have advanced degrees in science, who are in the leading institutions that are spending billions of dollars, collectively, on research. They're supposed to be advancing us into a new generation of precision medicine. And you can't think about another way of doing your research? It's so mind-boggling that this centuries-old way of classifying human beings is holding up the imagination of people who are supposed to be on the front lines of the most brilliant and dazzling scientific future. But then, you think, how could that possibly be—because they have such an investment.

RB: It's entrenched.

DR: And it's because they don't want to think about what it would mean to face the fact that they—here I'm talking about white researchers—and their children have their privileged position because of suffering and injustice. That they have a moral obligation to address. So they think of all these other ways of trying to address it that don't really fundamentally challenge the notion of biological race or white biological superiority. I mean, why would a white researcher say, "I'm really concerned that the daughters of my babysitters can't escape poverty and achieve what my daughter can achieve," or "I'm really concerned that black children in Philadelphia are so involved in the juvenile justice system," and their solution is to study the amount of gray matter or causes of conduct disorder in the brains of poor black children. Why would they do that instead of focusing on all the institutionalized barriers and forms of state violence against these children?

I really don't think it's coming from "those children belong to an inferior race" as much as these white researchers can't face the fact their children are better off because they're privileged. And if they want to do something about it, they are going to have to actually engage in dismantling systems that have privileged them and their children. But instead, they have created a giant industry of research looking for biological explanations and technological fixes for black disadvantage. Just common sense would tell you that's not what's going to solve the problem. I've been in so many conversations with white scientists who are liberal. They say they're coming from a place of wanting to "serve" these populations.

But when I suggest that the path they're on is not a good one, it could even harm the people they're claiming to help, they dig in their heels. They resist questioning their own privileged positions. I just think, wow, what is their investment in this?

RB: So what research agendas and technological developments do you think are vital for younger scholars to pay close attention to?

DR: Well, one is gene editing. I'm very alarmed by how scientists and the media are painting human genetic modification as strictly beneficial. I think we both saw the *New York Times* headline this morning—"Breakthrough"—about the first genetically modified human embryo. It's like the view of foster care we were discussing. "It can only help us!"

RB: With a million caveats buried down in the story.

DR: Exactly. But there seems to be, I think, too little understanding and interest in how gene editing not only privileges certain elites because they can afford to have access to it, but it's deeper than that. It's that it privileges people who don't have a stake in social change. So it's not just a matter of, well, let them use it if they want to. The material, ideological, and political resources are going to go toward gene editing to improve future children and away from changing the unequal conditions that people are living under now. Not to mention the racist images associated with it. I'm so tired of blond-haired, blue-eyed, white babies being held up as the so-called perfect products of gene editing.

But the deeper issue, to me, is how it takes the attention away from institutionalized discrimination, to the suffering of people who are tangled in these—not only stingy programs, but institutions affirmatively targeting them for violence. Gene editing isn't going to solve that. And it takes attention away from it in a really profound way. Because it pinpoints the problem in a "dangerous mutation," as opposed to dangerous social structures. So that is, I think, something that we should be paying attention to.

RB: I agree. And I would add, going back to one of the points you were making about foster care and these algorithmic risk assessments—is that in addition to these big initiatives around things like gene editing, there's also a more mundane, everyday penetrance of these technologies that reinforce unjust systems that have been around for a while.

DR: Yes. Absolutely. I was going to mention that. Predictive algorithms are taking over so many domains. They're in law enforcement, they're in foster care, they're in education, they're in health care. And this pretense that they are another technological solution to bias when, in fact, as we were talking about, they import biases. Not just prejudices, but

Ruha Benjamin and Dorothy Roberts

the structural biases. The people creating the algorithms are importing structural biases that already exist.

RB: Why do you think predictive approaches to decision making and governance capture the imagination?

DR: I think this relates, in part, to why genetics is so alluring. There's this belief that there is such a thing as pure science, pure mathematics, and pure algorithms, and people seem to forget that human beings are creating all of it. I have to remind my students all the time when we talk about ancestry testing, for example, that DNA isn't labeled by race. Somebody has to figure out what is an ancestry-informative marker. Somebody has to program [the bioinformatics software platform] STRUCTURE to find clusters of genetic similarity. There is this view that the DNA itself has information that the expert scientist is discovering, and that's just not true. But it's a very common misperception.

RB: And it's interesting to think about how the desire for technology to make all the decisions is happening at a time when there's a growing loss of faith that humans can be trusted to make sound decisions, political leaders or otherwise. It's a kind of displacement of human agency. One response to this could be that we need to pour more energy into engendering governance structures and modes of collective decision making that are actually trustworthy.

DR: Right. That's true. But the thing is, though, part of the smokescreen is that when you say we don't trust human beings, we'll trust the robots, you're actually taking away agency from the most disadvantaged people who don't have control over the algorithms. So it's not that we don't trust human agency. We're trusting the people that are doing the genetic engineering and creating the algorithms and building the robots. So we're actually increasing the agency of the most elite and advantaged, whose decisions are going into all of that technology. What we need is to give people who have been shut out more agency. So, for example, with gene editing, what we need is for the most disadvantaged people, who are going to be hurt by the switch to gene editing, as opposed to social change, to have a say in scientific development. In biomedical research, the research participants who are going through the brain scan to discover how the reduction in their brain matter is claimed to be the cause of their poverty—they should be the ones having a say in how this research is being designed and conducted.

You know, one of the things in the back of my mind as we've been talking about issues at the intersection of technology and society is the importance of a black feminist abolitionist approach because it expands our imagination of what is possible. For example, not relying on law enforcement to address domestic violence, but also envisioning what is going to replace carceral approaches. How can we deal with violence without relying on state violence? And that's the answer to the algorithms that are going to incorporate all of the institutionalized discrimination against people of color back into who is captured by the carceral state. The answer, to me, is the leadership and vision and strategizing and thinking and organizing of women of color, who want to abolish those structures going into the algorithms. You know, it really relates, I think, to what you were saying about human agency. What would it mean to give agency to the survivors of state and private violence to imagine and implement the best way to deal with it? That's such a different way of thinking.

RB: Absolutely. As we wind down and come full circle, one of the things that I really appreciate in talking to you is how the fire of fifteen-year-old Dorothy [Laughter] and the nineteen-year-old Dorothy in Chicago, in Colombia, is still here. I think so often we get schooled out of our idealism and our fire, with the more people learn about unjust social structures, we often become cynical and disillusioned. But you've retained the fire! That is something that I think we both want for our students, that the more they know, it shouldn't dampen their determination and desire for change—

DR: I agree with you that I want students to come out of my classes more enlightened about how inequality operates. Then that enlightenment leads them to, number one, have the tools to articulate what they felt, but they didn't quite know how to identify it, how to say it. Then to think about how they're going to move forward in their education and their future lives to do something about it. But the first thing is, you have to have a mind-set to imagine that you can do something. It's the opposite of what we were talking about, the people who clench their fists and say, "I can't imagine that. I can't imagine getting past race." You know, well, try.

RB: Precisely! This reminds me of the words of one of my favorite writers, Arundhati Roy, when she says, "The first step towards reimagining a world gone terribly wrong, is to stop making war on those who have a different imagination." This speaks to the way that those who monopolize power, epistemic and otherwise, try to shut down certain ways of thinking. For instance, the way that black feminist approaches to prison abolition are seen as unrealistic. That's a way of making war on those who have a different, *liberatory* imagination. And we have to really resist that urge.

Ruha Benjamin and Dorothy Roberts

Bibliography

Abel, Emily K. *Tuberculosis and the Politics of Exclusion: A History of Public Health and Migration to Los Angeles*. New Brunswick, NJ: Rutgers University Press, 2007.

Ahmed, Sara. *The Cultural Politics of Emotion*. Edinburgh: Edinburgh University Press, 2004.

Ahmed, Sara. *Queer Phenomenology: Orientations, Objects, Others*. Durham, NC: Duke University Press, 2006.

Ahmed, Sara, and Jackie Stacey, eds. *Thinking through the Skin*. London: Routledge, 2001.

Ajunwa, Ifeoma, Kate Crawford, and Jason Schultz. "Limitless Worker Surveillance." *California Law Review* 105, no. 3 (2016): 735–76.

Albanesius, Chloe. "HP Responds to Claim of 'Racist' Webcams," 2009. Pcmag.com. Accessed January 14, 2018. https://www.pcmag.com/article2/0,2817,2357429,00.asp.

Alexander, Michelle. *The New Jim Crow: Mass Incarceration in the Age of Colorblindness*. New York: New Press, 2012.

Almaguer, Tomás. *Racial Fault Lines: The Historical Origins of White Supremacy in California*. Berkeley: University of California Press, 1994.

Altieri, Miguel. "Agroecology versus Ecoagriculture: Balancing Food Production and Biodiversity Conservation in the Midst of Social Inequity." Commission on Environmental, Economic and Social Policy Occasional Paper No. 3 (2004): 8–28.

Alvarez, Luis. *The Power of the Zoot: Youth Culture and Resistance during World War II*. Berkeley: University of California Press, 2008.

Amar, Paul. "Introduction. New Racial Missions of Policing: Comparative Studies of State Authority, Urban Governance, and Security Technology in the Twenty-First Century." *Ethnic and Racial Studies* 33, no. 4 (2010): 575–92.

Amoore, Louise. "Algorithmic War: Everyday Geographies of the War on Terror." *Antipode* 41, no. 1 (January 2009): 49–69.

Amoore, Louise. *The Politics of Possibility: Risk and Security Beyond Probability*. Durham, NC: Duke University Press, 2013.

Amoore, Louise. "Security and the Incalculable." *Security Dialogue* 45, no. 5 (2014): 423–39.

Anderson, Reynaldo, and John Jennings. "Afrofuturism: The Visual Imagery of Kanye West." In *The Cultural Impact of Kanye West*, edited by Julius Bailey. New York: Palgrave Macmillian, 2013.

Aneesh, Aneesh. "Global Labor: Algocratic Modes of Organization." *Sociological Theory* 27, no. 4 (2009): 347–70.

Anglin, Sallie. "Generative Motion: Queer Ecology and Avatar." *Journal of Popular Culture* 48, no. 2 (2015): 341–54.

Angwin, Julia, Jeff Larson, Surya Mattu, and Lauren Kirchner. "Machine Bias." ProPublica, May 23, 2016. Accessed January 25, 2018. https://www.propublica.org /article/machine-bias-risk-assessments-in-criminal-sentencing.

Anteby, Michel, and Curtis K. Chan. "Being Seen and Going Unnoticed: Working under Surveillance." Paper presented at the Annual Meeting of the American Sociological Association, New York, August 13, 2013.

Appadurai, Arjun. *Modernity at Large: Cultural Dimensions of Globalization*. Minneapolis: University of Minnesota Press, 1996.

Arkin, Ronald. *Governing Lethal Behavior in Autonomous Robots*. Boca Raton, FL: Chapman and Hall, 2009.

Armour, Stephanie. "Borrowers Hit Social-Media Hurdles." *Wall Street Journal*, January 8, 2014. Accessed January 3, 2017. https://www.wsj.com/articles/borrowers-hit -socialmedia-hurdles-1389224469.

Association of Correctional Food Service Affiliates. "About ACFSA." Accessed July 8, 2017. http://www.acfsa.org/about.php.

Association of Correctional Food Service Affiliates. "Invitation to Attend 2017 Conference." Accessed July 8, 2017. http://www.acfsa.org/documents/2017Conf /2017InvitationToAttend.pdf.

Atanasoski, Neda, and Kalindi Vora. "Surrogate Humanity: Posthuman Networks and the (Racialized) Obsolescence of Labor." *Catalyst: Feminism, Theory, Technoscience* 1, no. 1 (2015): 1–40.

Atkins, Carolyn Peluso. "Do Employment Recruiters Discriminate on the Basis of Nonstandard Dialect?" *Journal of Employment Counseling* 30 (September 1993): 108–19.

Avila, Eric. *Popular Culture in the Age of White Flight: Fear and Fantasy in Suburban Los Angeles*. Berkeley: University of California Press, 2004.

Azavea. "Beyond the Box: Towards Prescriptive Analysis in Policing," 2014. Accessed June 30, 2017. https://www.youtube.com/watch?v=NCXFDfQsYBE&feature=youtu .be&t=33m41s.

Azavea. "HunchLab: Under the Hood," 2015. Accessed June 30, 2017. https://cdn.azavea .com/pdfs/hunchlab/HunchLab-Under-the-Hood.pdf.

Azavea. "Resources," 2016. Accessed June 30, 2017. https://www.hunchlab.com /resources/.

Azavea. "Announcing Our New User Interface," 2017. Accessed June 30, 2017. https:// www.youtube.com/watch?v=2mdqTAX4Yz0&t=2521s.

Azavea. "Features," 2017. Accessed June 30, 2017. https://www.hunchlab.com/features/.

Bailey, Moya, and Ayana A. H. Jamieson. "Palimpsests in the Life and Work of Octavia E. Butler." *Palimpsest: A Journal on Women, Gender, and the Black International* 6, no. 2 (2017): v–xiii.

Baker, Houston A. *Blues, Ideology, and Afro-American Literature: A Vernacular Theory*. Chicago: University of Chicago Press, 1984.

Ball, Kirstie. "Workplace Surveillance: An Overview." *Labor History* 51, no. 1 (April 1, 2010): 87–106. https://doi.org/10.1080/00236561003654776.

Ball, Kirstie, and Laureen Snider. *The Surveillance-Industrial Complex: A Political Economy of Surveillance*. New York: Routledge, 2013.

Baptist, Edward E. *The Half Has Never Been Told: Slavery and the Making of American Capitalism*. New York: Basic Books, 2014.

Baraka, Amiri. "Technology and Ethos." In *Raise, Race, Rays, Raze: Essays since 1965*. New York: Random House, 1971.

Bargu, Banu. *Starve and Immolate the Politics of Human Weapons*. New York: Columbia University Press, 2015.

Barndt, Deborah. *Tangled Routes: Women, Work, and Globalization on the Tomato Trail*. Lanham, MD: Rowman and Littlefield, 2008.

Bauman, Dan. "Campus Police Acquire Military Weapons." *New York Times*, September 21, 2014. https://www.nytimes.com/2014/09/22/world/americas/campus-police -acquire-military-weapons.html.

Bebout, Lee. *Whiteness on the Border: Mapping the U.S. Racial Imagination in Brown and White*. New York: NYU Press, 2016.

Beck, Charlie, and Colleen McCue. "Predictive Policing: What Can We Learn from Wal-Mart and Amazon about Fighting Crime in a Recession?" *Police Chief*, November 2009.

Becker, Gary. "Crime and Punishment: An Economic Approach." In *Essays in the Economics of Crime and Punishment*, edited by Gary Becker and William M. Landes, 1–55. New York: Columbia University Press, 1974.

Beckett, Katherine, and Naomi Murakawa. "Mapping the Shadow Carceral State: Toward an Institutionally Capacious Approach to Punishment." *Theoretical Criminology* 16, no. 2 (2012): 221–44.

Bell, Derrick A. "Who's Afraid of Critical Race Theory?" *University of Illinois Law Review* (1995): 893–910.

Bell, Susan E., and Anne E. Figert. *Reimagining (Bio)Medicalization, Pharmaceuticals, and Genetics: Old Critiques and New Engagements*. New York: Routledge, 2015.

Beller, Jonathan. *The Message Is Murder: Substrates of Computational Capital*. London: Pluto Press, 2017.

Benjamin, Ruha. *People's Science: Bodies and Rights on the Stem Cell Frontier*. Stanford, CA: Stanford University Press, 2013.

Benjamin, Ruha. "Informed Refusal: Toward a Justice-Based Bioethics." *Science, Technology, and Human Values* 41, no. 6 (2016): 967–90.

Benjamin, Ruha. "Innovating Inequity: If Race Is a Technology, Postracialism Is the Genius Bar." *Ethnic and Racial Studies* 39, no. 13 (2016): 1–8.

Benjamin, Ruha. *Race after Technology: Abolitionist Tools for the New Jim Code*. Cambridge: Polity, 2019.

Benkler, Yochai, and Helen Nissenbaum. "Commons-Based Peer Production and Virtue." *Journal of Political Philosophy* 4, no. 14 (2006): 394–419.

Bernstein, Elizabeth. "The Sexual Politics of the 'New Abolitionism.'" *Differences* 18, no. 3 (2007): 128–51.

Bertrand, Marianne, and Sendhil Mullainathan. "Are Emily and Greg More Employable Than Lakisha and Jamal? A Field Experiment on Labor Market Discrimination." *American Economic Review* 94, no. 4 (2004): 991–1013.

Birgitvanhout. "Black Doll White Doll." YouTube, 2007. Accessed December 30, 2017. https://www.youtube.com/watch?v=ybDaogSuAcg.

Bittel, Carla Jean. *Mary Putnam Jacobi and the Politics of Medicine in Nineteenth-Century America*. Chapel Hill: University of North Carolina Press, 2009.

Blas, Zach. "Informatic Opacity." *Journal of Aesthetics and Protest*, May 31, 2013. http://www.joaap.org/issue9/zachblas.htm.

Bliss, Catherine. *Race Decoded: The Genomic Fight for Social Justice*. Palo Alto, CA: Stanford University Press, 2012.

Bond-Graham, Darwin, and Ali Winston. "All Tomorrow's Crimes: The Future of Policing Looks a Lot Like Good Branding." *SF Weekly*, October 30, 2013. Accessed June 30, 2017. https://archives.sfweekly.com/sanfrancisco/all-tomorrows-crimes-the-future-of-policing-looks-a-lot-like-good-branding/Content?oid=2827968.

Bonilla-Silva, Eduardo. *Racism without Racists*, 5th ed. Lanham, MD: Rowman and Littlefield, 2018.

Borneman, John. *Cruel Attachments: The Ritual Rehab of Child Molesters in Germany*. Chicago: University of Chicago Press, 2015.

Boucher, Dave. "Aramark Lone Bidder for Tennessee Food Service Contract." *Tennessean*, August 12, 2016. Accessed July 8, 2017. http://www.tennessean.com/story/news/2016/08/12/aramark-lone-bidder-tennessee-prison-food-contract/88446156/.

Bouldin, Joanna. "The Body, Animation and the Real: Race, Reality and the Rotoscope in Betty Boop." In *Conference Proceedings for Affective Encounters: Rethinking Embodiment in Feminist Media Studies*, edited by Anu Koivunen and Susanna Paasonen. Turku, Finland: University of Turku, 2001.

Bouldin, Joanna. "Cadaver of the Real: Animation, Rotoscoping and the Politics of the Body." *Animation Journal* 12 (2004): 7–31.

Bowditch, Vincent Yardley. *Life and Correspondence of Henry Ingersoll Bowditch*. Boston: Houghton Mifflin, 1902.

Bowker, Geoffrey C., and Susan Leigh Star. *Sorting Things Out: Classification and Its Consequences*. Cambridge, MA: MIT Press, 2000.

Bowman, Theron. "Defining Terms and Introducing Issues." Paper presented at the first Predictive Policing Symposium, Los Angeles, November 18, 2009.

boyd, danah, and Kate Crawford. "Critical Questions for Big Data: Provocations for a Cultural, Technological, and Scholarly Phenomenon." *Information, Communication and Society* 15, no. 5 (2012): 662–79.

boyd, danah, Karen Levy, and Alice Marwick. "The Networked Nature of Algorithmic Discrimination." In *Data and Discrimination*, 53–57. New York: Open Technology Institute, 2014.

Brace, C. L. *Race Is a Four-Letter Word*. New York: Oxford University Press, 2005.

Brantingham, P. Jeffrey, and Martin B. Short. "Crime Emergence." In *When Crime Appears*, edited by Jean Marie McGlorin, Christopher J. Sullivan, and Leslie W. Kennedy, 73–96. London: Routledge, 2012.

Bratton, Benjamin H. *The Stack: On Software and Sovereignty*. Cambridge, MA: MIT Press, 2016.

Braun, Lundy. *Breathing Race into the Machine: The Surprising Career of the Spirometer from Plantation to Genetics*. Minneapolis: University of Minnesota Press, 2014.

Brayne, Sarah. "Surveillance and System Avoidance: Criminal Justice Contact and Institutional Attachment." *American Sociological Review* 79, no. 3 (2014): 367–91.

Brayne, Sarah. "Big Data Surveillance: The Case of Policing." *American Sociological Review* 82, no. 5 (2017): 997–1008.

Bridges, Khiara M., Terence Keel, and Osagie K. Obasogie. "Introduction: Critical Race Theory and the Health Sciences." *American Journal of Law and Medicine* 43 (2017): 179–82.

Brock, André. "From the Blackhand Side: Twitter as a Cultural Conversation." *Journal of Broadcasting and Electronic Media* 56, no. 4 (2012): 529–49.

Brock, André, Lynette Kvasny, and Kayla Hales. "Cultural Appropriations of Technical Capital: Black Women, Weblogs, and the Digital Divide." *Information, Communication, and Society* 13, no. 7 (2010): 1040–59.

Brophy, Enda. "The Subterranean Stream: Communicative Capitalism and Call Centre Labour." *Ephemera* 10, no. 3/4 (2010): 470–83.

Brown, Wendy. *States of Injury: Power and Freedom in Late Modernity*. Princeton, NJ: Princeton University Press, 1995.

Browne, Simone. "Race and Surveillance." In *Routledge Handbook of Surveillance Studies*, edited by Kirstie Ball, Kevin Haggerty, and David Lyon, 72–79. New York: Routledge, 2012.

Browne, Simone. *Dark Matters: On the Surveillance of Blackness*. Durham, NC: Duke University Press, 2015.

Brunton, Finn, and Helen Nissenbaum. "Vernacular Resistance to Data Collection and Analysis: A Political Theory of Obfuscation." *First Monday* 16, no. 5 (May 2, 2011). http://firstmonday.org/ojs/index.php/fm/article/view/3493.

Brush, Stephen B., and Doreen Stabinsky, eds. *Valuing Local Knowledge: Indigenous People and Intellectual Property Rights*. Washington, DC: Island Press, 1996.

Brustien, Joshua. "This Guy Trains Computers to Find Future Criminals." *Bloomberg*, July 18, 2016. Accessed June 30, 2017. https://www.bloomberg.com/features/2016-richard-berk-future-crime/.

Bueerman, Jim. "What Chiefs Expect from Predictive Policing: Perspectives from Police Chiefs." Paper presented at the first Predictive Policing Symposium, Los Angeles, November 18, 2009.

Butler, Bethonie. "Grandmaster Flash on 'The Get Down' and How He Used Science to Pioneer DJ Techniques." *Washington Post*, August 23, 2016. Accessed June 26, 2017.

https://www.washingtonpost.com/news/arts-and-entertainment/wp/2016/08/23
/grandmaster-flash-on-the-get-down-and-how-he-used-science-to-pioneer-dj
-techniques/?utm_term=.b655cac2b.

Byrnes, W. Malcolm. "E. E. Just and Creativity in Science: The Importance of Diversity." *Journal of African American Studies* 19, no. 3 (2015): 264–78.

Cacho, Lisa Marie. *Social Death: Racialized Rightlessness and the Criminalization of the Unprotected.* New York: NYU Press, 2012.

Camp, Camille Graham, ed. *Corrections Yearbook: Adult Corrections 2002.* Middletown, VA: Criminal Justice Institute, 2003.

Camp, Jordan T., and Christina Heatherton, eds. *Policing the Planet: Why the Policing Crisis Led to Black Lives Matter.* London: Verso, 2016.

Campanelli, Vito. "Technological Unconscious." *Streaming Egos, Digital Identities.* Goethe Institute, n.d.. Accessed December 30, 2017. http://blog.goethe.de/streamingegos/archives/76-Technological-Unconscious.html.

Camplin, Erika. *Prison Food in America.* Lanham, MD: Rowman and Littlefield, 2017.

Cannon, Walter B. *Biographical Memoir: Henry Pickering Bowditch 1840–1911.* Washington, DC: National Academy of Sciences, 1922.

Carlson, Holly K., and Monica A. McHenry. "Effect of Accent and Dialect on Employability." *Journal of Employment Counseling* 43 (June 2006): 70–84.

Carney, Jordain. "Paul: Police Should Give Back Military Gear." *The Hill*, May 27, 2015. http://thehill.com/blogs/floor-action/senate/243203-rand-paul-police-should-be-forced-to-give-back-military-gear.

Carrns, Ann. "Little Credit History? Lenders Are Taking a New Look at You." *New York Times*, February 24, 2017. Accessed April 18, 2017. https://www.nytimes.com/2017/02/24/your-money/26money-adviser-credit-scores.html?rref=collection%2Ftimestopic%2FFair%20Isaac%20Corporation&action=click&contentCollection=business&region=stream&module=stream_unit&version=latest&contentPlacement=2&pgtype=collection.

"Case Study: Mall of America's Enhanced Service Portal." Geofeedia, 2015. https://vdocuments.site/download/geofeedia-casestudy-mallofamerica-55d6c211ce10d.

Castañeda, Claudia. "Robotic Skin: The Future of Touch?" In *Thinking Through the Skin*, edited by Sara Ahmed and Jackie Stacey, 223–36. London: Routledge, 2001.

Chairman of the Joint Chiefs of Staff. *DoD Dictionary of Military and Associated Terms.* Washington, DC: Department of Defense, April 2018. http://www.jcs.mil/Portals/36/Documents/Doctrine/pubs/dictionary.pdf?ver=2018-05-02-174746-340.

Chamayou, Grégoire. "Patterns of Life: A Very Short History of Schematic Bodies by Grégoire Chamayou." *The Funambulist: Bodies, Designs and Politics*, December 14, 2014. http://thefunambulist.net/2014/12/04/the-funambulist-papers-57-schematic-bodies-notes-on-a-patterns-genealogy-by-gregoire-chamayou/.

Chamayou, Grégoire. *A Theory of the Drone.* Translated by Janet Lloyd. New York: New Press, 2015.

Champagne, Christine. "Anatomy of a Cannes Contender: Becoming Sweetie, the Little Girl Who Took on Child Predators." *Fast Company*, 2014. https://www.fastcompany.com/3031676/anatomy-of-a-cannes-contender-becoming-sweetie-the-little-girl-who-took-on-child-predators?partner=newsletter.

Charlesworth, Jessica. "Primer 2017: A Speculative Futures Conference." Core77, March 21, 2017. Accessed January 25, 2018. http://www.core77.com/posts/63489/Primer-2017-A-Speculative-Futures-Conference.

Chen, Mel. *Animacies: Biopolitics, Racial Mattering, and Queer Affect*. Durham, NC: Duke University Press, 2012.

Cheney-Lippold, John. *We Are Data: Algorithms and the Making of Our Digital Selves*. New York: NYU Press, 2017.

Chew, Matthew, and Andrew L. Hamilton. "The Rise and Fall of Biotic Nativeness: A Historical Perspective." In *Fifty Years of Invasion Ecology: The Legacy of Charles Elton*, edited by David M. Richardson, 35–47. Oxford: Blackwell, 2011.

Chun, Wendy H. K. "Race and/as Technology or How to Do Things with Race." In *Race After the Internet*, edited by Lisa Nakamura and Peter Chow-White, 38–69. New York: Routledge, 2011.

Citron, Danielle Keats. *Hate Crimes in Cyberspace*. Cambridge, MA: Havard University Press, 2014.

Citron, Danielle Keats, and Frank Pasquale. "The Scored Society: Due Process for Automated Predictions." *Washington Law Review* 89 (2014): 1–33.

Clark, Kenneth. *Prejudice and Your Child*. Boston: Beacon Press, 1955.

Clarke, Adele, Laura Mamo, Jennifer Ruth Fosket, Jennifer R. Fishman, and Janet K. Shim. *Biomedicalization: Technoscience, Health, and Illness in the U.S.* Durham, NC: Duke University Press, 2010.

Clarke, Peleg. "Dr Clarke's Case of Haematemesis." *New-England Medical Review and Journal* 15 (1827): 99–102.

Clough, Patricia Ticineto. "The Digital, Labor, and Measure Beyond Biopolitics." In *Digital Labor: The Internet as Playground and Factory*, edited by Trebor Scholz. New York: Routledge, 2013.

Clough, Patricia Ticineto, Karen Gregory, Benjamin Haber, and Josh Scannell. "The Datalogical Turn." In *Non-Representational Methodologies: Re-Envisioning Research*, edited by Phillip Vannini, 146–64. New York: Routledge, 2015.

Clough, Patricia Ticineto, and Craig Willse. "Gendered Security/National Security: Political Branding and Population Racism." *Social Text* 28, no. 4 (2010): 45–63.

Clover, Joshua. *Riot. Strike. Riot. The New Era of Uprisings*. Brooklyn, NY: Verso, 2016.

CNN. "A Look at Race Relations through a Child's Eyes." YouTube, 2012. Accessed December 30, 2017. https://www.youtube.com/watch?v=GPVNJgfDwpw.

Cole, Simon A. *Suspect Identities: A History of Fingerprinting and Criminal Identification*. Cambridge, MA: Harvard University Press, 2009.

Coleman, Beth. "Race as Technology." *Camera Obscura* 24, no. 1 (2009): 177–207.

Collins, Patricia Hill. *Black Feminist Thought: Knowledge, Consciousness, and the Politics of Empowerment*, 2nd ed. New York: Routledge, 2000.

Comolli, Jean-Louis. "Technique and Ideology: Camera, Perspective, Depth of Field." In *Film Reader 2*, edited by P. Erens and B. Horrigan, 128–40. Evanston, IL: Northwestern University Press, 1977.

Comolli, Jean-Louis. "Technique and Ideology: Camera, Perspective, Depth of Field (Parts 3 and 4)." In *Narrative, Apparatus, Ideology: A Film Theory Reader*, translated by Diana Matias, edited by Philip Rosen, 421–43. New York: Columbia University Press, 1986.

Comolli, Jean-Louis, and Jean Narboni. "Cinema/Ideology/Criticism." Translated by Susan Bennett. *Screen* 12, no. 1 (1971): 27–36.

Comolli, Jean-Louis, and Jean Narboni. "Cinema/Ideology/Criticism (2)." Translated by Susan Bennett. *Screen* 12, no. 2 (1971): 145–55.

Connor, Kathy. Author interview, Rochester, NY, August 16, 1997.

Consumer Financial Protection Bureau. "Analysis of Differences between Consumer-and-Creditor-Purchased Credit Scores," 2012. Accessed April 17, 2017. http://files.consumerfinance.gov/f/201209_Analysis_Differences_Consumer_Credit.pdf.

Cook, Rhonda. "Davis' Last Day: A Goodbye to Family." *Atlanta Journal-Constitution*, September 21, 2011. Accessed on August 5, 2016. http://www.ajc.com/news/news/local/davis-last-day-a-goodbye-to-family/nQL2s/.

Cooper, Melinda. *Life as Surplus: Biotechnology and Capitalism in the Neoliberal Era*. Seattle: University of Washington Press, 2008.

Cooper, Steven J. "From Claude Bernard to Walter Cannon: Emergence of the Concept of Homeostasis." *Appetite* 51, no. 3 (2008): 419–27.

Corkery, Michael. "Treasury to Examine Online Lending Industry." *New York Times*, July 16, 2015. Accessed January 3, 2017. https://www.nytimes.com/2015/07/17/business/dealbook/treasury-examines-whether-to-regulate-online-lenders.html.

Courtois, Stéphane, ed. *The Black Book of Communism: Crimes, Terror, Repression*. Translated by Jonathan Murphy and Mark Kramer. Cambridge, MA: Harvard University Press, 1999.

Cousins, Ben. "Capitalism Obscured: The Limits of Law and Rights-Based Approaches to Poverty Reduction and Development." *Journal of Peasant Studies* 36, no. 4 (2009): 893–908.

Crawford, Kate. "Artificial Intelligence's White Guy Problem." *New York Times*, June 25, 2016. https://www.nytimes.com/2016/06/26/opinion/sunday/artificial-intelligences-white-guy-problem.html?_r=1.

Creary, Melissa. "Biocultural Citizenship and Embodying Exceptionalism: Biopolitics for Sickle Cell Disease in Brazil." *Social Science and Medicine* 199 (2017): 123–31. Accessed January 25, 2018. https://www.sciencedirect.com/science/article/pii/S0277953617302654.

Crenshaw, Kimberlé. "Demarginalizing the Intersection of Race and Sex: A Black Feminist Critique of Antidiscrimination Doctrine, Feminist Theory, and Antiracist Politics." *University of Chicago Legal Forum* 1989, no. 1: 139–67.

Crosby, Alfred. *Ecological Imperialism: The Biological Expansion of Europe, 900–1900.* Cambridge: Cambridge University Press, 2004.

Cueto, Marcos. "An Asymmetrical Network: National and International Dimensions of the Development of Mexican Physiology." *Journal of the History of Medicine and Allied Sciences* 71, no. 1 (2015): 43–63.

Curtin, Deane. "Making Peace with the Earth: Indigenous Agriculture and the Green Revolution." *Environmental Ethics* 17, no. 1 (1995): 59–73.

"Cyberbabe to the Read the News." BBC, January 17, 2000. Accessed December 19, 2016. http://news.bbc.co.uk/2/hi/entertainment/606855.stm.

Dabney, Dean A., Joshua Page, and Volkan Topalli. "American Bail and the Tinting of Criminal Justice." *The Howard Journal of Crime and Justice* 56, no. 4 (2017): 397–418.

Dahad, Nitin. "Africa Tech Hub Promotes Tech Innovation." *The Next Silicon Valley,* September 12, 2013.

Dahl, Darren. "The Six-Minute Loan: How Kabbage Is Upending Small Business Lending—And Building a Very Big Business," *Forbes,* May 6, 2015, 56–60.

Davis, Angela Y. *Are Prisons Obsolete?* New York: Seven Stories Press, 2011.

Davis, Angela Y. *The Meaning of Freedom: And Other Difficult Dialogues.* San Francisco: City Lights Publishers, 2012.

Davis, Angela Y. *Freedom Is a Constant Struggle: Ferguson, Palestine, and the Foundations of a Movement.* Chicago: Haymarket Books, 2016.

Davis, Mike, Kelly Mayhew, and Jim Miller. *Under the Perfect Sun: The San Diego Tourists Never See.* New York: New Press, 2005.

Davis, Mike. *City of Quartz: Excavating the Future in Los Angeles.* London: Verso, 2006.

D'Cruz, Premilla. *Workplace Bullying in India.* New Delhi: Routledge, 2014.

D'Cruz, Premilla, and Ernesto Noronha. "The Interface between Technology and Customer Cyberbullying: Evidence from India." *Information and Organization* 24, no. 3 (2014): 176–93.

Dean, Jodi. *Democracy and Other Neoliberal Fantasies: Communicative Capitalism and Left Politics.* Durham, NC: Duke University Press, 2009.

de la Cadena, Marisol. "Anterioridades y externalidades: Más allá de la raza en América Latina." *E-Misférica* 5, no. 2 (2008). http://hemisphericinstitute.org/hemi/en/e-misferica-52/delacadena.

de la Cadena, Marisol. "Runa: Human but *Not Only.*" HAU: *Journal of Ethnographic Theory* 4, no. 2 (2014): 253–59.

de la Cadena, Marisol. *Earth Beings: Ecologies of Practice Across Andean Worlds.* Durham, NC: Duke University Press, 2015.

De La Ray, Rick. "Mamba Bamba." *Issuu,* March 2015. Accessed October 25, 2017. https://issuu.com/thelakeco/docs/the_lake_3.

Del Carmen Consulting. "Annual Contact Report 2016." Accessed June 30, 2017. http://www.arlington-tx.gov/police/wp-content/uploads/sites/9/2017/03/Arlington-Raciall-Profiling-Report-2016-.pdf.

Deleuze, Gilles. "Postscript on the Societies of Control." *October* 59 (1992): 3–7.

Deleuze, Gilles. *Difference and Repetition*. Translated by Paul Patton. New York: Columbia University Press, 1995.

Demos, Telis, and Deepa Seetharaman. "Facebook Isn't So Good at Judging Your Credit After All." *Wall Street Journal*, February 16, 2016. Accessed January 3, 2017. https://www.wsj.com/articles/lenders-drop-plans-to-judge-you-by-your-facebook-friends-1456309801.

Derrida, Jacques. "Force of Law: The 'Mystical Foundation of Authority.'" In *Acts of Religion*, edited by Gil Anidjar, 231–98. New York: Routledge, 2002.

Dery, Mark. "Culture Jamming: Hacking, Slashing, and Sniping in the Empire of Signs." *Open Magazine Pamphlet Series*, 1993. http://markdery.com/?page_id=154.

Dery, Mark. *Flame Wars: The Discourse of Cyberculture*. Durham, NC: Duke University Press, 1994.

Desmond, Adrian, and James Moore. *Darwin's Sacred Cause: How a Hatred of Slavery Shaped Darwin's Views on Human Evolution*. London: Penguin Books, 2009.

Deterville, Duane. "Defining the Afriscape through Ground Drawings and Street Altars." Paper presented at the Visual and Creative Studies Thesis Symposium, San Francisco, April 4, 2009.

Dick, Philip K. *The Minority Report and Other Classic Stories*. New York: Citadel, 2002.

Dilts, Andrew. *Punishment and Inclusion: Race, Membership, and the Limits of American Liberalism*. New York: Fordham University Press, 2014.

Dilts, Andrew. "To Build a World That Is Otherwise: Andrew Dilts on Abolition." *Abolition Journal*, July 2, 2015. Accessed January 25, 2018. https://abolitionjournal.org/andrew-dilts-abolition-statement/.

Dilts, Andrew, and Perry Zurn, eds. *Active Intolerance: Michel Foucault, the Prisons Information Group, and the Future of Abolition*. New York: Palgrave Macmillan, 2015.

Doezema, Jo. "Ouch! Western Feminists' 'Wounded Attachment' to the 'Third World Prostitute.'" *Feminist Review* 67 (2001): 16–38.

Doezema, Jo. "Now You See Her, Now You Don't: Sex Workers at the UN Trafficking Protocol Negotiations." *Social and Legal Studies* 14, no. 1 (2005): 61–89.

Doleac, Jennifer L., and Luke C. D. Stein. "The Visible Hand: Race and Online Market Outcomes." Stanford Institute for Economic Policy Research, Discussion Paper No. 10-025, 2010.

Donahue, Christopher. "Franz Boas and His Contemporaries." *Ether Wave Propaganda*, October 15, 2013. Accessed May 1, 2017. https://etherwave.wordpress.com/2013/10/15/franz-boas-on-the-instability-of-human-types/.

Dormandy, Thomas. *The White Death: A History of Tuberculosis*. New York: NYU Press, 2000.

Douglass, Frederick. "The Claims of the Negro, Ethnologically Speaking." An address before the literary societies of Western Reserve College, at commencement July 12, 1854.

Douglass, Frederick. *The Life and Times of Frederick Douglass*. Hartford, CT: Park Publishing Company, 1881.

Bibliography

Droit, Roger-Pol. "Michel Foucault, on the Role of Prisons." *New York Times*, August 5, 1975. Accessed January 25, 2018. http://www.nytimes.com/books/00/12/17/specials /foucault-prisons.html.

Duster, Troy. *Backdoor to Eugenics*, 2nd ed. New York: Routledge, 2003.

Duster, Troy. "The Combustible Intersection: Genomics, Forensics, and Race." In *Race after the Internet*, edited by Lisa Nakamura and Peter Chow-White, 310–27. New York: Routledge, 2011.

Duster, Troy. *The Legislation of Morality: Law, Drugs, and Moral Judgement*. New York: Free Press, 1970.

Duster, Troy. "Race and Reification in Science." *Science* 307, no. 5712 (2005): 1050–51.

Edelman, Benjamin, and Michael Luca. "Digital Discrimination: The Case of Airbnb .com." Harvard Business School, Working Paper No. 14-054, 2014.

Edelman, Benjamin, Michael Luca, and Dan Svirsky. "Racial Discrimination in the Sharing Economy: Evidence from a Field Experiment." *American Economic Journal: Applied Economics* 9, no. 2 (2016): 1–22.

Edelman, Lee. *No Future: Queer Theory and the Death Drive*. Durham, NC: Duke University Press, 2004.

Eglash, Ron. "Cybernetics and American Youth Subculture." *Cultural Studies* 12, no. 3 (1998): 382–409.

Eglash, Ron. "Computation, Complexity and Coding in Native American Knowledge Systems." In *Changing the Faces of Mathematics: Perspectives on Indigenous People of North America*, edited by Judith Hankes and Gerald Fast, 251–62. Reston, VA: National Council of Teachers of Mathematics, 2002.

Eglash, Ron. "Race, Sex, and Nerds: From Black Geeks to Asian American Hipsters." *Social Text* 20, no. 2 (2002): 49–64.

Eglash, Ron. "An Ethnocomputing Comparison of African and Native American Divination Systems." In *Reviewing Reality: Dynamics of African Divination*, edited by Walter E. A. van Beek, and Philip M. Peek, 295–312. Zurich: LIT Verlag, 2013.

Eglash, Ron. "A Generative Perspective on Engineering: Why the Destructive Force of Artifacts Is Immune to Politics." Paper delivered at Engineering a Better Future: Interplay of Social Science, Engineering and Innovation, Carnegie Mellon University, April 2016.

Eglash, Ron. "An Introduction to Generative Justice." *Revista Teknokultura* 13, no. 2 (2016): 369–404.

Eglash, Ron, and David Banks. "Recursive Depth in Generative Spaces: Democratization in Three Dimensions of Technosocial Self-Organization." *Information Society* 30, no. 2 (2014): 106–15.

Eglash, Ron, Audrey Bennett, Casey O'Donnell, Sybillyn Jennings, and Margaret Cintorino. "Culturally Situated Design Tools: Ethnocomputing from Field Site to Classroom." *American Anthropologist* 108, no. 2 (2006),: 347–62.

Eglash, Ron, Jennifer L. Croissant, Giovanna Di Chiro, and Rayvon Fouché. *Appropriating Technology: Vernacular Science and Social Power*. Minneapolis: University of Minnesota Press, 2004.

Eglash, Ron, and Colin Garvey. "Basins of Attraction for Generative Justice." In *Chaos Theory in Politics: Understanding Complex Systems*, edited by S. Banerjee, Ş. Erçetin, and A. Tekin, 75–88. Dordrecht: Springer, 2014.

Eichelberger, Erika. "Your Deadbeat Facebook Friends Could Cost You a Loan." *Mother Jones*, September 18, 2013. Accessed January 3, 2017. http://www.motherjones.com /politics/2013/09/lenders-vet-borrowers-social-media-facebook/.

Electronic Frontier Foundation. "Georgia Tech Police Department Drone Records," 2009. https://www.eff.org/document/georgia-tech-police-dept.

El-Haj, Nadia A. "The Genetic Reinscription of Race." *Annual Review of Anthropology* 36 (2007): 283–300.

Emdin, Christopher. "Exploring the Contexts of Urban Science Classrooms, Part 1: Investigating Corporate and Communal Practices." *Cultural Studies of Science Education* 2 (2007): 319–50.

Engel, Pamela. "The City of Camden, New Jersey Is under Intense, Military-Style Surveillance." *Business Insider*, December 30, 2013. Accessed January 25, 2018. http://www.businessinsider.com/camden-new-jersey-police-surveillance-2013-12.

Epstein, Steven. *Inclusion: The Politics of Difference in Medical Research*. Chicago. University of Chicago Press, 2007.

Escobar, Arturo. *Encountering Development: The Making and Unmaking of the Third World*. Princeton, NJ: Princeton University Press, 1995.

Esposito, Maurizio. *Romantic Biology, 1890–1945*. New York: Routledge, 2015.

Esteva, Gustavo. "Development as a Threat: The Struggle for Rural Mexico." In *Peasants and Peasant Societies*, edited by Teodor Shanin, 452–57. Oxford: Blackwell, 1987.

Eubanks, Virginia. *Automated Inequality: How High-Tech Tools Profile, Police, and Punish the Poor*. New York: St. Martin's, 2018.

Fanon, Frantz. *Black Skin, White Masks*. New York: Grove, 1967.

Farivar, Cyrus. "We Know Where You've Been: Ars Acquires 4.6M License Plate Scans from the Cops." *Ars Technica*, March 24, 2015. https://arstechnica.com/tech-policy /2015/03/we-know-where-youve-been-ars-acquires-4-6m-license-plate-scans -from-the-cops/.

Favret, Mary. *War at a Distance: Romanticism and the Making of Modern Wartime*. Princeton, NJ: Princeton University Press, 2010.

Federal Deposit Insurance Corporation. "2015 FDIC National Survey of Unbanked and Underbanked Households," 2016. Accessed January 3, 2017. https://www.fdic.gov /householdsurvey/.

Federal Trade Commission. "Prepared Statement of the Federal Trade Commission on Credit Scoring before the House Banking and Financial Services Committee Subcommittee on Financial Institutions and Consumer Credit," 2000. http:// docplayer.net/15225942-Prepared-statement-of-the-federal-trade-commission -credit-scoring.html.

Federal Trade Commission. "Credit Scores," 2013. Accessed January 3, 2017. https:// www.consumer.ftc.gov/articles/0152-credit-scores#what.

Feldman, Keith. "Empire's Verticality: The Af/Pak Frontier, Visual Culture, and Racialization from Above." *Comparative American Studies* 9, no. 4 (2011): 325–41.

Fergus, Devin. "The Ghetto Tax: Auto Insurance, Postal Code Profiling, and the Hidden History of Wealth Transfer." In *Beyond Discrimination: Racial Inequality in a Postracist Era*, edited by Fredrick C. Harris and Robert C. Lieberman, 277–316. New York: Russell Sage Foundation, 2013.

Fergus, Devin. "Financial Fracking in the Land of the Fee, 1980–2008." In *The Assets Perspective: The Rise of Asset Building and Its Impact on Social Policy*, edited by Reid Cramer and Trina R. Williams Shanks, 67–95. New York: Palgrave Macmillan, 2014.

Fergus, Devin, and Tim Boyd. "Introduction—Banking without Borders: Culture and Credit in the New Financial World." *Kalfou* 1 (2014): 7–28.

Ferguson, Andrew Guthrie. *The Rise of Big Data Policing: Surveillance, Race, and the Future of Law Enforcement*. New York: NYU Press, 2017.

Ferguson, Andrew Guthrie, and Damien Bernache. "The High Crime Area Question: Requiring Verifiable and Quantifiable Evidence for Fourth Amendment Reasonable Suspicion Analysis." *American University Law Review* 57, no. 6 (2008): 1587–1644.

Ferguson, Roderick A. *Aberrations in Black: Towards a Queer of Color Critique*. Minneapolis: University of Minnesota Press, 2004.

FICO. "Learn about the FICO® Score and Its Long History," n.d. Accessed January 15, 2017. http://www.fico.com/25years/.

Finnegan, Cara A. *Recognizing Lincoln: Image Vernaculars in Nineteenth-Century Visual Culture*. Thousand Oaks, CA: Sage, 2005.

Foucault, Michel. *Discipline and Punish: The Birth of the Prison*. Translated by Adam Sheridan. New York: Vintage, 1977.

Foucault, Michel. *Security, Territory, Population: Lectures at the Collège de France, 1977–1978*. Edited by Michel Senellart. New York: Picador, 2007.

Foucault, Michel. *The Birth of Biopolitics: Lectures at the Collège de France 1978–1979*. Translated by Adam Sheridan. New York: Vintage, 2008.

Fouché, Rayvon. "Not Made for Black History Month: Lewis Latimer and Technological Assimilation." In *Appropriating Technology: Vernacular Science and Social Power*, edited by Ron Eglash, Jennifer Croissant, Giovanna Di Chiro, and Rayvon Fouché, 315–30. Minneapolis: University of Minnesota Press, 2004.

Fouché, Rayvon. "Say It Loud, I'm Black and I'm Proud: African Americans, American Artifactual Culture, and Black Vernacular Technological Creativity." *American Quarterly* 58, no. 3 (2006),: 639–61.

Fouché, Rayvon. "From Black Inventors to One Laptop Per Child: Exporting a Racial Politics of Technology." In *Race after the Internet*, edited by Lisa Nakamura and Peter A. Chow-White. New York: Routledge, 2011.

Fourcade, Marion, and Kieran Healy. "Classification Situations: Life Changes in the Neoliberal Era." *Accounting, Organizations and Society*. 38 (2013): 559–72.

Fraser, Nancy. "Rethinking Recognition." *New Left Review* 3 (May–June 2000): 107–20. http://www.newleftreview.org/?view=2248.

Frey, Chris. "Revealed: How Facial Recognition Has Invaded Shops — And Your Privacy." *The Guardian*, March 3, 2016. https://www.theguardian.com/cities /2016/mar/03/revealed-facial-recognition-software-infiltrating-cities-saks -toronto.

Friedmann, Harriet. "The Political Economy of Food: A Global Crisis." *New Left Review* 197 (1993): 29–57.

Fujimura, Joan H., and Ramya Rajagopalan. "Different Differences: The Use of 'Genetic Ancestry' versus Race in Biomedical Human Genetic Research." *Social Studies of Science* 41, no. 1 (2010): 5–30.

Fullwiley, Duana. "The Biologistical Construction of Race: 'Admixture' Technology and the New Genetic Medicine." *Social Studies of Science* 38, no. 5 (2008): 695–735.

Gacheru, Margaretta. "The Kenyan Art Scene." *ArtAfrica*, 2017. Accessed January 11, 2018. https://artsouthafrica.com/220-news-articles-2013/2846-kenyan-art-scene-by -margaretta-wa-gacheru.html.

Gajjala, Venkataramana, Radhika Gajjala, Anca Birzescu, and Samara Anarbaeva. "Microfinance in Online Space: A Visual Analysis of Kiva.org." *Development in Practice* 21, no. 6 (2011): 880–93.

Gamber, John. *Positive Pollutions and Cultural Toxins: Waste and Contamination in Contemporary U.S. Ethnic Literatures*. Lincoln: University of Nebraska, 2012.

Gandy, Oscar. *Coming to Terms with Chance: Engaging Rational Discrimination and Cumulative Disadvantage*. New York: Routledge, 2009.

Gandy, Oscar, and Lemi Baruh. "Racial Profiling: They Said It Was against the Law!" *University of Ottawa Law and Technology Journal* 3, no. 1 (2006): 297–327.

García-Martínez, Marc. *The Flesh-and-Blood Aesthetics of Alejandro Morales: Disease, Sex, and Figuration*. San Diego: San Diego State University Press, 2014.

Garvey, Sean. "Atlanta Police Receive Counterterrorism Training in Israel." WABE, July 10, 2015. http://news.wabe.org/post/atlanta-police-receive-counterterrorism -training-israel.

Garza, José. "Social Turbulence as Reflected in Alejandro Morales' Novelistic Techniques." PhD dissertation, Indiana University, 2006.

Gaskins, Nettrice. "Hair Braiding Is Technology." *Recess*, August 2014. Accessed June 19, 2017. https://www.recessart.org/nettrice-gaskins-critical-writing.

Gaskins, Nettrice. "Techno-Vernacular Creativity, Innovation and Learning in Underrepresented Ethnic Communities of Practice." PhD dissertation, Georgia Institute of Technology, 2014.

Gates, Henry L. *The Signifying Monkey: A Theory of African-American Literary Criticism*. Oxford: Oxford University Press, 1988.

Gaul, Jerry. "Aramark Wins Food Services Contract for Prisons; Pa. Says Deal Saves Taxpayers Millions." *Philly Voice*, February 15, 2017. Accessed July 9, 2017. http:// www.phillyvoice.com/aramark-awarded-food-services-contract-prisons-pa-says -deal-saves-taxpayers-16-million/.

Ge, Yanbo, Christopher R. Knittel, Don MacKenzie, and Stephen Zoepf. "Racial and Gender Discrimination in Transportation Network Companies." National Bureau of Economic Research, Working Paper No. 22776, 2016.

Gee, Alistair. "More Than One-Third of Schoolchildren Are Homeless in Shadow of Silicon Valley." *The Guardian*, December 28, 2016. Accessed January 25, 2018. https://www.theguardian.com/society/2016/dec/28/silicon-valley-homeless-east -palo-alto-california-schools.

German, Mike, and Jay Stanley. "Fusion Center Update." American Civil Liberties Union, July 2008. https://www.aclu.org/files/pdfs/privacy/fusion_update _20080729.pdf.

Gilmore, Ruth Wilson. "Globalisation and US Prison Growth: From Military Keynesianism to Post-Keynesian Militarism." *Race and Class* 40, no. 2/3 (1999): 171–88.

Gilmore, Ruth Wilson. *Golden Gulag: Prisons, Surplus, Crisis, and Opposition in Globalizing California*. Berkeley: University of California Press, 2007.

Gilroy, Paul. *The Black Atlantic: Modernity and Double Consciousness*. Cambridge, MA: Harvard University Press, 1993.

Glanville, Doug. "Doug Glanville on Why He Still Gets Shunned by Taxi Drivers." *The Atlantic*, October 24, 2015. http://www.theatlantic.com.

Glazer, Nona Yetta. *Women's Paid and Unpaid Labor: The Work Transfer in Health Care and Retailing*. Philadelphia: Temple University Press, 1993.

Glissant, Édouard. *Poetics of Relation*. Ann Arbor: University of Michigan Press, 1997.

Godrej, Farah. "Spaces for Counter-Narratives: The Phenomenology of Reclamation." Paper presented at the Midwest Political Science Association meeting, Chicago, April 3–5, 2003.

Goldberg, David Theo. *The Racial State*. Hoboken, NJ: Wiley-Blackwell, 2002.

Goldmark, Alex. "Micro-Bias: If You Want a Kiva Loan, It Helps to Be Pretty and Light-Skinned." Good, Inc., March 29, 2012. Accessed December 19, 2016. www.goodis .com.

Gonzalez, Gilbert G. *Chicano Education in the Era of Segregation*. Dallas: University of North Texas Press, 2013.

Gordon, Avery. *Ghostly Matters: Haunting and the Sociological Imagination*. Minneapolis: University of Minnesota Press, 1997.

Gordon, Leslie. "New Report Faults California's Electronic Monitoring of Youth." University of California–Berkeley School of Law, July 11, 2017. Accessed January 25, 2018. https://www.law.berkeley.edu/article/new-report-faults-californias -electronic-monitoring-youth/.

Gossett, Che. "Pulse, Beat, Rhythm, Cry: Orlando and the Queer and Trans Necropolitics of Loss and Mourning." Verso Books, July 5, 2016. https://www.versobooks .com/blogs/2747-pulse-beat-rhythm-cry-orlando-and-the-queer-and-trans -necropolitics-of-loss-and-mourning.

Gould, Stephen Jay. *The Mismeasure of Man*. New York: W. W. Norton and Company, 1981.

Gowdy, John. *Limited Wants, Unlimited Means: A Reader on Hunter-Gatherer Economics and the Environment.* Washington, DC: Island Press, 1998.

Grant, Melissa Gira. *Playing the Whore: The Work of Sex Work.* New York: Jacobin.

Green, Laurie B., John Raymond McKiernan-González, and Martin Anthony Summers. "Introduction: Making Race, Making Health." In *Precarious Prescriptions: Contested Histories of Race and Health in North America,* edited by Laurie B. Green, John Raymond McKiernan-González, and Martin Anthony Summers, vii–xxviii. Minneapolis: University of Minnesota Press, 2014.

Greenberg, Reesa. "'Remembering Exhibitions': From Point to Line to Web." Tate Papers, No. 12 (autumn 2009). http://www.tate.org.uk/research/publications/tate -papers/12/remembering-exhibitions-from-point-to-line-to-web.

Greenwald, Glenn. "The Militarization of the U.S. Police: Finally Dragged into the Light by the Horrors of Ferguson." *The Intercept,* August 14, 2014. https:// theintercept.com/2014/08/14/militarization-u-s-police-dragged-light-horrors -ferguson/.

Gregg, Melissa. *Work's Intimacy.* Cambridge: Polity, 2011.

Gregory, Derek. *The Colonial Present: Afghanistan, Palestine, Iraq.* Malden, MA: Blackwell, 2004.

Gregory, Derek. "Drone Geographies." *Radical Philosophy* 183 (January/February 2014): 7–19.

Grewal, Inderpal. "Drone Imaginaries: The Technopolitics of Visuality in Postcolony and Empire." In *Life in the Age of Drone Warfare,* edited by Lisa Parks and Caren Kaplan, 343–65. Durham, NC: Duke University Press, 2017.

Griffiths, Josie. "Losing Face: What Is FaceApp, What Were the 'Race Change' Filters and Has the App Been in Accused of Racism Before?" *The Sun,* August 10, 2017. Accessed January 14, 2018. https://www.thesun.co.uk/tech/3410186/faceapp-selfie-app -race-change-filters-change/.

Groen, Jacco (dir.). *Lilet Never Happened.* London: Spring Film, 2012.

Grossberg, Lawrence. "On Postmodernism and Articulation: An Interview with Stuart Hall." In *Stuart Hall: Critical Dialogues in Cultural Studies,* edited by Kuan-Hsing Chen and David Morley, 131–50. London: Routledge, 1996.

Gurpegui Palacios, José Antonio. *Alejandro Morales: Fiction Past, Present, Future Perfect.* Tempe, AZ: Bilingual Review/Press, 1996.

Gustavsson, Eva. "Virtual Servants." *Gender, Work and Organization* 12 (5): 400–419.

Gutiérrez, David. *Walls and Mirrors: Mexican Americans, Mexican Immigrants, and the Politics of Ethnicity.* Berkeley: University of California Press, 1995.

Guzik, Keith. "Discrimination by Design: Predictive Data Mining as Security Practice in the United States' 'War on Terrorism.'" *Surveillance and Society* 7, no. 1 (2009): 1–17.

Gwynn, Charles W. *Imperial Policing.* London: Macmillan, 1934.

Haas, Peter M. "Do Regimes Matter? Epistemic Communities and Mediterranean Pollution Control." *International Organization* 43, no. 3 (1989): 377–403.

Hall, Rachel. "Terror and the Female Grotesque: Introducing Full-Body Scanners to U.S. Airports." In *Feminist Surveillance Studies*, edited by Rachel E. Dubrofsky and Shoshana Amielle Magnet, 127–49. Durham, NC: Duke University Press, 2015.

Hall, Ron E. "The Bleaching Syndrome: Implications of Light Skin for Hispanic American Assimilation." *Hispanic Journal of Behavioral Sciences* 16, no. 3 (1994): 405–18.

Hall, Ron E. "The Bleaching Syndrome: African Americans' Response to Cultural Domination vis-à-vis Skin Color." *Journal of Black Studies* 26, no. 2 (1995): 172–84.

Hall, Stuart. "The Whites of Their Eyes: Racist Ideologies and the Media." In *The Media Reader*, edited by M. Alvarado and J. O. Thompson, 7–23. London: British Film Institute, 1990.

Hall, Stuart. "Race, Culture, and Communications: Looking Backward and Forward at Cultural Studies." *Rethinking Marxism* 5, no. 1 (1992): 10–18.

Hall, Stuart, Chas Critcher, Tony Jefferson, John Clarke, and Brian Roberts. *Policing the Crisis: Mugging, the State and Law and Order*, 2nd ed. New York: Palgrave Macmillan, 2013.

Hammonds, Evelynn M. "New Technologies of Race." In *Processed Lives: Gender and Technology in Everyday Life*, edited by Melodie Calvery and Jennifer Terry, 74–85. New York: Routledge, 1997.

Haraway, Donna. *Crystals, Fabrics, and Fields: Metaphors That Shape Embryos*. Berkeley, CA: North Atlantic, 1976.

Haraway, Donna. *Simians, Cyborgs and Women: The Reinvention of Nature*. New York: Routledge, 1991.

Haraway, Donna. "Situated Knowledges: The Science Question in Feminism and the Privilege of Partial Perspective." *Feminist Studies* 14, no. 3 (1988): 575–99.

Haraway, Donna. *Staying with the Trouble: Making Kin in the Chthulucene*. Durham, NC: Duke University Press, 2016.

Haraway, Donna. "The Virtual Speculum in the New World Order." *Feminist Review* 55 (1997): 22–72.

Harcourt, Bernard E. *Against Prediction: Profiling, Policing, and Punishing in an Actuarial Age*. Chicago: Chicago University Press, 2006.

Harcourt, Bernard E. *The Illusion of Free Markets: Punishment and the Myth of Natural Order*. Cambridge, MA: Harvard University Press, 2011.

Harcourt, Bernard E. *Exposed: Desire and Disobedience in the Digital Age*. Cambridge, MA: Harvard University Press, 2015.

Harrington, Anne. *Reenchanted Science: Holism in German Culture from Wilhelm II to Hitler*. Princeton, NJ: Princeton University Press, 1996.

Harris, Brian. Author interview, Washington, DC, July 3, 1997.

Hartman, Saidiya V. *Scenes of Subjection: Terror, Slavery, and Self-Making in Nineteenth-Century America*. New York: Oxford University Press, 1997.

Harvey, David. "The New Imperialism: Accumulation by Dispossession." *Socialist Register* 40 (2004): 43–87.

Hasegawa, Toru. Author interview, New York, May 27, 1996.

Hatch, Anthony Ryan. *Blood Sugar: Racial Pharmacology and Food Justice in Black America*. Minneapolis: University of Minnesota Press, 2016.

Hatch, Anthony, and Kym Bradley. "Prisons Matter: Psychotropics and the Trope of Silence in Technocorrections." In *Mattering: Feminism, Science, and Materialism*, edited by Victoria Pitts-Taylor, 224–40. New York: NYU Press, 2016.

Hayes, L. J. B., and Sian Moore. "Care in a Time of Austerity: The Electronic Monitoring of Homecare Workers' Time." *Gender, Work & Organization* 24, no. 4 (2016): 329–44.

Heims, Steve J. *John von Neumann and Norbert Wiener*. Cambridge, MA: MIT Press, 1984.

Herbert, Steve. *Policing Space: Territoriality and the Los Angeles Police Department*. Minneapolis: University of Minnesota Press, 1997.

Hernández, Kelly Lytle. *Migra! A History of the U.S. Border Patrol*. Berkeley: University of California Press, 2010.

Hernández, Kelly Lytle. *City of Inmates: Conquest, Rebellion, and the Rise of Human Caging in Los Angeles, 1771–1965*. Chapel Hill: University of North Carolina Press, 2017.

Hicks, Marie. *Programmed Inequality: How Britain Discarded Women Technologists and Lost Its Edge in Computing*. Cambridge, MA: MIT Press, 2017.

Hill, Ally Rao, and Alastair Tombs. "The Effect of Accent of Service Employee on Customer Service Evaluation." *Managing Service Quality* 21, no. 6 (2011): 649–66.

Hindmarsh, Richard, and Barbara Prainsack, eds. *Genetic Suspects: Global Governance of Forensic DNA Profiling and Databasing*. Cambridge: Cambridge University Press, 2010.

Hinton, Elizabeth. *From the War on Poverty to the War on Crime: The Making of Mass Incarceration in America*. Cambridge, MA: Harvard University Press, 2016.

Hollibaugh, Amber, and Margot Weiss. "Queer Precarity and the Myth of Gay Affluence." *New Labor Forum* 24 (2015): 18–27.

Hornblum, Allen M. *Acres of Skin: Human Experiments at Holmesburg Prison: A Story of Abuse and Exploitation in the Name of Medical Science*. New York: Routledge, 1998.

Horowitz, Emily. *Protecting Our Kids? How Sex Offender Laws Are Failing Us*. Santa Barbara, CA: Praeger, 2015.

Hosoda, Megumi, and Eugene Stone-Romero. "The Effects of Foreign Accents on Employment-Related Decisions." *Journal of Managerial Psychology* 25, no. 2 (2010): 113–32.

Hu, Tung-Hui. *A Prehistory of the Cloud*. Cambridge, MA: MIT Press, 2015.

Human Rights Watch. "Irreparable Harm," 2013. Accessed July 2017. https://www.hrw.org/report/2013/05/01/raised-registry/irreparable-harm-placing-children-sex-offender-registries-us.

Hussain, Nasser. "The Sound of Terror: A Phenomenology of a Drone Strike." *Boston Review*, October 16, 2013. https://bostonreview.net/world/hussain-drone-phenomenology.

Hynes, Casey. "How Social Media Could Help the Unbanked Land a Loan." *Forbes*, April 25, 2017. Accessed May 20, 2017. https://www.forbes.com/sites/chynes/2017/04/25/how-data-will-help-drive-universal-financial-access/.

Illman, Erin. "CFPB Focused on Financial Technology in 2016—Expect More for 2017." *Banking & Financial Services Policy Report* 36 (2017): 1–2.

Imarisha, Walidah, and adrienne maree brown. *Octavia's Brood: Science Fiction Stories from Social Justice Movements.* Oakland, CA: AK Press, 2015.

Immergluck, Dan, and Jonathan Law. "Speculating in Crisis: The Intrametropolitan Geography of Investing in Foreclosed Homes in Atlanta." *Urban Geography* 35, no. 1 (2014): 1–24.

Irving, Washington. *The Kaaterskill Edition of Washington Irving.* New York: Pollard and Moss, 1882.

Jackson, Zakiyyah Iman. "Animal: New Directions in the Theorization of Race and Posthumanism." *Feminist Studies* 39, no. 3 (2013): 669–85.

JafariNaimi, Nassim. "Our Bodies in the Trolley's Path, or Why Self-driving Cars Must *Not* Be Programmed to Kill." *Science, Technology, & Human Values* (2017). Accessed January 25, 2018. http://journals.sagepub.com/doi/pdf/10.1177/0162243917718894

JafariNaimi, Nassim, Lisa Nathan, and Ian Hargraves. "Values as Hypotheses: Design, Inquiry, and the Service of Values." *Design Issues* 31, no. 4 (2015): 91–104.

James, Joy. *Warfare in the American Homeland: Policing and Prison in a Penal Democracy.* Durham, NC: Duke University Press, 2007.

James, William. "The Energies of Men." Delivered as the presidential address the American Philosophical Association at Columbia University, December 28, 1906..

Jaquez, Nefertiti. "Atlanta Police's High-Tech Cameras Helping Catch Criminals." WSBTV. February 24, 2017,. http://www.wsbtv.com/news/local/atlanta/atlanta -polices-high-tech-cameras-helping-catch-criminals/494039551.

Jasanoff, Sheila. *States of Knowledge: The Co-Production of Science and the Social Order.* New York: Routledge, 2004.

Jasanoff, Sheila, and Sang-Hyun Kim. *Dreamscapes of Modernity: Sociotechnical Imaginaries and the Fabrication of Power.* Chicago: University of Chicago Press, 2015.

Jenkins, Bill. "Phrenology, Heredity and Progress in George Combe's Constitution of Man." *British Journal for the History of Science* 48, no. 3 (2015): 455–73.

Jenq, Christina, Jessica Pan, and Walter Theseira. "Beauty, Weight, and Skin Color in Charitable Giving." *Journal of Economic Behavior and Organization* 119 (2015): 234–53.

Jerkins, Morgan. "The Quiet Racism of Instagram Filters." *Racked,* July 7, 2015. Accessed on July 7, 2015. https://www.racked.com/2015/7/7/8906343/instagram -racism.

Jirón-King, Shimberlee. "Illness, Observation, and Contradiction: Intertext and Intrahistory in Alejandro Morales's *The Captain of All These Men of Death.*" *Bilingual Review/La Revista Bilingüe* 29, no. 1 (2008): 3–13.

Joh, Elizabeth E. "The New Surveillance Discretion: Automated Suspicion, Big Data, and Policing." *Harvard Law and Policy Review* 10, no. 1 (2016): 15–42.

Johnson, Alan. "Union Says Its Prison Food Contract Would Save Ohio Taxpayers 44 Million." *Columbus Dispatch,* February 1, 2017. Accessed July 9, 2017. http://www

.dispatch.com/news/20170201/union-says-its-prison-food-contract-would-save
-ohio-taxpayers-44-million.

Johnson, Walter. *River of Dark Dreams: Slavery and Empire in the Cotton Kingdom*. Cambridge, MA: Harvard University Press, 2013.

Johnson, Walter. "Ferguson's Fortune 500 Company." *The Atlantic*, April 26, 2015.
Accessed January 25, 2018. https://www.theatlantic.com/politics/archive/2015/04
/fergusons-fortune-500-company/390492.

Jones, David S., and Ian Whitmarsh, eds. *What's the Use of Race? Modern Governance and
the Biology of Difference*. Cambridge, MA: MIT Press, 2010.

Jones, Nikki. *Between Good and Ghetto: African American Girls and Inner-City Violence*.
New Brunswick, NJ: Rutgers University Press, 2009.

Kage, Earl. Author interview, Rochester, NY, August 21, 1995.

Kahn, Jonathan. *Race in a Bottle: The Story of BiDil and Racialized Medicine in a Post-
Genomic Age*. New York: Columbia University Press, 2014.

Kanaboshi, Naoki. "Prison Inmates' Right to Hunger Strike." *Criminal Justice Review* 39,
no. 2 (2014): 121–39.

Kaplan, Amy. *The Anarchy of Empire in the Making of U.S. Culture*. Cambridge, MA: Harvard University Press, 2002.

Kaplan, Caren. *Aerial Aftermaths: Wartime from Above*. Durham, NC: Duke University
Press, 2017.

Kaplan, Caren. "Drone-o-Rama." In *Life in the Age of Drone Warfare*, edited by Lisa Parks
and Caren Kaplan, 161–77. Durham, NC: Duke University Press, 2017.

Kasoff, Jan. Author interview, New York, November 20, 1994.

Kasoff, Jan. Author interview, New York, February 15, 2016.

Katz, Stephen. "What It's Like to Actually Eat the Food in Oakland County Jail." *Detroit
Metro Times*, July 8, 2015. Accessed November 10, 2016. https://www.metrotimes
.com/detroit/what-ts-like-to-actually-eat-the-food-in-oakland-county-jail
/Content?oid=2354552.

Kearney, Richard. "Walter Benjamin." In *Modern Movements in European Philosophy:
Phenomenology, Critical Theory, Structuralism*, 151–68. Manchester: Manchester
University Press, 1994.

Keeling, Kara. *The Witch's Flight: The Cinematic, the Black Femme, and the Image of Common Sense*. Durham, NC: Duke University Press, 2007.

Kelkar, Kamala. "Prison Strike Organizers to Protest Food Giant Aramark." PBS *Newshour*, January 8, 2017. Accessed July 7, 2017. http://www.pbs.org/newshour/updates
/prison-strike-protest-aramark/.

Kelley, Robin D. G. "'We Are Not What We Seem': Rethinking Black Working-Class Opposition in the Jim Crow South." *Journal of American History* 80 (1993): 75–112.

Kelley, Robin D. G. *Freedom Dreams: The Black Radical Imagination*. Boston: Beacon,
2003.

Kendi, Ibram X. *Stamped from the Beginning: The Definitive History of Racist Ideas in
America*. New York: Nation, 2016.

Bibliography

Kerr, Ian R. "Bots, Babes and the Californication of Commerce." *University of Ottawa Law & Technology Journal* 1 (2004): 285–324.

Khalek, Rania. "Atlanta Mayor Rejects Demand to End Israel Police Training." *Electronic Intifada*, July 21, 2016. https://electronicintifada.net/blogs/rania-khalek/atlanta-mayor-rejects-demand-end-israel-police-training.

King, James. "IMF World Bank: Credit Scoring—Friends, Followers, and Settling Scores." *The Banker*, (2014).

King, Joyce E. "Dysconscious Racism: Ideology, Identity, and the Miseducation of Teachers." In *Racism: Essential Readings*, edited by E. Cashmore and J. Jennings, 295–303. London: SAGE, 2001.

King, Shaun. "Predictive Policing Is 'Technological Racism." *New York Daily News*, November 5, 2015. Accessed December 28, 2017. http://www.nydailynews.com/new-york/king-predictive-policing-technological-racism-article-1.2425028.

Kirsky, Eben, ed. *The Multispecies Salon*. Durham, NC: Duke University Press, 2014.

Kish, Zenia, and Justin Leroy. "Bonded Life: Technologies of Racial Finance from Slave Insurance to Philanthrocapital." *Cultural Studies* 29, no. 5–6 (2015): 630–51.

Kleeman, Sophie. "Here Are the Microsoft Twitter Bot's Craziest Racist Rants." Gizmodo.com, March 24, 2016.

Kleinman, Alexis. "Meet the Woman Who Says She's the Voice of Siri." *Huffington Post*, October 4, 2013.

Koper, Christopher S. "Just Enough Police Presence: Reducing Crime and Disorderly Behavior by Optimizing Patrol Time in Crime Hotspots." *Justice Quarterly* 12, no. 4 (1995): 649–72.

Krupar, Shiloh, and Nadine Ehlers. "'When Treating Patients Like Criminals Makes Sense': Medical Hot Spotting, Race, and Debt." In *Subprime Health: The American Health-Care System and Race-Based Medicine*, edited by Nadine Ehlers and Leslie Hinkson, 31–54. Minnesota: University of Minnesota Press, 2017.

Kumar, Kavita. "When MOA Shoppers Talk in Cyberspace, the Mall's Likely to Talk Back." *Minneapolis Star Tribune*, November 22, 2015. http://www.startribune.com/when-you-talk-about-the-mall-of-america-in-cyberspace-these-days-it-s-likely-to-talk-back/35297320.

Kuznick, Peter J. "The Birth of Scientific Activism." *Bulletin of the Atomic Scientists* 44, no. 10 (1988): 39–43.

Lachney, Michael. "Culturally Responsive Computing as Brokerage: Toward Asset Building with Education-Based Social Movements." *Learning, Media, and Technology* 42, no. 4 (2016): 420–39.

Lafrance, Adrienne. "Why Do So Many Digital Assistants Have Feminine Names?" *The Atlantic*, March 30, 2016.

Lamble, Sarah. "Queer Necropolitics and the Expanding Carceral State: Interrogating Sexual Investments in Punishment." *Law and Critique* 24, no. 3 (2013): 229–53.

Lancaster, Roger N. *Sex Panic and the Punitive State*. Berkeley: University of California Press, 2011.

Langewiesche, William. "Meet G4S, the Contractors Who Go Where Governments and Armies Can't—or Won't." *The Hive*, March 18, 2014.

Langworth, Robert H., ed. *Measuring What Matters: Proceedings from the Policing Research Institute Meetings*. Washington, DC: National Institute of Justice, 1999.

Lansing, Stephen J., and James N. Kremer. "Emergent Properties of Balinese Water Temple Networks: Coadaptation on a Rugged Fitness Landscape." *American Anthropologist* 95, no. 1 (1993): 97–114.

Laouenan, Morgane, and Roland Rathelot. "Ethnic Discrimination on an Online Marketplace of Vacation Rentals." University of Paris, Working Paper, 2016. http://rolandrathelot.com/wp-content/uploads/Laouenan.Rathelot.Airbnb.pdf.

Latour, Bruno. "On Recalling ANT." *Sociological Review* 47, no. S1 (1999): 15–25.

Lauter, David. "In China, App Aims to Shame Polluters by Showing Who Is Fouling Air." *Los Angeles Times*, December 30, 2014. Accessed June 10, 2017. http://www.latimes.com/world/asia/la-fg-china-bad-air-20141230-story.html.

Le Brun, Thierry. Author interview, Montreal, Quebec, November 27, 2006.

Lee, James Kyung-Jin. *Urban Triage: Race and the Fictions of Multiculturalism*. Minneapolis: University of Minnesota Press, 2004.

Leovy, Jill. "Breathing New Life: Olive View: Opened as a TB Sanitarium in 1920, the Hospital, Now a Modern Facility, Turned 75 This Week." *Los Angeles Times*, October 28, 1995. http://articles.latimes.com/1995-10-28/local/me-62120_1_olive-view.

Lev-Aretz, Yafit, and Nizan Geslevich Pachkin. "Don't Let Facebook Likes Sway Credit Decisions." *American Banker*, June 17, 2016. Accessed January 3, 2017. https://www.americanbanker.com/opinion/dont-let-facebook-likes-sway-credit-decisions.

Levy, Karen E. C. "Digital Surveillance in the Hypermasculine Workplace." *Feminist Media Studies* 16, no. 2 (2016): 361–65.

Lokko, Mae-ling. "Investigation of Coconut Agrowaste Upcycling for Ecologically Efficacious Building Lifecycles." PhD dissertation, Rensselaer Polytechnic Institute, 2016.

Lowe, Lisa. *Immigrant Acts: An Asian American Cultural Politics*. Durham, NC: Duke University Press, 1996.

Lowe, Lisa. *The Intimacies of Four Continents*. Durham, NC: Duke University Press, 2015.

Luce, Stephanie, Sasha Hammad, and Darrah Sipe. "Short Shifted." Retail Action Project, September 2014. http://retailactionproject.org/wp-content/uploads/2014/09/ShortShifted_report_FINAL.pdf.

Ludwig, Sarah. "Credit Scores in America Perpetuate Racial Injustice. Here's How." *The Guardian*, October 13, 2015. Accessed July 4, 2017. https://www.theguardian.com/commentisfree/2015/oct/13/your-credit-score-is-racist-heres-why.

Lum, K. and Isaac, W. "To Predict and Serve?" *Significance* 13 (2016): 14–19. doi: 10.1111/j.1740–9713.2016.00960.x.

Lupton, Deborah. "Food, Memory and Meaning: The Symbolic and Social Nature of Food Events." *Sociological Review* 42, 4 (1994): 664–85.

Lydon, Jason, et al. "Coming Out of Concrete Closets: A Report on Black and Pink's National LGBTQ Prisoner Survey." Black and Pink, October 2015.

Lyon, David, ed. *Surveillance as Social Sorting: Privacy, Risk, and Digital Discrimination.* New York: Routledge, 2003.

Lyon, David. *Surveillance Society: Monitoring Everyday Life.* London: Open University Press, 2011.

Magnet, Shoshana. *When Biometrics Fail: Gender, Race, and the Technology of Identity.* Durham, NC: Duke University Press, 2011.

Mailloux, Steven. "Re-Marking Slave Bodies: Rhetoric as Production and Reception." *Philosophy and Rhetoric* 35, no. 2 (2002): 96–119.

Maltz, Earl M., and Fred H. Miller. "The Equal Credit Opportunity Act and Regulation B." *Oklahoma Law Review* 31 (1978): 1–62.

Mamo, Laura, and Jennifer Fishman. "Why Justice? Introduction to the Special Issue on Entanglements of Science, Ethics, and Justice." *Science, Technology, and Human Values* 38, no. 2 (2013): 159–75.

Mann, Steve, Jason Nolan, and Barry Wellman. "Sousveillance: Inventing and Using Wearable Computing Devices for Data Collection in Surveillance Environments." *Surveillance & Society* 1, no. 3 (2003): 331–55.

Manning, Patrick. *The African Diaspora: A History Through Culture.* New York: Columbia University Press, 2010.

Manning, Peter K. *The Technology of Policing: Crime Mapping, Information Technology, and the Rationality of Crime Control.* New York: NYU Press, 2011.

Marez, Curtis. *Drug Wars: The Political Economy of Narcotics.* Minneapolis: University of Minnesota Press, 2004.

Marron, Donncha. "'Lending by Numbers': Credit Scoring and the Constitution of Risk within American Consumer Credit." *Economy and Society* 36 (2007): 103–33.

Marx, Gary T. *Windows into the Soul: Surveillance and Society in an Age of High Technology.* Chicago: University of Chicago Press, 2016.

Masciandaro, Nicola, ed. *Hideous Gnosis: Black Metal Theory Symposium I* (2010). http://www.radicalmatters.com/metasound/pdf/Hideous.Gnosis.Black.Metal.Theory.Symposium.I.pdf.

Massumi, Brian. *Parables for the Virtual: Movement, Affect, Sensation.* Durham, NC: Duke University Press, 2002.

Massumi, Brian. "The Future Birth of the Affective Fact." In *The Affect Theory Reader,* edited by Melissa Gregg and Gregory J. Seigworth, 53–70. Durham, NC: Duke University Press, 2011.

Massumi, Brian. *Ontopower: War, Power, and the State of Perception.* Durham, NC: Duke University Press, 2015.

Mathiesen, Thomas. "The Viewer Society: Michel Foucault's 'Panopticon' Revisited." *Theoretical Criminology* 1, no. 2 (1997): 215–34.

Mayo, Katherine. *Justice to All: The Story of the Pennsylvania State Police*. New York: G. P. Putnam's Sons, 1917.

Mbembe, Achille. "Necropolitics." *Public Culture* 15, no. 1 (2003): 11–40.

McArdle, Andrea, and Tanya Erzen, eds. *Zero Tolerance: Quality of Life and the New Police Brutality in New York City*. New York: NYU Press, 2001.

McCormack, Derek. "Remotely Sensing Affective Afterlives: The Spectral Geographies of Material Remains." *Annals of the Association of American Geographers* 100, no. 3 (July 2010): 640–54.

McFadden, Syreeta. "Teaching the Camera to See My Skin: Navigating Photography's Inherited Bias against Dark Skin." *Buzzfeed*, April 2, 2014. www.buzzfeed.com /syreetamcfadden/teaching-the-camera-to-see-my-skin.

M'Charek, Amade. "Beyond Fact or Fiction: On the Materiality of Race in Practice." *Cultural Anthropology* 28, no. 3 (2013): 420–42.

McKittrick, Katherine. *Demonic Grounds: Black Women and the Cartographies of Struggle*. Minneapolis: University of Minnesota Press, 2007.

McKittrick, Katherine. "Plantation Futures." *Small Axe* 342 (2013): 1–15.

McKittrick, Katherine, ed. *Sylvia Wynter: On Being Human as Praxis*. Durham, NC: Duke University Press, 2014.

McMichael, Phillip D. "A Food Regime Genealogy." *Journal of Peasant Studies* 36 (2009): 139–69.

McNeill, Maggie. "Lies, Damned Lies, and Sex Work Statistics." *Washington Post*, March 27, 2014.

McWilliams, Carey. *North from Mexico: The Spanish-Speaking People of the United States*. Philadelphia: J. B. Lippincott, 1949.

McWilliams, Carey. *California: The Great Exception*, rev. ed. Berkeley: University of California Press, 1999.

Mead, Louise S., Judi Brown Clarke, Frank Forcino, and Joseph L Graves. "Factors Influencing Minority Student Decisions to Consider a Career in Evolutionary Biology." *Evolution: Education and Outreach* 8, no. 1 (2015): 6.

Melamed, Jodi. *Represent and Destroy: Rationalizing Violence in the New Racial Capitalism*. Minneapolis: University of Minnesota Press, 2011.

Merkley, Jeff. "Brown, Merkley Press Federal Agencies on Oversight of Financial Technology." Press release, July 21, 2016. Accessed January 3, 2017. https://www .merkley.senate.gov/news/press-releases/brown-merkley-press-federal-agencies -on-oversight-of-financial-technology.

Mester, Loretta J. "What's the Point of Credit Scoring?" *Business Review*, September/ October 1997. Accessed January 3, 2017. https://pdfs.semanticscholar.org/4ccd/81d6 4e04ac7cadd9936a703543075fa24846.pdf.

Mignolo, Walter. *Local Histories/Global Designs: Coloniality, Subaltern Knowledges, and Border Thinking*. Princeton, NJ: Princeton University Press, 2012.

"Migratory Agricultural Workers of California: Their Health Care." *California and Western Medicine* 60, no. 2 (1944): 49–50.

Miller, Andrea. "(Im)Material Terror: Incitement to Violence Discourse as Racializing Technology in the War on Terror." In *Life in the Age of Drone Warfare*, edited by Lisa Parks and Caren Kaplan, 112–33. Durham, NC: Duke University Press, 2017.

Miller, Andrea. "Protocological Violence and the Colonial Database." *Antipode*. May 19, 2017. https://radicalantipode.files.wordpress.com/2017/05/6-andrea-miller.pdf.

Miller, Brittany. "Atlanta Neighbors Fed Up with Crime in Zone 4." CBS46.com, October 25, 2016. http://www.cbs46.com/story/33043327/neighbors-fed-up-with-crime-in-zone-4#ixzz4m4rKJIbL.

Miller, Reuben Jonathan, and Forrest Stuart. "Carceral Citizenship: Race, Rights and Responsibility in the Age of Mass Supervision." *Theoretical Criminology* 21, no. 4 (2017): 532–48.

Mintel. "FinTech Is Helping Lenders Move Away from FICO Scores," 2016.

Minton, Todd D., and Zhen Zheng. "Jail Inmates at Midyear 2014." U.S. Department of Justice, June 2015. Accessed January 25, 2018. https://www.bjs.gov/content/pub/pdf/jim14.pdf.

Mirchandani, Kiran, and Winifred R. Poster, eds. *Borders in Service: Enactments of Nationhood in Transnational Call Centers*. Toronto, ON: University of Toronto Press, 2016.

Mitlin, Diana, and David Satterthwaite. *Urban Poverty in the Global South: Scale and Nature*. New York: Routledge, 2013.

Mohandesi, Salar. "Who Killed Eric Garner?" *Jacobin*, December 12, 2014. http://jacobinmag.com/2014/12/who-killed-eric-garner/.

Molina, Natalia. *Fit to Be Citizens? Public Health and Race in Los Angeles, 1879–1939*. Berkeley: University of California Press, 2006.

Molina, Natalia. *How Race Is Made in America: Immigration, Citizenship, and the Historical Power of Racial Scripts*. Berkeley: University of California Press, 2013.

Moncada, Eduardo. "Counting Bodies: Crime Mapping, Policing and Race in Colombia." *Ethnic and Racial Studies*. 33, no. 4 (2010): 696–716.

Montgomery, Reid H., Jr., Gordon A. Crews, and William Crawley. *A History of Correctional Violence: An Examination of Reported Causes of Riots and Disturbances*. Washington, DC: American Correctional Association, 1998.

Montoya, Michael J. "Bioethnic Conscription: Genes, Race, and Mexicana/o Ethnicity in Diabetes Research." *Cultural Anthropology* 22, no. 1 (2007): 94–128.

Moore, Daniel. "Food, Dairy Companies Supplying State Prisons Unhappy with Contract Changes." *Pittsburgh Post-Gazette*, May 30, 2017. Accessed July 9, 2017. http://www.post-gazette.com/news/state/2017/05/30/aramark-pittsburgh-Food-dairy-companies-supplying-state-prisons-unhappy-with-contract-changes/stories/201704230011.

Moore, Linda. "Shelby County Employees Plead While Commissioners Ponder Food Service Contract." *Commercial Appeal*, March 16, 2015. Accessed July 10, 2017. http://archive.commercialappeal.com/news/government/county/shelby-county-employees-plead-while-commissioners-ponder-food-service-contract-ep-993775200-324443731.html.

Morales, Alejandro. *The Captain of All These Men of Death*. Tempe, AZ: Bilingual Press/ Editorial Bilingüe, 2008.

Morgan, Thomas M. "The Education and Medical Practice of Dr. James McCune Smith (1813–1865), First Black American to Hold a Medical Degree." *Journal of the National Medical Association* 95, no. 7 (2003): 603–14.

Morin, Rich, and Renee Stepler. "The Racial Confidence Gap in Police Performance." Pew Research Center for Social and Demographic Trends, September 29, 2016. Accessed June 30, 2017. http://www.pewsocialtrends.org/2016/09/29/the-racial -confidence-gap-in-police-performance/.

Morning, Ann. *The Nature of Race: How Scientists Think and Teach and Human Difference*. Berkeley: University of California Press, 2011.

Moten, Fred. "The Case of Blackness." *Criticism* 50, no. 2 (2008): 177–218.

Moten, Fred. "Blackness and Nothingness (Mysticism in the Flesh)." *South Atlantic Quarterly* 112, no. 4 (2013): 737–80.

Moten, Fred, and Stefano Harney. *The Undercommons: Fugitive Planning and Black Study*. New York: Minor Compositions, 2013.

Muehlmann, Shaylih. "How Do Real Indians Fish? Neoliberal Multiculturalism and Contested Indigeneities in the Colorado Delta." *American Anthropologist* 111, no. 4 (2009): 468–79.

Muhammad, Khalil Bigran. *The Condemnation of Blackness: Race, Crime, and the Making of Modern Urban America*. Cambridge, MA: Harvard University Press, 2010.

Mukundan, Harshini, Mark Chambers, Ray Waters, and Michelle H. Larsen. *Tuberculosis, Leprosy and Other Mycobacterial Diseases of Man and Animals: The Many Hosts of Mycobacteria*. Boston: CABI, 2015.

Muñiz, Ana. *Police, Power, and the Production of Racial Boundaries*. New Brunswick, NJ: Rutgers University Press, 2015.

Murakawa, Naomi. *The First Civil Right: How Liberals Built Prison America*. Oxford: Oxford University Press, 2014.

Myers, Peter C. *Frederick Douglass: Race and the Rebirth of American Liberalism*. Lawrence: University Press of Kansas, 2008.

NAACP. "The NAACP Filed an Historic Lawsuit Against Mortgage Lenders Alleging Racial Discrimination." NAACP.org, July 11, 2007. Accessed March 28, 2017. http:// www.naacp.org/latest/the-naacp-filed-an-historic-lawsuit-against-mortgage -lenders-alleging-racial-discrimination/.

Nakamura, Lisa. *Cybertypes: Race, Ethnicity, and Identity on the Internet*. New York: Routledge, 2002.

Nakamura, Lisa. *Digitizing Race: Visual Cultures of the Internet*. Minneapolis: University of Minnesota Press, 2007.

Nakamura, Lisa, and Peter Chow-White, eds. *Race after the Internet*. New York: Routledge, 2011.

National Telecommunications and Information Administration. *Falling through the Net: A Survey of the "Have Nots" in Rural and Urban America*. Washington, DC: U.S. Department of Commerce, 1995.

Neff, Gina, and Peter Nagy. "Talking to Bots: Symbiotic Agency and the Case of Tay." *International Journal of Communication* 10 (2016): 4915–31.

Negarestani, Reza. "The Labor of the Inhuman, Part II: The Inhuman." *e-flux* 53 (March 2014). http://www.e-flux.com/journal/53/59893/the-labor-of-the-inhuman -part-ii-the-inhuman/.

Nelson, Alondra. *The Body and Soul: The Black Panther Party and the Fight against Medical Discrimination*. Minneapolis: University of Minneapolis Press, 2013.

Nelson, Alondra. *The Social Life of DNA: Race, Reparations, and Reconciliation after the Genome*. New York: Beacon Press, 2016.

Nelson, Alondra, Thuy Linh N. Tu, and Alicia Headlam Hines, eds. *Technicolor: Race, Technology, and Everyday Life*. New York: NYU Press, 2001.

Neocleous, Mark. "Air Power As Police Power." *Environment and Planning D: Society and Space* 31, no. 4 (2013): 578–93.

Neocleous, Mark. *War Power, Police Power*. Edinburgh: Edinburgh University Press, 2014.

Neocleous, Mark, George Rigakos, and Tyler Wall. "On Pacification: Introduction to the Special Issue." *Socialist Studies/Études socialistes* 9, no. 2 (winter 2013): 1–6.

Newport, Frank. "Gallup Review: Black and White Attitudes toward Police." Gallup, August 20, 2014. Accessed June 30, 2017. http://www.gallup.com/poll/175088/gallup -review-black-white-attitudes-toward-police.aspx.

Ngai, Mai M. "The Strange Case of the Illegal Alien: Immigration Restriction and Deportation Policy in the United States, 1921–1965." *Law and History Review* 21, no. 1 (spring 2003): 69–107.

Nixon, Rob. 2011. *Slow Violence and the Environmentalism of the Poor*. Cambridge, MA: Harvard University Press, 2011.

Noble, Safiya Umoja. "Google Search: Hyper-Visibility as a Means of Rendering Black Women and Girls Invisible." *Invisible Culture* 19 (October 29, 2013). http://ivc.lib .rochester.edu/google-search-hyper-visibility-as-a-means-of-rendering-black -women-and-girls-invisible/.

Noble, Safiya Umoja. 2018. *Algorithms of Oppression: How Search Engines Reinforce Racism*. New York: NYU Press, 2018.

Noble, Safiya Umoja, and Brendesha M. Tynes, eds. *The Intersectional Internet: Race, Class, and Culture Online*. New York: Peter Lang, 2016.

Office of Economic Adjustment. "Defense Spending by State Fiscal Year 2015." U.S. Department of Defense, 2016. http://www.oea.gov/resource/defense-spending -state-fiscal-year-2015.

O'Neil, Cathy. *Weapons of Mass Destruction: How Big Data Increases Inequality and Threatens Democracy*. New York: Broadway, 2017.

Ordover, Nancy. *American Eugenics: Race, Queer Anatomy, and the Science of Nationalism.* Minneapolis: University of Minnesota Press, 2003.

"Orlando Gay Nightclub Shooting: Who Was Omar Mateen?" BBC, June 14, 2016. http://www.bbc.com/news/world-us-canada-36513468.

Packer, Jeremy, and Joshua Reeves. "Romancing the Drone: Military Desire and Anthropophobia from SAGE to Swarm." *Canadian Journal of Communication* 38 (2013): 309–331.

Packer, Jeremy, and Joshua Reeves. "Taking People Out: Drones, Media/Weapons, and the Coming Humanectomy." In *Life in the Age of Drone Warfare*, edited by Lisa Parks and Caren Kaplan, 261–81. Durham, NC: Duke University Press, 2017.

Pager, Devah. "The Mark of a Criminal Record." *American Sociological Review* 103 (March 2003): 937–75.

Panofsky, Aaron. *Misbehaving Science: Controversy and the Development of Behavior Genetics.* Chicago: University of Chicago Press, 2014.

Parham, Jason. "Why Black Mirror's Most Controversial New Episode Is Its Most Important." *Wired*, January 6, 2018. Accessed January 6, 2018. https://www.wired.com/story/black-mirror-black-museum.

Parks, Liz. "Putting Buzz to Work." National Retail Federation, June 6. 2016. https://nrf.com/news/putting-buzz-work.

Pasquale, Frank. *The Black Box Society: The Secret Algorithms That Control Money and Information.* Cambridge, MA: Harvard University Press, 2014.

Paulson, Steve. "Sherman Alexie on 'Flight,'" 2009. To the Best of Our Knowledge. Accessed June 20, 2017. http://www.ttbook.org/book/sherman-alexie-flight.

Pauly, Philip J. "The Beauty and Menace of the Japanese Cherry Trees: Conflicting Visions of American Ecological Independence." *Isis* 87, no. 1 (1996): 51–73.

Perkins, Tom. "Something Still Stinks in Michigan and Ohio's Prison Kitchens." *Detroit Metro Times*, February 17, 2016. Accessed July 6, 2017. https://www.metrotimes.com/detroit/something-still-stinks-in-michigan-and-ohios-prison-kitchens/Content?oid=2396672.

Pernet, Corinne A. "Between Entanglements and Dependencies: Food, Nutrition, and National Development at the Central American Institute of Nutrition (INCAP)." In *International Organizations and Development, 1945–1990*, edited by Marc Frey, Sönke Kunkel, and Corinna R. Unger, 101–25. New York: Palgrave Macmillan, 2014.

Perry, Walter L., Brian McInnis, Cart C. Price, Susan C. Smith, and John S. Hollywood. *Predictive Policing: The Role of Crime Forecasting in Law Enforcement Operations.* Santa Monica, CA: RAND Corporation, 2013.

Pettypiece, Shannon, and David Voreacos. "Walmart's Out-of-Control Crime Problem Is Driving Police Crazy." *Bloomberg Businessweek*, August 17, 2016.

Philip, Kavita, Lilly Irani, and Paul Dourish. "Postcolonial Computing: A Tactical Survey." *Science, Technology, and Human Values* 37, no. 1 (2012): 3–29.

Phillips, Sandra. "The Subprime Mortgage Calamity and the African American Woman." *Review of Black Political Economy* 39 (2012): 227–37.

Pieterse, Jan Nederveen. *White on Black: Images of Africa and Blacks in Western Popular Culture*. New Haven, CT: Yale University Press, 1992.

Pine, Greg. Author interview, Breda, Netherlands, September 10, 1997.

Pohl, J. Otto. *Ethnic Cleansing in the USSR, 1937–1949*. Westport, CT: Greenwood, 1999.

Pollan, Michael. "Against Nativism," *New York Times Magazine*, May 15, 1994.

Pollock, Anne. *Medicating Race: Heart Disease and Durable Preoccupations with Difference*. Durham, NC: Duke University Press, 2012.

Pollock, Anne. "On the Suspended Sentences of the Scott Sisters: Mass Incarceration, Kidney Donation, and the Biopolitics of Race in the United States." *Science, Technology, & Human Values* 40, no. 2 (2015): 250–71.

Poon, Martha. "Scorecards as Devices for Consumer Credit: The Case of Fair, Isaac & Company Incorporated." *Sociological Review* 55 (2007): 284–306.

Porter, Theodore M. *Trust in Numbers: The Pursuit of Objectivity in Science and Public Life*. Princeton, NJ: Princeton University Press, 1995.

Poster, Winifred R. "Who's on the Line? Indian Call Center Agents Pose as Americans for U.S.-Outsourced Firms." *Industrial Relations* 46, no. 2 (2007): 271–304.

Poster, Winifred R. "Emotion Detectors, Answering Machines and E-Unions: Multisurveillances in the Global Interactive Services Industry." *American Behavioral Scientist* 55, no. 7 (2011): 868–901.

Poster, Winifred R. "The Virtual Receptionist with a Human Touch: Opposing Pressures of Digital Automation and Outsourcing in Interactive Services." In *Invisible Labor*, edited by Marion G. Crain, Winifred R. Poster, and Miriam A. Cherry, 87–112. Berkeley: University of California Press, 2016.

Poster, Winifred R. "Multisurveillances: Technological Agency in Global Interactive Service Work." Unpublished monograph, Washington University, St. Louis, 2017.

Poster, Winifred R. "Sound Bites, Sentiments, and Accents: Digitizing Communicative Labor in the Era of Global Outsourcing." In *DigitalSTS: A Handbook and Fieldguide: Theorizing the Role of the Digital in Science and Technology Studies*, edited by David Ribes and Janet Vertesi. Princeton, NJ: Princeton University Press, forthcoming.

Poster, Winifred R., Marion G. Crain, and Miriam A. Cherry. "Conclusion." In *Invisible Labor*, edited by Marion G. Crain, Winifred R. Poster, and Miriam A. Cherry, 279–92. Berkeley: University of California Press, 2016.

Poster, Winifred R., and Zakia Salime. "Limits of Micro-Credit: Transnational Feminism and USAID Activities in the United States and Morocco." In *Women's Activism and Globalization*, edited by Nancy A. Naples and Manisha Desai, 189–219. New York: Routledge, 2002.

Povinelli, Elizabeth. *Geontologies: A Requiem to Late Liberalism*. Durham, NC: Duke University Press, 2016.

Pozo, Nathalie. "Veterans Help Put More Atlanta Police Officers on the Street." Fox5Atlanta, June 30, 2017. http://www.fox5atlanta.com/news/265040835-story.

President's Task Force on 21st Century Policing. *Final Report of the President's Task Force on 21st Century Policing*. Washington, DC: Office of Community Oriented Policing Services, 2015.

Price, Rob. "Microsoft Took Its New A.I. Chatbot Offline after It Started Spewing Racist Tweets." *Slate*, March 24, 2016.

"Project Sweetie." YouTube channel, last modified September 7, 2015. http://www .youtube.com/Sweetie.

Puar, Jasbir. *Terrorist Assemblages: Homonationalism in Queer Times*. Durham, NC: Duke University Press, 2007.

Puar, Jasbir. "The 'Right' to Maim: Disablement and Inhumanist Biopolitics in Palestine. *Borderlands* 14, no. 1 (2015). http://www.borderlands.net.au/vol14no1_2015 /puar_maim.pdf.

Purvis, June. "Suffragette Hunger Strikes, 100 Years On." *The Guardian*, July 6, 2009. Accessed March 10, 2017. https://www.theguardian.com/commentisfree /libertycentral/2009/jul/06/suffragette-hunger-strike-protest.

Quittner, Jeremy. "Banks to Use Social Media Data for Loans and Pricing." *American Banker*, January 26, 2012. Accessed January 3, 2017. https://www.americanbanker .com/news/banks-to-use-social-media-data-for-loans-and-pricing.

Raher, Stephen. "Paging Anti-Trust Lawyers: Prison Giants Prepare to Merge." Prison Policy Initiative, July 5, 2016. Accessed July 14, 2017. http://www.prisonpolicy.org /blog/2016/07/05/commissary-merger/.

Rakia, Raven. "Alton Sterling, Eric Garner, and the Criminalization of Black Business." *Complex*, July 7, 2016. http://www.complex.com/life/2016/07/criminalization-black -business.

Rancière, Jacques. *Disagreement: Politics and Philosophy*. Translated by Julie Rose. Minneapolis: University of Minnesota Press, 2004.

Rao, Leena. "California Regulators to Put Spotlight on Marketplace Lenders." *Fortune*, December 11, 2015. Accessed March 28, 2017. http://fortune.com/2015/12/11 /california-regulators-online-lending/.

Reardon, Jenny. *Race to the Finish: Identity and Governance in an Age of Genomics*. Princeton, NJ: Princeton University Press, 2002.

Reddy, Chandan. *Freedom with Violence: Race, Sexuality, and the US State*. Durham, NC: Duke University Press, 2011.

Reed, Alison, and Amanda Phillips. "Additive Race: Colorblind Discourses of Realism in Performance Capture Technologies." *Digital Creativity* 24, no. 2 (2013): 130–44.

Rhee, Nissa. "Study Casts Doubt on Chicago Police's Secretive 'Heat List.'" *Chicago Magazine*, August 17, 2016. Accessed June 30, 2017. http://www.chicagomag.com /city-life/August-2016/Chicago-Police-Data/.

Richards, Paul. "Alternative Strategies for the African Environment: Folk Ecology as a Basis for Community Oriented Agricultural Development." In *African Environment: Problems and Perspectives*, edited by Paul Richards. London: IAI, 1975.

Richardson, Sarah S., and Hallam Stevens. *Postgenomics: Perspectives on Biology after the Genome*. Durham, NC: Duke University Press, 2015.

Rios, Victor M. *Punished: Policing the Lives of Black and Latino Boys*. New York: NYU Press, 2011.

Rivera, Lauren A., and Andras Tilcsik. "Class Advantage, Commitment Penalty: The Gendered Effect of Social Class Signals in an Elite Labor Market." *American Sociological Review* 81, no. 6 (2016): 1097–1131.

Roberts, Dorothy. *Killing the Black Body: Race, Reproduction, and the Meaning of Liberty*. New York: Vintage, 1999.

Roberts, Dorothy. *Fatal Invention: How Science, Politics and Big Business Re-Create Race in the 21st Century*. New York: New Press, 2011.

Robinson, Cedric. *Black Marxism: The Making of the Black Radical Tradition*. Chapel Hill: University of North Carolina Press, 1983.

Robinson, Cedric. *Forgeries of Memory and Meaning: Blacks and the Regimes of Race in American Theater and Film before World War II*. Chapel Hill: University of North Carolina Press, 2007.

Robinson, Laurie O. "Predictive Policing Symposium: Opening Remarks." Paper presented at the first Predictive Policing Symposium, Los Angeles, November 18,2009.

Rodriguez, Dylan. *Forced Passages: Imprisoned Radical Intellectuals and the US Prison Regime*. Minneapolis: University of Minnesota Press, 2006.

Roe, Daphne A. *A Plague of Corn: The Social History of Pellagra*. Ithaca, NY: Cornell University Press, 1973.

Rose, Adam. "Are Face-Detection Cameras Racist?" *Time*, January 22, 2010. http://content.time.com/time/business/article/0,8599,1954643,00.html.

Rosenblat, Alex, Karen E. C. Levy, Solon Barocas, and Tim Hwang. "Discriminating Tastes: Uber's Customer Ratings as Vehicles for Workpalce Discrimination." *Policy & Internet* 9, no. 3 (2017): 256–79.

Rosenblat, Alex, and Luke Stark. "Algorithmic Labor and Information Asymmetries: A Case Study of Uber's Drivers." *International Journal of Communication* 10 (2016): 3758–84.

Roth, Lorna. "Looking at Shirley, the Ultimate Norm: Color Balance, Image Technologies, and Cognitive Equity." *Canadian Journal of Communication* 34, no. 1 (2009): 111–36.

Roth, Lorna. "Face Value, Skin Color and Intelligent Technologies." Gerard Reteiglezing 25th Jubilee Lecture presented at the National Multicultural Television Network, Amsterdam, February 17, 2010.

Roth, Lorna. "Bodies by Design: Hey, Look! They Painted That White Girl Black." Paper presented at The Body Eclectic: Exploring the Diversity of Bodily Being Conference held at Thompson Rivers University Gallery, Kamloops, BC, March 11–13, 2016.

Roth, Lorna. "Questão de Pele" (A Matter of Skin). *Zum* 10 (June 23, 2016). https://revistazum.com.br/en/revista-zum-10/questao-de-pele/.

Roy, Arundhati. *Capitalism: A Ghost Story*. Chicago: Haymarket, 2014.

Rudegeair, Peter. "Silicon Valley: We Don't Trust FICO Scores." *Wall Street Journal*, January 11, 2016. Accessed January 3, 2017. https://www.wsj.com/articles/silicon-valley -gives-fico-low-score-1452556468.

Rudolph, Adam. "Music and Mysticism, Rhythm and Form: A Blues Romance in 12 Parts." In *Arcana V: Music, Magic and Mysticism*, edited by John Zorn, 327–35. New York: Distributed Art Publishers, 2010.

Ruíz, Vicki. *Cannery Women, Cannery Lives: Mexican Women, Unionization, and the California Food Processing Industry, 1930–1950*. Albuquerque: University of New Mexico Press, 1987.

Rusert, Britt. "The Science of Freedom: Counterarchives of Racial Science on the Antebellum Stage." *African American Review* 45, no. 3 (2012): 291–308.

Rusli, Evelyn M. "Bad Credit? Start Tweeting." *Wall Street Journal*, April 1, 2013. Accessed January 3, 2017. https://www.wsj.com/articles/SB10001424127887324883604 578396852612756398.

Russell, Kathy, Midge Wilson, and Ronald Hall. *The Color Complex: The Politics of Skin Color in a New Millennium*. New York: Anchor, 2013.

Ryan, Vincent. "Fast Money." CFO, February 18, 2016. Accessed January 28, 2017. http://ww2.cfo.com/credit/2016/02/fast-money/.

Sagoff, Mark. *Price, Principle, and the Environment*. Cambridge: Cambridge University Press, 2005.

Salzinger, Leslie. *Genders in Production: Making Workers in Mexico's Global Factories*. Berkeley: University of California Press, 2003.

Sammond, Nicholas. *Birth of an Industry: Blackface Minstrelsy and the Rise of American Animation*. Durham, NC: Duke University Press, 2015.

Samuel, Henry. "French City Installs Anti-Homeless Cages around Benches." *The Telegraph*, December 26, 2014. Accessed January 25, 2018. http://www.telegraph.co .uk/news/worldnews/europe/france/11314081/French-city-installs-anti-homeless -cages-around-benches.html.

Santo, Alysia, and Lisa Iaboni. "What's in a Prison Meal?" The Marshall Project, July 7, 2015. Accessed November 10, 2016. https://www.themarshallproject.org/2015/07/07 /what-s-in-a-prison-meal?ref=collections#.oG4UiMzq9.

Satia, Priya. "The Defense of Inhumanity: Air Control and the British Idea of Arabia." *American Historical Review* 111, no. 1 (2006): 16–51.

Saul, Heather. "Homeless Spikes outside London Flats Spark Outrage on Twitter." *The Independent*, June 7, 2014. Accessed January 25, 2018. http://www.independent.co.uk /news/uk/home-news/homelessness-spikes-outside-london-flats-spark-outrage -on-twitter-9506390.html.

Sbicca, Joshua. "Eco-Queer Movement(s): Challenging Heteronormative Space through (Re)Imagining Nature and Food." *European Journal of Ecopsychology* 3, no. 1 (2012): 33–52.

Scanlan, Stephen J., Laurie Cooper Stoll, and Kimberly Lumm. "Starving for Change: The Hunger Strike and Nonviolent Action, 1906–2004." In *Research in Social Move-*

Bibliography

ments, Conflicts and Change, vol. 28, edited by Patrick G. Coy, 275–323. Bingley: Emerald Group, 2008.

Schlaepfer, Martin. A., Dov F. Sax, and Julian D. Olden. "The Potential Conservation Value of Non-Native Species." *Conservation Biology* 25 (2011): 428–37.

Schmidt, Gordon B. "How Social Media Can Impact the Organizational Political Process." In *Handbook of Organizational Politics: Looking Back and to the Future*, edited by Erin Vigoda-Gadot and Amos Drory. Cheltenham, UK: Edward Elgar, 2016.

Scholz, Trebor. *Uberworked and Underpaid: How Workers Are Disrupting the Digital Economy*. Cambridge: Polity, 2017.

Scholz, Trebor, and Nathan Schneider, eds. *Ours to Hack and to Own*. New York: OR Books, 2016.

Schulman, Miriam. "Little Brother Is Watching You." *Business and Society Review* 100–101, no. 1 (1998): 65–69.

Schwartz-Marin, Ernesto, and Peter Wade. "Explaining the Visible and the Invisible: Public Knowledge of Genetics, Ancestry, Physical Appearance, and Race in Colombia." *Social Studies of Science* 45, no. 6 (2015): 886–906.

Scott, Kimberly A., Kimberly M. Sheridan, and Kevin Clark. "Culturally Responsive Computing: A Theory Revisited." *Learning, Media and Technology* 40, no. 4 (2014): 412–36.

Segal, David. "Prison Vendors Continue to See Signs of a Captive Market." *New York Times*, August 29, 2015. Accessed July 10, 2017. https://www.nytimes.com 2015 /08/30/business/prison-vendors-see-continued-signs-of-a-captive-market.html ?mcubz=3.

Seivold, Garett. "Readying Retail for Terrorism's New Battleground." LPM, May 16, 2016. http://losspreventionmedia.com/loss-prevention-magazine/m-retail-security /readying-retail-for-terrorisms-new-battleground.

Selbst, Andrew. "Disparate Impact in Big Data Policing." *Georgia Law Review* 52 (2017): 109–96.

Serle, Jack, and Jessica Purkiss. "Drone Wars: The Full Data." Bureau of Investigative Journalism. 2017. https://www.thebureauinvestigates.com/stories/2017–01–01 /drone-wars-the-full-data.

Shabazz, Rashad. *Spatializing Blackness: Architecture of Confinement and Black Masculinity in Chicago*. Champaign: University of Illinois Press, 2015.

Shah, Nayan. *Contagious Divides: Epidemics and Race in San Francisco's Chinatown*. Berkeley: University of California Press, 2001.

Shapiro, Thomas M. *Toxic Inequality: How America's Wealth Gap Destroys Mobility, Deepens the Racial Divide, and Threatens Our Future*. New York: Basic Books, 2017.

Sharpe, Christina. *In the Wake: On Blackness and Being*. Durham, NC: Duke University Press, 2016.

Shaw, Ian. *Predator Empire*. Minneapolis: University of Minnesota Press, 2016.

Shaw, Ian. "The Urbanization of Drone Warfare: Policing Surplus Populations in the Dronepolis." *Geographica Helvetica* 71 (2016): 19–28.

Shaw, Ian, and Majed Akhter. "The Dronification of State Violence." *Critical Asian Studies* 46, no. 2 (2014): 211–34.

Shedd, Carla. "Countering the Carceral Continuum: The Legacy of Mass Incarceration." *Criminology and Public Policy* 10, no. 3 (2011): 865–971.

Shedd, Carla. *Unequal City: Race, Schools, and Perceptions of Injustice*. New York: Russell Sage Foundation, 2015.

Sheets, Connor. "Incarcerated Alabama Prison Strike Leader Goes on Hunger Strike as Advocates Decries 'Human Torture.'" AL.com, October 28, 2016. Accessed July 10, 2017. http://www.al.com/news/index.ssf/2016/10/alabama_prisoner_strike_organi.html.

Sheets, Connor. "I'm Not a Dog: Hunger Strikes inside Alabama Prisons, from Protests to Force Feeding." AL.com, April 30, 2017. Accessed on July 10, 2017. http://www.al.com/news/index.ssf/2017/04/im_not_a_dog_hunger_strikes_in.html.

Shen, Danni. "Sinofuturism: An Interview with Lawrence Lek." *Screen*, March 6, 2017. Accessed January 6, 2018. http://www.onscreentoday.com/conversation/sinofuturism.

Shifman, Mark A., Jeffrey I. Clyman JI, John A. Paton, Seth M. Powsner, Nancy K. Roderer, and Perry L. Miller. "NetMenu: Experience in the Implementation of an Institutional Menu of Information Sources." Proceedings of the 17th Annual Symposium on Computer Application in Medical Care, Washington, DC (1993): 554–58.

Shim, Janet K. *Heart-Sick: The Politics of Risk, Inequality, and Heart Disease*. New York: NYU Press, 2014.

Shiva, Vandana. "The Violence of Reductionist Science." *Alternatives* 12 (1987): 243–61.

Singh, Nikil Pal. *Race and America's Long War*. Berkeley: University of California Press, 2017.

Smith, Andrea. "Not Seeing: State Surveillance, Settler Colonialism, and Gender Violence." In *Feminist Surveillance Studies*, edited by Rachel E. Dubrofsky and Shoshana Amielle Magnet. Durham, NC: Duke University Press, 2015.

Smith, Eric R. *American Relief Aid and the Spanish Civil War*. Columbia: University of Missouri Press, 2013.

Smith, James McCune. *The Works of James McCune Smith: Black Intellectual and Abolitionist*. Oxford: Oxford University Press, 2006.

Smitherman, Geneva. *Talkin and Testifyin: The Language of Black America*. Detroit: Wayne State University Press, 1977.

Smithers, Gregory D. *Science, Sexuality, and Race in the United States and Australia, 1780–1940*. Lincoln: University of Nebraska Press, 2017.

Smoyer, Amy B., and Giza Lopes. "Hungry on the Inside: Prison Food as Concrete and Symbolic Punishment in a Women's Prison." *Punishment & Society* 19, no. 2 (2017): 240–55.

Smuts, Jan. *Africa and Some World Problems*. Oxford: Oxford University Press, 1930.

Snead, James A. "Repetition as a Figure of Black Culture." In *Out There: Marginalization and Contemporary Cultures*, edited by Russell Ferguson. Cambridge, MA: MIT Press, 1990.

Solway, Jacqueline S. *The Politics of Egalitarianism: Theory and Practice*. New York: Berghahn, 2006.

Spade, Dean. *Normal Life: Administrative Violence, Critical Trans Politics and the Limits of Law*. New York: South End, 2011.

Spillers, Hortense. *Black, White, and in Color: Essays on American Literature and Culture*. Chicago: University of Chicago Press, 2003.

Spivey, Yolanda. "Should the Keishas of the World Put Karen on Their Resume?" *Ms. Magazine*, November 11, 2012.

Sridhar, Kamal K. "Customer Attitudes to Non-Native Accented Outsource Service." Unpublished presentation, Asian and Asian American Studies, Stony Brook University, Stony Brook, NY, 2008.

Srnicek, Nick. *Platform Capitalism*. Cambridge: Polity, 2016.

Stacey, Jackie, and Lucy Suchman. "Animation and Automation: The Liveliness and Labours of Bodies and Machines." *Body & Society* 18, no. 1 (2012): 1–46.

Stanley, Eric, and Nat Smith. *Captive Genders: Trans Embodiment and the Prison Industrial Complex*. Oakland, CA: AK Press, 2015.

Staples, Amy. *The Birth of Development. How the World Bank, Food and Agriculture Organization, and World Health Organization Changed the World, 1945–1965*. Kent, OH: Kent State University Press, 2006.

Stark, Luke, and Karen E. C. Levy. "The Surveillant Consumer." *Media, Culture & Society*, 2018. https://doi.org/10.1177%2F0163443718781985.

State of Michigan. "Department of Corrections Testimony," March 3, 2016. Accessed July 9, 2017. http://house.michigan.gov/hfa/PDF/Corrections/DOC_Subcmte_Testimony(DetroitMetroTimesArticle_3-3-16).pdf.

State of Pennsylvania. "Governor's Office GO-TIME Announcement," 2017. Accessed July 10, 2017. https://www.governor.pa.gov/go-time-department-of-corrections-food-procurement-services-and-management-software-system-contract-to-save-an-estimated-16-6-million-over-three-years/.

Stern, Alexandra. *Eugenic Nation: Faults and Frontiers of Better Breeding in Modern America*. Berkeley: University of California Press, 2005.

Stoker, Elsbeth. "All the Men Were Naked and Playing with Themselves." *De Volkskrant*, May 29, 2012.

Stone, Sandy. "Split Subjects, Not Atoms; Or, How I Fell in Love with My Prosthesis." In *The Cyborg Handbook*, edited by C. H. Gray. New York: Routledge, 1991.

Strathern, Marilyn. *Partial Connections*. Walnut Creek, CA: AltaMira, 2005.

Subramaniam, Banu. *Ghost Stories for Darwin: The Science of Variation and the Politics of Diversity*. Chicago: University of Illinois Press, 2014.

Sweeney, Latanya. "Discrimination in Online Ad Delivery." *Queue* 11, no. 3 (2013): 10–29.

Sweeney, Miriam E. "The Ms. Dewey 'Experience': Technoculture, Gender, and Race." In *Digital Sociologies*, edited by Jessie Daniels, Gregory Kelson, and Tressie McMillan Cottom, 401–20. Bristol, UK: Polity, 2017.

Sweeney, Miriam E., and André Brock. "Critical Informatics: New Methods and Practices." *Proceedings of the Association for Information Science and Technology* 51, no. 1 (2014): 1–8.

Tahir, Madiha. "The Containment Zone." In *Life in the Age of Drone Warfare*, edited by Lisa Parks and Caren Kaplan, 220–40. Durham, NC: Duke University Press, 2017.

Tahir, Madiha. "The Ground Was Always in Play." *Public Culture* 29, no. 1 (2017): 5–16.

TallBear, Kim. *Native American DNA: Tribal Belonging and the False Promise of Genetic Science*. Minneapolis: University of Minnesota Press, 2013.

TallBear, Kim. "Dossier: Theorizing Queer Inhumanisms: An Indigenous Reflection on Working beyond the Human/Not Human." *GLQ: A Journal of Lesbian and Gay Studies* 21, no. 3 (2015): 230–35.

Taussig, Michael. *Mimesis and Alterity: A Particular History of the Senses*. New York: Psychology Press, 1993.

Taylor, Astra. "Non-Cooperativism." In *Ours to Hack and Own*, edited by Trebor Scholz and Nathan Schneider, 233–38. New York: OR Books, 2016.

Terry, Jennifer. *Attachments to War: Biomedical Logics and Violence in Twenty-First-Century America*. Durham, NC: Duke University Press, 2017.

Thacker, Eugene. *The Global Genome: Biotechnology, Politics, and Culture*. Cambridge, MA: MIT Press, 2005.

Thakor, Mitali. "The Allure of Artifice." In *Queer Feminist Science Studies: A Reader*, edited by Cyd Cipolla, Kristina Gupta, David A. Rubin, and Angela Willey, 141–56. Seattle: University of Washington Press, 2017.

Thakor, Mitali. "How to Look: Apprehension, Forensic Craft, and the Classification of Child Exploitation Images." *IEEE Annals of the History of Computing* 39, no. 2 (2017): 6–8.

Thakor, Mitali, and danah boyd. "Networked Trafficking: Reflections on Technology and the Anti-Trafficking Movement." *Dialectical Anthropology* 37, no. 2 (2013): 277–90.

Thomas, Sherri. "2016 Best Career Apps and Websites to Land Your Dream Job." *Huffington Post*, November 2, 2016.

Thompson, Charis. *Making Parents: The Ontological Choreography of Reproductive Technologies*. Cambridge, MA: MIT Press, 2007.

Thompson, Robert F. *Flash of the Spirit: African and Afro-American Art and Philosophy*. New York: Random House, 1985.

Toon, John. "Case Study: Swarms of Autonomous Aerial Vehicles Test New Dogfighting Skills." Georgia Tech Research Institute, April 21, 2017. http://www.news.gatech.edu/2017/04/21/swarms-autonomous-aerial-vehicles-test-new-dogfighting-skills.

Trinity Services Group. "Correctional Food Service, 2016." Accessed July 9, 2017. https://www.trinityservicesgroup.com/food-service-2/.

Turner, George, Jeff Brantingham, and George Mohler. "Technology Talk: Predictive Policing in Action in Atlanta, Georgia." *Police Chief Magazine*, 2014. http://www.policechiefmagazine.org/predictive-policing-in-action-in-atlanta-georgia/.

Bibliography

Ulloa, Astrid. *The Ecological Native: Indigenous Peoples' Movements and Eco-Governmentality in Colombia*. New York: Routledge, 2005.

United Nations General Assembly. "Protocol to Prevent, Suppress and Punish Trafficking in Persons, Especially Women and Children, Supplementing the United Nations Convention against Transnational Organized Crime." Organization for Co-Operation and Security in Europe, November 15, 2000. https://www.osce.org/odihr/19223.

U.S. Census Bureau. "Wealth and Asset Ownership Data Tables," 2017. Accessed June 15, 2017. https://www.census.gov/topics/income-poverty/wealth/data/tables.html.

U.S. Department of the Treasury. "Treasury Seeks Public Comments on Marketplace Lenders," July 16, 2016. Accessed January 3, 2017. https://www.treasury.gov/press-center/press-releases/Pages/jl0116.aspx.

Vaccari, Franco. *La photographie et l'inconscient technologique*. Paris: Créatis, 1981.

Valentine, Gill. "In-Corporations: Food, Bodies and Organizations." *Body & Society* 8, no. 2 (2002): 1–20.

Valentine, Gill, and Beth Longstaff. "Doing Porridge: Food and Social Relations in a Male Prisons." *Journal of Material Culture* 3, no. 2 (1998): 131–52.

Van Rooy, Jan. Author interview, Breda, Netherlands, September 10, 1997.

Van Rooy, Jan. "F-900 Skin Detail Adjustment Advice," May 14, 2004. Accessed January 15, 2009. http://www.cinematography.net/edited-pages/%5Bcml-hdtv%5D%20F-900%20skin%20detail%20adjustment%20advice.htm.

Villa-Nicholas, Melissa, and Miriam E. Sweeney. "Race, Gender, and the Perfect Digital Latina Worker." Presentation at 4S: Society for the Social Study of Science and Technology, September 2017.

Visser, Margaret. *Much Depends on Dinner*. Toronto, ON: McClelland & Stewart, 1986.

Wack, Kevin. "Subprime Specialist LendUp Raises $150M." *American Banker*, January 20, 2016. Accessed January 3, 2017. https://www.americanbanker.com/news/subprime-specialist-lendup-raises-150m.

Wacquant, Loïc. "Pugs at Work: Bodily Capital and Bodily Labour among Professional Boxers." *Body & Society* 1 (1995): 65–93.

Wacquant, Loïc. *Punishing the Poor: The Neoliberal Government of Social Insecurity*. Durham, NC: Duke University Press, 2009.

Waddell, Kaveh. "The Algorithms That Tell Bosses How Employees Are Feeling." *The Atlantic*, September 29, 2016. https://www.theatlantic.com/technology/archive/2016/09/the-algorithms-that-tell-bosses-how-employees-feel/502064/.

Wade, Peter, Carlos López Beltrán, Eduardo Restrepo, and Ricardo Ventura Santos. *Mestizo Genomics: Race Mixture, Nation, and Science in Latin America*. Durham, NC: Duke University Press, 2014.

Wagner, Wolfgang. "Vernacular Science Knowledge: Its Role in Everyday Life Communication." *Public Understanding of Science* 16, no. 1 (2007): 7–22.

Wahlman, Maude S. *Signs and Symbols: African Images in African-American Quilts*. New York: Museum of American Folk Art, 2001.

Wailoo, Keith, Alondra Nelson, and Catherine Lee. *Genetics and the Unsettled Past: The Collision of DNA, Race, and History*. New Brunswick, NJ: Rutgers University Press, 2012.

Walby, Kevin, and Seantel Anais. "Research Methods, Institutional Ethnography, and Feminist Surveillance Studies." In *Feminist Surveillance Studies*, edited by Rachel E. Dubrofsky and Shoshana Amielle Magnet, 208–20. Durham, NC: Duke University Press, 2015.

Wall, Tyler. "Ordinary Emergency: Drones, Police, and Geographies of Legal Terror." *Antipode* 48, no. 4 (September 2016): 1122–39.

Wall, Tyler. "Unmanning the Police Manhunt: Vertical Security As Pacification." *Socialist Studies/Études socialistes* 9, no. 2 (2013): 32–56.

Walsh, James. "Mall of America Protest Attracts Thousands on Busy Shopping Day." *Minneapolis Star Tribune*, January 6, 2015. http://www.startribune.com/dec-20-mall -of-america-protest-attracts-thousands/286443781/.

Walton, A. "Technology versus African-Americans." *Atlantic Monthly* 283, no. 1 (1999): 14–17.

Wang, Ze, Aaron Arndt, Surendra Singh, and Monica Biernat. "The Impact of Accent Stereotypes on Service Outcomes and Its Boundary Conditions." *Advances in Consumer Research* 36 (2009): 940–41.

Warhurst, Chris. "From Invisible Work to Invisible Workers: The Impact of Service Employers' Speech Demands on the Working Class." In *Invisible Labor*, edited by Marion G. Crain, Winifred R. Poster, and Miriam A. Cherry, 214–36. Berkeley: University of California Press, 2016.

Washington, Harriet A. *Medical Apartheid: The Dark History of Medical Experimentation on Black Americans from Colonial Times to the Present*. New York: Doubleday, 2006.

Watkins, Caitlin. "Industrialized Bodies: Women, Food, and Environmental Justice in the Criminal Justice System." In *Addressing Environmental and Food Justice toward Dismantling the School-to-Prison Pipeline Poisoning and Imprisoning Youth*, edited by Anthony Nocella, K. Animashaun Ducre, and John Lupinacci, 137–60. New York: Palgrave Macmillan, 2017.

Wattles, Jackie. "Chipotle under Fire for Illegal Workplace Policies." CNNMoney, August 24, 2016. http://money.cnn.com/2016/08/24/pf/jobs/chipotle-social-media -nlrb/.

Weber, Jutta. "Keep Adding: On Kill Lists, Drone Warfare and the Politics of Databases." *Environment and Planning D: Society and Space* 34, no. 1 (2016): 107–25.

Weber, Samuel. *Targets of Opportunity: On the Militarization of Thinking*. New York: Fordham University Press, 2005.

Weheliye, Alexander G. *Habeas Viscus: Racializing Assemblages, Biopolitics, and Black Feminist Theories of the Human*. Durham, NC: Duke University Press, 2014.

Weisburd, David A., and Anthony Braga. *Police Innovation: Contrasting Perspectives*. Cambridge: Cambridge University Press, 2006.

Wenger, Etienne. *Communities of Practice: Learning, Meaning, and Identity*. Cambridge, MA: Cambridge University Press, 1998.

Wertz, S. K. "Maize: The Native North American's Legacy of Cultural Diversity and Biodiversity." *Journal of Agricultural and Environmental Ethics* 18, no. 2 (2004): 131–56.

Western, Bruce. *Punishment and Inequality in America*. New York: Russell Sage Foundation, 2006.

"What Is My Credit Score, and How Is It Calculated?" *Time*, May 26, 2014. Accessed January 28, 2017. http://time.com/2791957/what-is-my-credit-score-and-how-is-it-calculated/?iid=sr-link1.

"What's Not in My FICO Scores." MyFICO.com, n.d. Accessed January 15, 2017. http://www.myfico.com/credit-education/whats-not-in-your-credit-score/.

White, Gillian B. "Uber and Lyft Are Failing Black Riders." *The Atlantic*, October 31, 2016. http://www.theatlantic.com.

White, Martha C. "Can a Payday Lending Start-Up Use Facebook to Create a Modern Community Bank?" *Time*, November 16, 2012. Accessed January 3, 2017. http://business.time.com/2012/11/16/can-a-payday-lending-start-up-use-facebook-to-create-a-modern-community-bank/.

Wien, Richard. Author interview, Rochester, NY, August 18, 1997.

Wilderson, Frank. *Red, White and Black: Cinema and the Structure of U.S. Antagonisms*. Durham, NC: Duke University Press, 2010.

Williams, Christine L., and Catherine Connell. "The Invisible Consequences of Aesthestic Labor in Upscale Retail Stores." In *Invisible Labor*, edited by Marion G. Crain, Winifred R. Poster, and Miriam A. Cherry, 193–213. Berkeley: University of California Press, 2016.

Williams, Johnny Eric. *Decoding Racial Ideology in Genomics*. Lanham, MD: Lexington Books, 2016.

Williams, Patricia J. *Seeing a Color-Blind Future: The Paradox of Race*. New York: Noonday, 1998.

Wing, Nick. "Our Bail System Is Leaving Innocent People to Die in Jail Because They're Poor." Justice Policy Institute, July 14, 2016. Accessed January 25, 2018. http://www.justicepolicy.org/news/10585.

Wingfield, Adia Harvey, and John Harvey Wingfield. "When Visibility Hurts and Helps: How Intersections of Race and Gender Shape Black Professional Men's Experiences with Tokenization." *Cultural Diversity and Ethnic Minority Psychology* 20, no. 4 (2014): 483–90.

Winner, Langdon. "Do Artifacts Have Politics?" *Daedalus* 109, no. 1 (1980): 121–36.

Winters, Robert. "Evaluating the Effectiveness of Prison Farm Programs." Corrections.com, September 23, 2013. Accessed July 18, 2017. http://www.corrections.com/news/article/33907-evaluating-the-effectiveness-of-prison-farm-programs.

Wong, Nicole C. "Voice Recognition: They Speak Thereby They Brand." *San Jose Mercury News*, March 21, 2005.

Woods, Tryon. "Surrogate Selves: Notes on Anti-Trafficking and Anti-Blackness." *Social Identities* 19, no. 1 (2013): 120–34.

Wynter, Sylvia. "The Ceremony Must Be Found: After Humanism." *boundary 2* 12, no. 3 (1983): 19–70.

Wynter, Sylvia. "Unsettling the Coloniality of Being/Power/Truth/Freedom: Towards the Human, after Man, Its Overrepresentation—An Argument." *CR: The New Centennial Review* 3, no. 3 (2003): 257–337.

Wzamen01. "HP Computers Are Racist." YouTube, December 10, 2009. Accessed December 30, 2017. https://www.youtube.com/watch?v=t4DT3tQqgRM.

YosemiteCCD. "The Barbie Doll Test." YouTube, June 9, 2009. Accessed December 30, 2017. https://www.youtube.com/watch?v=YOHbtM9463c.

Yue, Genevieve. "The China Girl on the Margins of Film." *October* 153 (2015): 95–116.

Zeynup, Tufeki. *Twitter and Teargas: The Power and Fragility of Networked Protest.* New Haven, CT: Yale University Press, 2017.

Zhang, Maggie. "Google Photos Tags Two African-Americans as Gorillas through Facial Recognition Software." *Forbes*, July 1, 2015. Accessed May 2015. https://www.forbes.com/sites/mzhang/2015/07/01/google-photos-tags-two-african-americans-as-gorillas-through-facial-recognition-software/#2494cba8713d.

Zhang, Wei, Songlin Fu, and Changding Zhang. "Fast Face Beautifying Method for Digital Images." U.S. Patent No. 9501843B2 filed March 24, 2016, and issued November 22, 2016.

Zhou, Shi-Sheng, and Yiming Zhou. "Excess Vitamin Intake: An Unrecognized Risk Factor for Obesity." *World Journal of Diabetes* 5, no. 1 (2014): 1–13.

Zoukis, Christopher, and Rod L. Bower. "Aramark's Correctional Food Services: Meals, Maggots, and Misconduct." *Prison Legal News*, December 2, 2015. Accessed March 10, 2017. https://www.prisonlegalnews.org/news/2015/dec/2/aramarks-correctional-food-services-meals-maggots-and-misconduct/.

Contributors

RUHA BENJAMIN is Associate Professor of African American Studies at Princeton University. She is the author of *People's Science: Bodies and Rights on the Stem Cell Frontier* (2013) and *Race After Technology* (2019) among other works that examine the tension between innovation and inequity.

TROY DUSTER, Chancellor's Professor Emeritus, University of California, Berkeley, is past president of the American Sociological Association, Emeritus Silver Professor of Sociology and former Director of the Institute for the History of the Production of Knowledge at New York University, and author of *The Legislation of Morality: Law, Drugs, and Moral Judgment* and *Backdoor to Eugenics*, among many other works.

RON EGLASH is Professor of Science and Technology Studies at Rensselaer Polytechnic Institute, with a secondary appointment in computer science. He received his BS in cybernetics, his MS in systems engineering, and his PhD in history of consciousness, all from the University of California. His work as a Fulbright scholar was published as *African Fractals: Modern Computing and Indigenous Design*. His NSF-funded research on "generative STEM" seeks ways to shift science and innovation toward a just and sustainable circular economy.

NETTRICE GASKINS received a PhD in digital media from Georgia Tech in 2014. Her model for "Techno-Vernacular Creativity" is an area of practice that investigates the characteristics of this production and its application in STEAM. She blogs for Art21, the producer of the Peabody Award–winning PBS series *Art in the Twenty-First Century*, and has published in several journals and books. She was the director of the STEAM Lab at Boston Arts Academy, lectures, and leads maker workshops internationally. She is currently a program manager at the Fab Foundation.

ANTHONY RYAN HATCH is Associate Professor of Science in Society, Sociology, and African American Studies at Wesleyan University. He is the author of *Blood Sugar: Racial Pharmacology and Food Justice in Black America* (2016).

ANDREA MILLER is a PhD candidate in cultural studies at the University of California, Davis. She received her MA in women's, gender, and sexuality studies at Georgia State University in 2014, and her research examines policing, surveillance, race, and infrastructure in the U.S. war on terror.

ALONDRA NELSON, President of the Social Science Research Council and Professor of Sociology at Columbia University, is the author of *The Social Life of DNA: Race, Reparations, and Reconciliation after the Genome* (2016) and *Body and Soul: The Black Panther Party and the Fight against Medical Discrimination* (2011), among many other works.

TAMARA K. NOPPER is Assistant Professor in the Department of Sociology at Rhode Island College. Her research focuses on racial and economic inequality, immigrant entrepreneurship, government policies toward minority business development, and ethnic banking.

CHRISTOPHER PERREIRA is Assistant Professor of American Studies and Latina/o Studies at the University of Kansas. His work can be found in the *Journal of Transnational American Studies*. He is completing his book *Manufacturing Prisoner-Patient Consent: Race, Memory, and Violence in the Medical Archive* with the support of a Ford Foundation Postdoctoral Fellowship.

WINIFRED R. POSTER teaches in International Affairs at Washington University, St. Louis. Her research explores digital globalization, feminist and critical race labor theory, and Indian outsourcing. Recent projects concern the labors of surveillance, crowdsourcing, cybersecurity, and artificial intelligence, and her latest coauthored books are *Invisible Labor* and *Borders in Service*.

LORNA ROTH is Professor Emeritus and former Chairperson of the Department of Communication Studies, Concordia University in Montréal. She is the author of *Something New in the Air: The Story of First Peoples Television Broadcasting in Canada* (2005) and is currently working on several articles and her second book entitled *Skinvisible: Race, Technologies, and "Intelligent Design."*

DOROTHY E. ROBERTS is George A. Weiss University Professor of Law and Sociology, Raymond Pace and Sadie Tanner Mossell Alexander Professor of Civil Rights, and 14th Penn Integrates Knowledge at University of Pennsylvania. She is the author of *Killing the Black Body: Race, Reproduction, and the Meaning of Liberty* (1997), *Shattered Bonds: The Color of Child Welfare* (2002), and *Fatal Invention: How Science, Politics, and Big Business Re-Create Race in the Twenty-First Century* (2011), among many other works.

BRITT RUSERT is the author of *Fugitive Science: Empiricism and Freedom in Early African American Culture* and coeditor of *W. E. B. Du Bois's Data Portraits: Visualizing Black America* (2018). She teaches in the W. E. B. Du Bois Department of Afro-American Studies at the University of Massachusetts, Amherst.

R. JOSHUA SCANNELL teaches sociology and women, gender, and sexuality studies at Hunter College. He is the author of *Cities: Unauthorized Resistances and Uncertain Sovereignty in the Urban World.*

MITALI THAKOR is Assistant Professor in the Science and Society Program at Wesleyan University and a former Postdoctoral Fellow in the Sexualities Project at Northwestern University. She earned her PhD from MIT's program in history, anthropology, and science, technology, and society, and her research and teaching cover issues of global policing, the use of artificial intelligence to resolve sexual violence cases, and queer studies of robotics.

MADISON VAN OORT received her PhD in sociology at the University of Minnesota–Twin Cities. Van Oort's writing has been published in the journals *Ethnography* and *Signs: Journal of Women in Culture and Society*.

Index